16th International Conference on Interfaces and Human Computer Interaction (IHCI2022) and 15th International Conference on Game and Entertainment Technologies (GET2022)

Held at the 16th Multi-Conference on Computer Science and Information Systems (MCCSIS 2022)

Lisbon, Portugal
19-22 July 2022

Editors:

Katherine Blashki
Piet Kommers
Pedro Isaías
Luís Rodrigues

ISBN: 978-1-7138-6090-7

Printed from e-media with permission by:

Curran Associates, Inc.
57 Morehouse Lane
Red Hook, NY 12571

Some format issues inherent in the e-media version may also appear in this print version.

International Association for Development of the Information Society (IADIS)
Rua Sao Sebastiao Da Pedreira
No. 100, 30, 1050-209
Lisbon, Portugal

Phone: 351 21 3151373
Fax: 351 21 3151244

secretariat@iadis.org

Additional copies of this publication are available from:

Curran Associates, Inc.
57 Morehouse Lane
Red Hook, NY 12571 USA
Phone: 845-758-0400
Fax: 845-758-2633
Email: curran@proceedings.com
Web: www.proceedings.com

INTERNATIONAL CONFERENCES

ON

INTERFACES AND HUMAN COMPUTER INTERACTION 2022

and

GAME AND ENTERTAINMENT TECHNOLOGIES 2022

part of the

MULTI CONFERENCE ON COMPUTER SCIENCE

AND INFORMATION SYSTEMS 2022

PROCEEDINGS
OF THE
INTERNATIONAL CONFERENCES
ON

INTERFACES AND HUMAN COMPUTER INTERACTION 2022

and

GAME AND ENTERTAINMENT TECHNOLOGIES 2022

JULY 20 - 22, 2022

Organised by

iadis

international association for development of the information society

As a member of Crossref (a non-profit membership organization for scholarly publishing working with the purpose to make content easy to find, link, cite and assess) each published paper in this book of proceedings will be allocated a DOI (Digital Object Identifier) number for its fast and easy citation and indexation.

Volume Editor:
Katherine Blashki

Computer Science and Information Systems Series Editors:
Piet Kommers and Pedro Isaías

Associate Editor: Luís Rodrigues

TABLE OF CONTENTS

FOREWORD ix

PROGRAM COMMITTEE xiii

KEYNOTE LECTURE xv

FULL PAPERS

INTERFACES AND HUMAN COMPUTER INTERACTION

A PSYCHOPHYSIOLOGICAL INVESTIGATION OF EMOTIONS EXPERIENCED IN A VIRTUAL REALITY 3D-LEARNING SIMULATION 3
Sadaf H. Khan, Abhijeet Kujur and Jyoti Kumar

UNDERSTANDING VIRTUAL REALITY GAME PLAYERS' SATISFACTION, LOYALTY, AND EXPERIENCE VALUE: A CASE STUDY OF THE BEATSABER 11
Guan Zhi Wang and Wen Huei Chou

USING EMOTIONAL DESIGN TO RAISE AWARENESS OF INFORMATION SECURITY 18
Frauke Prott and Margit Scholl

PATIENT USER INTERFACES FOR DETERMINING PAIN LEVEL THROUGH EVERYDAY SMARTPHONE TASKS AND WEARABLE PHYSIOLOGICAL SIGNAL SENSORS 27
Ashraf Khalil, Suha Glal and Salam Abdallah

THE IMPACT OF TEST ELEMENTS ON STUDENTS' PERFORMANCE IN EFL ASSESSMENT 34
Joma Alrzini, Diane Rasmussen Pennington and Mark D. Dunlop

ESTIMATION OF HUMAN EMOTION DEFINED WITH RUSSELL'S CIRCUMPLEX MODEL USING LIGHTWEIGHT FNIRS DEVICE 41
Daisuke Fukui, Takushige Katsura, Masashi Egi, Norihisa Komoda and Takenao Ohkawa

CONTRIBUTIONS OF AUGMENTED REALITY IN ARCHITECTURAL PROJECT REVIEW 49
Gaëlle Baudoux, Maxime Grella and Pierre Leclercq

METHODS FOR THE EVALUATION OF UX OVER TIME 57
Emmanuel O. C. Mkpojiogu, Obianuju E. Okeke-Uzodike and Victor Omopariola

IDENTIFICATION OF FACTORS AFFECTING THE LEARNERS' MOTIVATION IN AN E-LEARNING SCENARIO FOR INDUSTRIAL DESIGN EDUCATION 66
Naveen Kumar, Abhijeet Kujur and Jyoti Kumar

UNDERSTANDING USERS' UX NEEDS THROUGH THE LENSES OF PSYCHOLOGICAL NEEDS THEORIES: USERS' EXPECTATIONS AND FELT EXPERIENCES 75
Emmanuel O. C. Mkpojiogu, Obianuju E. Okeke-Uzodike and Victor Omopariola

A FRAMEWORK FOR ETHICS EDUCATION IN PERSUASIVE UX DESIGN 84
Sanju Ahuja and Jyoti Kumar

CORPORATE DIGITAL RESPONSIBILITY AND ACCESSIBILITY IN DIGITAL SERVICES 92
Terhi Kärpänen

GENDER CLASSIFICATION USING SINGLE IMAGE PER PERSON 99
Rubata Riasat, Abdul Hannan Sadiq and Faizan Ahmad

USING INFORMATION VISUALIZATION TO SUPPORT THE SELF-MANAGEMENT OF TYPE 2 DIABETES MELLITUS 107
Janet Wesson and Meggan Naude

TELEINCLUSIVE LEARNING: AN EXPLORATORY STUDY ON STUDENTS' EXPECTATIONS OF USING TELEPRESENCE ROBOT FOR ATTENDING CLASSES 115
Luciano Gamberini, Gabriella Francesca Amalia Pernice, Valeria Orso and Daniela Mapelli

COMBINED UX/UXI TAXONOMY FOR PROSUMER COMMONS IN SMART SUSTAINABLE CITIES 122
Aleksi Kajander and Maria Claudia Solarte-Vasquez

A COMBINED APPROACH FOR USABILITY EVALUATION OF AN E-COMMERCE WEBSITE: REMOTE USABILITY TESTING, EYE-TRACKING, AND SUS TECHNIQUES 131
Thanaa Saad Alsalem, Maymunah Abdullatif Alismail and Majed Aadi Alshamari

RETHINKING THE SHOPPING EXPERIENCE: A QUALITATIVE EXPLORATIVE STUDY ON 3D WEB AND AR FOR DISPLAYING AND SELLING GOODS 142
Valeria Orso, Giovanni Portello, Leonardo Pierobon, Alice Bettelli, Merylin Monaro and Luciano Gamberini

ON THE IMPACT OF THE USER CONTEXT CRITERIA IN THE DETECTION OF MOBILE USER INTERFACES DEFECTS 149
Mabrouka Chouchane and Makram Soui

GAME AND ENTERTAINMENT TECHNOLOGIES

GAMIFICATION OF DISCUSSOO: AN ONLINE AI-BASED FORUM FOR SERIOUS DISCUSSIONS 157
Elena Bakhanova, Madiha Anjum, Jaime A. Garcia, William L. Raffe and Alexey Voinov

GAME GRAPHICS AND EFFECTIVE LEARNING: A REVIEW OF VISUAL COMMUNICATION RESEARCH IN SERIOUS GAMES 165
Hua Bai, Ran Zhang, Björn Berg Marklund and Ulf Wilhelmsson

THE EMERGENT ASPECT OF CLIMATE CHANGE IN VIDEO GAMES: A HISTORICAL REVIEW 174
Khalil Morad El Ghilali, Spiros Papadopoulos and Iman Meriem Benkirane

GAMING SKILL DEMOGRAPHICS: AN ANALYSIS OF CONSISTENCY IN VIDEO GAME RESEARCH 184
Elizabeth A. Matthews, Irina Koleva and Sujana Basnet

SHORT PAPERS

INTERFACES AND HUMAN COMPUTER INTERACTION

USING AN INTENTION PREDICTION ALGORITHM TO DISPLAY ADAPTIVE WARNINGS OF CYCLISTS 195
Lisa Graichen, Matthias Graichen and Leon Gärtner

RESEARCH ON LOW CARBON DESIGN STRATEGY OF CATERING TAKEOUT FROM THE PERSPECTIVE OF "DOUBLE CARBON" 200
Shen Chuanyue

FORMAL EDUCATION AND THE READINESS FOR WORK IN UX: THE RESULTS FROM A MIXED-METHODS RESEARCH STUDY 205
Ladislava Zbiejczuk Suchá, Jáchym Kubáček and Jitka Bartošová

SPEAKING, TOUCHING OR GESTICULATING? HOW DOES IN-VEHICLE INTERACTION TYPE AFFECT DRIVER DISTRACTION? 211
Lisa Graichen, Matthias Graichen and Lena Hanstein

GAME AND ENTERTAINMENT TECHNOLOGIES

A DEEP REINFORCEMENT LEARNING APPROACH TO THE ANCIENT INDIAN GAME - CHOWKA BHARA 216
Annapurna P. Patil, Sanjay Raghavendra, Shruthi Srinarasi and Reshma Ram

FLOW, ITS STRANDS AND MICROFLOW IN THE GAME DESIGN OF HORROR GAMES 221
Reinaldo Augusto de Oliveira Ramos and Rafael Diogo Rossetti

REFLECTION PAPERS

GAME AND ENTERTAINMENT TECHNOLOGIES

THE LUDIC SPECTACLE AND MEDIATIZED PARTICIPATION IN ESPORTS: POLAND AND HONG KONG 229
Mateusz Felczak

WE NEED TO FOCUS ON RULES 233
Luiz Cláudio Silveira Duarte and Adriano Furtado Holanda

POSTERS

INTERFACES AND HUMAN COMPUTER INTERACTION

CO-EXPERIENCE AND DIGITAL INCENTIVES: UNDERSTANDING PURCHASE INTENTION IN THE P2E METAVERSE 239
Sujin Bae, Qiyuan Tang and Ohbyung Kwon

COMPARATIVE STUDY ON THE CHARACTERISTICS OF METAVERSE EXPERIENCE: AN EXPERIENCE ECONOMY MODEL PERSPECTIVE 243
Qiyuan Tang, Sujin Bae and Ohbyung Kwon

FOREWORD

These proceedings contain the papers of the: 16th International Conference on Interfaces and Human Computer Interaction 2022 and 15th International Conference on Game and Entertainment Technologies 2022, which were organised by the International Association for Development of the Information Society, from 20 - 22 July, 2022. These conferences are part of the 16th Multi Conference on Computer Science and Information Systems 2022, 19 - 22 July, which had a total of 608 submissions.

The Interfaces and Human Computer Interaction (IHCI) 2022 conference aims to address the main issues of concern within Interface Culture and Design with a particular emphasis on the affective aspects of design, development and implementation of interfaces and the generational implications for design of human and technology interaction. This conference aims to explore and discuss innovative studies of technology and its application in interfaces and welcomes research in progress, case studies, practical demonstrations and workshops in addition to the traditional submission categories.

This conference seeks to cover both technological as well as non-technological issues related to these developments.

Submissions were accepted under the following topics:

- Affective User-Centred Analysis, Design and Evaluation
- The Value of Affective Interfaces / Systems / Application / Interaction
- Generational differences and technology design
- Measurement of success of emotional technology / interfaces
- Supporting user populations from specific Generations
- Supporting user populations with Physical Disabilities
- Supporting user populations with Intellectual Disabilities
- Creativity Support Systems
- Emotional Design issues / methods / experiences for novel interfaces including tangible, Mobile and Ubiquitous computing, mixed reality interfaces and multi-modal interfaces
- Usability
- User studies and fieldwork
- Methodological implications of Emotional User Studies
- Participatory design and Cooperative design techniques
- Ethical issues in emotional design
- HCI and Design education
- Eliciting User Requirements

The Game and Entertainment Technologies (GET) 2022 conference aims to bring together research and practice from creative, social and business practitioners and researchers in this challenging field. The focus of this conference is on design, development and evaluation of games, entertainment technologies and the nature of play.

Known to have been enjoyed since at least 30 BC, games and entertainment are a universal part of human experience and present in all cultures. Games and entertainment activities contribute to the social, emotional, psychological and physical well-being of human society. As game and entertainment technologies become increasingly more pervasive we are continually challenged in our work, learning and personal life by increased access to virtual spaces and communities that offer opportunities for everyday needs and aesthetic experiences. The 'Creative Industries' require design and development structures, techniques and methodologies that enrich, enhance and encourage new interaction modes, metaphors and in-depth co-creation.

Topics of interest include, but are not limited to the following areas:

- Development methodologies
- Design issues
- Controversial issues – we welcome debate and dissension, for example; games as art, entertainment as purely for monetary returns etc
- Special Effects
- Animation
- Mobile and ubiquitous games and entertainment
- Serious Games –applications, critiques
- Philosophical issues
- Prototypes
- Social and cultural uses of/for Play
- Tools and technologies
- Skills, strategy, rules and chance
- Genre
- Immersiveness and engagement
- Research methodologies in creative practice
- Usability and playability
- User/player centered design
- Psychological, social, and cultural differences in perception and participation
- Communities, networks, social interaction and social capital
- Cross-cultural and intercultural approaches
- Assessment of exploratory learning approaches
- Emerging practices

These events received 147 submissions from more than 24 countries. Each submission has been anonymously reviewed by an average of five independent reviewers, to ensure that accepted submissions were of a high standard. Consequently, only 23 full papers were published. The overall acceptance rate corresponds to about 16%. A few more papers were accepted as short papers, reflection papers and posters. An extended version of the best papers will be published in the IADIS International Journal on WWW/Internet (ISSN: 1645-7641) and also in other selected journals.

Besides the papers' and posters' presentation, the conferences also included a keynote presentation from an internationally distinguished researcher. We would therefore like to express our gratitude to Professor Xiaoru Yuan, School of AI, Peking University, China, for accepting our invitation to be the keynote speaker.

This volume has taken shape as a result of the contributions from a number of individuals. We are grateful to all authors who have submitted their papers to enrich these conferences proceedings. We wish to thank all members of the organizing committee, delegates, invitees and guests whose contribution and involvement are crucial for the success of the conference.

Last but not the least, we hope that everybody enjoyed the presentations, and we invite all participants for the next years´ edition of these conferences.

Katherine Blashki, Noroff University College, Norway
Interfaces and Human Computer Interaction 2022
& Game and Entertainment Technologies 2022 Program Chair

Piet Kommers, University of Twente, The Netherlands
Pedro Isaías, The University of New South Wales (UNSW – Sydney), Australia
MCCSIS 2022 General Conference Co-Chairs

July 2022

PROGRAM COMMITTEE

INTERFACES AND HUMAN COMPUTER INTERACTION CONFERENCE 2022 & GAME AND ENTERTAINMENT TECHNOLOGIES CONFERENCE 2022 PROGRAM CHAIR

Katherine Blashki, Noroff University College, Norway

MCCSIS 2022 GENERAL CONFERENCE CO-CHAIRS

Piet Kommers, University of Twente, The Netherlands
Pedro Isaías, The University of New South Wales (UNSW – Sydney), Australia

INTERFACES AND HUMAN COMPUTER INTERACTION CONFERENCE 2022 COMMITTEE MEMBERS

Alexander Kröner, Technische Hochschule Nürnberg Georg Simon Ohm, Germany
Ana Cristina Bicharra Garcia, Universidade Federal do Estado do Rio de Janeiro, Brazil
Anastasija Nikiforova, University of Tartu, Estonia & European Open Scien, Belgium
Andre Constantino da Silva, Instituto Federal de Sao Paulo, Brazil
Arianna D Ulizia, Irpps-cnr, Italy
Asterios Leonidis, Foundation For Research & Technology – Hellas, Greece
Bridget Kane, 1954, Sweden
Celia Martinie, Université Toulouse III - Paul Sabatier, France
Chee Weng Khong, Multimedia University, Malaysia
Connie Veugen, Vrije Universiteit Amsterdam, Netherlands
Eduardo Tanaka, Eldorado Research Institute, Brazil
Eleni Mangina, University College Dublin (UCD), Ireland
Janet Wesson, Nelson Mandela Metropolitan University, South Africa
Jesuk Ko, Universidad Mayor de San Andres (UMSA), Bolivia
José Antonio Macías Iglesias, Universidad Autónoma de Madrid, Spain
José Luis Tapia Fabela, Universidad Autónoma del Estado de México, Mexico
Kal Dhou, Texas A&M University Central Texas, USA
Kamila Rios Rodrigues, Universidade de São Paulo, Brazil
Larbi Esmahi, Athabasca University, Canada
Leonelo Almeida, Federal University of Technology, Paraná, Brazil
Linghan Zhang, George Mason University, USA
Maki K. Habib, The American University in Cairo, Egypt
Mark Apperley, University of Waikato, New Zealand
Mathieu Raynal, University of Toulouse, France
Michael Hobbs, Deakin University, Australia
Michael Hohl, HS Anhalt/FB Design, Germany
Nadine Vigouroux, IRIT, CNRS, Paul Sabtier University, France
Nuno Otero, Linnaeus University, Sweden
Otniel Portillo Rodriguez, Universidad Autonóma del Estado de México, Mexico
Rüdiger Heimgärtner, Intercultural User Interface Consulting, Germany
Sheng Tan, Trinity University, USA
Silvio Cazella, UFCSPA , Brazil
Xiaokun Zhang, Athabasca University, Canada
Yacine Bellik, LISN Laboratory, Paris-Saclay University, France

GAME AND ENTERTAINMENT TECHNOLOGIES 2022

COMMITTEE MEMBERS

Abdennour El Rhalibi, Liverpool John Moores University, United Kingdom
Alf Inge Wang, Norwegian University of Science and Technology, Norway
Castulus Kolo, Macromedia University of Applied Sciences, Germany
Christos Bouras, University of Patras and Computer Technology Institute, Greece
Connie Veugen, Vrije Universiteit Amsterdam, Netherlands
Damon Daylamani Zad, Brunel University, United Kingdom
Daniel Cermak-Sassenrath, It University of Copenhagen, Denmark
Etienne Armand Amato, Gobelins L École de L Image, France
Gabriele D`Angelo, University of Bologna, Italy
Harry Agius, Brunel University London, United Kingdom
Kendra Cooper, Independent Scholar, Canada
Laura Ricci, University of Pisa, Italy
Marcia Medeiros, UniFANOR (Devry Brasil), Brazil
Mei-kei Lai, Macao Polytechnic Institute, China
Michael Katchabaw, University of Western Ontario, Canada
Michel Simatic, Telecom Sudparis, France
Mikael Collan, Lappeenranta University of Technology, Finland
Monica Gavrielidou, University of Thessaly, Greece
Panagiotis Kyriakoulakos, University of the Aegean, Greece
Pilar Lacasa, University of Alcala, Spain
Thrasyvoulos Tsiatsos, Aristotle University of Thessaloniki, Greece
Vlasios Kasapakis, University of The Aegean, Greece
Xiong Shuo, Huazhong Univerisity of Science and Technology, China
Yoshihiro Okada, Kyushu University, Japan
Zuo Long, Chang An University, China

KEYNOTE LECTURE

VISUALIZING THE COVID-19 PANDEMIC

Professor Xiaoru Yuan, School of AI, Peking University, China

ABSTRACT

During the still ongoing COVID-19 pandemic, visualization has demonstrated its unique power in communication of the information era. In this talk, I will first present a series of visualizations done by my team and collaborators in the beginning of 2020 on the theme of COVID-19. Among them, some visualizations have been broadcasted by the media with a large audience. Then a visual analytical platform for collaboratively collecting, annotating, and analyzing a global collection of visualizations related to the COVID-19 pandemic will be introduced. The visualization samples we have collected through this platform could inspire further research in the direction of understanding how visualizations interact with the society. Key findings from this systematic approach will be discussed.

FULL PAPERS

A PSYCHOPHYSIOLOGICAL INVESTIGATION OF EMOTIONS EXPERIENCED IN A VIRTUAL REALITY 3D-LEARNING SIMULATION

Sadaf H. Khan, Abhijeet Kujur and Jyoti Kumar
Department of Design,
Indian Institute of Technology Delhi, India

ABSTRACT

Virtual Reality (VR) technology is being used as a tool in a range of sectors, including emotional research and academia. To date, research has investigated the efficacy of virtual reality in a variety of emotional-related health treatments, learning phobia therapy, and the provision of virtual support to students throughout the globe. The immersive environments and experiences of virtual reality have a significant psychological influence on VR users. The emotional state is related to a person's educational background. Therefore, it would be intriguing to explore the effect of virtual reality on the emotional states of learners. The emotional impact of VR-3D learning environments is investigated in this study. It employs neurophysiological techniques, such as the Galvanic Skin Response (GSR), semi-structured interviews, and self-reporting questionnaires, to evaluate the emotional states, VR experiences, and other behavioral elements of students. The participants in the research were asked to engage in virtual reality learning situations, and their physiological responses were recorded simultaneously. According to the findings, Virtual 3D-Environments in educational settings may aid students in reducing stress and evoking positive emotions, resulting in an enhanced learning experience.

KEYWORDS

VR 3D-Learning Simulation, Emotion, Learning Experiences, GSR

1. INTRODUCTION

Emotions are important in rational decision-making, perception, and learning, along with a range of other processes that influence both physiological and psychological health (Picard, 1997). As emotions are mediated through attention, self-regulation, and motivation, they have an immediate impact on learning and accomplishment (Pekrun, 1992). They guide a person's attention toward or away from learning issues in learning contexts, resulting in self-regulated learning. According to research, learners who are in a happy emotional state make more constructive judgments because they perceive events more favourably than they would at other times (Isen and Reeve, 2005). In addition, past research has shown that emotions may influence learners' performance and achievement while using computer-assisted learning and emotional variables should be included throughout the learning process (Järvenoja and Järvelä, 2005) (Nummenmaa et al., 2008). Thus, emotional comprehension and recognition are critical parts of human behavior study especially while learning. Affective states must be elicited in laboratory contexts to research human emotions. Emotion elicitation methods such as visuals, sounds, films, and, more recently, virtual reality (VR) have been used recently in literature. (Cipresso et al., 2018). Virtual Reality (VR) headsets, give a level of immersion that may facilitate more consistent emotional elicitation than less-immersive displays, and can provide a powerful but reasonably safe platform for eliciting negative emotions like fear and rage. In both scientific and commercial contexts, virtual reality has grown in popularity in recent years. Emotions strengthen our sensory cortices, according to a review performed by Vuilleumier (2005). According to the studies that have involved neuroimaging, our sensory cortices activate more in reaction to emotion (Vuilleumier, 2005). Today, many students struggle with comprehension owing to the quality and requirement of abstract thought and concepts. VR plays a crucial part in pedagogy, providing a wonderful and engaging way to acquire knowledge. However, in order to explore emotions while learning subjective surveys, such as the Positive and Negative Affect Schedule (PANAS), Self-Assessment Manikin (SAM), and Differential Emotions Scale, are currently the most popular techniques.

Emotion can also be expressed through the autonomous nervous system, which regulates physiological cues such as skin conductance, facial expression, heart rate, body temperature, and pupil dilation (Chen et al., 2017). Immersion is another VR phenomenon tied to emotional experience. Immersion is a three-dimensional concept that expresses how present a user feels in a virtual reality environment (Slater and Wilbur, 1997). Three aspects of immersion have been found by researchers: spatial immersion, engagement, and realness (Schubert et al., 2001). These models seek to explain how the mind generates the feeling of immersion. These theories are based on cognitive processes, and they assume that focusing attention on the VR world and building a mental picture of it are required for humans to feel immersion (Sheridan, 1999). A virtual reality learning environment (VRLE) is one in which the participant (for example, a student) actively engages with what is going on rather than being a passive recipient of the information that is being presented to them. Additionally, it promotes facilitation between students' emotional well-being and their surrounding environments. This might be in the form of a desktop setup, or it could entail the student donning virtual reality glasses or some other type of head mounted display (HMD) together with an input device. Due to this virtual immersion, they are able to participate in the activities taking place in that environment. The use of an embodiment in a VR setup, which is a three-dimensional representation of a person, is yet another approach that may be taken. A student may first conceptualize and create his or her virtual being before employing him or her to get exposed to a simulated setting. Their physical manifestation may be tailored to their specifications and style of operation (Bricken, 1991). Therefore, the purpose of the study is to observe that VR learning environments elicit positive emotions that are helpful in learning.

2. LITERATURE SURVEY

2.1 Emotions Induced in Virtual Built-Environments in an Academic Context

Students' learning outcomes are significantly influenced by the VR academic environment (Gilmore and Warren, 2007). Emotions are thought to play an important influence in computer and technology-assisted academic learning (Plass and Kaplan, 2016). Exploration of emotions generated during interactions with the learning environment, (ii) measurement of emotional experience in the learning environment, and (iii) causes and effects of the emotional state of the learner in the learning environment are the three main areas of research on emotions during learning (Mayer, 2020). The first step is to pinpoint the major emotions that learners experience when engaging in an educational activity. In a technology-rich learning environment, three types of emotions have been discovered (Loderer et al., 2020). Positive emotions like pleasure, and negative feelings like stress and boredom (Duffy et al., 2020). However, in an experiment involving learning in augmented reality (Harley et al., 2020), the pleasant emotions of joy and interest were the highest intensity emotional states discovered.

The next step is to determine methods to explore the key emotions that students experience when using VR based learning. Interviews, scale-based questionnaires, and neurophysiological methods for measuring arousal, using GSR (Tichon and Mavin, 2019), have all been employed in the literature to identify emotions. The last step is to determine what kinds of causal linkages, factors and effects between the learning environment and emotions (Loderer et al., 2020). Researchers have uncovered evidence of links between emotional processing (e.g emotions experienced during e-learning) and cognitive processing (such as involvement level and strategy use), as well as between affective processing and learning outcomes (Deaux and Philogène, 2001).

Emotions are mental and emotional states that affect behavior and thought. They are initiated by external or internal stimuli and are followed by physical and physiological reactions. Two characteristics of emotions are arousal, or activity, and valence, or pleasantness (Lang, 1995). The intensity of emotions have been linked to neurological and physiological activity, as well as ideas and culture. From a physiological viewpoint, it is believed that physiological reactions to events cause emotions. Since the physiological signals associated with emotional states are automatic, the majority of individuals are unaware of them. Consequently, physiological signal analysis may be utilized to determine emotions with precision. Therefore, the purpose of this research was to explore the effect of virtual reality learning environments on students' emotional being. In this experiment, the HTC vive pro-eye VR Headset and Empatica-E4 GSR are employed for stimulus exposure and data collection, respectively. The objective was to examine the participants' positive and negative emotional states, as well as their level of arousal, while exposed to a VR learning environment.

2.2 Validation for Utilizing Virtual Reality in Learning Environments

In a simulated environment, the ability to elicit a response from the user is similar to that elicited by a physical environment (Rohrmann and Bishop, 2002). As a result, direct comparisons of virtual and real environments are required. Psychological responses and cognitive performance have been used in some comparisons to assess the validity of virtual environments (Kort et al., 2003). The subjective perceptions of daylit spaces were compared by Chamilothori, Wienold, and Andersen, who found no significant differences between the real and virtual environments (Chamilothori et al., 2019). Researchers investigated psycho-physiological responses elicited by real-world and VR scenarios with varying levels of immersion using electrodermal activity (EDA) and found correlations in physiological dynamics between real-world and 3D environments (Higuera-Trujillo et al., 2017). Marn-Morales et al investigated the emotional responses elicited in subjects in a real and virtual museum, finding no differences in self-assessment but differences in brain dynamics (Marín-Morales et al., 2019). Therefore, more research is required to determine the validity of virtual reality in terms of physiological responses and behavioral performance.

3. METHODS AND MATERIALS

3.1 Stimuli

A 3D virtual environment was created with a collaborative pedagogical approach in mind, allowing for greater reciprocal learning in academic settings but also requiring learners to work and perform autonomously. The 3D-VR learning environment was used as a stimulus in order to assess the emotional responses of the participants in this study. The softwares 'Sketchup-Pro VR' and 'Simlab Composer-10 VR' were used to create this stimulation. The stimulus was delivered to the subjects through an HTC Vive Pro-Eye VR Headset. The Virtual Classroom was developed keeping in mind the Collaborative Pedagogical approach. The non-rigid flexible arrangement style was applied within a four-walled enclosure provided with modernistic materials and textures like steel, glass, thermoplastic, acrylic, wood etc. The space of the VR classroom was 24 sq. m. The design of the VR learning space may be categorised as a modernist classroom setting.

Figure 1. 3D-VR learning environment to evaluate learner's emotional responses

3.2 Participants

The participants in this study were nine males and two females, with a mean age of 23.15 years and a standard deviation of 2.98 years. All of the participants were IIT Delhi undergraduate students with design and non-design backgrounds.

3.3 Procedure

Participants in this experiment were instructed to wear virtual reality headgear, a galvanic skin response (GSR) sensor wristwatch, and interact with a 3D virtual environment that was designed with a collaborative pedagogical approach in mind. They were told to familiarize themselves with the headgear, observe their virtual surroundings, and get immersed in it. They were then virtually transported to the virtual simulation for a time interval of 6 minutes. Each participant was given 15 minutes to complete the experiment, including the time for preparation of the experiment and the time spent experiencing the VR simulation. During the experiment, their GSR data was also being recorded. Soon after the experiment, a questionnaire was asked to be filled out by the participants based on their experiences in the virtual classroom setting, as well as a few questions were asked of them in a form of semi-structured interview.

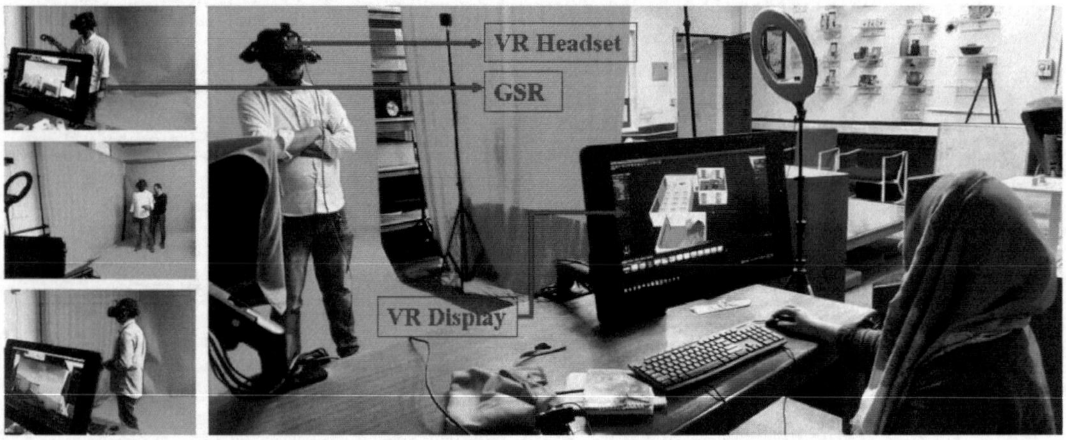

Figure 2. Participant activity during the VR Experiment

4. ANALYSIS AND RESULTS

For this study, there were three primary methods of data collection. In-person semi-structured interviews are the first approach. Participants expressed and described their experiences in a 3D-VR learning setting. The questionnaire, which participants were requested to complete, provided the second source of data. Galvanic skin responses to emotional arousal, captured as the subjects interacted with the VR environment, was the third source of data. Finally, as described earlier in this section, the three sources of data were assessed and analyzed.

4.1 Interview Findings

When exposed to the virtual classroom simulation, participants reported their feelings of 'Engagement', 'Calmness', and 'Stress'. These reports included their emotional reactions to the virtual classroom setting, as well as their likes and dislikes. As shown in Figure 3, 60% of the participants described the VR environment as engaging, 30% as calm, and 10% as stressful.

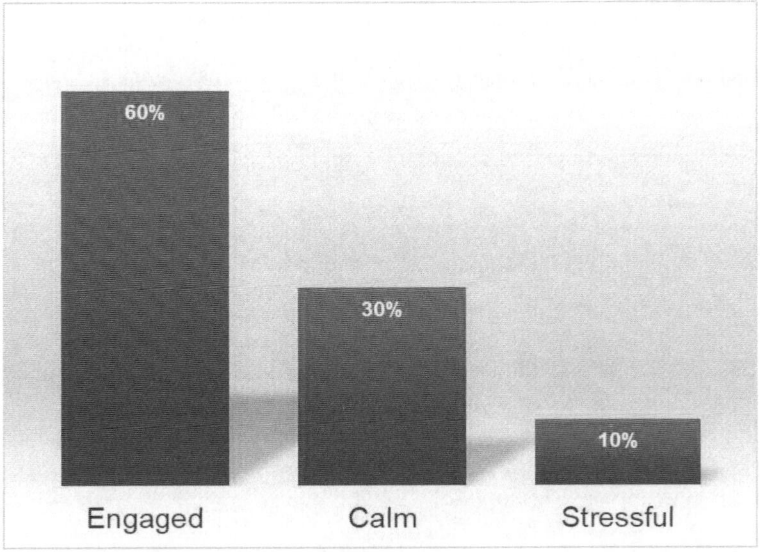

Figure 3. No. of mentions for the kind of feeling in the simulated VR-Environment

4.2 Questionnaire Findings

According to the questionnaire, the participants felt both pleasant and unpleasant feelings when interacting with the 3D VR environment. 'Distress', 'Fear', 'Calmness' and 'Engagement' were the most common feelings felt by nearly all of the participants. Positive learning emotions were expressed by all individuals, who felt calm and engaged while they were experiencing the simulation. As seen in Figure 4, negative emotions such as distress and fear are represented by red, while positive emotions such as calmness and engagement are represented by blue in the graph.

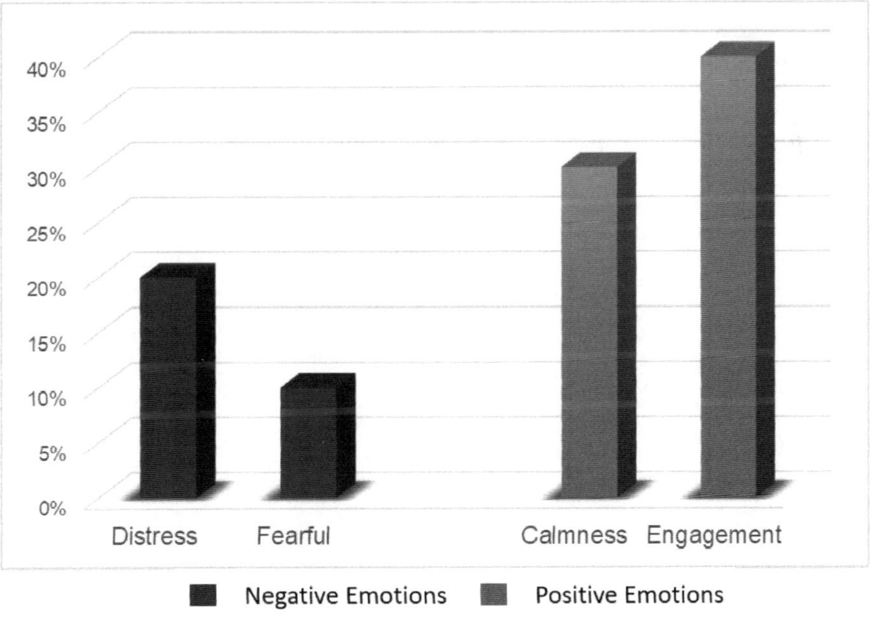

Figure 4. Emotional Data from the Questionnaire

The behavioural data out of the questionnaire resulted in 50% of people being found to be 'satisfied' with this kind of VR learning environment, 30% mentioned that the VR environment can enhance their 'performance' and 20% felt that these kinds of virtual environments have great 'importance' in learning.

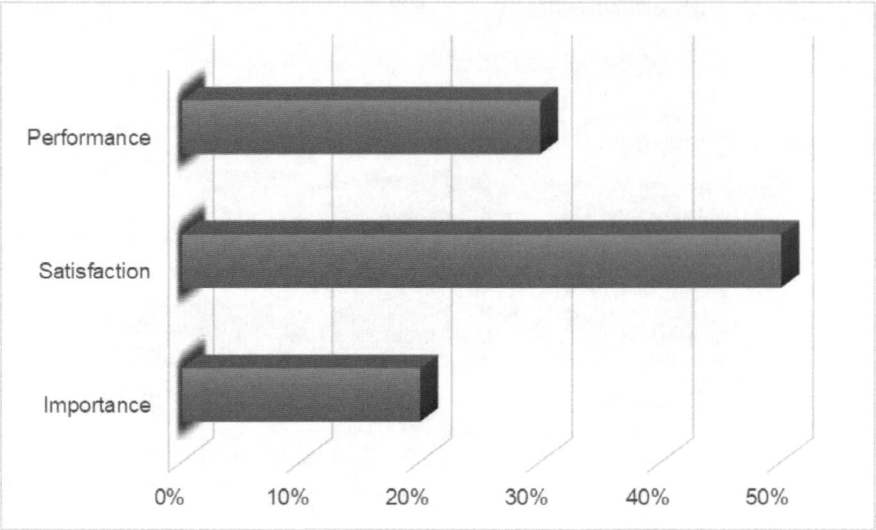

Figure 5. Behavioural Data from the Questionnaire

4.3 Psychogalvanic Reflex Findings

The change in electrical resistance of the skin is a response for emotional arousal and is measured via the galvanic skin response. It changes when the activity of sweat glands regulated by the ANS changes. Previous research has found that skin conductivity rises in synchrony with emotional arousal (Handri et al., 2010). To measure the GSR signal, a commercial sensor was used (Empatica E4 wristwatch sensor). The sensor was attached to the individual's wrist (figure 2). In order to determine the variability of the GSR signal, the temporal domain was explored and evaluated. Using normalization methods, data was filtered. Using the following formula, normalized data was obtained:

Normalized GSR = Experimental GSR - Baseline GSR

The rise in the rate of emotional arousal as measured by the GSR sensor during the 3D learning simulation is seen in Figure 6. It is evident that with the commencement of the stimulus, which is VR immersion and along with VR components such as the brightness of the virtual learning environment, the openness of the room, the sharp edges of the furniture, and the texture, arousal level is increased. After a noticeable latency (((Alexander et al., 2005)), the mean arousal level of all participants peaked. The skin conductance level increases according to the duration of VR exposure.

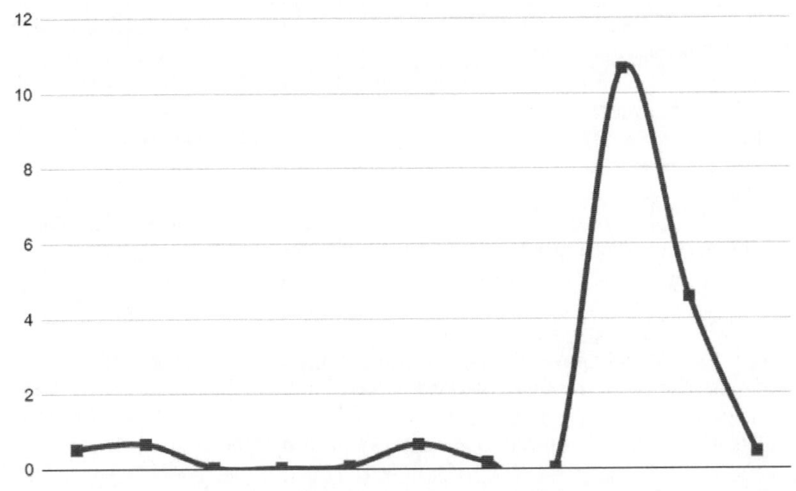

Figure 6. Increase in the rate of emotional arousal during interaction with 3D-VR learning environment

5. DISCUSSION AND CONCLUSION

As the stimulation in a constructed 3D-VR environment is prominent, the study's results indicate that there is a critical link between the built-environment of a learning space and the emotional states of students. These pleasant and unpleasant emotional states impact the learner's learning capacity and results. Though the limited sample size is a significant drawback for the purpose of this research, the experiment's results give a wealth of information for evaluating the likelihood of emotional arousal on learning. This experiment demonstrates that behavioural information, such as interview data and questionnaire data, may be used to determine what sort of 3D VR learning simulation learners need in terms of their emotions. In addition, the GSR signal may be useful for investigating the causes of emotional arousal. Even though great progress has been made in approaches for detecting emotional states, further research is required to uncover effective VR classroom features to trigger emotions that strongly affect learning via cognitive factors such as expectancies and perceptions. Basic emotions are universal, but those which elicit strong emotions in the VR classroom should be examined. We also urge that participants actively and deliberately engage in the selection of what triggers their emotions, and are educated about the study's goal, so that they may help trigger their own emotions.

REFERENCES

Alexander, D. M., Trengove, C., Johnston, P., Cooper, T., August, J. P., & Gordon, E. (2005). Separating individual skin conductance responses in a short interstimulus-interval paradigm. Journal of Neuroscience Methods, 146(1), 116–123. https://doi.org/10.1016/j.jneumeth.2005.02.001

Bricken M (1991) Virtual reality learning environments: potentials and challenges. SIGGRAPH Comput. Graph. 25(3). New York, NY, USA: Association for Computing Machinery: 178–184.

Chamilothori K, Wienold J and Andersen M (2019) Adequacy of Immersive Virtual Reality for the Perception of Daylit Spaces: Comparison of Real and Virtual Environments. LEUKOS 15(2-3). Taylor & Francis: 203–226.

Chen H, Dey A, Billinghurst M, et al. (2017) Exploring pupil dilation in emotional virtual reality environments. Available at: http://ir.canterbury.ac.nz/handle/10092/15404.

Cipresso P, Giglioli IAC, Raya MA, et al. (2018) The Past, Present, and Future of Virtual and Augmented Reality Research: A Network and Cluster Analysis of the Literature. Frontiers in psychology 9: 2086.

Deaux K and Philogène G (2001) Representations of the Social: Bridging Theoretical Traditions. Wiley.

Duffy MC, Lajoie SP, Pekrun R, et al. (2020) Emotions in medical education: Examining the validity of the Medical Emotion Scale (MES) across authentic medical learning environments. Learning and Instruction. DOI: 10.1016/j.learninstruc.2018.07.001.

Gilmore S and Warren S (2007) Themed article: Emotion online: Experiences of teaching in a virtual learning environment. Human relations; studies towards the integration of the social sciences 60(4). SAGE Publications Ltd: 581–608.

Handri S, Yajima K, Nomura S, et al. (2010) Evaluation of Student's Physiological Response Towards E-Learning Courses Material by Using GSR Sensor. 2010 IEEE/ACIS 9th International Conference on Computer and Information Science. DOI: 10.1109/icis.2010.92.

Harley JM, Lajoie SP, Tressel T, et al. (2020) Fostering positive emotions and history knowledge with location-based augmented reality and tour-guide prompts. Learning and Instruction 70: 101163.

Higuera-Trujillo JL, Maldonado JL-T and Millán CL (2017) Psychological and physiological human responses to simulated and real environments: A comparison between Photographs, 360° Panoramas, and Virtual Reality. Applied Ergonomics. DOI: 10.1016/j.apergo.2017.05.006.

Isen AM and Reeve J (2005) The Influence of Positive Affect on Intrinsic and Extrinsic Motivation: Facilitating Enjoyment of Play, Responsible Work Behavior, and Self-Control. Motivation and emotion 29(4): 295–323.

Järvenoja H and Järvelä S (2005) How students describe the sources of their emotional and motivational experiences during the learning process: A qualitative approach. Learning and Instruction 15(5): 465–480.

Kort YAW de, de Kort YAW, IJsselsteijn WA, et al. (2003) Virtual Laboratories: Comparability of Real and Virtual Environments for Environmental Psychology. Presence: Teleoperators and Virtual Environments. DOI: 10.1162/105474603322391604.

Lang PJ (1995) The emotion probe. Studies of motivation and attention. The American psychologist 50(5): 372–385.

Loderer K, Pekrun R and Lester JC (2020) Beyond cold technology: A systematic review and meta-analysis on emotions in technology-based learning environments. Learning and Instruction 70: 101162.

Marín-Morales J, Higuera-Trujillo JL, Greco A, et al. (2019) Real vs. immersive-virtual emotional experience: Analysis of psycho-physiological patterns in a free exploration of an art museum. PloS one 14(10): e0223881.

Marín-Morales J, Llinares C, Guixeres J, et al. (2020) Emotion Recognition in Immersive Virtual Reality: From Statistics to Affective Computing. Sensors 20(18). DOI: 10.3390/s20185163.

Mayer (2020.) Searching for the role of emotions in e-learning. Learning and instruction. Available at: https://www.sciencedirect.com/science/article/pii/S095947521930324X.

Nummenmaa L, Hirvonen J, Parkkola R, et al. (2008) Is emotional contagion special? An fMRI study on neural systems for affective and cognitive empathy. NeuroImage 43(3): 571–580.

Pekrun R (1992) The impact of emotions on learning and achievement: Towards a theory of cognitive/motivational mediators. Applied psychology = Psychologie appliquee 41(4). Wiley: 359–376.

Picard (1997.) Affective Computing Cambridge. MA: MIT Press [Google Scholar].

Plass JL and Kaplan U (2016) Chapter 7 - Emotional Design in Digital Media for Learning. In: Tettegah SY and Gartmeier M (eds) Emotions, Technology, Design, and Learning. San Diego: Academic Press, pp. 131–161.

Rohrmann B and Bishop I (2002) SUBJECTIVE RESPONSES TO COMPUTER SIMULATIONS OF URBAN ENVIRONMENTS. Journal of environmental psychology 22(4): 319–331.

Schubert T, Friedmann F and Regenbrecht H (2001) The experience of presence: Factor analytic insights. Presence 10(3). MIT Press - Journals: 266–281.

Sheridan TB (1999) Descartes, Heidegger, Gibson, and God: Toward an eclectic ontology of presence. Presence 8(5). MIT Press - Journals: 551–559.

Slater M and Wilbur S (1997) A framework for immersive virtual environments (FIVE): Speculations on the role of presence in virtual environments. Presence 6(6). MIT Press - Journals: 603–616.

Tichon JG and Mavin T (2019) Using the Experience of Evoked Emotion in Virtual Reality to Manage Workplace Stress. Human Performance Technology. DOI: 10.4018/978-1-5225-8356-1.ch011.

Vuilleumier P (2005) How brains beware: neural mechanisms of emotional attention. Trends in cognitive sciences 9 (12): 585–594.

UNDERSTANDING VIRTUAL REALITY GAME PLAYERS' SATISFACTION, LOYALTY, AND EXPERIENCE VALUE: A CASE STUDY OF THE BEATSABER

Guan Zhi Wang and Wen Huei Chou
Department of Digital Media Design
National Yunlin University of Science and Technology
123 University Road, Section 3, Douliou, Yunlin 64002, Taiwan, R.O.C

ABSTRACT

In recent years, the emergence of VR technology provides game players immersive experience in a 3D virtual world. This study investigated virtual reality gamers' experience value, customer satisfaction, and customer loyalty in China with online questionnaires. A total of 383 valid questionnaires were collected and which were analyzed by factor analysis and reliability analysis. The results show that the experience value of VR game players has a positive and significant impact on both customer satisfaction and customer loyalty. In addition, customer satisfaction has a positive and significant influence on customer loyalty. Furthermore, there are significant differences in players' experience value among different genders. Therefore, it is suggested that when designing games or VR products, the gamming industry should consider the differences in the intrinsic factors of customer experience value between male and female to achieve the goal of improving customer's satisfaction and their loyalty.

KEYWORDS

Virtual Reality, Game Player, Experience Value, Customer Satisfaction, Customer Loyalty

1. INTRODUCTION

Virtual reality (VR) uses computers and headware devices to generate a realistic three-dimensional visual, tactile, and auditory sensory environment (Bierbaum, 2000), giving people a sense of immersion, which is formed by the high degree of integration and unification between humans and computers (Yang, 2016). Due to the rapid development of VR in the early 21st century, the cost down of the VR products has become more and more popular. For the first-time user of VR games, good experience value will make them more likely to purchase VR products in the future (Chen, 2016).

There are relatively few studies addressing the relationships about user experience and their loyalty and satisfaction in VR scenario. Among them, there is even rare literature to be found on discussing customer satisfaction, customer loyalty and customer experience value based on different genders. "BeatSaber is the best-selling VR game to date, with 4 million units sold on all platforms. Therefore, this paper takes it as an example to explore VR game players' satisfaction, loyalty and experience value in different genders. VR game players' responses were collected by the online questionnaire, and then analized by the statistical software to understand the relationships of the constructs. This paper was divided into introduction, literature review, research design, statistical analysis, and conclusions and discussions.

2. LITERATURE REVIEW

2.1 Characteristics of Virtual Reality

Dalgarno & Lee (2010) stated that multi-perception is the aspects of VR technology that give users multi-perceptual capabilities, such as auditory perception, visual perception, tactile perception or motion perception. With the advance of VR technology, human-computer interaction and multi-sensory ccould produce the similiar feeling as in real life in the virtual environment. According to Mikropoulos (2006), interactivity refers to the degree to which users can manipulate objects in an analogous environment and receive the feedbacks from the environment. Immersion is a psychological state mainly referring to the user's feeling of being surrounded by an environment that provides continuous stimulating information to the user. To increase the user's immersion, the connection between the real world and the virtual world can be used to enhance the user's sense of immersion, which enables the user to quickly integrate into the virtual environment. Thus, the integration between the user and the virtual environment is rapidly enhanced (Duan, Wu, and Jin, 2015). Van de Vall (2002), argued that input and immersion are essential factors for experiencing presence. In order to effectively measure the degree of immersion, the factors that affect input and immersion should be accurately analyzed. This view is similar to the cognitive process of immersion proposed by Parong & Mayer (2021).

2.2 Customer Satisfaction and Loyalty

Customer satisfaction of VR products is a key factor in promoting VR technology because it is beneficial to increase the market share of products, which in turn generate income for the R&D of VR companies (Ru, 2017). To increase customers' satisfaction, VR products must meet the needs of the customers in terms of cost-performance ratio and price flexibility (Bierbaum, 2000). If the VR products is pricing too high, then customers would not be satisfied to support them. In terms of price elasticity, high-tech products are high in price but their retention rate is relatively low, so the users' satisfaction of the products decrease. Tsai (2016) stated that value demand is the overall feeling of customer payoff and reward. Gartner (2016) specified products need to have novel features, reasonable price, and sufficient attractiveness to meet the needs of their customers.

Customer loyalty is inseparable from custom satisfaction. Customer loyalty can be determined by the following two dimensions: 1. Quality requirements: In experiencing a product, customers will first realize the performance and applicability of the product (Chennamma, 2013); followed by the reliability and safety of the product (Chen, 2016). This means that the design of VR devices needs to consider various aspects in order to meet the user's demand for product quality. 2. Functional requirements: customers will consider the product's dominant functions and assistance tools. Dominant function refers to the technology and comfort that the product can provide to customers in the process of device use. In terms of VR products, electronic devices should be able to play the role of creating virtual space graphics. Secondly, they should enhance the user's product experience through vision, hearing or touch, so the user can feel all the functional experiences that occur in the real world in the virtual environment.

2.3 Customer Experience Value

Mathwick, Malhotra and Rigodon (2001) believed that experience value can be divided into four criterias such as customer return on investment, service superiority, aesthetic sense, and fun. Among which, customer return on investment mainly refers to the psychological input of financial investment and the return on investment. These factors affect the customer's pursuit of product function and the service return of product efficiency. The service superiority mainly refers to the customer's passive feeling of the service and the degree of service professionalism. The aesthetic sense is only a passive reaction to the external situation generated by the customer subjectively. The reaction is mainly the impact of visual effects produced by customers attracted in the consumption situation. Fun is an intrinsic experience value with self-expression value formed by customers through their own preferences, which mainly includes two aspects including escape and enjoyment.

When comparing different gaming experiences, Christensen, Mathiesen, Poulsen, Ustrup & Kraus (2018) pointed out most aspects of the gaming experience were rated significantly higher in the VR version than in the non-VR version. In a tourism study, Wu, Ai & Cheng (2019) found that satisfaction with the VR experience is positively related to loyalty. In addition, the VR experience is positively related to satisfaction with the VR experience and loyalty to the VR experience.

2.4 Gender Differences in Gaming

The VR world is a cyberspace that full of fantasy and with a sense of modernity. In the game, dreams and reality are mixed together to form a creative world. The VR players could be male or female. MacCallum-Stewart (2010) pointed out that female players prefer romantic, cute, social, and even pink as the main theme of the game. This also explains why men and women show different thoughts and personalities when playing games. Therefore, this study investigates gender difference in experience value, customer satisfaction, and customer loyalty.

2.5 Research Hypotheses

Tseng and Chang (2012) found that experience value has a positive and significant effect on customer satisfaction. Therefore, hypothesis H1 is proposed: VR game customer experience value will have a positive and significant impact on customer satisfaction. The study of Tseng and Zhang (2012) found that experience value has a significant impact on customer loyalty. Therefore, hypothesis H2 is proposed: VR game customer experience value will have a positive and significant impact on customer loyalty.

Singh (2006) stated that increasing customer satisfaction can increase future customer loyalty. Strenitzerová and Gaňa (2018) argued that there is a positive effect of customer satisfaction on customer loyalty and that satisfaction will spread with the positive effect to attract potential consumers. Therefore, hypothesis H3 is proposed: VR game customer satisfaction has a positive and significant effect on customer loyalty.

Liu (2018) found that online games are different for men and women in terms of the experience value. Lin, Lin and Jiang (2015) mentioned that players with different genders could gain and enhance friendships, challenge mission levels, and relax through gaming attributes such as social interaction, scenario simulation, mission design, and animation effects. Based on the above literature, hypothesis H4 is proposed: customers with different genders have significant differences in customer experience value.

Zhang (2014) believed that different genders will choose different types of games. Lowrie and Jorgensen (2011) found that male teammates prefer games to be more action, visual and spatial, while females prefer problem solving and quantitative calculation related games. Therefore, hypothesis H5 is proposed: There is a significant difference in customer loyalty among customers of different genders.

Yu (2010) pointed out male are significantly more addicted to online games than female, and there are significant gender differences in the satisfaction of different online games. Chuang, Liu and Hsieh (2021) studied survival shooting game players and found that there were significant gender differences in satisfaction with the game, and males had higher satisfaction levels comparing with female. Therefore, based on the above literature, hypothesis H6 is proposed: there is a significant difference in customer satisfaction by gender.

The research model is shown in Figure 1.

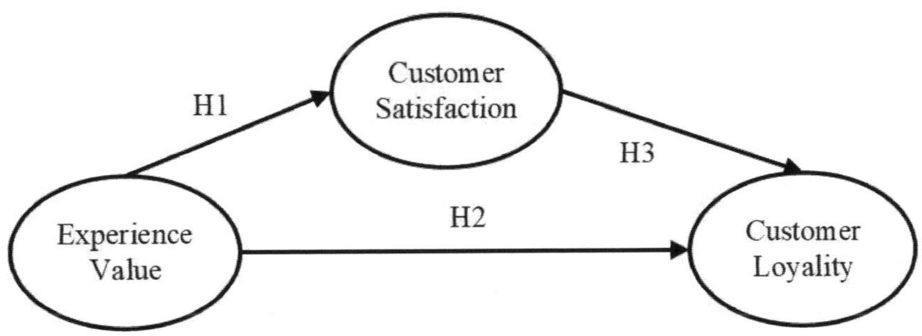

Figure 1. Research model

3. RESEARCH DESIGN

3.1 Questionnaire Development

In this study, the questionnaire was designed based on the above-mentioned research variables and definitions, as well as with reference to the research of past scholars. The first part of the questionnaire is customer experience value, which includes 15 questions on return on investment, superiority, aesthetics, fun, and immersion; the second part is customer satisfaction, which includes 13 questions on safety and reliability, five senses, cost-performance ratio, interactivity, and applicability; the third part is customer loyalty, which includes 15 questions on flexible price, multi-sensory game environment, inner thoughts, immersion, and attention; the fourth part is respondents' background information (age, age, age of the respondents, and age of the respondents). The questionnaire was measured on a five-point Likert scale, with five categories: very satisfied, satisfied, average, dissatisfied, and very dissatisfied, and was given scores of 5, 4, 3, 2, and 1 in that order.

3.2 Sampling Process

A total of 383 valid questionnaires were collected during the 5-day survey period from 2021/11/20 to 2021/11/25.

3.3 Questionnaire Validity and Reliability

This study adopted factor analysis to examine the survey items of the constructs. Questions were retained if their eigen values is greater than 1, and factor loading is greater than .5 (Hair, Anderson, Babin & Black, 2010). The constructs to be measured includes return on investment, superiority, aesthetics, fun, immersion, safety and reliability, five senses, cost-price ratio, interactivity, applicability, flexible price, multi-sensory game environment, internal thinking, strength of immersion tendency, and attention. In the reliability analysis, the Cronbach's α of all the components ranged from 0.74 to 0.95, which all met the standard of 0.7. Therefore, the questionnaire has good validity and reliability.

4. STATISTICAL ANALYSIS

4.1 Gender Differences

The sample of this study consisted of 285 (54.91%) males and 234 (45.09%) females. The mean of the customer experience value was 4.34 (standard deviation .60) for male and 4.21 (standard deviation .59) for female. The test result reached a significant level ($t=2.37$, $p=.018<0.05$), indicating that there is a significant difference between male and female students' perceptions of experience value. However, there was no significant difference in gender regarding customer satisfaction and customer loyalty. The comparative analysis of different constrcuts by gender is shown in Table 1.

Table 1. The differences of constructs by gender

Constructs	Gender	N	Mean	Std. Deviation	t	p-value
Customer Experience Value	Male	285	4.34	.60	2.37	.018
	Female	234	4.21	.59		
Customer Satisfaction	Male	285	4.27	.67	.41	.679
	Female	234	4.24	.64		
Customer Royality	Male	285	4.17	.64	-.07	.947
	Female	234	4.17	.59		

4.2 Regression Analysis

The non-standardized coefficient of experience value on customer satisfaction is 0.967, and the t-value is 43.147 (p=.000<0.05). Therefore, hypothesis 1 is supported. The experience value has a significant impact on customer satisfaction. The R2 is 0.783, which means that it has high explanatory power, as shown in Table 2.

Table 2. Regression of experience value on customer satisfaction

Dependent Variable	Indenpent Variable	Non-standarized Coefficient		Standarized Coefficient	t	p-value	Explainable Variation
		B	Standard error	β			R^2
	Constant	0.085	0.041		2.073	0.039	0.783
Customer Satisfaction	Experience Value	0.967	0.022	0.885	43.147	0.000	

The non-standardized coefficient of experience value on customer loyalty is 0.885, and the t-value was 37.923 (p=.000 < 0.05). Hence, hypothesis 2 is supported. The experience value has a significant influence on customer loyalty. The R2 is 0.736 indicating a high degree of explanatory power, as shown in Table 3.

Table 3. Regression of experience value on customer loyality

Dependent Variable	Indenpent Variable	Non-standarized Coefficient		Standarized Coefficient	t	p-value	Explainable Variation
		B	Standard error	β			R^2
	Constant	0.311	0.042		7.335	0.000	0.736
Customer Loyality	Experience Value	0.885	0.023	0.858	37.923	0.000	

The non-standardized coefficient of customer satisfaction on customer loyalty is 0.852 and the t-value is 47.732 (p=.000<0.05), so hypothesis 3 holds. There is a significant effect of customer satisfaction on customer loyalty. The R2 is 0.815 meaning there is a a high degree of explanatory power, as shown in Table 4.

Table 4. Regression of customer satisfaction on customer loyality

Dependent Variable	Indenpent Variable	Non-standarized Coefficient		Standarized Coefficient	t	p-value	Explainable Variation
		B	Standard error	β			R^2
	Constant	0.344	0.033		10.331	0.000	0.815
Customer Loyality	Customer Satisfaction	0.852	0.018	0.903	47.732	0.000	

5. CONCLUSIONS AND SUGGESTIONS

The results of the regression analysis show that hypotheses 1, 2 and 3 are all supported. VR gammers' experience value have positively and significantly effects on both customer satisfaction and customer loyality. Namely, VR head-mounted displays could ehnacne users' experience value, and increase both their satisfaction and loyality. In addition, VR game customer satisfaction has a positive and significant impact on customer loyalty. When VR players are satisfied with the VR experiences that head-mounted displays brought to them, their loyalty were increased, so they would use the VR device continuously.

There are significant differences in gender regarding experience value. Male players are more willing to pay for the game than female players. In terms of aesthetics, male customers are more acceptable thatn than female customers when playing the game. In terms of pleasure, male players believe the game is more interesting than female players. The overall experience value of male customers is higher than that of female customers. Therefore, when designing VR games or products, the VR company should consider the differences of the intrinsic factors in the experience value between male and female customers in order to achieve the goal of improving customer satisfaction and customer loyalty.

REFERENCES

Bierbaum, A. D. (2000). VR Juggler: A Virtual Platform for Virtual Reality Application Development (Master dissertaion, Iowa State University). Retrieved from http://citeseerx.ist.psu.edu/viewdoc/summary?doi=10.1.1.18.4512

Chen, C. L. (2016). Regurgitation of VR virtual reality technology. Electronic Technology and Software Engineering, 16, 16-17.

Chennamma, H. R., & Yuan, X. (2013). A survey on eye-gaze tracking techniques. arXiv preprint arXiv, 14, 1312-6410.

Christensen, J. V., Mathiesen, M., Poulsen, J. H., Ustrup, E. E., & Kraus, M. (2018, April). Player experience in a VR and non-VR multiplayer game. In *Proceedings of the virtual reality international conference-Laval virtual*, 1-4.

Chuang, C. W., Liu, C. F., & Hsieh, P. C. (2021). A study on the satisfaction of survival game shooting course - A case study of National Taichung University of Science and Technology. 20, 79-91.

Dalgarno, B., & Lee, M. (2010). What are the learning affordances of 3-D virtual environments? *British Journal of Educational Technology*, *1*, 10-32.

Dooley, K. (2020). A question of proximity: Exploring a new screen grammar for 360-degree cinematic virtual reality. *Media Practice and Education*, *21*(2), 81-96.

Duan, Y. F., Wu, X. L., & Jin, F. (2015). Research progress on the etiology and treatment of autism. *Chinese Science: Life Sciences*, 9, 820-844.

Gartner, W. B. (2016). *Entrepreneurship as organizing: Selected papers of William B. Gartner*. Edward Elgar Publishing.

Hair, J. F., Anderson, R. E., Babin, B. J., & Black, W. C. (2010). Multivariate data analysis: A global perspective (Vol. 7).

Lin, Y. L., Lin, H. W., & Jiang, Y. W. (2015). Value structure and clustering of social web game players. Marketing Review/Xing Xiao Ping Lun, *12*(3).

Lowrie, T.& Jorgensen, R. (2011). Gender differences in students'mathematics game playing. *Computer & Education*, *57* (4), 2244-2248.

MacCallum-Stewart, E. (2010). Lost on a desert island: The sims 2 castaway as convergence text. *Games and Culture*, *5*(3), 278-297

Mathwick, C., & Malhotra, N., & Rigodon, E. (2001). Measurement and Application in the Catalog and Internet Shopping Enviroament. *Experiential Value Conceptualization*, 1, 9-16.

Mikropoulos, T.A. (2006). A Unique Characteristic in Educational Virtual Environments.*Virtual Reality*, 3, 197-206.

Parong, J., & Mayer, R. E. (2021). Cognitive and affective processes for learning science in immersive virtual reality. *Journal of Computer Assisted Learning*, *37*(1), 226-241.

Ru Zuofei (2017). Application and prospect of virtual reality technology. *China Science and Technology Expo*, 35, 75-77.

Singh, H. (2006). The importance of customer satisfaction in relation to customer loyalty and retention. *Academy of Marketing Science*, *60*(193-225), 46.

Strenitzerová, M., & Gaňa, J. (2018). Customer satisfaction and loyalty as a part of customer-based corporate sustainability in the sector of mobile communications services. *Sustainability*, *10*(5), 1657.

Tsai, Ching-Lam (2016). What do teachers say? A study on the interference effect of school selection of senior high school students by the degree of teachers' opinions. *South Asia Journal*, 36, 290-321.

Tseng, L.C., and Zhang Y.R. (2012), A study of the relationship between customer perception quality, experience value, satisfaction, and loyalty: A case study of hotels in Kaohsiung and Tainan. *Jia Nan Journal*, 38, 347-365.

Van de Vall, R. (2002). Immersion and distance in virtual spaces. In *Mobilizing Place, Placing Mobility* (pp. 141-153). Brill.

Wu, H. C., Ai, C. H., & Cheng, C. C. (2019). Virtual reality experiences, attachment and experiential outcomes in tourism. *Tourism Review*.

Yang, Chien-Huei (2016). A study on customer satisfaction of online games and next-generation hosts in Hsinchu area (Unpublished master's thesis). Yuanpei University of Science and Technology, Taiwan.

Yu, J. W. (2010). A study on the relationship between school life satisfaction and online game addiction among secondary school students. *Journal of Chengdu University of Chinese Medicine: Education Science Edition*, 4, 6-69.

Zhang, Wan-Hui (2014). The effect of gender differences on the loyalty and willingness to pay for mobile games. Master's thesis, Department of Information Management, National Taichung University of Science and Technology, Taichung, Taiwan. Retrieved from https://hdl.handle.net/11296/j3eb75.

USING EMOTIONAL DESIGN TO RAISE AWARENESS OF INFORMATION SECURITY

Frauke Prott and Margit Scholl
Technical University of Applied Sciences Wildau
Hochschulring 1, 15745 Wildau, Germany

ABSTRACT

Awareness raising is a crucial step in achieving a higher level of information security (InfoSec), which is needed, in turn, for successful digitization. To encourage employees to feel positive toward InfoSec and as a means to support their learning process, awareness-raising measures can make use of the principles of emotional design. In this paper, we present the development and evaluation of digital serious games that use emotional design principles, such as personalization, the possibility of identification, appealing multimedia elements, and storytelling. The results of the user tests indicate that the digital serious games that have been developed are positively accepted by employees and moderately enhance and intensify InfoSec-related knowledge.

KEYWORDS

Emotional Design, Digital Serious Games, Awareness, Information Security

1. INTRODUCTION

Successful digitization relies on a high level of information security (InfoSec) (BMI, 2021). The latest Data Breach Investigations Report (DBIR) of Verizon states that 82 percent of the breaches were made possible by unconscious behavior and/or active decisions by humans involving the theft of credentials, phishing, misuse, or error (Verizon, 2022). Thus, the training and education of users to promote awareness of InfoSec and the appropriate behavior required to protect the information and data of their organization should be a critical and very important component of an organization's InfoSec strategy, besides technical advances and the designing of security guidelines that do not hinder but rather support the carrying out of daily work (Azeroual and Nikiforova, 2022; Sasse et al., 2022; ENISA, 2018).

Accordingly, the focus of this paper is on measures to raise awareness of InfoSec. InfoSec awareness (ISA) in the organizational context is defined as the extent to which every member of staff understands the importance of information security, the levels of information security appropriate to the organization, their individual security responsibilities, and acts accordingly (ISF, 2003). A literature review of ENISA (2018) suggests that measures that empower people to respond appropriately to InfoSec threats in the belief that their actions will be successful are more effective in provoking security-conscious behavior than measures that emphasize threats and trigger a feeling of fear. Thus, it is important to arouse positive emotions in employees when raising their awareness. This can be done by integrating emotional design into awareness-raising measures. "Emotional design is the concept of how to create designs that evoke emotions which result in positive user experiences" (Interaction Design Foundation, n.d.). In recent years, serious games have emerged as a new educational approach in InfoSec that creates a fun, enjoyable environment in which users can experience attacks and practice appropriate behavior to protect information assets (Hart et al., 2020).

Against this background, the present paper delineates the development and evaluation of digital serious games using the principles of emotional design as a means to raise awareness of InfoSec for employees working in small and medium-sized enterprises (SMEs). The digital serious games are part of the extensive research project Awareness Lab SME (ALARM) Information Security, which sets out to innovate a complete scenario that can be used to support SMEs in raising their InfoSec level and fostering a sustainable InfoSec culture within their organizations (https://alarm.wildau.biz/en). This scenario comprises analog and digital learning scenarios (serious games), on-site attacks (such as phishing simulations), and scientific testing, including awareness measurements, quizzes, and tests. The idea is to make InfoSec tangible and to forge an emotional relationship with it at the experiential level. The focus of the results presented here is on digital serious games.

The paper continues as follows: in section two we give an overview of the relevant literature on the emotional design of learning materials, game-based learning, and raising InfoSec awareness. In section three, we explain the development and story concept of the digital serious games and then present the results of the user tests of two games. Section four discusses the contribution and limitations of the paper and highlights further research activities.

2. LITERATURE REVIEW

2.1 Emotional Design of Learning Materials

Emotional design is characterized by, amongst other things, the personalization of the user experience, the possibility of identification, appealing multimedia elements (e.g., visual design, layout, color, sound), and storytelling (Interaction Design Foundation, n.d.; Um et al., 2011).

Um et al. (2011) demonstrate that the positive emotional design of multimedia learning materials, comprising saturated, bright warm color combinations and illustrations and characters with round shapes, increases comprehension and transfer and reduces the perceived difficulty of the learning task. In turn, the positive emotions that are elicited increase motivation and satisfaction and enhance perceptions of the learning materials. These findings are confirmed in different ways by further studies (e.g., Mayer and Estrella, 2014; Heidig et al., 2015; Li et al., 2020). Using emotional design principles in the design of a PowerPoint lesson—such as designing key learning elements with humanoid features and appealing colors—improves learning outcomes in terms of retention, as compared with standard black-and-white graphics, whereby marginally lower levels of perceived difficulty and marginally higher levels of learning effort are observed (Mayer and Estrella, 2014). In their attempt to identify relevant emotional design features, Heidig et al. (2015) find that learners' emotional states are influenced not so much by the objective but rather by the perceived aesthetics and usability of the material. While the emotional state has only a minor effect on learning outcomes, it impacts people's intrinsic motivation to learn and to continue working with the learning material (Heidig et al., 2015). By contrast, Li et al. (2020) do not find there to be any differences in students' emotions between the experimental and control group when confronted with learning materials with either a positive or neutral design. However, the learning performance differs in that students in the experimental group performed better in the retention and transfer tests. When emotional design principles are applied in learning contexts, it is important to make the essential learning content more appealing rather than just adding pretty graphical elements that are irrelevant to the learning content. This practice can impede learning instead of supporting it (Mayer and Estrella, 2014).

2.2 Game-Based Learning

Emotional design can also be integrated into the learning materials through the use of games and game elements. "The ability to play is critical not only to being happy, but also to sustaining social relationships and being a creative, innovative person" (Brown and Vaughan, 2009, p. 6). Playing is described as being ostensibly purposeless and voluntary, having an inherent attraction, a sense of freedom from time, a diminished consciousness of self, and improvisational potential, and prompting the desire to continue (Brown and Vaughan, 2009). It is suggested that playing affects brain development—for example, by creating new neural connections and benefiting learning (Brown and Vaughan, 2009). "While playing, the brain is able to experience situations without threatening its physical or emotional integrity" (Pavlidis and Markantonatou, 2018, p. 322).

Given the positive effects of play, games and game elements are increasingly being introduced into learning and working environments. Game-based learning (GBL) is described as an enjoyable and motivating form of learning (Linek and Albert, 2009). Serious games are (computer) games used to raise awareness of a topic and to develop knowledge and skills by allowing learners/players to delve into situations that are seldom or hardly ever experienced (Ypsilanti et al., 2014). In contrast to entertaining games, serious games aim to convey educational content in addition to providing entertainment (Mildner and Mueller, 2016).

Games that are supposed to support learning are characterized by clear objectives and direct feedback (Fang et al., 2013). The participants work toward a specific goal, choose and perform actions, and experience the immediate consequences. GBL and serious games provide learners with an environment in which they can make mistakes and experiment in a protected space (Trybus, 2014). The lived experiences are transferable from the simulated to the real world (Trybus, 2014).

Studies reveal the positive effects of using games in learning: GBL environments are highly involving and therefore effectively support the learning process (Buffum et al., 2015). Games as a learning method improve short- and long-term learning results (Wouters et al., 2013). Game-based learning scenarios increase motivation and stimulate behavioral change (Bösche and Kattner, 2011; Hsu et al., 2008). It is important to align the games to the everyday reality of the target group, as the connection to real situations and challenges enhances learning success (Lombardi, 2007). Serious games promote learning success through the active involvement of the learners who are able, as a result, to refer to real situations (Ypsilanti et al., 2014). Meaningful narratives support the immersion in serious games, which is crucial for learning success. Narratives invite the player to participate in the story and decide on the development of the story, thus encouraging the intrinsic motivation to learn. It is recommended that the narratives stimulate the imagination and include characters with whom learners can empathize (Naul and Liu, 2020).

2.3 Raising InfoSec Awareness

A literature review revealed that self-efficacy is a moderately strong predictor of security-conscious behavior (ENISA, 2018). The concept of self-efficacy describes a person's subjective perception of their own ability to complete a task or achieve a goal. If a person is confident of their own skills, it is more likely that they will successfully complete tasks and achieve goals (Bandura, 1995). Self-efficacy is enhanced by positive personal experiences, a positive perception of other people's experience, and positive feedback and encouragement (Bandura, 1995). Hence, awareness-raising measures should strengthen the perception of self-efficacy in relation to security-conscious behavior. However, ISA often only involves the transfer of knowledge—e.g., via a web-based training or a lecture (Hart et al., 2020; ACS, 2016; Beyer et al., 2015). Yet the complexity of an issue like InfoSec and the relevance of self-efficacy underline the importance of actively involving users in awareness-raising measures so that they are able to protect sensitive information in case of an InfoSec threat or attack. Thus, employees should be given the possibility of experiencing InfoSec threats in a protected space, where they can try out and practice security-conscious behavior. Game-based learning in the form of serious games is a learning method that enables exactly that (Ghazvini and Shukur, 2018).

Thus, in recent years an increasing number of both research projects and commercial providers have been developing serious games to complement knowledge-based security trainings. Hart et al. (2020) provide an overview of the most established security-related serious games, majoritarian analog (card and board) games, as documented in the literature. Hart et al. (2020) identify the limitations of the security games they review, stating that the games often focus on a particular category of threats, are developed for a specific context, and do not offer the possibility of considering the security threats from the perspective both of the attacker and of the defender. By contrast, a previous overview and evaluation of serious games in cybersecurity training only focused on digital games in academic and commercial settings (Hendrix et al., 2016). From the perspective of Hendrix et al. (2016) the digital games under review seldom target IT professionals and managers, and the evaluations of them are not sufficiently rigorously. In the case of commercial games, no information about their effectiveness is generally given.

Research projects report the positive effects of both analog and digital serious security games on participants' engagement and participation in the learning scenarios as well as on learning outcomes (see, for example, Hart et al, 2020; Yasin et al., 2019; Ghazvini and Shukur, 2018). Moreover, commercial providers of security serious games highlight the positive effects of these awareness-raising and training measures for InfoSec but, as Hendrix et al. (2016) point out, provide no evidence proving these positive outcomes (see Kaspersky, 2022; Fabula Games, 2022).

3. METHODOLOGICAL APPROACH

3.1 Development and Story Concept of the Present Digital Serious Games

Even if the developer of a serious game cannot accommodate all the qualities of play (Brown and Vaughan, 2009)—e.g., purposelessness—we hope to benefit from these characteristic features in raising awareness of InfoSec and in transferring the relevant knowledge. Thus, we expect that the inherent attraction of play will motivate participants to engage with the serious games. The temporal freedom experienced while playing—which we interpret as forgetting time—may encourage users to delve deeper into the topic and learning content than they would with more classical learning materials such as presentations or web-based trainings. The diminished consciousness of self may support identification with the game characters, allowing learners to slip into these roles in the serious games and thus experience problems and situations from their perspectives. We also hope to benefit from participants' desire to continue, whereby participants of one digital serious game will want to play further serious games dealing with InfoSec issues.

The digital serious games we are developing are immersive stories that represent daily work situations in SMEs. The participants experience the stories from a first-person perspective. This entails intensive involvement and enables identification with the learning content. It is expected that it will make the development of knowledge and skills particularly effective and long-lasting. It also enables positive personal experiences and positive feedback as a means to enhance self-efficacy. As a format, we have chosen the visual novel—a kind of interactive book, in which the players make decisions and thus determine the further course of the story (Choi, 2019). Hence, our digital serious games are characterized by pictures in the form of colorful drawings, written dialogues in boxes with rounded corners, and descriptions of the situation. Three-dimensionality is created with the help of ambient music and sound effects (e.g., a person clearing their throat, the phone ringing, a door slamming).

The story concept of the (in total) seven digital serious games is characterized by diversity, individuality, and continuity. Each game focuses on a different InfoSec issue, such as passwords, CEO Fraud, cloud applications, and data protection. To actively involve participants, it is critical that the topic and the problem addressed by the game are relevant and interesting for them (Schell, 2019). Thus, the topics covered in the seven digital games emerge from a qualitative study within SMEs (Pokoyski et al., 2021). Within these games, the players take on a variety of roles—they may switch from being a security expert to being a hacker, while at another time they may be a detective or even slip inside an AI entity. This not only ensures variety but also enables learners to gain insight into the topics from different perspectives.

Our seven digital games can be played independently of one another and in any order. The individual stories and learning contents are self-contained. The specific topics can thus be explored in greater depth and breadth than is possible in a more comprehensive game that includes all the different aspects. Nevertheless, the stories are interconnected by an overall storyline that plays out in a fictional organization. As a result, the participants meet the same people (boss, accounting manager, trainee, production manager) in each serious game and get to know them better. Each digital serious game offers a personalized learning experience. At the beginning, the participants choose a character and a name. With every decision that has an impact on the course of the game, the players embark on their very own learning journey based on their knowledge and preferences. Each game includes two to three learning paths that the users follow based on their decisions. The paths that are chosen determine the learning content that the participants are confronted with and the challenges they have to meet. In each game the users can enhance different skills (e.g., social competence) and areas of knowledge (e.g., security understanding) that are important for InfoSec.

One character in the overall story welcomes the participants at the beginning of a digital game and alerts them to the topic of the game, to the skills and knowledge that are evaluated within the game, and to aspects the users should concentrate on. At the end of the game, the same character gives feedback on what has been achieved. This feedback includes an explanation of how the score was calculated and recommendations and suggestions for the user. Other feedback messages are shown during the game and indicate positive and negative decisions and behavior. In addition, a glossary module allows learners to read important InfoSec terms before and after the digital game. Hence, the users are not left to their own devices but are supported while learning. Figure 1 shows screenshots of a decision option within the digital game and of feedback at the end of it, as well as an example of a decision tree for one of the digital serious games.

Figure 1. Sample screenshots of alternative decisions, feedback, and a decision tree of our digital serious games

3.2 User Test

The digital serious games developed in the present project are particularly tailored to employees of SMEs who work in different departments—performing different sets of tasks—and are not experts in information technology. Employees from the pilot companies and other partner organizations test and evaluate the digital serious games from a practical perspective. The contact persons at these organizations receive the information about the user test and forward it to employees. Staff participation is voluntary so we have no influence over which employees ultimately take part. The responses by the test users form the basis for the final development of these serious games. The user test also includes short, standardized, written pre- and post-surveys that are analyzed descriptively. The participants are asked about the extent to which they agree with given statements on a five-point Likert scale—focusing, for example, on content, the realism of the presentations, the playing time, and the level of difficulty. Learning success is measured by self-assessments reflecting on InfoSec experience and the acquisition of knowledge.

In the following, we present the results of the user tests of two digital serious games. In the first, called *Hacker Attack*, the users slip into the role of a hacker who tries to log in to the server of the fictional company. The scores in this game relate to efficacy (Do the users succeed in the hack?) and variability (How many different approaches have the users tried in attempting to achieve their goal?). In the second, *Search for Clues*, the users take on the role of a detective who is trying to solve a case of CEO Fraud in the fictional company. Here, the users are assessed in terms of their efficacy (Do they manage to solve the case?), social competence (Do they treat the employees of the company in an empathic and friendly manner?), and discovered learning content (How much learning content do they encounter on their way through the game?).

The participants of the first user test of the game *Hacker Attack* were mostly male (65%, n=26[1]) with two predominant age ranges: 25–34 (35%) and 35–50 (35%, n=26). They mostly worked in the fields of sales (23%), information technology (IT) (19%), and human resources (19%) (n=26). By contrast, the participants in the second user test of the digital game *Search for Clues* were predominantly female (57%, n=23), and most of them were between 35 and 50 years old (43%). They were primarily employees in the human resources (30%), customer service (17%), and sales (17%) departments (n=23). The participants in both user tests needed an average of ten minutes to complete the game (*Hacker Attack*: n=42; *Search for Clues*: n=31). The users evaluated the playing time on average as “exactly right” on a five-point Likert scale (1=too short, 3=exactly right, 5=too long) (*Hacker Attack*: mean=3, n=31; *Search for Clues*: mean=3.44, n=25). The perceived level of difficulty is between “easy” and “exactly right” with a mean of 2.81 for *Hacker Attack* (n=31) and 2.52 for *Search for Clues* (n=25) (scale: 1=too easy, 3=exactly right, 5=too difficult).

[1] The differing sample size (n) is determined by the fact that not all participants took part in both the pre- and post-questionnaire or answered all the questions.

The following figure shows the overall assessment of the two selected digital serious games from the perspective of the test users. Studies indicate that the left end of a response scale is selected more often than the right (Menold and Bogner, 2015). We therefore take the midpoint of the scale (=3) to mean "good" in the user evaluation, expressing satisfaction on the part of respondents. Both serious games thus have a relatively positive evaluation, as almost all the aspects score an average value of over 3.

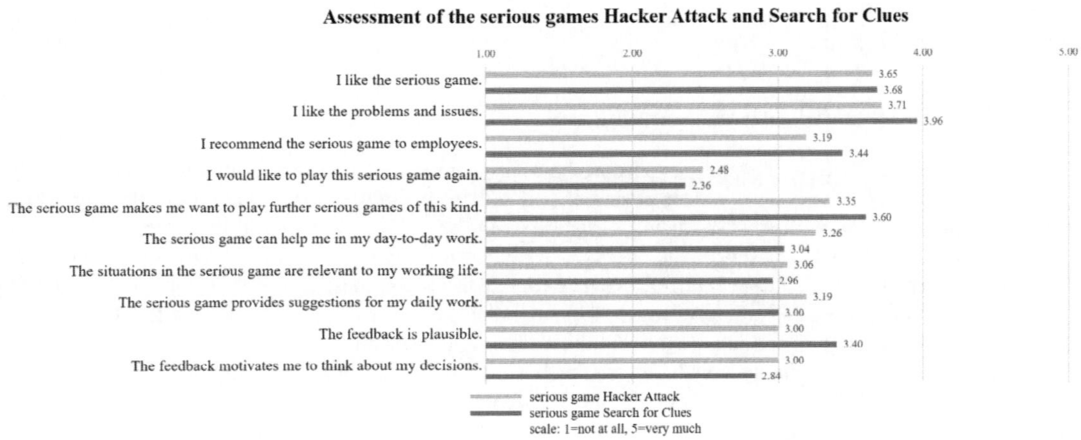

Figure 2. Overall assessment of the two digital serious games *Hacker Attack* and *Search for Clues*

The overall positive evaluation of the two digital serious games and, in particular, the relatively high level of agreement with the statement that users would like to play further serious games of this kind show that users enjoy such games as awareness-raising measures. However, as users are less motivated to play the same digital serious game again, it is important to integrate these games in a broader awareness-raising measure that includes other materials to reinforce the process.

Figure 2 also shows that the narratives of the digital serious games moderately reflect the working lives of users and that they—and therefore the learning content provided—moderately support them in their daily working life. When analyzing the three questions about the effect of the games on the daily work of the three departments most represented in the user tests, it is striking that human resources agreed most strongly with the given statements and sales least strongly. Bearing in mind the different demographics of those taking part in the *Hacker Attack* and *Search for Clues* user tests, it is evident that the digital serious games that have been developed appeal to a wide range of users.

The participants have a sense of learning success when playing the digital serious games. On the one hand, they acquired new knowledge or reinforced what they already knew (*Hacker Attack*: mean=3.17, n=30; *Search for Clues*: $mean_{new\_knowledge}$=2.92; $mean_{reinforce\_knowledge}$=3.2; n=25) (answer scale: 1=not at all, 5=very much). On the other hand, they felt more experienced in InfoSec after completing the serious game *Hacker Attack* ($mean_{pre}$=3.12, $mean_{post}$=3.32, n=25). With *Search for Clues*, no difference was found between the pre- and post-survey (mean=3.43; n=23) (answer scale: 1=beginner, 3=advanced, 5=expert).

4. DISCUSSION

4.1 Research and Practical Contribution

The preliminary results of the user tests indicate that digital serious games that use emotional design principles, such as personalization, the possibility for identification, appealing multimedia elements, and storytelling, are positively accepted by employees and moderately help to enhance and intensify knowledge in InfoSec. The digital serious games also support users to some degree in their daily work. These games are thus a promising measure for raising awareness of InfoSec.

The two digital serious games that are presented here have been developed as part of a research project designed for employees in SMEs—raising awareness of InfoSec topics is relevant for their professional life in general and, to a certain extent, for their private life (passwords, phone fraud, etc.). The serious games and the underlying research project have added social value, as the games and other materials developed in the project are available on the dedicated website free of charge for anyone interested. Thus, for example, organizations can raise employee awareness of InfoSec while expending fewer resources. The digital serious games can also become part of the education of young adults, enabling apprentices and students to start their professional life with an awareness of InfoSec.

4.2 Limitations and Further Research

InfoSec is an issue that is constantly evolving. Thus, it is important that the serious games cover different topics—as is the case here—and are, if possible, updated from time to time. In addition, the digital games should be part of a wider awareness-raising measure, as in the present research project. We intend to include further recommendations for users at the end of a digital serious game. Based on their results in the specific digital game, the users should be referred to other digital serious games, which they can use to practice the same or other InfoSec skills and knowledge. They will also be invited to participate in a test where they can broaden their knowledge of the subject that the digital game focuses on.

It is not possible to reliably conclude, on the basis of the questionnaire presented and the descriptive analysis, that the digital serious games enhance and intensify knowledge while also raising awareness and ultimately encouraging safe behavior. A more elaborated scientific methodological approach to measure InfoSec awareness and behavior (intention) is warranted to validate the first preliminary findings of these user tests. We are therefore using the current research project to develop and test an instrument for measuring InfoSec awareness including security-conscious behavior on the basis of an extensive literature review.

Lacruz and Américo (2018) demonstrate that the quantum of learning is on average 18% higher if participants are involved in a debriefing after a business game. In our own tests and evaluations, we also observed that the discursive exchange of experiences and knowledge during and after a session playing analogue serious games, which are also being developed in the project, is critical to raising awareness of InfoSec. Even though users are supported during the learning process by a familiar character from the digital serious games, further research is needed into ways of achieving an exchange of ideas between the participants of the different digital learning scenarios.

ACKNOWLEDGEMENT

We thank the Federal Ministry for Economic Affairs and Climate Action for funding the project. We are grateful to Gamebook Studio HQ for developing the digital serious games and the pilot companies for their active involvement in the project. Finally, we would like to acknowledge the anonymous reviewers for their helpful critical comments. Many thanks, too, to Simon Cowper for his detailed and professional proofreading of the text.

REFERENCES

Allianz für Cyber-Sicherheit (ACS) (alliance for cyber security), 2016. *Awareness-Umfrage 2015: Ergebnisse (awarenss survey 2015: results)*. Bonn, Germany.

Azeroual, O. and Nikiforova, A., 2022. Apache Spark and MLlib-Based Intrusion Detection System or How the Big Data Technologies Can Secure the Date. *Information*, Vol. 13, No. 2, article 58.

Bandura, A., 1995. Exercise of Personal and Collective Efficacy in Changing Societies. *In Bandura, A. (ed). Self-efficacy in Changing Societies*. Cambridge University Press, Cambridge, England, pp. 1-45.

Beyer, M., S. et al., 2015. *Awareness is Only the First Step: A Framework for Progressive Engagement of Staff in Cyber Security*. Hewlett Packard, Business white paper.

Bösche, W. and Kattner, F., 2011. Fear of (Serious) Digital Games and Game-based Learning? Causes, Consequences and a Possible Countermeasure. *International Journal of Game-Based Learning*, Vol. 1, No. 3, pp. 1-15.

Brown, S. and Vaughan, C., 2009. *Play. How It Shapes the Brain, Opens the Imagination, and Invigorates the Soul.* Avery, Penguin Group, New York, USA.

Buffum, P. S. et al., 2015. Mind the Gap: Improving Gender Equity in Game-Based Learning Environments with Learning Companions. *AIED: International Conferences on Artificial Intelligence in Education*.

Bundesministerium des Innern, für Bau und Heimat (BMI) (Federal Ministry of the Interior and Community), 2021. *Cybersicherheitsstrategie für Deutschland 2021 (Cyber Security Strategy for Germany 2021)*. Berlin, Germany.

Choi, C., 2019. *Bigger on the Inside: A History of Visual Novels.* https://medium.com/@cecilchoi/bigger-on-the-inside-a-history-of-visual-novels-981e42f43608, 22. Februar 2019, accessed May 6, 2022.

European Union Agency for Network and Information Security (ENISA), 2018. *Cybersecurity Culture Guidelines: Behavioural Aspects of Cybersecurity*. Heraklion, Greece.

Fabula Games, 2022. *Serious Games: Incredibly Effective.* https://fabula-games.de/en/, accessed June 28, 2022.

Fang, X. et al., 2013. Development of an Instrument for Studying Flow in Computer Game Play. *International Journal of Human-Computer Interaction*, Vol. 29, No. 7, pp. 456-470.

Ghazvini, A. and Shukur, Z., 2018. A Serious Game for Healthcare Industry: Information Security Awareness Training Program for Hospital Universiti Kebangsaan Malaysia. *International Journal of Advanced Computer Science and Application*, Vol. 9, No. 9, pp. 236-245.

Hart, S. et al., 2020. Riskio: A Serious Game for Cyber Security Awareness and Education. *Computer & Security*, Vol. 95, August 2020, article 101827.

Heidig, S. et al., 2015. Emotional Design in Multimedia Learning: Differentiation on Relevant Design Features and Their Effects on Emotions and Learning. *Computers in Human Behavior*, Vol. 44, March 2015, pp. 81-95.

Hendrix, M. et al., 2016. Game Based Cyber Security Training: Are Serious Games suitable for cyber security training? *International Journal of Serious Games,* Vol. 3, No. 1, pp. 53-61.

Hsu, S. H. et al., 2008. From Traditional to Digital: Factors to Integrate Traditional Game-based Learning into Digital Game-based Learning Environment. *Proceedings 2nd IEEE International Conference on Digital Game and Intelligent Toy Enhanced Learning, DIGITEL*, pp. 83-89.

Interaction Design Foundation, n.d.. *Emotional Design.* https://www.interaction-design.org/literature/topics/emotional-design, accessed May 8, 2022.

ISF, 2003. *The standard of good practice for information security.* Version 4.0. Information Security Forum.

Kaspersky, 2022. *[Dis]connected. A mobile cybersecurity quest.* https://media.kaspersky.com/en/business-security/enterprise/Kaspersky_[dis]connected_datasheet_0121EN_Gl.pdf, accessed June 28, 2022.

Lacruz, A. J. and Américo, B. L., 2018. Debriefing's Influence on Learning in Business Game: An Experimental Design. *BBR. Brazilian Business Review*, Vol. 15, No. 2, pp. 192-208.

Li, J., et al., 2020. Can Emotional Design Really Evoke Emotion in Multimedia Learning?. *International Journal of Educational Technology in Higher Education*, Vol. 17, article 24.

Linek, S. B. and Albert, D., 2009. Game-based Learning: Gender-Specific Aspects of Parasocial Interaction and Identification. *International Technology, Education and Development Conference (INTED)*.

Lombardi, M., 2007. *Authentic Learning for the 21st Century: An Overview.* http://www.lmi.ub.edu/cursos/s21/REPOSITORIO/documents/Lombardi_2007_Authentic_learning.pdf, accessed May 12, 2022.

Mayer, R. E. and Estrella, G., 2014. Benefits of Emotional Design in Multimedia Instruction. *Learning and Instruction*, Vol. 33, October 2014, pp. 12-18.

Menold, N. and Bogner, K., 2015. *Gestaltung von Ratingskalen in Fragebögen (Layout of rating scales in questionnaires).* GESIS – Leibniz-Institut für Sozialwissenschaften (SDM Survey Guidelines), Mannheim, Germany.

Mildner, P. and Mueller, F., 2016. Design of Serious Games. *In Dörner, R. et al. (eds). Serious Games: Foundations, Concepts and Practice*. Springer International Publishing, Cham, Switzerland, pp. 57-82.

Naul, E. and Liu, M., 2020. Why Story Matters: A Review of Narrative in Serious Games. *Journal of Educational Computing Research*, Vol. 58, No. 3, pp. 687-707.

Pavlidis, G. P. and Markantonatou, S., 2018. Playful Education and Innovative Gamified Learning Approaches. *In Koutsopoulos, K. C. et al. (eds). Handbook of Research on Educational Design and Cloud Computing in Modern Classroom Settings*. IGI Global, Hershey, Pennsylvania, USA, pp. 321-341.

Pokoyski, D. et al., 2021. *Qualitative Wirkungsanalyse Security Awareness in KMU: Tiefenpsychologische Grundlagenstudie im Projekt Awareness Labor KMU (ALARM) Informationssicherheit (Qualitative Impact Study Security Awareness in SME: Deepthpsychology Fundamental Study in the Project Awareness Lab SME (ALARM) Information Security).* Scholl, M. (ed), Technische Hochschule Wildau (Technical University of Applied Sciences Wildau), Wildau, Germany. https://alarm.wildau.biz/static/d6490e49f8d31adfa35259134b8d1b9d/220316-alarm-studie-final.pdf, accessed May 6, 2022.

Sasse, A. et al., 2022. Warum IT-Sicherheit in Organisationen einen Neustart braucht (Why IT-Security in Organizations needs a restart). *18. Deutscher IT-Sicherheitskongress des BSI (18. German IT-Security Convention of the BSI (Federal Office for Information Security).*

Schell, J., 2019. *The Art of Game Design. A Book of Lenses*. 3rd edition. CRC Press, London, England.

Trybus, J., 2014. *Game-Based Learning: What it is, Why it Works, and Where it's Going.* New Media Institute.

Um, E. et al., 2012. Emotional Design in Multimedia Learning. *Journal of Educational Psychology*, Vol. 104, No. 2, pp. 485-498.

Verizon, 2022. *Data Breach Investigations Report (DBIR) 2022.* https://www.verizon.com/business/resources/reports/2022/dbir/2022-data-breach-investigations-report-dbir.pdf, accessed June 28, 2022.

Wouters, P. et al., 2013. A Meta-analysis of the Cognitive and Motivational Effects of Serious Games. *Journal of Educational Psychology*, Vol. 105, No. 2, pp. 249-265.

Yasin, A. et al., 2019. Improving software security awareness using a serious game. *IET Software*, Vol. 13, No. 2, pp. 159-169.

Ypsilanti, A. et al., 2014. Are Serious Video Games Something More than a Game? A Review on the Effectiveness of Serious Games to Facilitate Intergenerational Learning. *Education and Information Technologies*, Vol. 19, pp. 515-529.

PATIENT USER INTERFACES FOR DETERMINING PAIN LEVEL THROUGH EVERYDAY SMARTPHONE TASKS AND WEARABLE PHYSIOLOGICAL SIGNAL SENSORS

Ashraf Khalil[1], Suha Glal[1] and Salam Abdallah[2]
[1]College of Technological Innovation, Zayed University, Abu Dhabi, United Arab Emirates
[2]College of Business, Abu Dhabi University, Abu Dhabi, United Arab Emirates

ABSTRACT

Tracking patients' pain is a critical issue for clinical caregivers, particularly among staff responsible for providing analgesic relief. However, collecting regularly scheduled pain measurements from patients can be cumbersome and time-consuming for clinicians. Additionally, Opiophobia among patients and physician is a well-documented barrier for effective pain management. With the ever-growing popularity of smartphones, physiological wearable sensors and their potential effectiveness for medical assessment and diagnostic, we created Pain Sense: a mobile application that measure how pain affects a person's motor coordination, cognition, and physiological markers using performance metrics and sensor data. We developed and evaluated the usability and acceptability of a smartphone app to support objective pain intensity measure to permit effective pain management and relief. We employed iterative process for app development and testing. Patient and clinicians participated in alpha testing of the final prototype to assess usability and acceptability. The current Pain Sense app include the following user interfaces to assess situational impairment: Typing UI, Swiping UI, Balancing UI, Reaction UI and Choice UI. We ran randomized controlled trial to validate the effectiveness of human performance metrics and features derived from mobile embedded sensors and physiological sensing technologies in developing an objective metric for pain intensity assessment.

KEYWORDS

Pain Sense Mobile Application, Pain Reporting Tasks, Physiological Signals, Physiological Markers, Perceived Pain Intensity, User Interface

1. INTRODUCTION

Healthcare is an immense matter that challenges all nations, developed and developing, both economically and socially. From an economic viewpoint, worldwide spending on health is anticipated to rise from US$7·83 trillion in 2013 to $18·28 trillion in 2040 (Dieleman et al., 2016). In fact, approximately 70–78% of health-care budgets are expend-ed on the controlling of chronic diseases such as heart disease, cancer, stroke, type 2 diabetes, obesity, and arthritis (CDC, 2015)— and its complications (Celler & Sparks, 2015). In UAE, cancer is the second leading cause of death -according to the World Health Organization (WHO) report published in 2018- accounting for 12% of all mortalities in the country. Pain management plays an integral role in maintaining well-being and good quality of life for individuals with cancer, therefore, a huge part of cancer treatment programs is directed towards it (Robb et al., 2006). There are several barriers for effective pain management, namely, Opiophobia (fear of drug prescription) among patients and physicians, lack of effective communication amongst healthcare providers and patients, acceptance of the inevitability of chronic pain, poor or absent assessment procedures and lack of formal training in pain management (Howard, 2003). The problem is that the majority of contemporary pain scales are based on standards that were developed in the previous century. Although their effectiveness in assessing various types of pain clinically has been well proven over the years (Aitken, 1969; Lundeberg et al., 2001), this fact does not mean they do not need a serious up-grade since society and technologies have advanced. Second, most of these standards are grounded on subjective (self-reported pain) rating scales such as the Numerical Rating Scale (NRS), visual analog scales (VAS), and verbal rated scales (VRS) (Jost & Roila, 2009). Presently, there are no standardized, objective ways to utilize physiological markers, such as skin conductance response, heart rate, and temperature, to make a conclusive pain intensity assessment. Furthermore, the current pain rating scales do not support patients with cognitive disorders or communicative impairments, for example those suffering from complete or partial paralysis, adults with dementia and other mental disabilities, and young children. Moreover, in a study published in the Journal of Pain and Symptom Management, a positive correlation between patient satisfaction and self-reported pain intensity was reported, specifically, patients with the highest pain level were the least satisfied with the pain control they received (Miaskowski et al., 1994). Therefore, improving pain intensity assessment will improve patient satisfaction, which in turn, will help improve an essential proportion of healthcare quality. The use of software technologies in healthcare is on a rapid rise, where mobile-based applications can help both patients and healthcare staff gain a deeper understanding of the patient's condition (AlSalah et al., 2020). Mobile applications monitoring the blood sugar level of diabetic patients being one such example (Cedeno-Moreno & Vargas-Lombardo, 2020). Smartphones have now become the preferred communication, entertainment, educational devices due to the wide variety and range of prices and smartphones users are never long separated from their device (Jamalova & Constantinovits, 2020).

Therefore, in this study, we aim at developing an effective pain screening (quantification and characterization) methodology by harnessing the power and popularity of smartphones and the technological advancement of wearable sensing technologies. Specifically, we intend to develop the "Pain Sense" platform which uses machine learning models trained on human performance metrics and physiological sensor data to estimate a patient's pain intensity. This study also tries to identify design challenges and practical trade-offs important to take into account when developing computerized user interfaces for pain assessment.

2. METHOD

2.1 Setting

This study is currently being conducted at Burjeel Hospital in Al Ain city in UAE. The study was approved by Abu Dhabi University Institutional Review Board (IRB).

2.2 Procedure

The current study is divided into two main phases. Phase I (the study being described here) consisted of the mobile app development process and initial results of acceptability. Phase II, currently underway, consists of a randomized controlled trial (RCT) to test the efficacy of the mobile app in assessing pain intensity using mobile phone task and physiological signals. The 4-step iterative development process employed in phase I consisted of

Step 1: Ideation and Exploration
Step 2: Software Design and Hardware Integration
Step 3: Stakeholders Accessibility Testing
Step 4: Analysis and Evaluation.

2.2.1 Ideation and Exploration

In this step, various smartphone-based tasks, and user interfaces such as typing, swiping, balancing, short-term memory and tapping were evaluated and explored. For each task, a set of features were extracted to measure human performance. Furthermore, various physiological signals, clinically proven to correlate with pain were investigated such as HRV, respiration rate, oxygen saturation and galvanic skin response (GSR).

2.2.2 Software Design and Hardware Integration

In this step, the actual coding and implementation of Pain Sense mobile app has taken place. In addition, various wearable sensors for acquiring physiological signals were compared, evaluated and considered (refer to Table 1). Although, there is a huge number of physiological signals monitoring kits available in the market, we limited our hardware evaluation to the kits depicted in Table 1. This decision was made due to two reasons. First, those tool kits have Android APIs will facilitate the integration between the data generated by the kit and the developed app. Second, those kits support the continuous and real-time monitoring of a broad range of physiological signals. After considering tradeoffs between conveniences to wear, cost and number of physiological signals monitored, a decision was reached to utilize Microsoft Band 2. The only physiological signal the app doesn't allow us to monitor (or derive) is the respiration rate. Zephyr belt-type BioHarness provides respiration rate signal, but the user is required to wear it on a bare chest to get an accurate reading. This of course won't be convenient for the setting of the current study. The band sends the physiological signals data to the mobile via Bluetooth.

Table 1. Physiological signals measuring wearables toolkit

Name	Type	Biometric measured	Price
Zephyr belt-type BioHarness sensor	Chest belt	ECG, temperature, HR, HRV, respiration rate, Body motion	$631.4
MC10	patch	ECG, EMG, Body motion	$2,500
Empatica's E4	wristband	skin temperature, blood volume pulse (BVP), GSR	$1,690
Microsoft Band 2	wristband	HR, body motion, skin temperature, galvanic skin response, beat-to-beat interval	$250

The app was developed for Android supported mobile devices but the availability of iOS API for Microsoft Band 2 will allow us to create an iOS app in the future. The app was written in the native Android development language, Java. The app was designed to record the raw physiological signal data and the raw performance matrix. This design decision was made for two reasons. First, it will improve the app performance and will speed up the recording process. Second, recording raw signal vs. extracting specific features will give us more flexibility in signal processing. In other words, the raw signal can be analyzed with powerful processing units which will ensure the extraction of various information with great accuracy. The raw data (physiological signals and mobile tasks performance) were logged in CSV file. The CSV files were saved locally in the Tablet and a copy of each file was sent automatically via email at the end of each pain assessment session as a backup.

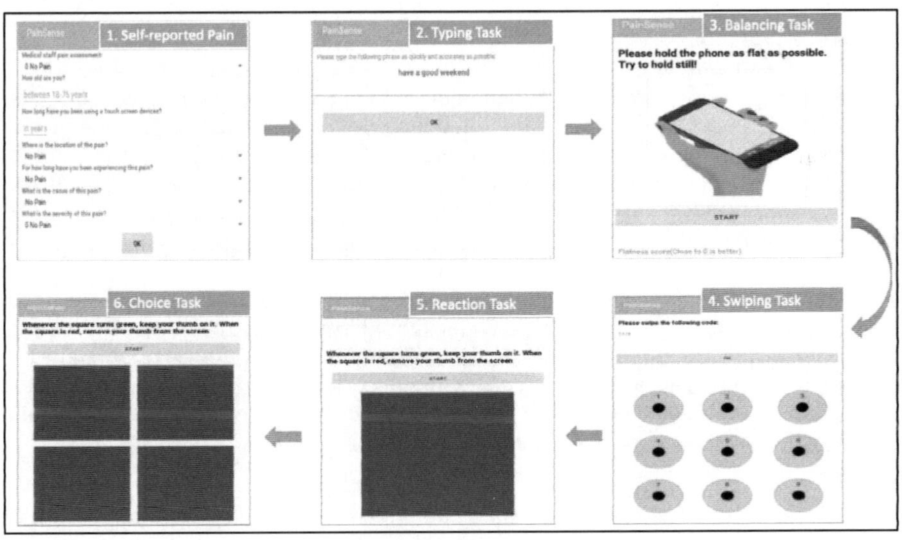

Figure 1. Pain Sense application 6 UI

Pain Sense application consist of 6 UI and 5 tasks. The 5 task are the same task employed by Mariakakis et al (Mariakakis et al., 2018), specifically, they included typing task, swiping task, balancing task, reaction task and choice task. In addition, we have included pain reporting task. The pain reporting task allow us to compare between the patient self-reported pain and the clinician perceived pain intensity. Furthermore, at this phase of the project the self-reported pain is the ground truth that will be utilized to build the machine learning model which will allow was to predicate pain intensity level in phase II of the project. Moreover, Mariakakis et al have only measured heart rate using the mobile camera and a technique called photoplethysmography (PPG). On the other hand, our application monitors 4 different physiological signals, namely, heart rate, GSR, beat-to-beat interval, and skin temperature. In addition, those signals are being recorded from the being of the pain assessment session to the end. The average pain assessment session duration was found to be 7.2 minutes. This will give us a better chance to correlate and quantify pain intensity using physiological signals. Figure 1 depicates the 6 UI and tasks of Pain Sense application. A short description of the implementing details of each task is presented below.

2.3 The Self-Reported Pain UI

This interface consists of text fields and spinners. The interface records the pain location, duration, cause and intensity according to the patient and the clinician.

2.4 Typing Task UI

In this task, the patient is presented with a random phrases from the MacKenzie-Soukoreff phrase set (MacKenzie & Soukoreff, 2003). Furthermore, in order to extract specific features from this task, we had to build a custom keyboard. Android build-in keyboard doesn't allow programmer to capture fine-details that we found to be important for the current study. Furthermore, without a custom-build keyboard we will not be able to acquire touch location in the soft keyboard, acceleration data due to typing and text change events simultaneously.

2.5 Balancing Task UI

This task requires the user to hold the mobile on their hand-balm as flat as possible. A flatness score which represents the standard deviation of the acceleration in the z-direction is represented to the user to help them achieve this task.

2.6 Swiping Task UI

In this task, the patient is presented with a 4-digit number that he has to swipe in a numbers pad. To allow the patient to validate his response, each number is presented in a text field as the patient touch center of each number (the black dot in Figure 1 task 4). A simple graphical image represented the numbers pad. In order to identify the number being touched we had to create another color-coded number pad and place it underneath the original number pad (refer to Figure 2). The overlay image has exactly the same size as the displayed image. It uses different colored regions to indicate each number. When the patient clicks on the primary image, code runs to check the pixel at the corresponding point in the color-coded image.

Furthermore, in order to speed the color matching task and avoiding comparing the touch location with all the 9 colors, the pad was divided into 9 different regions based on the image coordinates (Figure 2 green dashed lines shows the 9 regions). Using the touch location, the region is specified and therefore the color of the touched region is compared with one color. Furthermore, when comparing the touched location with the corresponding color for the region, the colors may not be exact match due to image scaling (scaling change the image resolution). A color matching tolerance value was used.

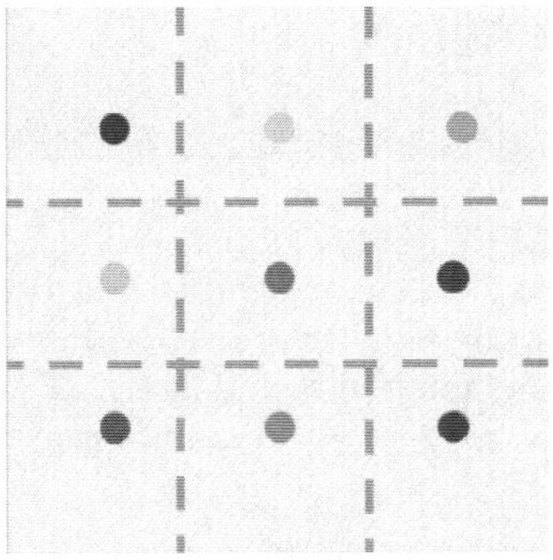

Figure 2. Color-coded numbers pad

2.7 Reaction Task UI

The reaction task displays a red square for the patient. The patient must touch the square when it turns green and left his finger when the square turns red again. The color change events were spaced within a 7-second period. Particularly, the red square turns into green randomly within the first 3 seconds. Then, it turns red again randomly within the last 3 seconds.

2.8 Choice Task UI

This task is similar to the pervious one with one exception. Instead of being presented with one single square the patient is presented with 4 squares. Only one square randomly changes its color from red to green. The user should pick the correct square as fast as possible.

3. USER STUDY

To evaluate the usability and acceptability of the implemented versions of the app and to improve its design and the study development, we conducted focus groups with key stakeholder groups. The 3 key stakeholder groups: (1) patient (n=2); (2) clinicians (n=2); (3) members of the community, and society (n=2). In this phase, stakeholders were included as consultants and therefore were not consented as participants. The focused group interviews allowed us to observe and question stakeholders as part of qualitatively appraising reactions and deriving design implications. The stakeholder interview guide included the following topics: (1) perceived importance of effective pain assessment; (2) barriers to communication between patients and clinicians regarding pain management; (3) potential feasibility, acceptability, and usability of Pain Sense app; and (4) feedback on the overall app design.

4. ANALYSIS AND EVALUATION

Based on the stakeholders' feedback certain mobile tasks were considered for exclusions such as the typing task and the balancing task. Also, the UI design of certain tasks was improved considerably following the guidance and the feedback of the stockholders. The details of the design and UI improvement will be specified in the result section. Toward the end of the development life cycle, patients were asked to participate in user acceptance testing (UAT). During UAT sessions, research and development staff observed participants during their initial interactions with Pain Sense. Participants were asked to complete specific tasks within the demo app. Participants were also promoted to share general feedback on Pain Sense at the end of the testing session, specifically on how intuitive the tasks were. Testers' feedbacks along with the developers notes and observation during the testing session informed the design in the following iteration.

5. RESULTS AND DISCUSSION

Feedback from stakeholders and Alpha testers highlighted specific features that needed to be incorporated in the app or to be removed. In the following lines, we will go through the various UI in Pain Sense and discuss how they were modified based on the received feedback. The pain reporting UI had a mixed and sometime contrasting feedback. Clinicians found the requested information to be useful and comprehensives, patients on the other hand did not like the fact that they have to fill all the details requested in this task. Furthermore, one of the clinics asked us to change the Numerical Rating Scale we are utilizing to represent pain intensity to visual analog rating scale companied with face pain rating scale. Figure 3 shows the UI for the task after modification.

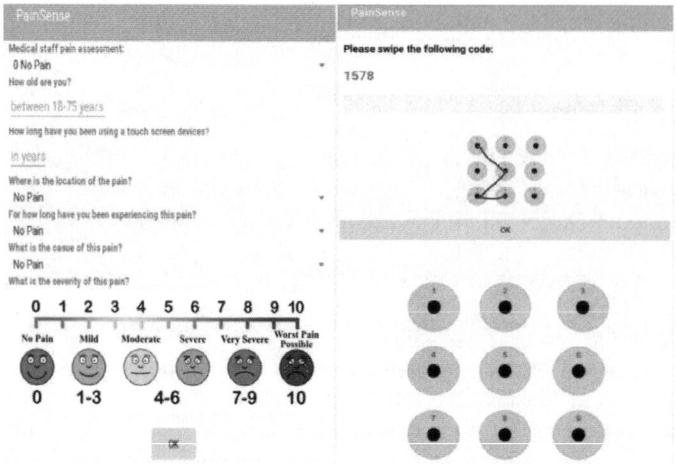

Figure 3. Modified Self-reported Pain UI (on the left) and swiping UI (on the right)

The patient thought that the typing task would be very hard if the patient is suffering from pain with high intensity and they asked us to remove it. Yet, we have not removed it. In work conducted by Mariakakis et al, they found that the typing task provide 4 important features to estimate a person's blood alcohol level (BAL) (Mariakakis et al., 2018). Specifically, they found that the mean touch radius while lifting, mean distance from key center, mean force during touch and mean touch duration features to be one of the most important extracted features needed to train the machine learning classifier. Therefore, we decided to keep this task at this phase of the project. We would like to see if this task would also play a significant role in estimating pain intensity. Also, we would like to see if we would get more negative feedback about the typing task UI in the clinical study as well. Then, we can make a better-informed decision with regards to keeping or removing this task from Pain Sense app. The balancing task was viewed as simple and feasible, but its effectiveness was doubted by number of participants. Therefore, the research team decided to swap this task with short memory task. In fact, in Mariakakis et al work found that balancing with heart rate task had the least accuracy when compared to the performance of the other tasks in estimating BAL. With a closer examination to the task features only the mean heart rate value was found to be a significant feature derived from this task. In our case, the physiological signals are recorded independently throughout the pain assessment session, therefore omitting the balancing task will not affect the heart rate reading as we are logging it separately.

In regard to the swiping task, the research team noticed that users frequently tap the displayed numbers in the screen instead of swiping them. This is maybe due to the fact that the UI was written in English, but all the participants were not English native speakers. Therefore, the UI was modified to include a small example showing a swiped number as depicted in Figure 3 the image on the right. No negative feedback was given for the choice task or reaction task. The two tasks were viewed as simple and appropriate.

6. CONCLUSIONS

To the best of our knowledge, we are the first to describe the development of an app designed for assessing pain intensity using performance metrics based on smartphone tasks. Usability and acceptability testing and the active involvement of stakeholders improved the app design tremendously and it will increase its potential benefit for patients and clinicians. We have highlighted specific implementation details to help other researchers who would like to study situational impairments in other scenarios. Furthermore, we have made the source code for the app open and available publicly via GitHub. Impending results from our randomized controlled trial will provide key data on the effectiveness of this app in assessing pain intensity.

REFERENCES

Aitken, R. C. B. (1969). A Growing Edge of Measurement of Feelings [Abridged]: Measurement of Feelings Using Visual Analogue Scales. *Journal of the Royal Society of Medicine*, *62*(10). https://doi.org/10.1177/003591576906201005

AlSalah, R. M., Salam, A. A., Alzamil, M. A., Alyemni, R. M. A. M. K., & Alahmdi, M. A. (2020). Thakirni Application: An Assistive Application for Alzheimer Patients. *International Journal of Online and Biomedical Engineering*, *16*(15). https://doi.org/10.3991/ijoe.v16i15.18063

CDC. (2015). *Chronic Disease Overview | Publications | Chronic Disease Prevention and Health Promotion | CDC.* Chronic Diseases: The Leading Causes of Death and Disability in the United States.

Cedeno-Moreno, D., & Vargas-Lombardo, M. (2020). Mobile Applications for Diabetes Self-Care and Approach to Machine Learning. *International Journal of Online and Biomedical Engineering*, *16*(8). https://doi.org/10.3991/ijoe.v16i08.13591

Celler, B. G., & Sparks, R. S. (2015). Home telemonitoring of vital signs - Technical challenges and future directions. *IEEE Journal of Biomedical and Health Informatics*, *19*(1). https://doi.org/10.1109/JBHI.2014.2351413

Dieleman, J. L., Templin, T., Sadat, N., Reidy, P., Chapin, A., Foreman, K., Haakenstad, A., Evans, T., Murray, C. J. L., & Kurowski, C. (2016). National spending on health by source for 184 countries between 2013 and 2040. *The Lancet*, *387*(10037). https://doi.org/10.1016/S0140-6736(16)30167-2

Howard, R. F. (2003). Current Status of Pain Management in Children. In *Journal of the American Medical Association* (Vol. 290, Issue 18). https://doi.org/10.1001/jama.290.18.2464

Jamalova, M., & Constantinovits, M. G. (2020). Attitudes toward smartphone characteristics: What do users pay for? *International Journal of Interactive Mobile Technologies*, *14*(9). https://doi.org/10.3991/ijim.v14i09.13089

Jost, L., & Roila, F. (2009). Management of cancer pain: ESMO Clinical Recommendations. *Annals of Oncology*, *20*(SUPPL. 4). https://doi.org/10.1093/annonc/mdp164

Lundeberg, T., Lund, I., Dahlin, L., Borg, E., Gustafsson, C., Sandin, L., Rosén, A., Kowalski, J., & Eriksson, S. v. (2001). Reliability and responsiveness of three different pain assessments. *Journal of Rehabilitation Medicine*, *33*(6). https://doi.org/10.1080/165019701753236473

MacKenzie, I. S., & Soukoreff, R. W. (2003). *Phrase sets for evaluating text entry techniques.* https://doi.org/10.1145/765968.765971

Mariakakis, A., Parsi, S., Patel, S. N., & Wobbrock, J. O. (2018). Drunk user interfaces: Determining blood alcohol level through everyday smartphone tasks. *Conference on Human Factors in Computing Systems - Proceedings*, *2018-April*. https://doi.org/10.1145/3173574.3173808

Miaskowski, C., Nichols, R., Brody, R., & Synold, T. (1994). Assessment of patient satisfaction utilizing the American Pain Society's quality assurance standards on acute and cancer-related pain. *Journal of Pain and Symptom Management*, *9*(1). https://doi.org/10.1016/0885-3924(94)90140-6

Robb, K. A., Williams, J. E., Duvivier, V., & Newham, D. J. (2006). A pain management program for chronic cancer-treatment-related pain: A preliminary study. *Journal of Pain*, *7*(2). https://doi.org/10.1016/j.jpain.2005.08.007

THE IMPACT OF TEST ELEMENTS ON STUDENTS' PERFORMANCE IN EFL ASSESSMENT

Joma Alrzini, Diane Rasmussen Pennington and Mark D. Dunlop
University of Strathclyde, Glasgow, UK

ABSTRACT

Students applying to study at a university in a country that does not use their native language typically have to sit a formal language assessment exam; This exam is now most commonly done electronically. This can be challenging for students if they do not have previous experience with online tools. While previous studies have shown that practice of some skills exam, such as writing tasks, help improve students' performance, while other test skills has to be investigated. Still, there are few scientific and published studies on the usability and the effect of the design of test elements and their effect on test accuracy and effectiveness. The purpose of this study is to investigate factors of online English as a foreign language (EFL) tests and how they can adversely affect students' performance during the test. To meet this aim, we investigated the correlation between test structure and some test-taker characteristics. The study's significance is considered a guideline for test designers to improve the test design, which should lead to a more accurate assessment of the student's performance. This research was conducted using an online survey of new University entrance students. The key findings of this study are that less confidence during the test may result in an artificially reduced test score, with a potentially significant impact on a student's career or need to retake repeatedly. Moreover, other facts have been measured about an English online test such as first language, subject area and previous training on such examination. These contribute to challenges during the exam, which were raised in participants' responses on having difficulty interacting with the test.

KEYWORDS

English Language Testing, Test Impact, Students' Performance, Test Elements

1. INTRODUCTION

With the increased use of digital technologies in the education sector, students are faced with challenges to adapt to diverse online learning systems. Such a system is utilized for learning the English language as a second language, and conducting the assessment online. Many factors influence the performance of students through an English online test such as their perception, motivation, knowledge, and desire as well as the delivery mode of the test (Budin 2014; Brunfaut et al 2018). Furthermore, some studies revealed there is an impact of the test method on writing results, by looking at the average obtained result of writing tasks on a computer-based (Breland, Lee & Muraki 2005). This may be due to the familiarity, prior knowledge and usability of the test which assist test-takers to obtain better scores(Breland, Lee & Muraki 2005).

Zheng et al (2018) stated that the integration of technology in language learning has become an essential trend in many language institutes, due to the renewal development and expanded applications of technology in learning tools. Particularly in an online learning environment, students are engaging with a new dynamic environment, so their interaction with technology becomes an effective factor in learning success. Moreover, the rehearsal activities may help in familiarising with the test structure which in turn leads to confidence during the test.

Objectives of the study:

- To define the level of confidence of students during English online tests and the difficulty they have.
- To investigate the relationship between usability of the test and the most preferred features of the test.
- To identify other variables that can improve the test.

Research Questions:

- What challenges students may face during the test?
- To what extent the confidence feeling of a student helps them to perform better in the online test?
- What is the level of confidence of students during the test?

The rest of the paper is organised as follows: Section 2 discusses the methodology being utilized for this research, including a detailed literature review; Section 3 describes the obtained results; Sections 4 and 5 present the discussion and conclusion

2. METHODS

This study is an initial part of the whole study investigating user experience with English online tests. A mixed-method is being utilized for the quantitative research approach. In this paper report, a scoping literature review and an online survey of non-native English speakers who are studying English courses or have done so recently have been recruited. This study is an initial part of the whole study investigating user experience with English online tests. A mixed-method is being utilized for the quantitative research approach.

2.1 Literature Review

We reviewed recently published studies following a scoping review format with searches on the following databases: ACM Digital Library, IEEE Digital Library, Google Scholar and Web of Science. In this literature, the used approach is identifying the relevant studies by the title of the paper and abstract. This approach is synthesizing evidence from recent studies to identify the knowledge gap and clarify concepts of the research (Munn et al, 2018).

The review has been done with the following guide of scoping review methodology and Prisma diagram which is an extension of scoping review (Hamel et al, 2021). The strategy of this review is to use separate search queries for each database for the review period of 2010 to 2020 (inclusive). The use of search queries provided a variety of retrieved results, and these results are filtered based on relevance. In this theoretical method, the main focus is on the interaction between students and an English test done online, which means in the field of human-computer interaction. The impact of learning English online has been highlighted in this literature. Computer-assisted language learning is still in its development phase, recent studies presented the correlation between the practical usage of a digital English learning environment with the psychological aspects of it such as motivation, confidence and effectiveness (Lai, 2019). Studies indicated also that there is an improvement in students' performance in grammar and vocabulary knowledge with digital English learning (Cole & Vanderplank 2016; Lee 2019). At the same time, these studies revealed that EFL (English as a Foreign Language) learners interact more with virtual learning environments as a result of the frequent use of technology tools. However, these studies did not investigate the impact of the test and the approach of interacting with the online test.

Test format can impact the performance of students during the test, with the effect of gender bias as well. A comparison study was done for pre-intermediate level students on two types of tests multiple-choice (MC) and Constructed Response (CR) EFL vocabulary test. It indicated that students perform better in MC format than in CR test format, with variation between genders in the two formats, which means males scored relatively better in MC format than females (Masoumi & Sadeghi, 2020). Furthermore, language testing may be affected by a variety of factors, some from test format and methods and others from the test-takers perspective. The test itself has some formats such as open-end, gap-filling, ordering, multiple-choice...etc., while none of these formats of the test has an ideal test format, the test administrators have to employ the format based on the purpose and context of the test. Moreover, the familiarity with the test content can help reading comprehension test, these two influenced elements lead to influence scours of a test-taker (Rezaei, Barati & Youhanaee, 2012).

Test structure and test design are the most items of test usability, get used to testing is not an easy task but needs more practice. As Saiful et al (2020) pointed out that students need to be trained on the TOEFL test which is one of the official English language tests, particularly for the writing section. This is not only for acquiring knowledge but for time management as well (Saiful et al 2020). This study is only for the witting section, so other sections need to investigate. In addition to the test structure, student-centred design is an essential element of the test to offer interaction via technology. This means learners' comfortability, level of confidence and ability to achieve a better result from real interaction with an English learning environment (Wu et al, 2011). Furthermore, previous studies in this field confirmed that interaction tools build the confidence of students which leads to a direct correlation between confidence and motivation of students with their learning ability (Wu et al 2010).

In terms of usability design, more research needs to be conducted to investigate the different test designs and how they are usable for test-takers. This also includes the validity and effectiveness of the test design. The development of a web application for the IELTS reading test done by Rokhaniyah and Putra (2021) evaluated the performance among test-takers, this development carried out the feasibility and the effectiveness of the test as essential phases of the development process. The results of this study show an enhancement on obtained better scores and test-takers are motivated more.

To sum up, the scoping review for this study is summarised in the following Prisma diagram.

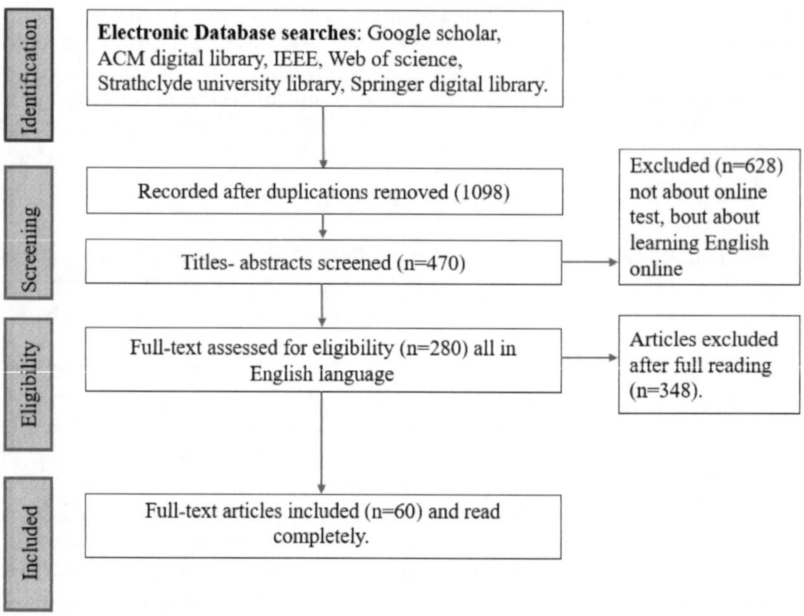

Figure 1. Prisma Flow Diagram of Reviewed Articles

2.2 Online Questionnaire

A survey questionnaire has been deployed to investigate the user experience with an English online test. A set of 21 questions were sent to language schools and first-year overseas students at universities in the UK for distribution through gatekeepers. The total number of submissions received was 132, mainly from university first-year students who studied English recently. After removing uncompleted responses we obtained 124 completed questionnaires. The survey was conducted under departmental ethical approval.

The questionnaire was composed of four sections:

1. An informed consent page
2. A demographic information page (age range, gender, subject study domain (e.g. science, engineering, humanities…)
3. Questions concerning language testing: background qualification levels, the experience of online testing, confidence level and comments on style and challenges in the use of test systems and training provided prior to testing.
4. A reduced version of the System Usability Scale (Brooke 1996) focussing on general impressions of online testing.

3. RESULTS

Some previous studies reported that there is an impact of the test types and question types as well. However, there are not many pieces of research that considered the impact from the user perspective of a test-taker performance. The survey questions are mainly to examine the user experience. Data is being analysed quantitatively using Qualtrics software in order to describe it statistically. This approach assists in classifying received responses from the participants based on the categories of the questions and builds a comprehensive picture of the observed results. Most of the participants at the undergraduate or postgraduate level of study are from the under-35 age group. They studied the English language as a second language and their top six first languages were Chinese, Arabic, French, Greek, and Hungarian. The background of the participant is mostly Engineering and science.

The 1st part of the questionnaire is about general information to classify the participants according to age, gender, first language and subject area. Moreover, most of the participants have done the test online, and only 14.7% of them have never done the online test before as shown in figure 2.

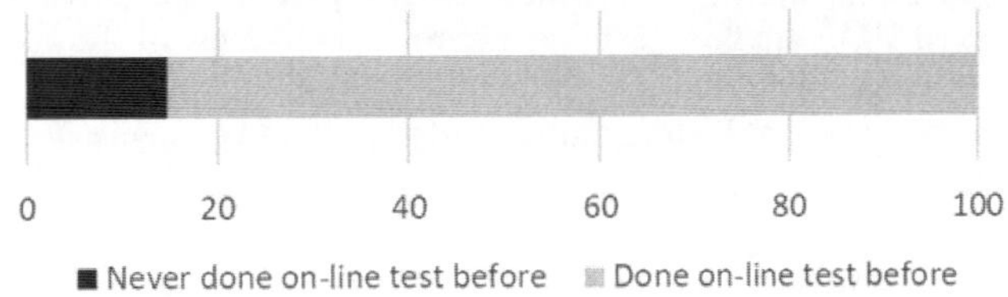

Figure 2. Percentage of Students Who Had an Online Test and Did Not

The 2nd part of the questionnaire is about the challenges of taking a test online and how test-takers feel during the test. For this purpose, we used an open-ended question to find out the correlation between some elements such as interaction difficulty and challenges that may be counted during the test. From the responses to the question of challenges students may face some of them have a problem related to familiarity with test structure and others do not have, meanwhile, most of them have challenges. These challenges can affect their performance in the test and it is summarized by frequently mentioned in responses (time, question type, technical problem, environment and vocabularies, etc.) as shown in the word cloud image.

Figure 3. Word Cloud of Most Affected Challenges on the Performance

The main focus is on the correlation between variables and the situation of test-takers during the test. For instance, the correlation between the first language of students and the level of confidence. As shown in the table most frequent mother language of the participants and level of confidence. It seems no significant effect from the first language side, but with the Chinese language, the shape of alphabetical characters may affect some of their stress and less confidence during the test.

Table 1. Level of Confidence Corresponding to the Language of Students

Students first language	Frequently	Level of confidence percentage
Chinese	36	27% unconfident
		21% less confident
		41% confident
Arabic	25	50% confident
		50% less confident
Spanish	3	All confident
Hungarian	4	All confident

In our investigation about the difficulty that test-takers may have, the results of the survey showed that 66% of the participants have difficulty with an online test and 34% do not have difficulty. This provides insight into figuring out reasons for that which will be for the rest of the project. Furthermore, training on how to use the online test systems plays a fundamental role in this part, 85% of participants have not been trained on the system before the test had difficulty during the test. In the last part of the questionnaire participants were asked about anything need be improved, and most of the answers were summarised as follows:

- Provide help tools such as highlighting or underlining and giving students note features so that they may put a mark on any question they did not understand or leave it to the end.
- Question and answer on the same page by making all questions and their answers on the same page.
- Test structure improvements to help students navigate through exam questions.
- Preferred questions some students prefer multiple-choice.
- Navigation icons and links should be obvious.

These improvements need to be done on the system side, however, from a user perspective, the system is in the middle of being easy to use as evaluated by the participants. Figure 4 shows.

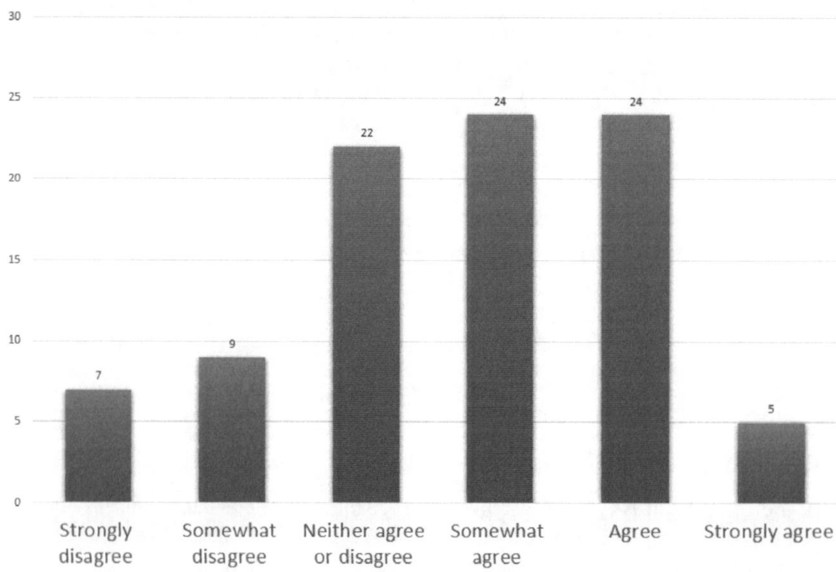

Figure 4. Participants' Opinions about Improve the Usability of the Test

4. DISCUSSION

The result towards the end of this study which is based on two used methods the questionnaire and the literature of previous research demonstrated that the impact of the test can be from the test structure or a test-taker aspect. This largely confirms the research questions as follows: the level of confidence is differentiated between students based on other factors such as the first language which is the most noticeable specifier. In addition, in writing tests students would prefer the online method rather than speaking tests (Wu et al 2010). In the questionnaire we have not measured the performance of students during the test but the correlation between confidence level and perform better can be extracted from the challenges mentioned by participants. This gives insight into affected elements of the test to help students become more confident during the test in order to get a better score.

Furthermore, as shown in the result section most of the students are at the normal confidence level. Firstly, test design has a limitation that can affect the performance of students such as page layout, question type, navigation icons and others. These futures are taken from test-takers experience and previous sties. However, it cannot be generalized due to the limited samples of participants and the variety of test designs. Secondly, from the user perspective, some factors can affect user performance. For instance, user background and subject area which is meant adapting to a computer for students who utilise computers mostly. From this side, we identify that prior experience with a computer helps students to perform better on online tests and improve user satisfaction. Additionally, training was raised as the most important issue, particularly for students who are not familiar with a test on a technology device. The training leads to answering the test easily and saves time as well. As a result, this would improve a student's score on the test.

5. LIMITATION

In addition to the literature review, this study was conducted with a relatively small number of participants (n=124) primarily those already in University courses completing a questionnaire online, but it was an in-depth study and in line with the previous studies in the area called the impact of online English testing. Although we do not believe there was a direct impact on responses, recruitment and study were carried out during international lockdowns due to the Covid-19 pandemic.

6. CONCLUSION AND FUTURE WORK

This paper has investigated the impact factors that may affect the performance of students on English as a Foreign Language online testing. It has provided insight into how the challenges of the test environment impact the performance of students. The main contribution of this research is summarizing the main challenges faced during an English online test. As presented in the result section, evaluating the user experience with English online tests shows a disparity between students depending on background, their first language, test design and others. The approach of training on how to do the test had been reported in a previous study about writing tasks only but in this study, we recommend prior test training should be taken for all English test skills. Preliminary findings of this study enable us to investigate the influence of additional factors from the test design and how can we overcome them. In particular, we are now investigating the impact of pre-test training to reduce the impact of tests on the accuracy of students' results. More participants and more personal studies may also report more factors and challenges of the English online test. These may play a fundamental role in improving the scores of a test-taker on an English online test. The recommendation of this continuing study also is to evaluate the accuracy and effectiveness of the test structure against the system usability scale.

REFERENCES

Breland, H., Lee, Y.-W. and Muraki, E. (2005). *Comparability of TOEFL CBT essay prompts: response-mode analyses.* Educational and Psychological Measurement, *65*(4), 577-595.

Brooke, J. (1996). "SUS: A "*quick and dirty" usability scale". In Usability evaluation in industry*, Edited by: Jordan, P. W., Thomas, B. A. Weerdmeester and McClelland, I. L. 189–194. London: Taylor & Francis.

Brunfaut, T., Harding, L. and Batty, A. O. (2018). *Going online: The effect of mode of delivery on performances and perceptions on an English L2 writing test suite.* Assessing Writing, 36, 3-18.

Budin, M., (2014). *Investigating the relationship between English language anxiety and the achievement of school-based oral English test among Malaysian Form Four students.* International Journal of Learning, Teaching and Educational Research, *2*(1).

Cole, J. and Vanderplank, R. (2016) *Comparing autonomous and class-based learners in Brazil: Evidence for the present-day advantages of informal, out-of-class learning.* System, 61, 31-42.

Hamel, C., et al. (2021). *Defining Rapid Reviews: a systematic scoping review and thematic analysis of definitions and defining characteristics of rapid reviews.* Journal of Clinical Epidemiology, 129, 74-85.

Lai, C., (2019). *The influence of extramural access to mainstream culture social media on ethnic minority students' motivation for language learning.* British Journal of Educational Technology, 50(4): p. 1929-1941.

Lee, J.S. and Lee, K. (2010) *Informal digital learning of English and English as an international language: The path less traveled.* British Journal of Educational Technology, 50(3), 1447-1461.

Munn, Z., et al., (2018). *Systematic review or scoping review? Guidance for authors when choosing between a systematic or scoping review approach.* BMC medical research methodology, 18(1): p. 1-7.

Masoumi, G.A. and Sadeghi, K. (2020). *Impact of test format on vocabulary test performance of EFL learners: the role of gender.* Language Testing in Asia, 10(1), 1-13.

Rezaei, O., Barati, H., and Youhanaee, M. (2012). *The Effect of Content Familiarity and Test Format on Iranian EFL Test Takers' Performance on Test of Reading Comprehension.* International Journal of Applied Linguistics and English Literature, 1(4): p. 1-14.

Rokhaniyah, H. and Putra, O. V. (2021). *Developing Web-Based Online Test System to Boost IELTS Academic Reading Score.* English Review: Journal of English Education, 9(2): p. 9-18.

Saiful, A., et al., (2020). *EFL Learners' Difficulties in the Structure and Written Expression Section of TOEFL Test In An Indonesian University.* Englisia. 7(2).

Wu, W.-c.V., Yen, L.L., and Marek, M. (2011). *Using online EFL interaction to increase confidence, motivation, and ability.* Journal of Educational Technology & Society, 14(3): p. 118-129.

Wu, W.-c.V. and Marek, M. (2010). *Making English a" Habit": Increasing Confidence, Motivation, and Ability of EFL Students through Cross-Cultural, Computer-Assisted Interaction.* Turkish Online Journal of Educational Technology-TOJET, 9(4): p. 101-112.

Zheng, C., et al. (2018). *The relationship between English language learners' motivation and online self-regulation: A structural equation modelling approach.* System, 76: p. 144-157.

ESTIMATION OF HUMAN EMOTION DEFINED WITH RUSSELL'S CIRCUMPLEX MODEL USING LIGHTWEIGHT FNIRS DEVICE

Daisuke Fukui[1], Takushige Katsura[2], Masashi Egi[1], Norihisa Komoda[3] and Takenao Ohkawa[4]
[1]*Hitachi, Ltd., Research & Development Group, Japan*
[2] *Graduate School of Integrative Science and Engineering Systems, Tokyo City University, Japan*
[3] *Codesolutions Co. Ltd., Japan*
[4] *Graduate School of System Informatics, Kobe University, Japan*

ABSTRACT

A method for estimating human emotions defined with the Russell's circumplex model using a lightweight functional near infrared spectroscopy (fNIRS) device is proposed. With the proposed method, from only 2-ch sensors measuring total-hemoglobin data with the lightweight fNIRS device, 35 features for estimating emotions are generated. Using the generated features, k-nearest neighbor models for estimating 20 emotions are constructed. The evaluation of the constructed models using measured 320 records from 20 participants showed that it is possible to estimate the emotions "excited" and "lethargic" with a classification rate of more than 60% by cross-validation.

KEYWORDS

fNIRS, Estimation of Emotions, K-Nearest Neighbor Model, Hemoglobin, Russell's Circumplex Model

1. INTRODUCTION

If the emotions evoked by people in various situations in their daily lives can be estimated at a high classification rate, they can be used to improve human computer interaction. This can be achieved by identifying the emotions people experience when using computers and accordingly optimizing computer behavior. As more emotions are estimated, the range of applications expands. Russell proposed a model in which various human emotions are arranged in a circle in a two-dimensional space with two axes: pleasant and unpleasant, and active and inactive (James, 2003).

Functional near infrared spectroscopy (fNIRS), which measures the increase or decrease in hemoglobin (Hb) in blood of the brain based on the absorption rate of near-infrared light, has been used to estimate pleasant and unpleasant emotions in humans (Daisuke, 2021, Kazuki, 2015). There is also a method using functional magnetic resonance imaging (fMRI), which measures the increase or decrease in Hb by the change in the magnetic force of deoxygenated Hb. Although these methods can estimate pleasant and unpleasant emotions, they cannot estimate more nuanced emotions as defined using Russell's circumplex model.

There is a method that uses electroencephalography (EEG) sensors to estimate more than two emotions: pleasant and unpleasant. Yuen (2009) computed six statistical features from EEG data and used a neural network to identify five emotions (anger, sad, surprise, happy, and neutral) with a 95% classification rate. Murugappann (2010) used the "db4" wavelet function to derive modified energy-based features from EEG data and identified five emotions (disgust, happy, surprise, fear, and neutral) with an 83.26% classification rate using a k-nearest neighbor (kNN) model. Islam (2021) converted one-dimensional EEG data into Pearson's correlation coefficient featured images of channel correlation of EEG sub-bands and used a convolutional neural network trained on these images to recognize three levels of valence and arousal (low/middle/high) with an accuracy of over 70%.

However, the EEG sensors used in these studies are equipped with 32 to 62 channels, making it difficult to measure EEG in daily life. Also, EEG signals measured at various locations on the scalp are usually contaminated with a large amount of noise. For example, potential changes caused by eye and muscle movements are included in the EEG data as noise. Several methods have been proposed to remove noise in EEG data, but it is difficult to remove it completely.

We propose a method for estimating emotions using a lightweight fNIRS device. Since fNIRS measurement is less affected by noise than EEG measurement, it is more suitable for measuring brain activity of people in their daily lives. On the basis of the results of a previous study (Daisuke, 2021), we evaluated the classification rate of the kNN model, which estimates 20 emotions defined with Russell's circumplex model, by cross-validation.

2. EMOTION ESTIMATION BY FNIRS

2.1 Definition of Emotions

On the basis of Russell's circumplex model (James, 1980, 2003) shown in Figure 1, we selected a total of 20 emotions, five in each of the four quadrants of pleasant/activation, pleasant/deactivation, unpleasant/activation, and unpleasant/deactivation. These emotions were selected to have moderate variations in the degree of valence (pleasant/unpleasant) and arousal (activation/deactivation) within each quadrant. The list of selected emotions is shown in Table 1. These 20 emotions were used as research targets in our study.

Figure 1. Russell's circumplex model

Table 1. Emotions selected for our study

Category	Emotions
Pleasant-Activation	exited, delighted, grad, happy, pleased
Pleasant-Deactivation	sleepy, calm, relaxed, content, serene
Unpleasant-Activation	angry, afraid, annoyed, distressed, frustrated
Unpleasant-Deactivation	miserable, sad, gloomy, bored, lethargic

2.2 Measurement Method

Figure 2 shows the method we used for measuring brain activity during image viewing using HOT-1000 (Yiheng, 2005, Takayuki, 2016), a lightweight fNIRS device manufactured by NeU Co[1]. The participant wears the HOT-1000 on his head and views the images on the display. By measuring total-Hb while the participant is viewing the image, we investigated the relationship between the emotion evoked by the participant and brain activity.

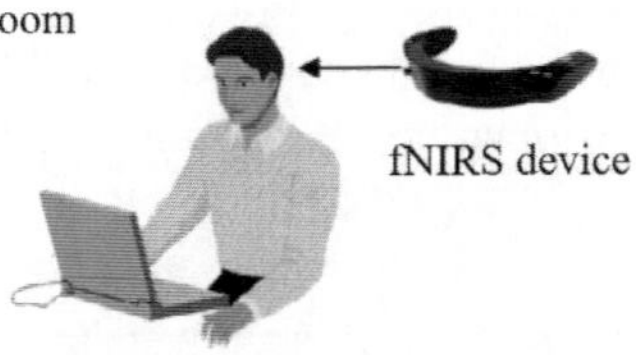

Figure 2. Measurement method

There are two types of data that can be measured with HOT-1000. One is the total-Hb measured at a depth of about 1 cm from the scalp (S), and the other is the total-Hb measured at a depth of about 3 cm from the scalp (D). During normal brain activity, the increase in total-Hb is not seen near the scalp but only deep in the brain. Therefore, the total-Hb calculated by subtracting S from D can be considered to indicate brain activity (B). However, the amount of change in total-Hb near the scalp and deep in the brain are both always affected by heartbeat and other factors as well as brain activity, so it is necessary to eliminate these factors.

First, the baselines of S_i and D_i waveform data are corrected after removing pin and step noise. Next, α, which represents the degree that heartbeat and other factors affect brain activity, is calculated using the following five formulas. The brain-activity waveform data (B_i) are then derived by subtracting α times S_i from D_i. In these formulas, *i* represents the elapsed time from the start of the brain-activity measurement. The measurement of brain activity begins when HOT-1000 is placed on the participant's head.

$$B_i = D_i - \alpha \cdot S_i$$

(1) $\alpha = 1$

(2) $\alpha = \frac{H_i}{h_i}$

(3) $\alpha = \frac{\sum_{i=T_0}^{T_2} d_i}{\sum_{i=T_0}^{T_2} s_i}$

(4) $\alpha = \frac{\sum_{i=T_0}^{T_1} d_i}{\sum_{i=T_0}^{T_1} s_i}$

(5) $\alpha = Corr(d_i, s_i)$

The H and h in Formula (2) represent the heartbeat components of D and S, respectively. The heartbeat components are calculated using a band-pass filter from 0.7 to 2.0 Hz, which indicates the frequency of the heartbeat. The d and s in Formulas (3) through (5) represent the values of D and S, respectively, in which the heartbeat component has been removed. The T_0 in Formulas (3) and (4) represents the start time of the rest period (see Chapter 3 for details). The T_2 in Formula (3) represents the end time of the image display. The T_1 in Formula (4) represents the end time of the rest period. The Corr function in Formula (5) calculates the correlation coefficient between d_i and s_i in the last 5 seconds.

---

[1] http://neu-brains.site/en/

The B_i derived using Formula (1) indicates the brain activity calculated simply from the difference between d_i and s_i without removing any effect of heartbeat and other factors. Formula (2) calculates the ratio of the heartbeat components of D and S to remove the effect of heartbeat. Formula (3) calculates the ratio of the integral values of d_i and s_i in the image-display period including the rest period to remove the effects of heartbeat and other factors (such as body movement). Formula (4) calculates the ratio of the integral values in Formula (3) from the rest period only. The reason the correlation coefficients between d_i and s_i for the past 5 seconds are calculated in Formula (5) is to derive the brain activity using the characteristic that the correlation between total-Hb near the scalp and deep in the brain becomes higher when there is no brain activity and lower when there is brain activity.

Finally, for each of the five types of brain-activity waveform data derived from the five formulas, the seven features shown in Table 2 are calculated. A total of 35 features are used to estimate 20 emotions. We used the kNN model, which is a machine-learning model that can obtain a better classification rate even with a small amount of training data.

Table 2. Features

ID	Feature
F1	Mean
F2	Standard deviation
F3	Median
F4	Maximum value
F5	Time required to reach maximum value
F6	Maximum change in time window (5 seconds)
F7	Rising slope (1 s from start)

3. EMOTION-ESTIMATION EXPERIMENT

We conducted an experiment using HOT-1000 to measure brain activity when a person viewed 20 images that evoked 20 different emotions. A total of 20 participants, who were asked to cooperate voluntarily, participated in this experiment. Twelve were in their 30s (8 men and 4 women) and 8 were in their 40s (6 men and 2 women). This experiment was approved by the Ethical Review Working Committee of the Research and Development Group, Hitachi, Ltd (Approval No. 20160905-0144).

An overview of the measurement procedure is shown in Figure 3. In the first five minutes, we explained the methods of the experiment, received informed consent, and attached HOT-1000 to the participants. Next, the 20 images and their descriptions were displayed to the participants in 2 sessions of 10 images each. Each image-display session was followed by a 1-min rest period. Before presenting the ten images to the participants, one neutral image (Figure 4) that was not used for analysis was displayed to the participants to suppress the response of brain activity to the first image displayed. A total of 11 images were displayed in a single "image display" session. The ten images displayed to the participants following the neutral image were arranged randomly. Finally, a questionnaire was administered to the participants to determine whether the images evoked the desired emotions. The reason the images were displayed in two separate sessions was to eliminate the effect of the order in which the images were displayed on the results. The ten images displayed to half the participants in the first image-display session were displayed to the other half in the second image-display session and vice versa.

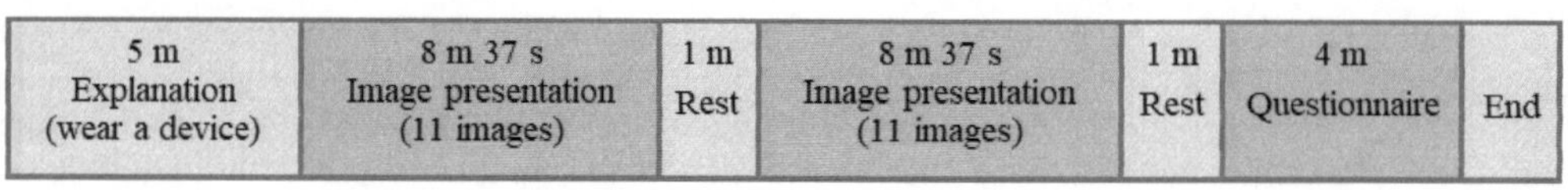

Figure 3. Measurement procedure

Figure 4. Neutral image

The image-display procedure is shown in Figure 5. First, a 30-s rest period was set up to calm brain activity. During the rest period, only the character "+", which is about 2 cm in length and width, was displayed in the center of the screen, and the participants were told to gaze at it. Next, the description of the image to be displayed was shown for 7 seconds. By displaying the description of the image immediately before the image display, the target brain activity was stimulated. Finally, an image was displayed to the participants for 10 seconds to evoke the target emotion. This procedure was repeated 11 times using 1 neutral image and 10 different experimental images.

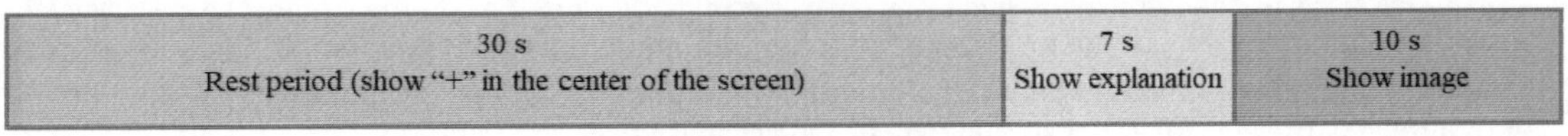

Figure 5. Image-display procedure

Figure 6. Example of description and image

Figure 6 shows an example of the descriptions displayed to the participants and those displayed following the descriptions. The 20 images used in the experiment were purchased from Getty Images[2]. The method of selecting the 20 images was as follows. First, for each of the 20 emotions (see Table 1), 5 evaluators (all Japanese nationals) selected one candidate image that evoked the emotion through keyword searches on Getty Images. Next, the 5 evaluators voted to select one image that would strongly evoke that particular emotion. Two evaluators were experts in the field of product and service evaluation (one man and one woman in their 40s). Another three were the researchers (men in their 40s) who have been engaged in fNIRS research for more than two years.

The content of the questionnaire given to the participants at the end of the experiment is shown in Figure 7. The participants were asked whether the emotion described in the description matched the content of the images. The visual analogue scale (VAS) values, which were obtained by normalizing the line lengths of the questionnaire responses to take values from 0 to 10 based on the left edge, were used as the teacher data. The 80 records with a VAS value of less than 5 (data that did not match the target emotion) were excluded from the analysis because the emotion evoked was unknown. The remaining 320 records were used for the analysis.

[2] https://www.gettyimages.com/

In general, a minimum of 50 records is required for training, and this experiment met that criterion. It is preferable to train 10 times the amount of data as the number of features, but we were able to obtain more than 90% of the recommended data, although it was slightly less than the 350 recommended records for the 35 features in this study.

Please draw a vertical line to indicate whether the emotion described in the description matched the content of the image.

Not matched ———————— Matched

Figure 7. Questionnaire content

4. EXPERIMENTAL RESULTS

On the basis on the above experimental data, we trained 20 different kNN models to classify each of the emotions shown in Table 1. The k in the kNN models was chosen to be 3, which is the most accurate among various k values. The models were evaluated using 10-fold cross-validation using the metrics of Matthews correlation coefficient (MCC), precision, recall, and accuracy.

The 10-fold cross-validation is a validation method with which the training data are randomly divided into 10 groups; 9 groups are trained and the remaining 1 group is validated, and repeated 10 times until all groups are validated. MCC is an evaluation metric that does not depend on data bias. Precision is an evaluation metric to evaluate whether the estimated result from the classification model is correct when the result is positive. Recall is an evaluation metric to evaluate whether the estimated result from the classification model is correct when the correct emotion is positive. Accuracy is an evaluation metric to evaluate whether the estimated result from the classification model is correct for all estimated results.

The formulas for calculating each evaluation metric are described below: TP (true positive) represents the amount of data when the result estimated from the classification model is positive and correct; FP (false positive) represents the amount of data when the result estimated from the classification model is positive and incorrect; TN (true negative) represents the amount of data when the result estimated from the classification model is negative and correct; FN (false negative) represents the amount of data when the result estimated from the classification model is negative and incorrect.

$$\cdot MCC = \frac{(TP \times TN) - (FP \times FN)}{\sqrt{(TP+FP) \times (TP+FN) \times (TN+FP) \times (TN+FN)}}$$

$$\cdot Precision = \frac{TP}{TP+FP}$$

$$\cdot Recall = \frac{TP}{TP+FN}$$

$$\cdot Accuracy = \frac{TP+TN}{TP+TN+FP+FN}$$

Table 3 shows the evaluation results of the kNN models. If there is a large bias in the amount of correct data (corresponding to the target emotion) and the amount of incorrect data (not corresponding to the target emotion), accuracy will be large. Therefore, the baseline value, which is obtained by dividing the greater amount of correct or incorrect data by the total data, is also described in the table. The baseline value represents the accuracy of a meaningless classification model that predicts all data as correct or incorrect and used as a metric to evaluate the validity of Accuracy.

The results of analysis showed that the "exited" kNN model's MCC was 0.695, precision was 68.8%, recall was 73.3%, and accuracy was 97.2% (baseline was 95.3%). The "lethargic" kNN model's MCC was 0.656, precision was 72.7%, recall was 61.5%, and accuracy was 97.5% (baseline was 95.9%). Both models had high

MCC with recall exceeding 50% and accuracy exceeding the baseline. All the other kNN models showed lower accuracy than the baseline and their recall was less than 50%.

"Excited" is placed as a highly active emotion in the "pleasant" direction in Russel's model, and "lethargic" is placed as a less active emotion in the "unpleasant" direction in Russel's model. It is possible that the degree of activation in Russel's model is reflected in the amount of total-Hb.

Tables 4 and 5 show the classification results when the VAS thresholds were changed from 6 to 9 for "excited" and "lethargic", respectively. For "excited", when the VAS threshold exceeded 8, recall improved to 0.8. There was no improvement in the recall for "lethargic" by changing the VAS threshold.

These results indicate that the proposed method can estimate brain activity when "excited" or " lethargic" is evoked with a classification rate of more than 60%. The results also indicate that "excited" with a VAS of more than 8 could be classified with a classification rate of 80%. It may be possible to classify the brain activity of people who feel strongly "excited" with a high classification rate.

Table 3. Classification results of k-NN models

Emotion	MCC	Precision	Recall	Accuracy (baseline)
excited	0.695	0.688	0.733	97.2(95.3)
lethargic	0.656	0.727	0.615	97.5(95.9)
calm	0.319	0.333	0.400	91.3(93.8)
frustrated	0.255	0.278	0.313	92.5(95.0)
afraid	0.234	0.250	0.273	94.7(96.6)
gloomy	0.211	0.273	0.214	94.1(95.6)
serene	0.154	0.211	0.200	90.3(93.8)
sad	0.156	0.182	0.235	90.3(94.7)
distressed	0.137	0.200	0.143	93.8(95.6)
content	0.132	0.200	0.158	91.3(94.1)
annoyed	0.118	0.130	0.214	90.3(95.6)
grad	0.103	0.182	0.111	92.2(94.4)
relaxed	0.099	0.150	0.158	89.7(94.1)
sleepy	0.097	0.143	0.133	92.2(95.3)
miserable	0.080	0.111	0.143	91.3(95.6)
pleased	0.065	0.100	0.133	90.3(95.3)
happy	0.063	0.111	0.118	90.3(94.7)
delighted	0.053	0.105	0.111	89.7(94.4)
angry	0.000	0.000	0.000	91.6(96.3)
bored	-0.013	0.048	0.053	88.1(94.1)

Table 4. Classification results of k-NN model for "excited"

Empathy threshold	MCC	Precision	Recall	Accuracy (baseline)
5 or more	0.695	0.688	0.733	97.2 (95.3)
6 or more	0.673	0.667	0.714	96.7 (94.9)
7 or more	0.648	0.667	0.667	96.4 (94.6)
8 or more	0.787	0.8	0.8	97.5 (93.8)
9 or more	0.714	0.667	0.8	96.9 (94.8)

Table 5. Classification results of k-NN model for "lethargic"

Empathy threshold	MCC	Precision	Recall	Accuracy (baseline)
5 or more	0.656	0.727	0.615	97.5 (95.9)
6 or more	0.264	0.4	0.2	96.0 (96.3)
7 or more	0.431	0.6	0.333	96.4 (95.9)
8 or more	0.28	0.286	0.333	94.4 (96.3)
9 or more	0.478	0.5	0.5	95.8 (95.8)

5. CONCLUSION

To estimate various emotions in daily life, we conducted an experiment to estimate 20 emotions defined with the Russell's circumplex model using HOT-1000, which is a lightweight fNIRS device. The 35 features representing brain activity were first calculated from the total-Hb data measured using HOT-1000. Using those 35 features, we then trained kNN models to predict the 20 measured emotions and evaluated the classification rate of those emotions by 10-fold cross validation. The proposed method estimated brain activity when "excited" or " lethargic" was evoked with a classification rate of more than 60%. It may be possible to classify the brain activity of people who feel strongly "excited" with a classification rate of 80%.

Previous studies have shown that EEG is effective in predicting various human emotions. However, the EEG sensors used in these studies are equipped with 32 to 62 channels, making it difficult to measure EEG in daily life. Also, EEG signals measured at various locations on the scalp are usually contaminated with a large amount of noise. Therefore, we attempted to estimate emotions using a lightweight device that can measure brain activity in daily life and measure fNIRS data, which is robust against noise. The results of this study indicate that certain emotions, such as "excited" and "lethargic", can be classified with a high classification rate, but the number of participants and amount of data collected are not sufficient, so continued data collection is necessary for future work.

REFERENCES

Daisuke, F. et al., 2021. Estimation of human emotion using total-hemoglobin data measured by a lightweight fNIRS device. *IEEJ Transactions on Electronics, Information and Systems*, Vol. 141, Issue 6, pp. 735-742. (written in Japanese)

Islam, M. R. et al., 2021. EEG channel correlation based model for emotion recognition. *Computers in Biology and Medicine*, 136, 104757.

James, A. R., 1980. A circumplex model of affect. *Journal of Personality and Social Psychology*, Vol. 39, No. 6, pp. 1161-1178.

James, A. R., 2003. Core affect and the psychological construction of emotion. *Psychological Review*, Vol. 110, pp. 145-172.

Murugappan, M. et al., 2010. Classification of human emotion from EEG using discrete wavelet transform. *Journal of biomedical science and engineering*, 3(04), pp. 390-396.

Kazuki, Y. and Hitoshi, T., 2015. Evaluation of pleasant and unpleasant emotion with visual stimulus using NIRS. *Transactions of the Japanese Society for Medical and Biological Engineering*, Vol. 53, Supplement, pp. S379-S382.

Takayuki, N. et al., 2016. Interpersonal frontopolar neural synchronization in group communication: An exploration toward fNIRS hyperscanning of natural interactions. *NeuroImage*, Vol. 133, June 2016, pp. 484-497.

Thomas, M. C. and Peter, E. H., 1967. Nearest neighbor pattern classification. *IEEE Transactions on Information Theory*, Vol. 13, Issue 1, pp 21-27.

Yiheng, Z. et al., 2005. Eigenvector-based spatial filtering for reduction of physiological interference in diffuse optical imaging. *J. Biomed Opt*, Vol.10, No. 1, pp. 11-14.

Yuen, C. T. et al., 2009. Classification of human emotions from EEG signals using statistical features and neural network. *International Journal of Integrated Engineering*, 1(3), pp. 71-79.

CONTRIBUTIONS OF AUGMENTED REALITY IN ARCHITECTURAL PROJECT REVIEW

Gaëlle Baudoux[1], Maxime Grella[2] and Pierre Leclercq[1]
[1]*LUCID-ULiège, Allée de la découverte, 9 - B4000 Liege - Belgium*
[2]*Université de Liège, Rue des Vennes, 312 - B420 Liege - Belgium*

ABSTRACT

Already present in the fields of medicine and video games, augmented reality is now being employed in architectural design. We explore here the role that this new digital tool can play, as a means of interaction, in the review of projects. To do so, we work through experiments that immerse designers in three different environments: (1) a 2D environment, composed of plans and sections, (2) an augmented reality environment on a tablet and, finally, (3) an environment combining the two approaches. We can thus dissect how augmented reality can be a relevant tool and which functionality(ies) can enrich its current potentialities in architectural design.

KEYWORDS

Architectural Design, Project Review, Augmented Reality, Evaluation of Solutions, External Representations

1. INTRODUCTION

Today, the digital revolution is everywhere, even in the design professions. Augmented reality (AR) and virtual reality (VR) also offer great opportunities in architecture, engineering and construction (Noghabaei *et al.*, 2020). However, new tools exploiting the possibilities of augmented reality are not yet commonly operated, neither in architectural agencies nor in academia (Noghabaei *et al.*, 2020). In particular, project review is still often carried out in a «traditional» way using 2D plans and sections on paper.

Therefore, could these new tools bring added value to the design and review process? Do they allow for a better representation of the project and thus a better understanding of the architectural elements?

Let us specify that we are in a *post-WIMP* approach. We are looking for an intuitive tool with a fluid interface that does not require software to be manipulated.

2. AUGMENTED REALITY

Ronald T. Azuma (1997) defines augmented reality, AR, « as the set of applications that verify the following three properties: (1) the combination of the real and the virtual, (2) real-time interaction, and (3) the integration of the real and the virtual. » This differs from other technologies and virtual reality, by the environment in which the user evolves that is real and enriched by the addition of virtual information (Azuma, 1997).

It is important to consider that this technology is not yet considered mature (Arnaldi *et al.*, 2018). Indeed, commonly used headsets only allow a field of view of 100-110° to date. The image resolution is also not sufficient for such a closely viewed screen. The need for high resolution also means that more equipment is required than the few square centimeters of display space available. The equipment must also have a sufficient battery life to allow for mobile use. It also requires constant calibration between reality and virtual elements. For these reasons, our experiments will mobilize tablets rather than headsets.

The fields in which the most articles on AR have been published between 2001 and 2019 are education, engineering, science, mobile applications and medicine. Most of the papers, nearly 16% of the 1008 papers surveyed, covered the design and development of augmented reality applications or mobile applications (Tezer *et al.*, 2019). Since 2016, 235,030 scientific articles have been published, in French or English, on augmented reality, while virtual reality amasses 137,310 publications. If we focus only on the literature that combines AR and architecture, the number drops to 53,220. Most articles rarely specify the tool used for the research, but 24,724 publications specify the use of the tablet.

Therefore, it seems relevant to feature the exploitation of AR on the tablet in architecture.

3. ISSUE

At this stage, we question the opportunities of this technology, no more as a communication medium, but as an aid for the review of architectural design projects. We are therefore observing the activities of solution evaluation and not the generation of these solutions. We assume that AR on the tablet is a relevant tool in architectural design review, that it provides a better level of understanding and analysis of the project than «traditional» methods and that the additional information provided by AR serves the evolution of the architectural project.

4. METHODOLOGY

To confirm these hypotheses, we implement an experiment comparing different project representation methods and analyses the understanding of the project. We carry out this experiment through a simulation: the review of the same project by different architects to detect a maximum of errors that have been previously inserted.

4.1 Choice of AR-Type and Modeling Software

The system must be accessible, both financially, in terms of availability and in ease of use, so that it can be employed by anyone. Secondly, since the employment of AR requires a 3D digital model of the architectural object, the system must have good software-hardware interoperability. Finally, as few applications allow interaction with digital models from architectural design, the system must be able to host a wide range of applications, to allow a greater choice. We conclude from these considerations that the use of a generalist system such as a digital tablet has several advantages. It is a mobile tool, whose onboard power is similar to a laptop and whose integrated components (camera, gyroscope, luminosity sensor, pressure sensor, etc.) make it possible to imagine all sorts of applications. This gives us a great freedom of choice when selecting the AR application to be used. This tool is also very fluid and does not require a training phase. The tablet is only a window into the virtual world.

As a software, we chose ArchiCAD because the 3D model is generated automatically which ensures consistency of information between the 2D and 3D deliverables. It also reduces the risk of uneven representations.

We consider the following criteria for the choice of the AR application: having a compatible import format to our modeling software (ArchiCAD), having a calibration system allowing to lock the 3D model in space, allowing resizing as well as movement in most possible axes, guaranteeing an accessible price or free availability and finally being able to generate sections in real-time, displaying textual information, interacting with the model by selecting elements or displaying a shading.

The Augment application[1], based on ARcore technology used in Industry 4.0 and especially studied by Jakl *et al.* (2018), best meets these criteria and is therefore chosen to generate the augmented reality model.

4.2 Choice of Representation Media

There are several categories of representations, that play different roles in our perception of architectural information. To conduct this experiment, we choose to apply two of the seven existing ones (Baudoux *et al.*, 2019): 2D plans and sections: this is the usual basic support in design, they are still today the most mobilized elements to support reflection and communication; and 3D immersion: this support allows the use of an AR application in analogy with the physical model, another usual support in design, and will be compared to our basic support. These two methods are thus integrated into 3 types of project review: an analysis using 2D plans and sections, an analysis using a 3D model in augmented reality and finally an analysis using both of the above methods.

1 Augment (2019). https://www.augment.com/

4.3 Choice of Project Composition and Incorporated Errors

The reviewed project is a fictive family dwelling. We made this choice because the designers are experts in the design and evaluation of this type of project and because its program remains fairly standard and compatible with the experiment.

As written above, this building incorporates errors that are deliberately slipped in. By errors we mean elements that generate a solution that is incompatible with the characteristics of the problem or with functionally, technically or culturally effective proposals (Blavier *et al*, 2008). Ten errors are included. They concern the architectural program (*e.g.* a requested room not appearing), the functionality of a place (*e.g.* a door not opening in the right direction), the implantation of the building (*e.g.* the access to the terrace not being possible from the living rooms) or the information necessary for any plan (*e.g.* an unspecified bay height). They can also be errors in representation (*e.g.* the inconsistency between the garage door drawn in plan and the solid wall at the same place in section). Figures 1 to 3 present the project and point out the errors that have been inserted. Note that the number of errors is not known to the participants. The subjective appreciation of the notion of error by each participant makes the number of errors to be pointed out variable. We will therefore not evaluate the percentage of errors detected.

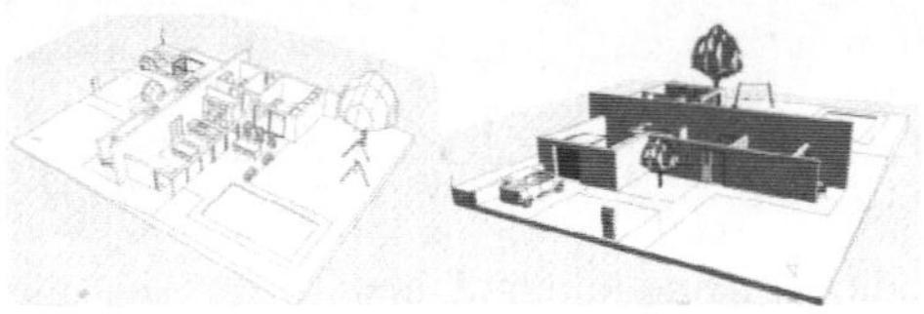

Figure 1. 3D views of the project (without roofs)

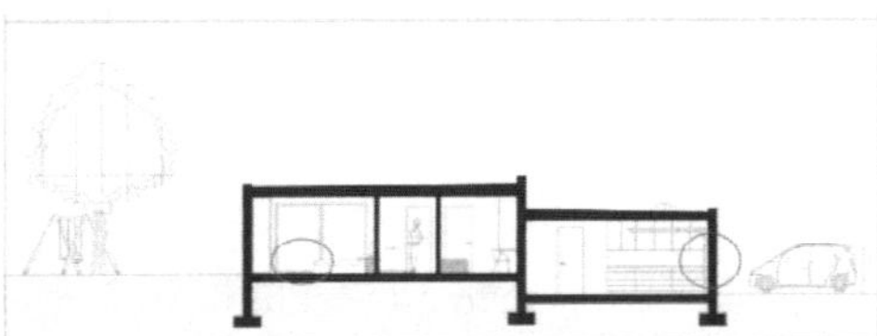

Figure 2. Longitudinal section of the project

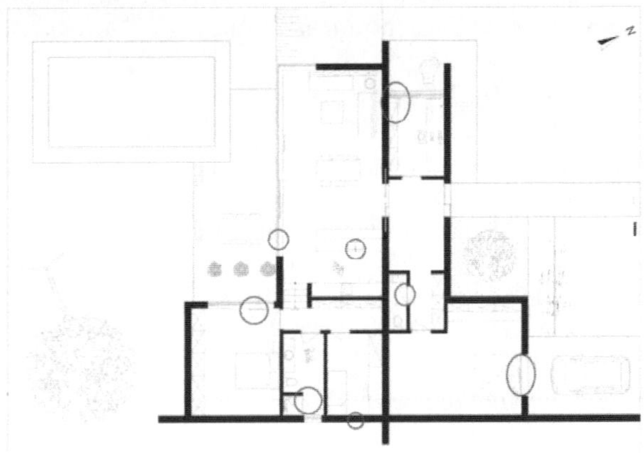

Figure 3. *Project* plan with the location of errors to be detected

4.4 Selection of Participants

Finally, we select the subjects for our experiment. We need designers who are trained in project review and have mastered the design of a family dwelling. Furthermore, designers under 25 years of age are more likely to be comfortable with technology (Elsen *et al.*, 2018). We therefore selected 15 students in 3rd bachelor and 2nd master, engineer-architects at the University of Liège.

5. EXPERIMENTAL PROTOCOL

5.1 Experimental Space and Data Collection

We carry out all three types of experiments at the same location. We prepare two different stations for this purpose:

- A 2D station: consisting of a desk on which a 1/50 scale plan and section are placed, as well as measuring and drawing tools and a computer acting as a timer.
- An RA station: consists of a desk, height-adjustable, on which a marker is fixed, a circulation area allowing movement around the model, and a tablet to work with the RA model.

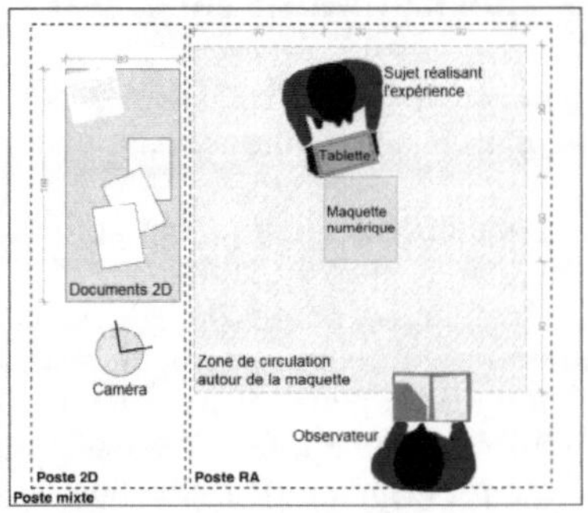

Figure 4. Schematic plan of the experimental space

We will proceed by observation as it appears to be the most suitable means to appraise such visual data. It is done through observation grid and camera recording. A few minutes informal interview is carried out immediately after the review session to collect the participants' feelings about their performance. We will not investigate the manipulations carried out on the tablet because we are not testing the software functions.

5.2 Typical Procedure

Each experiment takes about 30 minutes: 5' for experimental space preparation; 5' for subject installation and discovery of the AR application; maximum 15' for the review (from this point on, the participant can no longer interact with the observer); 5' for the debriefing. Before launching the observation, we carry out a preliminary experiment of each type which allows us to test the protocol, validate the time needed per subject, the understanding of the statement, the stability of the software, the experimental space, the structure of the note-taking grid and the video framing plans.

5.3 Collected Data

We carried out 3x5 experiments with a review time of 6' to 15'. The whole corpus constitutes 161 minutes of video, completed by 15 note-grids, 10 annotated plans and sections, 95 screen captures taken with the AR application and the informal interviews synthesized into 15x5 keywords. Based on these data and after coding, each temporal unit of each experiment can be characterized according to a series of parameters deriving from protocols of design processes analysis (Ben Rajeb & Leclercq, 2015). Theses analyzed data concern:

- The subject's actions trace his review activity (measure, draw, explore 3D, take a screenshot, comment).
- The the spatial scale of the reviewing activity (1. whole, 2. building, 3. interior or exterior, 4. room, 5. detail). An average level can be calculated.
- The focus of attention (implantation, program, structure, function, layout, light, aesthetics).
- The types of errors found (programmatic, functional, site, representational, informative).
- The additional tools used for the review (fine-liners, ruler, visualization software, screen capture).

6. RESULTS

6.1 2D Experiment

We start the analysis of the collected data with the comparative basis experiment: the 2D review. The general representation below summarizes the course of the 5 2D experiments. We can read the duration of each review, the moments when errors are detected and the cumulative error curve.

We can notice that these reviews present the three usual phases of an architecture review: a project discovery phase, before the detection of the first error, an error detection phase and a verification phase. This segmentation is logical since the subjects take time to get acquainted with the situation before doing the review and then checking their work. The discovery phase lasts on average one minute for the 2D review (Table 1). It should be noted that the subjects are experts in reviewing projects such as this one.

We also investigate the link between review time and number of errors found. Note that no time limit was given to the participants and that none of them exceeded the 15-minute review time. Table 1 illustrates that the longest reviews are also the ones where the highest number of detected errors. Furthermore, we see from Figure 5 that the longer the detection phase, the more errors are detected. As the other phases do not vary much, we can conclude that as the total review time increases, the detection time increases and more errors are detected.

Table 1. Summary table of the temporal analysis

Experiment Number	Exp. duration	Nb of errors	Time to 1st err. detect.
Exp 4	07'00''	2	01'30''
Exp 1	08'30''	2	01'00
Exp 2	10'00''	3	01'30"
Exp 5	11'30''	3	00'15''
Exp 3	14'30''	5	01'00''
TOTAL	**51'30''**	**15**	

Table 2. Table of spatial scale (level of abstraction)

Experiment Number	Average spatial scale level
Exp 1	1,71
Exp 2	2,20
Exp 3	3,14
Exp 4	3,29
Exp 5	2,30
Moyenne	**2,52**

Is the spatial scale level also related to the number of errors found? Our qualitative analyses do not allow us to establish a correlation, but they do advance some initial trends. Indeed, tables 1 and 2 evidence a relationship between these two parameters: except for experiment 4, the experiments characterized by the highest level of spatial scale are also those with the highest number of errors found. Nevertheless, an error may be detected, not because the subject analyses a plan in greater depth, but because he has been attracted by an element of representation different from what he is used to. We have observed this phenomenon several times: while a participant is evaluating a room, he suddenly detects an error elsewhere.

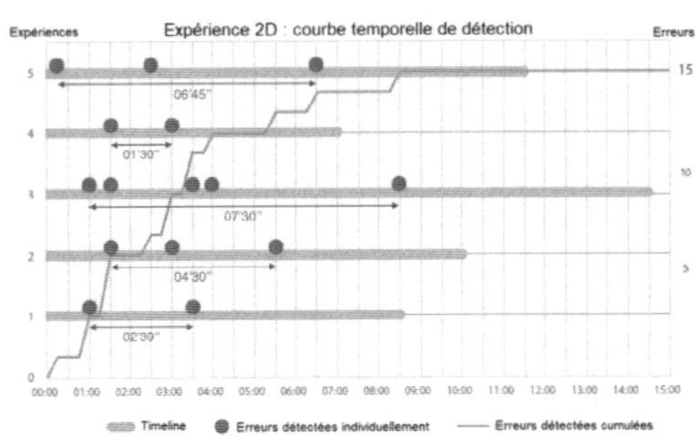

Figure 5. Graph of the timeline of the 2D experiment

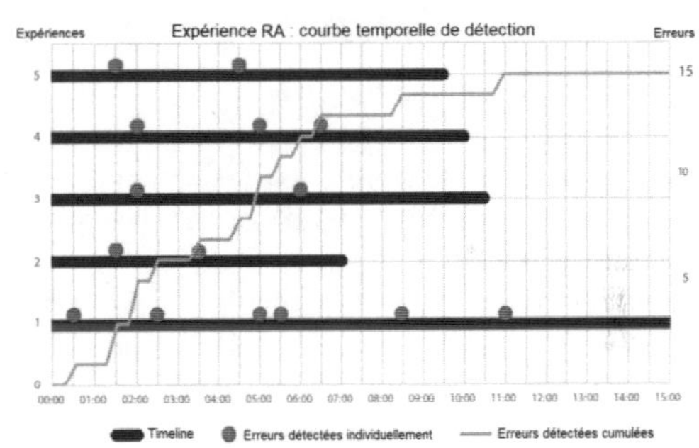

Figure 6. Graph of the timeline of the AR experiment

6.2 AR Experiment

For the review with AR, we can summarize the process in the Figure 6.

As before, we can divide the process into three phases: discovery, error detection and verification. The average time of discovery is 1'30", thus longer than in 2D. This additional time can be explained by a short learning stage. This stage being short, it is not a sign of a need for a preliminary tablet training phase. This loss of time being quite negligible on the scale of the review and not very disturbing for the user, we can interpret it as a positive sign regarding the usage of new tools.

In an intriguing way, the « implantation » error was detected in 100% of the cases. However, the implantation of the building is only the third or fourth focus on which the participants were looking and it only occurs a minor part of the time. Therefore, does the employment of an augmented reality model influence the focus? Does it help to focus attention on other elements than in a traditional review? First of all, the main focus of the subjects was similar in both experiments and concerned the layout and functionality (tables 3 and 4). Thus, AR does not seem to influence the focus. Nevertheless, we note that participants spend more time on the « implantation » focus in 2D than in AR while, at the same time, the proportion of implantation errors detected is higher in AR than in 2D. AR therefore seems to highlight certain errors associated with the characteristics of this technology. By doing so, it allows attention to be drawn to other elements than in a classic review.

Table 3. Main focus in 2D

Experiment Number	Average spatial scale level	Main focus
Exp 1	1,71	Functional
Exp 2	2,20	Lighting and implantation
Exp 3	3,14	Layout
Exp 4	3,29	Layout
Exp 5	2,30	Functional

Table 4. Main focus in AR

Expe Number	Average spatial scale level	Main focus
Exp 1	3,63	Functional > Layout
Exp 2	2,07	Layout > Implantation
Exp 3	2,62	Functional
Exp 4	2,90	Layout
Exp 5	2,68	Layout

Furthermore, none of the informative errors, in our case the absence of a graphic scale, were found. This lack of detection can be explained by the habit of being able to zoom in and out on a digital platform such as a computer or smartphone screen, which puts the notion of scale into perspective. We wonder then whether this lack of scale could constitute a handicap when it comes to error detection. It should be noted that the number and type of errors detected do not seem to differ in 2D or AR. In both types of review, participants make assumptions about the dimensions of the elements, due to the lack of scale. It should also be noted that the intention to measure was never mentioned. This can lead to damaging consequences, as uncertain approximations can lead to serious errors in the subsequent design. However, this is not related to the specific usage of AR.

6.3 Mixed Experiment

The mixed experiment presents the process illustrated in Figure 7. In terms of protocol, each participant reviews according to his affinity with the two proposed modalities, 2D or AR. Thus, some of them keep a single modality while others alternate between the two. We are therefore more vigilant in analyzing the data and basing our reasoning on a qualitative analysis of the elements observed.

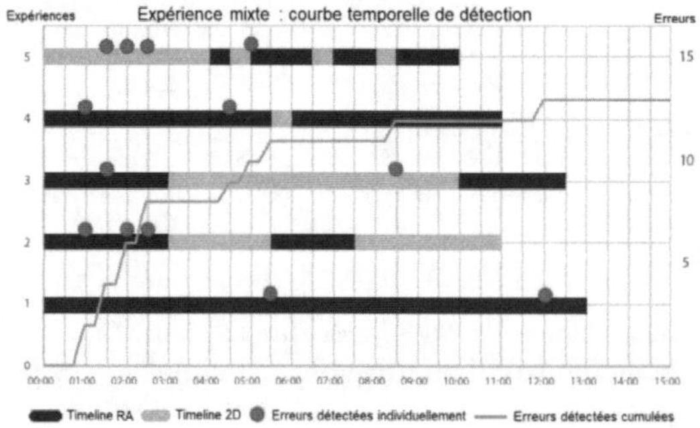

Figure 7. Graph of the timeline of the mixed experiment

We observe a detection phase with two different slopes: a strong slope with high density error detection (1'00-2'30), and a lower slope (4'30-12'00). This reflects a two-speed activity: a first modality is chosen and kept for 4 minutes on average, after which the number of errors decreases. This is due to the time lost in changing modality, which includes a media change, an adaptation and a new discovery phase. The 1'30" plateau seems to confirm our interpretation. Moreover, it is logical that the second detection phase has a lower slope than the first one: the subject having already found some errors, has statistically fewer chances to detect others.

This experiment leads to another outcome: 80% of the participants decide to start with AR and 80% finished with it. 65% of the review time was spent on AR compared to 35% on 2D. We investigate the causes that lead the subjects to prefer AR. We can see two factors: the desire to try out new tools with subjects describing AR as « fun » and « playful »; and the interest of subjects in using AR to understand the site and to check plans.

7. GENERAL DISCUSSION

The previous results and discussions enabled us to identify the interesting points of each type of experiment. This general discussion aims to extend our investigations by cross-referencing the results obtained and thus provide a concrete answer to the research questions formulated in section 3.

Does augmented reality provide a better level of understanding and analysis of the architectural project compared to « traditional » methods? In our experiment, AR does not provide added value in these aspects. Indeed, the 2D experiment seems to remain the most efficient review format. As the following table evidences, for the same number of errors found, the total review takes less time in 2D than in AR. The average effective time and the average duration of the active phase also confirm this conclusion. However, the time difference is relatively small. The number of errors detected is also identical, so we could consider AR and 2D on an equivalent level. This advances the idea that AR does not stand out positively from 2D.

Table 5. Summary table of temporal data for the three experiments

Exp. Type	Total duration	Av. duration	Nb detected err.	Spatial scale level	Av. effective time
2D	51’30’’	10’18’’	15	2,52	4’32’’
AR	52’00’’	10’24’’	15	2,78	4’42’’
AR + 2D	57’30’’	11’30’’	15	2,40	4’24’’

Does augmented reality provide an analysis of additional factors that do not usually appear? In other words, does the focus vary according to the reviewing media? Informative errors were more often detected in 2D than in AR, while the implantation error was more easily detected in the 3D AR model. Lack of scale was only detected once when moving from the 3D model to the 2D documents. These few facts suggest that the focus varies between review media. This is also seen by Cheng et al. (2001) and Kirsh (2010) who highlighted the use and benefits of multiple representations, typically in real contexts. However, more experiments are required to affirm this with certainty.

Is augmented reality a relevant tool for the preliminary design review? For all the above reasons, we believe that it is indeed a relevant tool. However, it is not a better tool than the existing solutions. We have seen that it influences the qualitative parameter rather than the quantitative one, the focus remaining different. Thus, it would be advisable to choose a modality according to the parameters that wish to be observed.

8. CONCLUSION

This study allowed us to explore augmented reality and its employment in architectural project reviews. Through 15 project evaluations, we tried to evaluate this technology’s contributions. The subjects had to identify a maximum of errors, deliberately included in the project, by use of 2D documents, augmented reality model, or a combination of these two. Thus, we found that this technology’s contributions are limited. Similar to a traditional solution, it does not seem to provide significant added value in error detection. However, we found that AR did influence the designer's focus. The experiments also highlighted the existence of three phases during a review: a discovery phase, an active phase and a verification phase. We found that the discovery and verification phases tend to be constant. This allowed us to notice a link between the time spent in active mode on a project review task and the final quality of this work characterized by a high number of errors detected.

The first limitation encountered is that AR system is yet fully mature. The second limitation is related to the sample, which is composed of 15 subjects with a similar profile. This already allows some results to be drawn, but the sample could be increased and diversified so that the conclusions can be more extensive and nuanced. Moreover, there is a possible effect of the participant's background knowledge, them being novices in AR usage while experts in traditional 2D documents usage. Nevertheless, the observed AR learning stage was short and didn't bias the results. Finally, the last limitation is linked to our analysis angle. The augmented reality review involves multiple notions including the notion of error, the design process, human behavior, human-machine interactions and real-time interaction. We have chosen to focus only on the notion of error.

As the field of study is currently in full expansion, we do not doubt that the possibilities for research will continue to grow. We are currently carrying out experiments under real conditions of review by professionals on large-scale integrated design projects to explore the use of AR on tablets, its added value in terms of communication and the handling of this new tool. Furthermore, the data collected allows us to go beyond the parameter of the notion of error and to analyze complementary factors such as the impact of interfaces or architectural project components. We could thus see if this confirms or refutes our statements.

REFERENCES

Arnaldi B., Guitton P., & Moreau G. (dir) (2018). *Réalité virtuelle et réalité augmentée. Mythes et réalités,* Iste Edition.

Azuma, R.T., (1997). A survey of augmented reality. *Presence: Teleoperators and Virtual Environments, vol. 6, no. 4,* pp.355-385.

Baudoux, G., Calixte, X., Leclercq, P. (2019). Analysis of instrumental practices in collaborative design: method of identifying needs, means and their effectiveness. *16th international conference Coopérative Design Visualization and Engineering,* University of Balearic Islands, 2019, Mallorca, Spain.

Ben Rajeb, S., & Leclercq, P. (2015). Co-construction of meaning via a collaborative action research approach. Yuhua Luo éd., In LNCS, Lecture Notes in Computer Sciences, vol 9320, Cooperative Design, Visualization, and Engineering, pp. 205-215

Blavier A., Leclerq P. & Safin S. (2008). Errors in architectural design process: Towards a cognitive model. Internation Design Conference - DESIGN 2008 Dubrovnik - Croatia.

Cheng, P. C., Lowe, R. K., & Scaife, M. (2001). Cognitive science approaches to understanding diagrammatic representations. Artif. Intell. Rev., 15(1), 79-94.

Elsen, C., Jancart, S. & Stals, A. (2017). Practical Trajectories of Parametric Tools in Small and Medium Architectural Firms.

Elsen, C., Jancart, S., & Stals, A. (2018). La complexité dans la pratique architecturale numérique : le cas des bureaux belges de petite et moyenne taille.

Jakl, A., Schöffer, L., Husinsky, M., & Wagner, M. (2018). Augmented Reality for Industry 4.0: Architecture and User Experience. In *FMT* (pp. 38-42).

Noghabaei, M., Heydarian, A., Balali, V., & Han, K. (2020). Trend Analysis on Adoption of Virtual and Augmented Reality in the Architecture, Engineering, and Construction Industry. *Data*, *5*(1), 26.

Tezer, M., Yıldız, E., Masalimova, A., Fatkhutdinova, A., Zheltukhina, M. & Khairullina, E. (2019). Trends of Augmented Reality Applications and Research throughout the World: Meta-Analysis of Theses, Articles and Papers between 2001-2019 Years. *International Journal of Emerging Technologies in Learning (iJET), 14*(22), 154-174.

METHODS FOR THE EVALUATION OF UX OVER TIME

Emmanuel O. C. Mkpojiogu[1,2], Obianuju E. Okeke-Uzodike[3] and Victor Omopariola[4]
[1]*School of Computing, Universiti Utara Malaysia, 06010 UUM, Sintok, Malaysia*
[2]*Department of Software Engineering, Veritas University, Abuja, Nigeria*
[3]*Department of Applied Management, Durban University of Technology, Pietermaritzburg, KwaZulu-Natal, South Africa*
[4]*Department of Computer and Information Technology, Veritas University Abuja, Nigeria*

ABSTRACT

In this paper a literature review strategy was utilized to assess the methods of evaluating UX longitudinally. The review revealed that studies on user experience evaluation over time are rare. This rareness is attributed to the cost involved in carrying out such studies. This research nonetheless suggests that lack of sufficient information and adequate knowledge on methods used for the evaluation of UX over time may also be the reason for the scarcity of studies on long-term user experience evaluation. On this note, this paper reviewed previous works on long-term evaluation of UX to elicit the methods employed in conducting such evaluation to inform possible researchers on the existing methods. The outcome of the study indicated a number of methods for the evaluation of UX over time.

KEYWORDS

Evaluation, Methods, Over Time, User Experience

1. INTRODUCTION

There are several studies and discussion in the user experience (UX) research domain and among UX practitioners that attempt to arrive at a harmonized or a generally accepted definition for UX (Bargas-Avila & Hornbæk, 2011; Hassenzahl & Tractinsky, 2006; Law et al., 2009; Roto et al., 2011). However, till date there is no harmonious definition of UX. UX nonetheless, encompasses the characteristics, dimensions, facets, attributes and processes attributed and associated to the notion of 'experience', but in scope it is narrowed down to users' interacting with digital products, applications and artifacts. UX involves and relates to human perceptions, responses and reaction that follow the anticipated or actual interaction with an interactive digital artifact (Karapanos, 2013). It probes to understand and get close to the user of a product as a human being and understand his person and feelings in relation to the product(s) he interacts with. It also consists of all emotions, sensations, sentiments, attitudes, beliefs, reactions, responses, preferences, feelings, perceptions, affects, physical and psychological reflections, behaviors, and achievements that happen before, during, and after interaction with an artifact. It questions what people do and why they do those things (Karapanos, 2013). UX describes the user's subjective experiences (such as, physical or behavioral, or affective (emotional) responses/reactions) that emerges while using a product (Olsson, 2012). With respect to the general background, subject and history of user experience, the features, and characteristics of human experience have progressively gained ground and interest in the practice, research, design and evaluation of digital products in the past couple of years. Oppelaar et al. (2008) opine that good product usability is now a manifest and obvious feature and its consideration is not enough when planning, designing and evaluating successful, result-oriented and well performing products. Likewise, Rifkin (2000) stresses and maintains that users do not necessarily value products as things in themselves per se but do so because of the quality of the experience these commodities give them.

The UX definition from the ISO indicates an equivalence betwixt "the use" (i.e., the actual use) and "the anticipated use" (i.e., the expected use) of a product (ISO 9241: 210, 2010), thus implying the congruence of users' expectations of experience and the felt (or actual) experience. User experience indicates the feeling or perception of users about the functionality, goodness, beauty and other qualities and characteristics of a software artifact (Wright & McCarthy, 2011; Kashfi et al., 2017). Interestingly, UX is not altogether new. More than 20 years ago, Carroll and Thomas (1988) looked into the associations existing betwixt 'ease of use' and 'fun', and then threw a clarion challenging call to the human-computer interaction community for a scientific and systematic study of fun (i.e., funology). The transition of technology from the workplace to the pervading of people's everyday life made boundaries of distinction blurred, as it created a prevailing dichotomy betwixt the product utilized as a work 'tool' and the ones used as leisure, relaxation, and pleasure 'toy' (Monk et al., 2002). Consequently, the idea of user experience emerged out of the belief and concern that the usual usability employed to assess the heavily utilitarian, instrumental, ergonomic, task- and goal-driven perspectives of work experience, did not provide explanation for or take into adequate cognizance the more emotional, affective and hedonic quality perceptions of use. This has led to an attention shift from the more objective and ergonomic aspects of interactive products (for example, perspicuity, function, simplicity, content, presentation, utility, ease of use, lucidity etc.), to incorporate the heavily subjective aspects of user's sentiments, feelings, sensuality, emotions, passion, attitudes, drives and motivational responses. This shift in paradigm and focus resulted in the slowness of UX developing as a research area (Hart, 2014). This is coupled with the fact that the subjective perceptions, and sentiments of users seemed too unclear (fuzzy) to be seen or taken as reliable (Monk et al., 2002), leading to the doubt on whether or not user experience can be measured on not. Nevertheless, Tractinsky et al.'s (2000) research paper: 'What is beautiful is usable' (Tractinsky et al., 2000), surged the significance of aesthetics in affecting decisive judgments and perceptions concerning the quality of a product, and ignited a rise in user experience research that investigated a compendium of UX aspects comprising the quality of hedonics (Hassenzahl, 2001), pleasure (Jordan, 2000), attractiveness (Norman, 2002), joy of use (Hassenzahl, Beu, & Burmester, 2001), and aesthetic beauty, etc. (Hassenzahl & Monk, 2010; Hussain et al., 2019f; Hart, 2014).

As a result, design and evaluation challenges have shifted from designing and evaluating products that provide reliable, secured, efficient, easy and usable functionalities (Hussain et al., 2018; 2019a; 2019b; Mkpojiogu et al., 2018; 2019) (with prices that are comparatively competitive) to the designing of products that provide users with pleasurable and desirable experiences (and improve their self-functioning and well-being), that have features that exceed and transcend their expectations and which support the fulfillment of their basic and important human psychological needs, like identifying or engaging with or socializing via a digital artifact and others through the mediation of technology (Hart, 2014). Hassenzahl (2003) thus posits that there is the need for a "more holistic perspectives and an enrichment of traditional quality models with non-utilitarian [non-ergonomic] concepts, such as individuation, fun, joy, pleasure, hedonic value or ludic value" in the designing and evaluating of software artifacts following both the global competition (that is, the economics viewpoint) and users' inherent needs for leisure and pleasure and their need to thrive, evolve and enjoy (that is, the humanism viewpoint). These premises served as precursor to the emergence of UX as a new conceptual idea to denote the aspects that deal with the experience of users in their interaction with digital artifacts. Generally, the advancement from research on human factors (ergonomics), Kansei engineering (Nagamachi, 2002), usability, user satisfaction, among other aspects has been a very interesting course. A reflective analysis of this development is in Mahlke (2008) and in Battarbee (2004). The notion of UX is eagerly been accepted by the human-computer interaction research domain. According to Olsson (2012), UX is vigorously been studied as a phenomenon with new practices and methodologies emerging and associated with it, and it is now a new tool used to further the practice of user or human-centered design and evaluation. Additionally, new conceptual ideas are regularly been developed and older applicable ones are combined and brought under the canopy of UX. Some instances include: aesthetics (Wright et al., 2008), pleasure (Jordan, 2002), emotions and hedonism (Hassenzahl, 2003; Hussain et al., 2019g; Olsson, 2012) etc.

UX has six main characteristics, namely: dynamic, subjective, context-dependent, holistic, worthwhile and multi-dimensional (Kashfi et al., 2017). It is majorly hinged on and characteristically dominated by the subjective perspectives of human perception of product quality. It relies on human reflective and subjective perception and judgment (Wright & McCarthy, 2011; Hassenzahl, 2010). For example, the perception of one user about a given product quality may be that it is simple, novel, interesting, enjoyable and admirable. Meanwhile, another user may see the product as complicated, uninteresting and old. Other product qualities (perceptions of quality) can be handled as being more objective, at least theoretically (Kashfi et al., 2017). The word subjective is utilized in requirements engineering literatures to indicate that since perceptions of product qualities are difficult to quantify and evaluate, practitioners in industry tend to consider or evaluate them on the basis of their (that is, users') sentiments and perceptions. Presently, the most efficient and feasible method to assess perceptions, affects and emotional responses of users is through the direct gathering of their sentiments, and allowing for free self-expression about a product from users. This is usually done using qualitative measures and psychometric instruments. However, to gain results that are externally valid and reliable, practitioners need to elicit responses from users that are heterogeneous and whose numbers are statistically significant (Hussain et al., 2019e; Law et al., 2014).

Furthermore, UX is holistic and comprehensive and cannot be totally reduced to inherent or latent quantifying variables (Hassenzahl, 2010). It develops following the inherent qualities of usability, functionality, utilitarian and other quality perceptions of products, and the sentiments of users about them in a specified time, context of interaction and situation of use (Hassenzahl, 2003). The holistic and comprehensive characteristic of user experience is akin to the cross-cutting characteristics of other quality attributes. In the two scenarios, two or more functionalities are influenced by the associated requirements. Nonetheless, with regard to UX, this inter-correlation is heavily intricate, particularly taking into consideration that user experience is dynamic (i.e., temporal and evolving) and thus users' judgment and opinion about their experience undergoes evolution in the course of time (Hassenzahl & Tractinsky, 2006). Also, research in user experience utilizes the term context-dependent (i.e., situated) to stress that any particular experience is unique, temporal, unrepeatable, non-replicable and situated both in time and in its context (Wright & McCarthy, 2011). In addition, UX is worthwhile (that is, it is positive), implying that it concentrates on delivering values for users as well as creating delightful, pleasurable and desirable experiences as opposed to just only preventing negative issues (frustrations/pains/disgusts), which happens to be the focus of usability. Finally, UX is multidimensional as it is a composite construct comprising of several other related constructs (Hassenzahl, 2010; Kashfi et al., 2017; Hussein et al., 2019; Hussain et al., 2019d).

There is currently no agreement in the research domain on how UX should be designed or evaluated or the methods for its evaluation and whether the UX of a product can be accounted for by mere manipulation and measurement of the UX attributes (Law et al., 2014). This is further compounded by the dynamic features of UX. UX is temporal and there is a complex association among the several experiential moments or episodes of experience (Kashfi et al., 2017). UX is also dynamic. It develops and evolves in the course of time (Hassenzahl, 2010). For instance, over time, a user may perceive a novel feature in a product as old, or a complex feature as simple. Therefore, in the design and evaluation of UX, practitioners should give/pay good attention to the varying episodes of experience (Hassenzahl, 2010); such as, experience before use (expected experience), momentary experience (during usage), remembered experience (that is, shortly after usage) and accumulated experience (that is, over longer period of usage) (Hassenzahl, 2010). Practitioners need to decide which episodes are more significant than others for the software that is being designed, developed (or evaluated) and why; for example, for an electronic marketing site, first impression is more vital than it is for a work app. This understanding can then assist practitioners to suggest more appropriate design solutions. Also, first time users may be confused by the range of icons and options featured on the interface of some smart phones. Nevertheless, once they become familiar with the phones, they may become captivated and enthralled by the new features and possibilities that the devices present when compared to the usual features in phones. Hence, an experience is thus unique, very likely to evolve with time, and cannot be repeated (Hassenzahl, 2010; McCarthy & Wright, 2004). After a first-time experience, smartphone users who are novices will never experience again in their life time the first-time encounter of smartphones usage again. The first-time experience is now in the past (Kraus, 2017; Kamal et al., 2019).

In addition, substantial UX studies have placed attention on short-term interactions and evaluations, hinged on users' first impressions, pre- and post-interaction experiences; however, limited and scanty research works have captured user experience from long-term usage perspective (Hart, 2014). Even for the few works that captured long-term usage, the length of use varies (Hart, 2014). Prior studies have concentrated principally on short-term assessments, with users' first perceptions of digital artifacts (i.e., after a first-time use), instead of in a long-term use. Studies show that the way a person perceives the quality of a product evolve with time (Kujala et al, 2019). However, only a limited number of works showed such evolutions in usability, hedonics and aesthetics perceptions (Karapanos et al., 2008; von Wilamowitz-¬Moellendorff et al., 2006).

Product evaluation practices have been traditionally focused on early interactions. Evaluators have been mainly concerned with product quality characteristics associated with initial product use (Karapanos, 2013). However, recent developments have stirred up the concerns for the evaluation of the UX of interactive products after prolonged use (Karapanos, 2013). Hence, several calls have been made for the need to look into the place of time in UX research (Courage, Jain, & Rosenbaum, 2009; Hassenzahl & Tractinsky, 2006; Karapanos, Zimmerman, Forlizzi, & Martens, 2009). Prior studies (Jain et al. (2010); Karapanos et al. (2009, 2010); Kujala et al. (2011)) show that UX is dynamic and evolving over time. According to Karapanos et al. (2009), as a result of the swift of development and growth in technological innovations, the understanding and designing of products for prolonged use is becoming a very critical issue of concern. These stated instances point to drift in emphasis of product success from its initial purchase to the outcome of the experiences emanating from prolonged use. The timeframes in prior UX longitudinal studies are relatively short, and the ideal timeframe for evaluating UX is still unknown (Yuhui et al., 2019).

In some studies (Hassenzahl et al., 2000; Tractinsky & Zmiri, 2006) the investigation or evaluation carried out was on short test tasks. In Courage et al.'s (2009) study, five weeks of usage was investigated. However, in Von Moellendorff et al.'s (2006) and Karapanos et al.'s (2009, 2010) studies, the evolving nature of UX was investigated over months. Kujala et al. (2011) employed the UX Curve approach to retrospectively evaluate the UX of mobile phones and Facebook users. A number of UX studies have concentrated on short-term evaluations, based on the first impressions that users have in their pre- and post-interactions, however, few of these studies captured long-term usage of interactive products (Hart, 2014). In addition, Hart's (2014) study reported on an ecological longitudinal inquiry into how UX perceptions change over time in long-term product use. However, longitudinal studies are time consuming and costly (Kujala et al., 2011; Law & van Schaik, 2010). In a study using day reconstruction method, it was found that UX evolved into three phases, from orientation to incorporation and then to identification. It showed clear temporal patterns. These transitions were motivated by three forces, namely: familiarity, functional dependency, and emotional attachment (Karapanos, 2013).

Just as it is for designing for UX, a holistic evaluation of UX is challenging as a result of its dynamic, subjective, and difficult-to-quantify nature. Consequently, Vermeeren et al. (2010) posit that there are no generally accepted standard approaches or methods for the evaluation of UX (Olsson, 2012). There is nonetheless a debate among academics on the way UX can and should be measured or evaluated (Law, 2011). While one part of researchers contends for a qualitative (holistic) approach, others argue in favor of a quantitative (reductionist) approach (Law, 2011; Kraus, 2017). However, some prefer to be in the middle and contend for mixed or hybrid (triangulation) approach (Hart, 2014). Kujala et al. (2011) posit that there are two main approaches for evaluating long-term UX. These are retrospective evaluation and repeated evaluation. The major distinction between them is that in retrospective evaluation, evaluators ask users to recall their long-term experience, whereas in repeated evaluation, evaluators perform continuous evaluation of UX over a period of time in a longitudinal field study repeatedly. Retrospective impressions can have a greater influence on later behavior. In Karapanos et al.'s (2010) and Norman's (2009) studies, it was observed that reported memories could guide the future behavior of the individual. Prior longitudinal studies though scarce, show that there is transition in experiences and that experience over time is not stable, but rather temporal and dynamic (Karapanos, 2013, Nakamura et al, 2021). Though the reason for the scarcity of longitudinal studies on UX evaluation is the cost involved in carrying out such research, ignorance and inadequate exposure to the UX methods used for long-term studies could be possible reason also. Most researchers do not have sufficient knowledge and adequate information on the methods used for the evaluation of user experience over time. This may be the reason for low (scarce) longitudinal studies on user experience evaluation. This study seeks to fill this gap by reviewing extant literature to find out the various methods used for the evaluation of UX over time.

2. METHODOLOGY

A literature review method was used to study the methods of evaluating the user experience of interactive systems over time from prior studies. The contents of several previous studies were analyzed and relevant information on the methods used for the longitudinal UX evaluation were extracted and synthesized. The procedure utilized in the review is as follows: i) download articles related to methods of evaluating UX over time; ii) analyze the downloaded articles for relevant information; iii) extract the methods used for evaluating UX over time from the downloads; iv) compare studies related to methods on evaluating UX over time. Figure 1 provide illustration of this procedure.

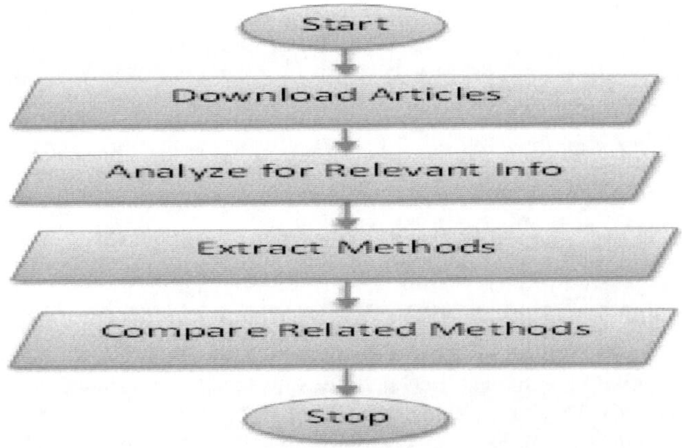

Figure 1. Research Method

The inclusion criteria for the review include all studies in English Language on UX evaluation methods, qualitative UX evaluation methods, quantitative UX evaluation methods, longitudinal UX evaluation methods. Any study outside the above criteria is excluded in the review. The search strings include: "UX evaluation methods", "longitudinal methods for UX evaluation", "method for evaluating UX over time"

3. RESULTS

This study observed a number of methods used in evaluating user experience. Table 1 shows specific UX evaluation approaches spread across qualitative, quantitative and combined methods.

Table 1. Studies on UX Evaluation Methods

Studies	**Methods**		
	Qualitative	Quantitative	Combined
Gaver et. al. (1999)	Cultural probes		
Buchenau & Suri (2000)	Experience prototyping		
Kahneman et. al. (2004)	Day reconstruction method		
Swallow et. al. (2005)	Persona matching		
Hektner, Schmidt & Csikszentmihalyi (2006)	Experience Sampling Method (ESM)		
Marshall & Rossman (2010)	Focus Group		
Kujala et al. (2011)	UX Curve (Used for UX over time)		
Mendoza, Novick & Paso (2005)	Diary method		
Von Wilamowitz--Moellendorff et al. (2006)	Retrospective interview method		
Karapanos (2013)	Experience Narratives		
Hassenzahl (2003); Diefenbach et al. (2014); Hassenzahl & Monk (2010)		AttrakDiff2	
Laugwitz's et al. (2008)		User Experience questionnaire	
Vermeeren et al. (2010)		Survey method	
Karapanos, Martens, & Hassenzahl (2010); Karapanos (2013)		iScale	
Desmet (2005)		Product Emotion Measurement instrument (PrEmo)	
Spangenberg, Voss, & Crowley (1997)		HED-UT Scale	

Väänänen-Vainio-Mattila & Segerståhl (2009)		Service User eXperience (ServUX)	
Watson et al. (1988)		PANAS questionnaire	
Fronemann & Peissner (2014); Sheldon et al. (2001)		UNeeQ questionnaire	
Karapanos et al. (2009); Karapanos (2013)	Day reconstruction method	AttrakDiff questionnaire	Combined approach (Studied UX over time)
Kraus (2017)	Experience Sampling Method (ESM)	Questionnaire	√
Hart (2014)			√

From the literature survey, more studies were conducted using qualitative approaches. This is followed by studies done with quantitative approach. Fewer studies utilized the combined approach (also known as mixed or triangulation approach). This may be due the cost of using this approach as it combines the effort of both qualitative and quantitative research. The cost is time, effort and finance related. Essentially, the use of combined methods is laborious, costly and time consuming. This notwithstanding, the combined approach is a better approach to handle the evaluation of UX on a long-term (Karapanos et al., 2009; Hart, 2014). Further, some studies conducted over time utilize day reconstruction method (DRM). The day reconstruct method requires study participants to reconstruct one or more most impactful experience they had during interaction. The study participants record down their experiences after an interaction and in addition also describe vividly one most impactful experience that they had in their order of impact and give a name to the experience(s). The choice of DRM method is because of its simplicity, ease of use and experience elicitation capability. There are several methods like experience sampling method, used in longitudinal studies (Table 1). Table 2 indicates a comparison of studies on user experience evaluation over time. The comparison show that prior studies used varying approaches (in various contexts) in conducting UX evaluation over time and the number of participants used for the evaluation and the time span of evaluation also varied.

Table 2. Comparison of Studies on UX Evaluation over Time

Studies on UX over Time	Time Span	No. of Participants	Method Used	Context
Mendoza, Novick & Paso (2005)	8 weeks			Tracked UX of middle school teachers with websites
Mendoza, Novick & Paso (2005)	5 weeks	10		Interactive TV pointing device
Karapanos et al., (2009); Karapanos (2013)	5 weeks	6	Experience Narratives; Day reconstruction method	Assess UX after their purchase of a mobile phone
Karapanos (2013)	4 weeks	10	AttrakDiff 2	To identify where users point at in an interactive TV
Karapanos (2013)	-	12	iScale (constructive method)	Participants draw a graph on how their opinion about three distinct qualities on their mobile phones evolved over time
Karapanos (2013)	Two sessions of 40 minutes each separated by approx. one week interval	48	iScale (value-account method)	Participants joined two sessions. In each session, they employed two tools to report on two product qualities
Von Wilamowitz--Moellendorff et al. (2006)	Nil	7	Retrospective interview technique	Utilizing a retrospective interview approach to capture the changes in users' opinions and perceptions to the usage of their mobile phones.

4. CONCLUSION

This study employed a literature review methodology to examine the methods of evaluating user experience over time. The review discovered that longitudinal studies on UX are scare. This scarcity is due to the cost of conducting such research. This study however allude that lack of adequate information and sufficient knowledge may also be responsible for the low level of studies on UX evaluation over time. Therefore, this study sought to review prior studies on the evaluation of user experience over time to capture methods used for such evaluation to expose potential researchers to available methods. The study reveals several methods for the longitudinal evaluation of user experience.

ACKNOWLEDGEMENT

The authors acknowledge the Durban University of Technology in South Africa for supporting this study.

REFERENCES

Battarbee, K. (2004). Co-experience: Understanding user experiences in social interaction. Doctoral dissertation, Helsinki: University of Art and Design.

Bargas-Avila, J.A., & Hornbæk, K. (2011). Old wine in new bottles or novel challenges: a critical analysis of empirical studies of user experience. In Proc of the SIGCHI Conf on Human Factors in Computing Systems, (pp.2689-2698).

Buchenau, M., & Suri, J. F. (2000). Experience prototyping. Proceedings of the 3rd Conference on Designing Interactive Systems: Processes, Practices, Methods, and Techniques -DIS '00, 424–433.

Carroll, J. M., & Thomas, J. C. (1988). Fun. SIGCHI Bulletin, 19(3), 21–24.

Courage, C., Jain, J., & Rosenbaum, S. (2009). Best practices in longitudinal research. In CHI'09 Extended Abstracts on Human Factors in Computing Systems (pp. 4791–4794). Boston, MA: ACM.

Desmet, P. (2005). Measuring emotion: development and application of an instrument to measure emotional responses to products." In Funology, edited by Mark A. Blythe, Kees Overbeeke, Andrew F. Monk, and Peter C. Wright, 111–23. Human-Computer Interaction Series Springer Netherlands.

Diefenbach, S., Kolb, N., & Hassenzahl, M. (2014). The 'hedonic' in human-computer interaction: history, contributions, and future research directions. In: Proceedings of the 2014 Conference on Designing Interactive Systems (DIS), (pp. 305– 314).

Fronemann, N., & Peissner, M. (2014). User experience concept exploration: user needs as a source for innovation. In Proceedings of the 8th Nordic Conf. on Human-Computer Interaction: Fun, Fast, Foundational, (pp. 727-736), ACM.

Gaver, B., Dunne, T., & Pacenti, E. (1999). Design: Cultural probes. Interactions, 6(1), 21–29.

Hart, J. (2014). Investigating user experience and user engagement for design. Doctoral Dissert., Manchester University.

Hassenzahl, M. (2001). The effect of perceived hedonic quality on product appealingness. International Journal of Human-Computer Interaction, 13(4), 481–499.

Hassenzahl, M. (2003). The thing and I: understanding the relationship between user and product. In Blythe, M., Monk, A.F., Overbeeke, K., Wright, P. (eds.), Funology: from usability to enjoyment, (pp. 31-42), Kluwer.

Hassenzahl, M. (2010). Experience design: technology for all the right reasons. Synthesis Lectures on Human-Centered Informatics, 3(1), 1–95.

Hassenzahl, M., Beu, A., & Burmester, M. (2001). Engineering joy. IEEE Software, 18(1), 70–76.

Hassenzahl, M., & Monk, A. (2010). The inference of perceived usability from beauty. Human–Computer Interaction, 25(3), 235–260.

Hassenzahl, M., Platz, A., Burmester, M., & Lehner, K. (2000). Hedonic and ergonomic quality aspects determine a software's appeal. In Proc. of the SIGCHI conference on Human Factors in Computing Systems (pp. 201-208). ACM.

Hassenzahl, M., & Tractinsky, N. (2006). User experience–a research agenda. Behaviour & Infor Tech. 25(2), 91–97.

Hektner, J.M., Schmidt, J.A., & Csikszentmihalyi, M. (2006). Experience Sampling Method: Measuring the Quality of Everyday Life. 1 edition. Thousand Oaks, Calif: SAGE Publications, Inc.

Hussain, A., Mkpojiogu, E.O.C. & Hassan, F. (2018). Dimensions and sub-dimensions for the evaluation of m-learning apps for children: A review. International Journal of Engineering & Technology (IJET), 7 (3.20), 291-295.

Hussain, A., Mkpojiogu, E.O.C. & Kutar, M. (2019a). The impact of software features' perceived importance on the perceived performance of software products' quality elements. Journal of Computational and Theoretical Nanoscience. 16 (5-6), 2135-2140.

Hussain, A., Shamala, P., & Mkpojiogu, E.O.C. (2019b). The effect of software features' perceived importance on the observed performance of software product qualities. Journal of Advanced Research in Dynamical and Control Systems (JARDCS), 11(08-SI), 1076-1082.

Hussain, A., Mkpojiogu, E.O.C., & Hussein, 1. (2019d). UXD community of practice: an interventionist participatory action research bridging the gap between industry and academics. Journal of Advanced Research in Dynamical and Control Systems (JARDCS), 11(05-SI), 1500-1505

Hussain, A., Mkpojiogu, E.O.C., & Hussein, I. (2019e). A taxonomy of frustration factors in UXD practice: experiences from a UXD community of practice. Journal of Advanced Research in Dynamical and Control Systems (JARDCS), 11(05-SI), 1479-1486

Hussain, A., Hussein, I., & Mkpojiogu, E.O.C. (2019f). Assessing the frustrations of practicing user experience design (UXD) among the UXD community of practice in Malaysia: a netnographic approach. Compusoft: An International Journal of Advanced Computer Technology (IJACT), 8(8), 3345-3355

Hussain, A., Hussein, I., Mahmud, M., & Mkpojiogu, E.O.C. (2019g). Understanding the characteristics of UX Malaysia UXD community of practice (CoP): a participants' observation. Test Engin. and Management, 81 (11-12), 3157-3171

Hussein, I., Hussain, A., Mkpojiogu, E.O.C., & Mahmud, M. (2019). A UX community of practice: design goals, practice motivations and values. Test Engineering and Management, 81 (11-12), 3144-3156.

ISO. (2010). FDIS 9241-210: Ergonomics of human-system interaction - Part 210: Human-centered design for interactive systems (formerly known as 13407). Switzerland: International Organization for Standardization (ISO).

Jordan, P. W. (2000). Designing pleasurable products: An introduction to the new human factors. Taylor & Francis.

Kahneman, D., Krueger, A.B., Schkade, D.A., Schwarz, N., & Arthur A Stone, A.A. (2004). A survey method for characterizing daily life experience: The day reconstruction method. Science 306(5702), 1776–1780.

Kamal, F.M., Hussein, I., Hussain, A., Mkpojiogu, E.O.C., & Baharin, H. (2019). User experience design (UXD) community of practice in Malaysia and their practice constraints: a participatory action research. International Journal of Innovative Technology and Exploring Engineering, 8(8S), 505-514

Kashfi, P., & Feldt, R. 2017). Integrating user experience practices into software development processes: implications of the UX characteristics. PeerJ Computer Science.

Karapanos, E. (2013). Modeling Users' Experiences with Interactive Systems, NY: Springer.

Karapanos, E., Hassenzahl, M., & Martens, J-B. (2008). User experience over time. In CHI '08 extended abstracts on Human factors in computing systems (pp. 3561–3566). Florence, Italy: ACM.

Karapanos, E., Martens, J. B., & Hassenzahl, M. (2010). On the retrospective assessment of users' experiences over time: memory or actuality?. In CHI'10 Extended Abstracts on Human Factors in Computing Systems (pp. 4075-4080). ACM.

Karapanos, E., Zimmerman, J., Forlizzi, J., & Martens, J. (2009). User experience over time: an initial framework. In Proceedings of CHI '09: The 27th international conference on Human factors in computing systems (pp. 729–738). ACM.

Kraus, L. (2017). User experience with mobile security and privacy mechanisms. Doctoral Dissertation, Technischen Universitat Berlin.

Kujala, S., Miron-Shatz, T., & Jokinen, J. J. (2019). The cross-sequential approach: A short-term method for studying long-term user experience. Journal of Usability Studies, 14(2)

Kujala, S., Roto, V., Väänänen-Vainio-Mattila, K., Karapanos, E., & Sinnelä, A. (2011). UX curve: a method for evaluating long-term user experience. Interacting with Computers, 23 (5), 473–83.

Laugwitz, B., Held, T., & Schrepp, M. (2008). Construction and evaluation of a user experience questionnaire (pp. 63-76). Springer Berlin Heidelberg.

Law, E.L. (2011). The measurability and predictability of user experience. In Proceedings of the 3rd ACM SIGCHI Symposium on Engineering Interactive Computing Systems (EICS).ACM, (pp. 1–10).

Law, E.L., Roto, V., Hassenzahl, M., Vermeeren, A., & Kort, J. (2009). Understanding, scoping and defining user experience: a survey approach. In Proceedings of the SIGCHI Conference on Human Factors in Computing Systems (CHI), (pp.719-728), ACM.

Law, E.L-C., & van Schaik, P. (2010). Modelling user experience - an agenda for research and practice. Interact. Comput. 22 (5), 313–22. doi:10.1016/j.intcom.2010.04.006.

Law, E.L-C., van Schaik, P., & Roto, V. (2014). Attitudes towards User Experience (UX) Measurement. International Journal of Human-Computer Studies 72 (6), 526–41, doi: 10.1016/j.ijhcs.2013.09.006.

Mahlke, S. (2008). User experience of interaction with technical systems: theories, methods, empirical results, and their application to the development of interactive systems. Doctoral dissertation, Belin: Berlin Univ. of Technology.

Marshall, C., & Rossman, G.B. (2010). Designing qualitative research. Sage publications.

Mendoza, V., Novick, D. G., & Paso, E. (2005). Usability over time. In Proceedings of the 23rd annual international conference on Design of communication: documenting & designing for pervasive information (pp. 151–158). ACM.

McCarthy, J., & Wright, P. (2004). Technology as experience. Interactions,11(5), 42-43.

Mkpojiogu, E.O.C., Hashim, N.L., Hussain, A., & Tan, K.L. (2019). The impact of user demographics on the perceived satisfaction and comfort of use of m-banking apps. Inter. J. Innov Techn and Exploring Engineering, 8(8S), 460-466.

Mkpojiogu, E.O.C., Hussain, A., & Hassan, F. (2018). A systematic review of usability quality attributes for the evaluation of mobile learning applications for children. ICAST 2018, AIP Conf. Proc. 2016

Mkpojiogu, E.O.C., Okeke-Uzodike, O.E., Emmanuel, E.I. & Eze, C. (2021). Understanding users' UX needs through the lenses of psychological needs theories: users' expectations and felt experiences. IHCI 2022.

Monk, A., Hassenzahl, M., Blythe, M., & Reed, D. (2002). Funology: designing enjoyment. In CHI'02 Extended Abstracts on Human Factors in Computing Systems (pp. 924–925). ACM.

Nakamura, W. T., Ahmed, I., Redmiles, D., Oliveira, E., Fernandes, D., de Oliveira, E. H., & Conte, T. (2021). Are UX evaluation methods providing the same big picture? Sensors, 21(10), 3480.

Nagamachi, M. (2002). Kansei engineering in consumer product design. Ergonomics in Design, 10(2), 5-9.

Norman, D.A. (2002). The design of everyday things, (p. 257). Basic Books.

Norman, D. A. (2009). The way I see it: memory is more important than actuality. Interactions, 16(2), 24-26.

Olsson, T. (2012). User expectations and experiences of mobile augmented reality services. Tampere University of Technology, Tampere.

Oppelaar E.R., Hennipman, E., & van der Veer, G.C. (2008). Experience design for dummies. Proc of ECCE'08, 27.

Rifkin, J. (2000). The age of access. The new culture of hypercapitalism, where all of life is paid-for experience. Tarcher, 320.

Roto, V., Law, E., Vermeeren, A., & Hoonhout, J. (2011). User experience white paper: Bringing clarity to the concept of user experience. http://www.allaboutux.org/files/UX-WhitePaper.pdf. 2011.

Sheldon, K. M., Elliot, A. J., Kim, Y., & Kasser, T. (2001). What is satisfying about satisfying events? Testing 10 candidate psychological needs. Journal of personality and social psychology, 80(2), 325.

Spangenberg, E.R., Voss, K.E., & Crowley, A.E. (1997). Measuring the hedonic and utilitarian dimensions of attitude: a generally applicable scale by Eric R. Spangenberg, Voss, K.E., & Crowley, A.E. (Ed.). Advances in Consumer Research 24, 235–41.

Swallow, D., Blythe, M., & Wright, P. (2005). Grounding experience: relating theory and method to evaluate the user experience of smartphones. In Proceedings of the 2005 annual conference on European association of cognitive ergonomics (pp. 91–98). University of Athens.

Tractinsky, N., Katz, A., & Ikar, D. (2000). What is beautiful is usable. Interacting with Computers, 13(2), 127–145.

Tractinsky, N., & Zmiri, D. (2006). Exploring attributes of skins as potential antecedents of emotion in HCI. In Aesthetic computing (pp. 405–422).

Väänänen-Vainio-Mattila, K., & Segerståhl, K. (2009). A Tool for evaluating service user eXperience (ServUX): development of a modular questionnaire.

Vermeeren, A. P., Law, E. L.C., Roto, V., Obrist, M., Hoonhout, J., & Väänänen-¬Vainio-Mattila, K. (2010). User experience evaluation methods: current state and development needs. In Proceedings of the 6th Nordic Conf on HCI

Von Wilamowitz-Moellendorff, M., Hassenzahl, M., & Platz, A. (2006). Dynamics of user experience: How the perceived quality of mobile phones changes over time. In User Experience – Towards a unified view, Workshop at the 4th Nordic Conference on Human-Computer Interaction (pp. 74–78).

Watson, D., Clark, L. A., & Tellegen, A. (1988). Development and validation of brief measures of positive and negative affect: the PANAS scales. Journal of personality and social psychology, 54(6), 1063.

Wright, P. & McCarthy, J. (2011). Experience-centered design, (p. 123), Morgan & Claypool.

Wright, P., Wallace, J., McCarthy, J. (2008). Aesthetics and experience-centered design. Trans on CHI, 15(4), 21.

Yuhui, W., Chunfu, L., Tian, L., & Qin, H. (2019). Longitudinal study on retrospective assessment of perceived usability: A new method and perspectives. Interacting with Computers, 31(4), 393-412.

IDENTIFICATION OF FACTORS AFFECTING THE LEARNERS' MOTIVATION IN AN E-LEARNING SCENARIO FOR INDUSTRIAL DESIGN EDUCATION

Naveen Kumar, Abhijeet Kujur and Jyoti Kumar
Department of Design, Indian Institute of Technology, Delhi, India

ABSTRACT

Industrial design has certain "niche" aspects illustrating precision and level of detail which are introduced to the students to fulfill real-world design expectations. As reported in literature, encouraging students to undergo an online industrial design course while simultaneously maintaining their motivation is a difficult task. Today, technological advancements in e-learning are being employed to make industrial design education and learning more engaging for students. The learners are rapidly changing their e-learning practices and motivations in response to new innovations. Research suggests that the technological advancements in e-learning are appealing primarily because they are novel and different. Later, when learners get used to them, they may lose their interest leading to loss of motivation. Motivational factors of an e-learning platform can be an aid to understand learners' motivation and knowledge gaining methods. However, there has been a dearth of literature featuring methods for assessing motivation of an online industrial design learning. Furthermore, complexity of learners' motivation, drives and variety of motivational theories has made the assessment more complicated particularly in the context of online industrial design education. Therefore, this study tries to investigate the relation between effectiveness of an online industrial design learning platform and learners' motivation. The study followed a mixed-method approach and used survey questionnaires and semi-structured interviews with 200 participants who underwent an online industrial design education. The study identifies various facets of industrial design learning and its relation with students' attitudes and motivations, which in turn may improve their performance in industrial design applications.

KEYWORDS

Industrial Design, Design Education, Motivation, e-Learning

1. INTRODUCTION

In this era of online teaching many issues about online teaching's efficacy and effects on instructors and students have arisen (Vikas & Mathur, 2022). Understanding student perspectives may assist educators make more learner oriented online modules. In a fast technological development, and knowledge-based economy, educators desire to educate learners with sophisticated technical skills and core competencies. Preparing learners for a fast-changing workplace requires an effective e-learning framework. Technology is routinely utilized to improve student engagement and educational accomplishments (Carle et al., 2009) (Carle et al., 2009). One such required field is industrial design competencies where prototypes are traditionally used to visualize and test designs. The lack of a clear separation between theoretical knowledge and practical abilities is also a feature of design as an educational discipline. Because industrial design is a technology-driven field, it needs a unique evaluation for learning motivation. Motivation to learn reveals that a student wants to learn through training (Garavan et al., 2010). Motivation is the degree of goal-directed effort (Garavan et al., 2010) and learning motivation is a student's endeavor to learn. Motivation may be inherent or external, depending on situational and environmental influences (Ryan & Deci, 2006).

In order to assess the factors influencing the motivation of learners in an online industrial design, an integrated computer aided design (CAD) and 3D-printing course was identified (Zardari et al., 2021)). Research suggests that learners prioritize e-learning quality (Fayed & Cummings, 2022). Many non-motivated adult learners leave e-learning in their early stages. This is due to the poor design and usability of e-learning platforms to a large part (Granić & Ćukušić, n.d.). The identified course programme offered basic skill training on computer aided design and 3D printing technology run by industry experts. In this study, end-user evaluations for motivational analysis and expert inspections are combined in the methodology, resulting in extensive input from students, instructors, and professionals. The programme aimed to enhance learners' skill set and find a potential business opportunity in the space of industrial designing and 3D printing. The mode of training was online and was delivered to all registered candidates. The Student journey flow is shown below:

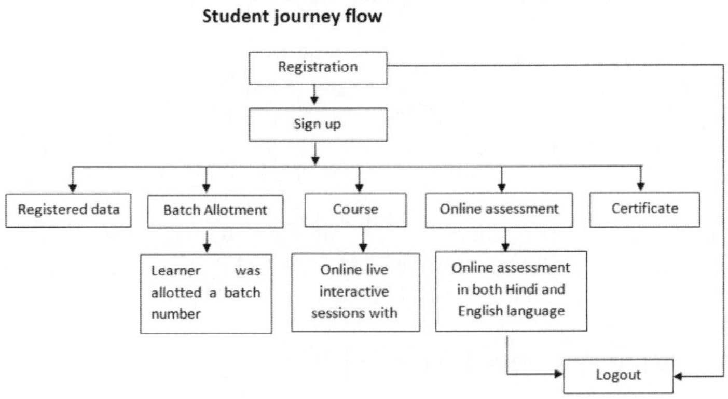

Figure 1. Student journey flow

This student flow breaks down the activities into tasks for the students, which generally results in a list of all the things an online learner may encounter chronologically in the simplest method.

The importance of e-learning interfaces that are more precisely matched to how people naturally learn, live, and gain information cannot be overstated. These interfaces also influence the motivation of the learners (Matsuo et al., 2008). (Barolli et al., 2006). If the interface is not clear and simple to use, learners' focus will be on interaction rather than content acquisition. Correspondingly, User experience (UX) has been defined as a result of the user's internal state (predispositions, expectations, needs, motivation, humor, etc.), the designed system's characteristics (e.g., complexity, purpose, usability, functionality, etc.), and the context (or environment) in which the interaction takes place (e.g., online, organizational environment, the importance of the activity, voluntary use, etc.) (Hassenzahl & Tractinsky, 2006). There are so many variables to user experience (UX) and motivation, evaluating it may be difficult. The quality of the user experience is a critical competitive component especially in any online industrial design course development. When a user interacts with an e-learning platform, he or she develops a subjective physical and emotional sensation which influences the motivation. The emotional domain of e-learning is concerned with how instructional information increases learners' internal perceptions, which drives them to learn. To enhance the UX and motivation of an e-learning platform, a strategic assessment methodology is required, since traditional approaches are insufficient for UX evaluation (Laugwitz et al., 2008). Industrial designers almost exclusively work with sketches, clay, and other traditional media, which gives them a unique perspective on digital prototype. Digital prototypes are critical to production processes. Transitioning between physical and digital representations of a prototype during design iterations is thus a major barrier in the industrial design process.

2. LITERATURE SURVEY

2.1 Types of Motivation in an Online Industrial Design Education

Educators of online industrial design learning argue that learners must have control over the interaction and be creative in their participation (Andrews, 1996). They recognise the learners' intuition and embody emotion and motivation. Educators may not have an abstract theory to explain these events, but they do have a clear commitment to accommodating a wide range of user perceptions that includes motivation. Intrinsically motivated activities corresponding to online industrial design learning are interfaces, digital interactions, multiple sensory-motor coordination, continuous learning and confidence (Krippendorff *, 2004). These characteristics of intrinsic motivation explains the drive of adopting industrial design education and defies causal/rational human behavior theories. Learners are allowed to choose how they want to spend their time. The learners' objective is not to arrive at a conclusion, but to engage in a process of intentional involvement and to solve design challenges that arise along the route.

2.2 Relationship of Motivation with Emotion and Cognition

Motivation is the driving force behind all human behavior, causing a cascade of changes both intellectually and emotionally. Motivational orientations influence and condition behavior, as well as the degree to which students assimilate knowledge during their instruction (Sánchez-Barroso et al., 2020). In industrial design learning, incorporating assessments and evaluation stimulates learners' and helps them achieve their learning objectives (Wilson & Choi, 2020). In e-learning contexts, learners' intrinsic motivation was found to be strong and motivation fosters self-determination and passion, which encourages students to put up greater effort in both personal and academic endeavors (Singh, n.d.) (Fırat et al., 2018). E-learning, hands-on and project-based learning are all popular active teaching methods presently. These learning techniques provide a pleasant emotional response (Terrón-López et al., 2017) ; (Jeong et al., 2019).

2.3 Impact of Motivation on e-Learning

Literature in educational psychology asserts that student motivation is a significant factor in e-learning (Jeong & González-Gómez, n.d.). Both intrinsic and extrinsic motivations can be conceptualized and measured as influential indicators for students' satisfaction, enjoyment and excitement. It has been found that the main cause of the incompleteness of an e-learning program is poor student motivation. A high motivation level is necessary for students to be successful in e-learning (Cain, 2008) In other words, students who are motivated will perceive greater success and satisfaction than those who are not (Cain, 2008)

3. RESEARCH METHODS

3.1 Procedures

This study followed a mixed method research technique with a descriptive approach. This method is helpful for capturing user's motivation, convictions, and attitudes. ((O'Brien & Lebow, 2013)). Additionally, mixed method approach is an emerging used research approach in the domain of UX ((Krawczyk et al., 2019)) Both Survey questionnaires as well as semi-structured interviews were conducted for the purpose of this study. The data has been collected in one phase which provided the scope of triangulation as well as additional insight ((Reio, 2009).) The population of the study are 'learners' who have gone through an online industrial design course. A convenience sampling method was used to select samples. The sampling group consisted of learners who completed an industrial design course named "Computer Aided Design (CAD) and 3D printing". The questionnaire consisted of five broad themes that were targeted to find out their motivation while undergoing the course. They are: 'Effectiveness of the course', 'Self-motivation', 'Career/academics oriented goals', 'Motivation and social cohesion' and 'Opportunity based emotional motivation'. A combination of statistical analysis and qualitative analysis approaches were followed for the data analysis purpose.

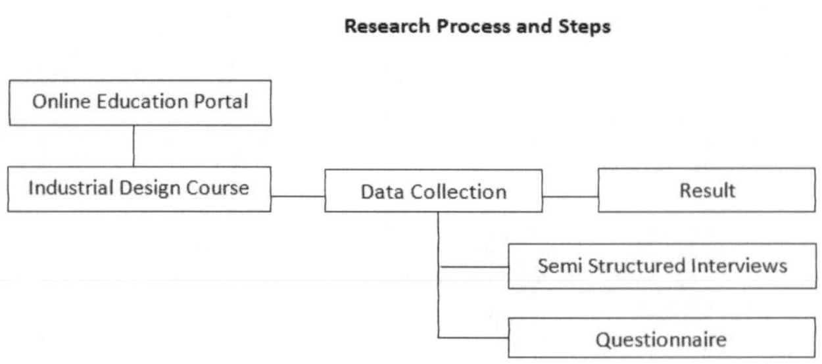

Figure 2. Research flow chart

3.2 Context and Participants

A total of 289 learners were contacted and were asked to respond to the survey questionnaire. Questionnaires were circulated multiple times to get maximum participation. A total of 200 responses for the survey questionnaire were received. 50 interviews were conducted to get in depth insight about motivation affecting learning of industrial design platforms.

4. ANALYSIS AND RESULTS

The survey questionnaire developed for this study was also tested for reliability. Cronbach alpha were calculated for an internal consistency check. The result of each section is given below:

Table 1. Cronbach alpha for the questionnaire data

Themes for Questionnaire	Effectiveness of the course	Self-motivation	career/Academic oriented goals	Motivation and social cohesion	Opportunity based emotional motivation
Cronbach's Alpha	0.79	0.82	0.81	0.92	0.82
Interpretation of score	Good	Good	Good	Excellent	Good

Questions under each of the themes have either near to 0.8 or more than o.8 score which is considered good. The acceptable score of Cronbach's alpha to be reliable is 0.7.

4.1 Demographic Analysis

A cross-sectional research was conducted to understand learners' background on the imposition of online learning of industrial design. The Total strength of students who underwent industrial design is approximately 200. The needed sample size was determined as 200, with a margin of error of 5%, a confidence interval of 95% and a response distribution of 25%. A self-designed qualitative questionnaire was used as a research tool. The questionnaire's components were selected based on the learners' academic background and accessible literature (Abbasi et al., 2020). Using the field pretest approach, a 7-item online questionnaire with three domains was planned and produced. Internal consistency (Cronbach's alpha) was computed using the data from the pilot research. Cronbach's alpha coefficient was calculated to be 0.83. Using a Likert scale, several features of learners' perspective that affect their learning were considered for the study based on evidence from numerous factors. The impact of demographic factors on several areas of students' learning are shown below.

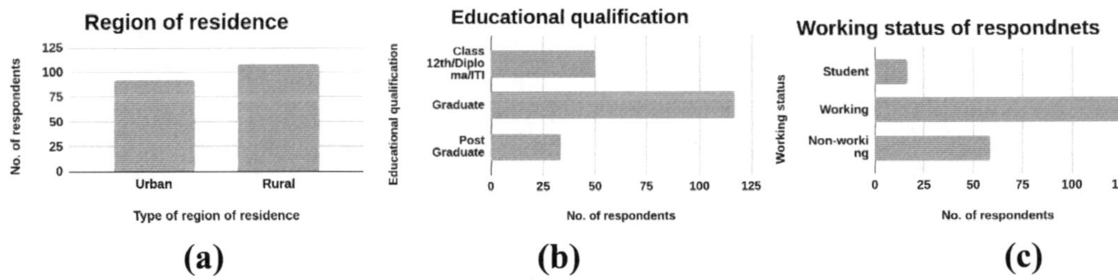

Figure 3 (a) (b) (c). Demographic data of the learners'

Through an online survey of 200 learners, we want to get a better understanding of students' perceptions and preferences for online industrial design learning. We also looked at the preferences of students for different aspects of online courses, which may help in creating a more successful online learning environment for industrial design courses. The responses for the perception about online courses are shown below.

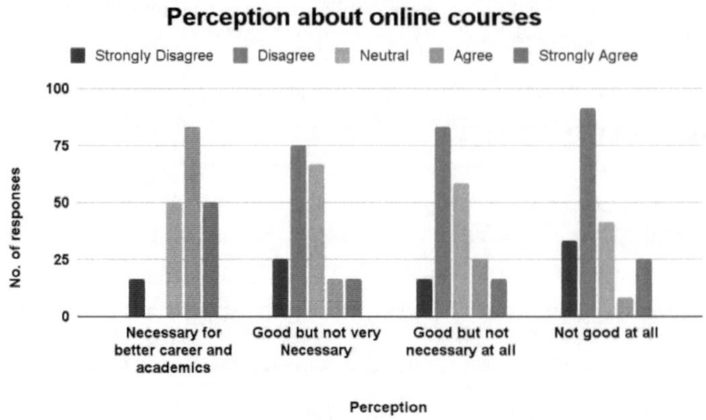

Figure 4. Perception of the learners

4.2 Interview Findings

Following the trial, participants rated their degree of motivation with the two indistinct factors of an online industrial design course namely ‘course content’ and ‘course prospectus’. The likes and dislikes of the course, as well as how it affects learners’ motivation, are included in these reports. The factors of course content affecting motivation were ‘course module’, ‘online assessment’, ‘downloadable notes’, ‘tool installation’, ‘live classes’ and ‘availability of recorded lectures’. Similarly, the factors of course prospectus affecting motivation were ‘peer discussion’, ‘lower fees’, ‘course structure’, ‘hands-on exercises’, ‘instructor quality’, ‘referrals’ and ‘certifications’. The frequency with which participants encountered these motivational factors related to the course, however, were varied. Figure 5 depicts the motivational features that were experienced, mentioned and discussed by the learners’.

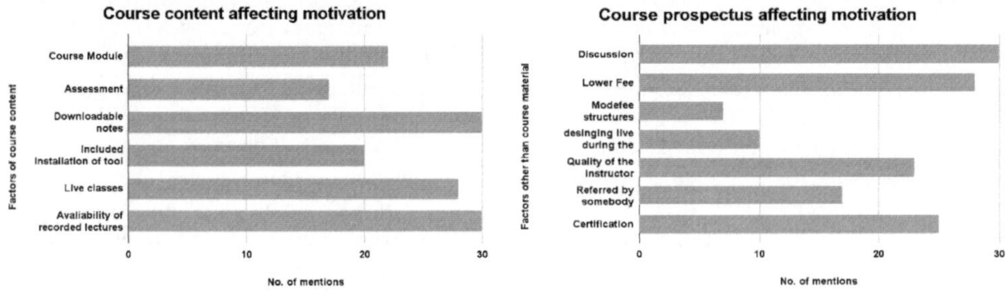

Figure 5. Motivational factors of the course as suggested by the learners’

4.3 Questionnaire Findings

4.3.1 Effectiveness of the Course

Few of the benefits of online industrial design courses are the effectiveness in educating students and its use as a professional development, in combating the rising need of technical skills and core competencies. Figure 6 below shows how effective factors of an online industrial design course influences motivation of the learners’. The factors for the effectiveness of this course are ‘level of difficulty’, ‘comprehensibility’, ‘usefulness’, ‘extent of effort’ and 'need for help’. Survey questions for the effectiveness of the course was; Whether this course was difficult for you to understand/comprehend? Were you sure about the usefulness of this course? etc.

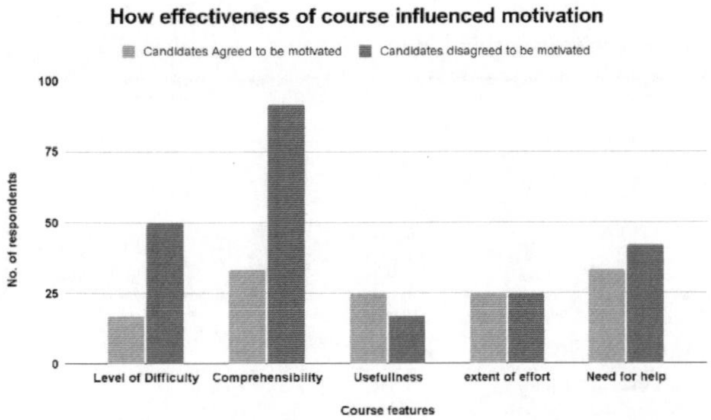

Figure 6. Effectiveness of course and motivation

4.3.2 Self-Motivation

Motivation has been highlighted as a crucial component impacting learning in the realm of education (Lim, 2004). Learner motivation has been linked to a number of significant learning outcomes, including perseverance, retention, success, and course satisfaction, according to previous research (Vallerand & Blssonnette, 1992) (Lepper & Cordova, 1992). Survey questions for self-motivation were: Do you like to learn new challenging things? Do you connect with the learning content and hands-on exercise? Motivational factors of learning attitudes like 'learning fervor', 'curiosity', 'acquiring new knowledge' and 'applying new knowledge' can be related to motivation as shown below.

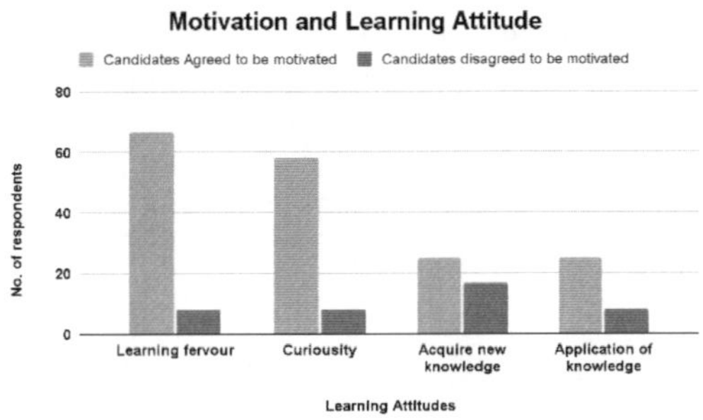

Figure 7. Learning attitudes and motivation

4.3.3 Career/Academics Oriented Goals

Through the fulfillment of the three fundamental needs, learners develop a more developed sense of self and improve their psychological well-being through academic achievements. Motivational factors related to career are 'satisfaction', 'job-ready', 'technology', 'exhibition of learning' and 'Online learning excitement'. Survey questions for career oriented goals were; Do you feel good and satisfied with the grades you got in this course? Do you like to show your caliber to your family, friends, employer, or others?

4.3.4 Motivation through Social Cohesion

Collaborative learning, among other things, may assist students develop their higher-level cognitive abilities, verbal communication skills, and self-management. The factors relating to social cohesion and motivation are 'frequent discussions', 'connection with instructor', 'team work', 'networking with instructor', 'peer networking' and 'peer review'. Survey questions for social cohesion influences motivation were: As a learner do you like to connect and discuss with fellow learners? Do you like to take group assignments or individual tasks?

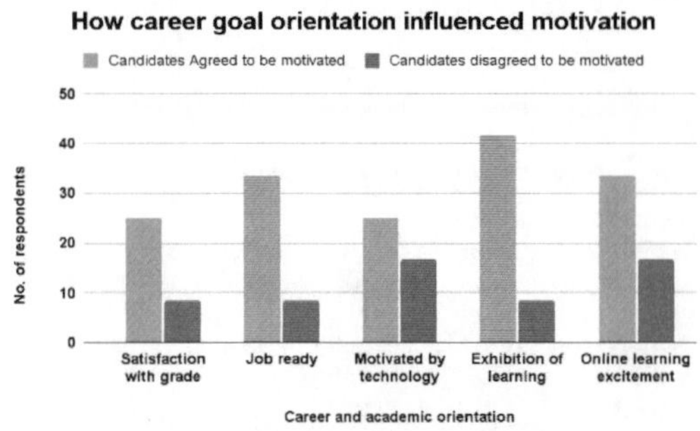

Figure 8. Career and motivation

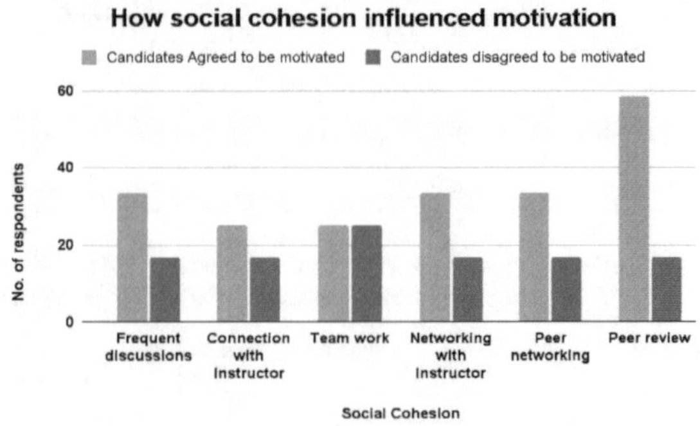

Figure 9. Social cohesion and motivation

4.3.5 Opportunity based Emotional Motivation

The structure of student participation is multi-dimensional. It is considered that learning occurs when students apply their emotional resources; hence, emotional engagement is crucial in learning. Emotions are made up of phenomenology, physiological, expressive, behavioral, and motivational components (Özgür & Altun, 2021). The opportunistic and emotional factors that influenced motivations for an online industrial design course are 'effort worthy', 'time worthy', 'emotionally exhaustive', 'rewarding', 'thought provoking' and 'persuasive'. Survey questions for emotional motivation were; Do you think that the outcome (in terms of learning) you received was worth the effort? Do you think that the time spent on this course can be better utilized somewhere else?

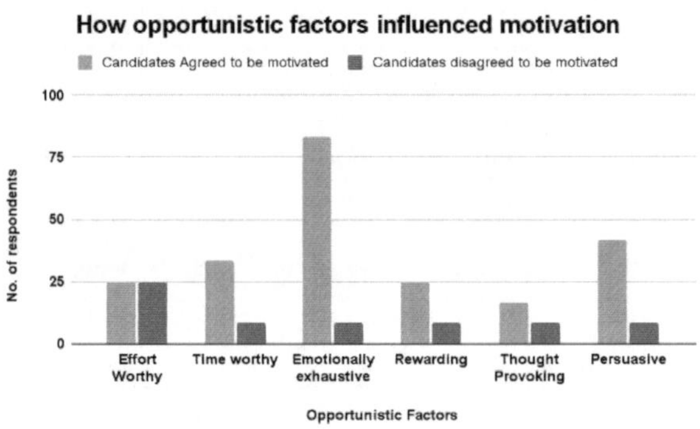

Figure 10. Opportunity based emotion and motivation

5. DISCUSSION AND CONCLUSION

The results produced from the data gathered throughout the research indicate that there exists a fundamental link between the e-learning course and students' motivational states. The majority of learners approve that they were motivated in the online industrial design course, according to the findings. These motivational states have an impact on the learner's learning capacities and results. Though the study's goal is limited by the small sample size, the data acquired from the experiment give valuable insight into the potential of motivational arousal in learning. As a result of this experiment, it has become clear that behavioral datasets such as interview and questionnaire data may aid in determining what sort of e-learning design the learners need in terms of their motivations. Even though techniques for identifying motivational states have progressed significantly, additional research is required to uncover effective industrial design e-learning features for eliciting motivations that are substantially influenced by cognitive characteristics such as expectations and perceptions. Although fundamental motivations are universal, online industrial design course features that elicit strong motivations may be scrutinized. As a consequence, processes should be adopted in which each industrial design learner actively and consciously participates in the selection of what provokes motivation.

REFERENCES

Abbasi, S., Ayoob, T., Malik, A., & Memon, S. I. (2020). Perceptions of students regarding E-learning during Covid-19 at a private medical college. *Pakistan Journal of Medical Sciences Quarterly*, *36*(COVID19-S4), S57–S61. https://doi.org/10.12669/pjms.36.COVID19-S4.2766

Andrews, A. P. (1996). *"Designing Instrinsically Motivating Interactivity: Interactive Technologies in Service to Their Users*. University of Pennsylvania.

Barolli, L., Koyama, A., Durresi, A., & De Marco, G. (2006). A web-based e-learning system for increasing study efficiency by stimulating learner's motivation. *Information Systems Frontiers*, *8*(4), 297–306. https://doi.org/10.1007/s10796-006-9004-5

Cain, J. A. (2008). *An analysis of motivation orientations and social interaction on successful and poor learners in an e-learning environment* [TUI University]. https://www.learntechlib.org/p/127325/

Carle, A. C., Jaffee, D., & Miller, D. (2009). Engaging college science students and changing academic achievement with technology: A quasi-experimental preliminary investigation. *Computers & Education*, *52*(2), 376–380. https://doi.org/10.1016/j.compedu.2008.09.005

Fayed, I., & Cummings, J. (2022). *Teaching in the Post COVID-19 Era: World Education Dilemmas, Teaching Innovations and Solutions in the Age of Crisis*. Springer International Publishing. https://play.google.com/store/books/details?id=CB9azgEACAAJ

Fırat, M., Kılınç, H., & Yüzer, T. V. (2018). Level of intrinsic motivation of distance education students in e-learning environments. *Journal of Computer Assisted Learning*, *34*(1), 63–70. https://doi.org/10.1111/jcal.12214

Garavan, T. N., Carbery, R., O'Malley, G., & O'Donnell, D. (2010). Understanding participation in e-learning in organizations: a large-scale empirical study of employees. *International Journal of Training and Development*, *14*(3), 155–168. https://doi.org/10.1111/j.1468-2419.2010.00349.x

Granić, & Ćukušić. (n.d.). Usability testing and expert inspections complemented by educational evaluation: A case study of an e-learning platform. *Journal of Educational Technology & Society*. https://www.jstor.org/stable/pdf/jeductechsoci.14.2.107.pdf?casa_token=buOOt0czPfsAAAAA:2AqGcPmasn7kKIsaQYVG0XV8A9UpCC6Inqs1atYTwINnASRJhB_u1UteANTsMrfn2nSkAIUoCpYTE7u9-mc4x74NiuahL2Pshd8mFheOUwaD6uK1iYAs

Hassenzahl, M., & Tractinsky, N. (2006). User experience - a research agenda. *Behaviour & Information Technology*, *25*(2), 91–97. https://doi.org/10.1080/01449290500330331

Jeong, & González-Gómez. (n.d.). Effects of active learning methodologies on the students' emotions, self-efficacy beliefs and learning outcomes in a science distance learning course. *JOTSE: Journal of*. https://upcommons.upc.edu/handle/2117/134429

Jeong, J. S., González-Gómez, D., Cañada-Cañada, F., Gallego-Picó, A., & Bravo, J. C. (2019). Effects of active learning methodologies on the students' emotions, self-efficacy beliefs and learning outcomes in a science distance learning course. In *Journal of Technology and Science Education* (Vol. 9, Issue 2, p. 217). https://doi.org/10.3926/jotse.530

Krawczyk, P., Maslov, I., Topolewski, M., Pallot, M., Lehtosaari, H., & Huotari, J. (2019). Threats to Reliability and Validity of Mixed Methods Research in User eXperience. In *2019 IEEE International Conference on Engineering, Technology and Innovation (ICE/ITMC)*. https://doi.org/10.1109/ice.2019.8792676

Krippendorff *, K. (2004). Intrinsic motivation and human-centred design. *Theoretical Issues in Ergonomics Science*, *5*(1), 43–72. https://doi.org/10.1080/1463922031000086717

Laugwitz, B., Held, T., & Schrepp, M. (2008). Construction and Evaluation of a User Experience Questionnaire. *HCI and Usability for Education and Work*, 63–76. https://doi.org/10.1007/978-3-540-89350-9_6

Lepper, M. R., & Cordova, D. I. (1992). A desire to be taught: Instructional consequences of intrinsic motivation. *Motivation and Emotion*, *16*(3), 187–208. https://doi.org/10.1007/bf00991651

Lim, D. H. (2004). Cross Cultural Differences in Online Learning Motivation. *Educational Media International*, *41*(2), 163–175. https://doi.org/10.1080/09523980410001685784

Matsuo, K., Barolli, L., Xhafa, F., & Koyama, A. (2008). New functions for stimulating learners' motivation in a web-based e-learning system. *International Journal of*. https://www.igi-global.com/article/new-functions-stimulating-learners-motivation/1734

O'Brien, H. L., & Lebow, M. (2013). Mixed-methods approach to measuring user experience in online news interactions. In *Journal of the American Society for Information Science and Technology* (Vol. 64, Issue 8, pp. 1543–1556). https://doi.org/10.1002/asi.22871

Özgür, A., & Altun, A. (2021). Emotional Design and Engagement With Multimedia Learning Materials in E-Learning. In *Motivation, Volition, and Engagement in Online Distance Learning* (pp. 168–191). IGI Global. https://doi.org/10.4018/978-1-7998-7681-6.ch008

Reio, T. G. (2009). Media Review: Hesse-Biber, S., & Leavy, P. (Eds.). (2008). *Handbook of Emergent Methods.* New York: Guilford Press. In *Journal of Mixed Methods Research* (Vol. 3, Issue 1, pp. 90–92). https://doi.org/10.1177/1558689808326122

Ryan, R. M., & Deci, E. L. (2006). Self-regulation and the problem of human autonomy: does psychology need choice, self-determination, and will? *Journal of Personality*, *74*(6), 1557–1585. https://doi.org/10.1111/j.1467-6494.2006.00420.x

Sánchez-Barroso, G., González-Domínguez, J., García-Sanz-Calcedo, J., & Zamora-Polo, F. (2020). Analysis of Learning Motivation in Industrial Engineering Teaching in University of Extremadura (Spain). *Sustainability: Science Practice and Policy*, *12*(12), 4987. https://doi.org/10.3390/su12124987

Singh. (n.d.). Study of achievement motivation in relation to academic achievement of students. *International Journal of Educational Policy Research and Review.* https://www.globalacademicstar.com/download/article/bb2kChnDp21z96C7oCVGj2GEWSKfgcwIKqg2ZiHG.pdf

Terrón-López, M.-J., García-García, M.-J., Velasco-Quintana, P.-J., Ocampo, J., Vigil Montaño, M.-R., & Gaya-López, M.-C. (2017). Implementation of a project-based engineering school: increasing student motivation and relevant learning. *European Journal of Engineering Education*, *42*(6), 618–631. https://doi.org/10.1080/03043797.2016.1209462

Vallerand, R. J., & Blssonnette, R. (1992). Intrinsic, extrinsic, and amotivational styles as predictors of behavior: A prospective study. *Journal of Personality*, *60*(3), 599–620. https://doi.org/10.1111/j.1467-6494.1992.tb00922.x

Vikas, S., & Mathur, A. (2022). An empirical study of student perception towards pedagogy, teaching style and effectiveness of online classes. *Education and Information Technologies*, *27*(1), 589–610. https://doi.org/10.1007/s10639-021-10793-9

Wilson, W., & Choi, Y. M. (2020). Leveraging Design Competitions to Enhance Learning Goals and Student Motivation Within a Studio Project. *Advances in Industrial Design*, 255–260. https://doi.org/10.1007/978-3-030-51194-4_34

Zardari, B. A., Hussain, Z., Arain, A. A., Rizvi, W. H., & Vighio, M. S. (2021). Development and Validation of User Experience-Based E-Learning Acceptance Model for Sustainable Higher Education. *Sustainability: Science Practice and Policy*, *13*(11), 6201. https://doi.org/10.3390/su13116201

UNDERSTANDING USERS' UX NEEDS THROUGH THE LENSES OF PSYCHOLOGICAL NEEDS THEORIES: USERS' EXPECTATIONS AND FELT EXPERIENCES

Emmanuel O. C. Mkpojiogu[1,2], Obianuju E. Okeke-Uzodike[3] and Victor Omopariola[4]
[1]*School of Computing, Universiti Utara Malaysia, 06010 UUM, Sintok, Malaysia*
[2]*Department of Software Engineering, Veritas University, Abuja, Nigeria*
[3]*Department of Applied Management, Durban University of Technology, Pietermaritzburg, KwaZulu-Natal, South Africa*
[4]*Department of Computer and Information Technology, Veritas University Abuja, Nigeria*

ABSTRACT

The purpose of this study was to conduct a literature review in order to gather material that would serve to underpin and support a link between UX requirements and psychological theories. In the paper, relevant sources from extant literature were accessed and synthesized. The outcome revealed that psychological theories support user experience needs. UX needs as psychological needs are fully supported by psychological theories. In the light of this, the search for ways to meet these needs should be done using psychological needs fulfillment strategies. Further studies will investigate ways of meeting these user experience needs and how these needs can be modeled for UX design and evaluation.

KEYWORDS

Psychological Needs, Psychological Theories, User Experience Needs

1. INTRODUCTION

User Experience (UX) is the totality of users' feelings, perceptions, motivations, preferences, beliefs, attitudes and emotional reactions that result from their mental or actual encounter or interaction with interactive technological artifacts. Users' needs and their experiences are interwoven. The meeting or not meeting of users' needs define the kind of experience such users will have with a product. Users' needs depict and include what they expect and actually experience before, during and/or after their interaction with an interactive product (Olsson, 2012; Hussein et al., 2019a; 2019b). In reality, the ISO definition of UX (ISO 9241: 210, 2010) can be understood as drawing a parallel between "the usage" (i.e., actual use) and "the anticipated use" (i.e., expected use) of a system, meaning that users' expectations of UX and the felt (actual) UX are in sync. Furthermore, as Karapanos et al. (2009) pointed out, the often-anticipated experiences with a product might be much more important, emotional, and memorable than the actual experiences. According to Kankainen (2003), UX is influenced by the user's previous experiences as well as their expectations for the product. The consumers' present experience affects their expectations during the encounter, resulting in a cyclic process of expectation revision over time. Wright et al. (2008) address anticipation and consider it to be one of the most important sense-making processes in humans. Experience is always shaped by what has happened previously, according to Wright et al. (2008). Baumeister as al. (2007) also claimed that people anticipate consequences by reflecting on previous and current experiences. Expectations are formed as a result of anticipating (or expecting) an experience based on previous experiences, encounters, and interactions. Expectations come before real usage experience (Olsson, 2012). Yogasara et al. (2011) used the phrase "expected user experience" to describe "the experiences and sentiments that the user anticipates to have while imagining utilizing an interactive product or system" (Hussain et al., 2021a; 2021b; 2021c).

Users' expectations in the domains of human-computer interaction (HCI) and user experience (UX), according to Olsson (2012), could be related to the product or service itself, its use, or the experiential outcomes of that use. People may expect the experience to provide specific options for action or conclusion, according to Wright et al. (2008), (for example, what new activities does a product allow). Furthermore, the temporal and spatial characteristics of the experience can be predicted to a degree — for example, how intense the experience will be and how long it will last (Olsson, 2012). Yogasara et al. (2011) found that users' anticipations included a variety of factors connected to the environment, experiential knowledge, and anticipated mood of the users. Furthermore, according to Demir et al. (2009), expectations may be regarding an unknown feature of a product (for example, performance prior to use/consumption) as well as the outcome of an action (for example, pushing a button to go to the menu of a cellular phone). What effect does the user's anticipation have on their experience? Diverse expectations elicit and promote different "shades of meaning" to the final users of a product, according to Wright et al. (2008). Expectations are the core of the user experience cycle, according to Hiltunen et al. (2002): expectations direct human interpretation, information collection, and attention when using a product. For example, a high anticipation of a novel interaction approach in a product (e.g., touch screen in its early days) may prevent other features from being seen or the device from being used for its intended purposes. Expectations, according to Arhippainen (2009), might influence users' impressions of a product's capabilities and overall quality. Expectations exist as a norm against which actual experience is measured, according to Bhattacherjee's (2001) expectation-confirmation theory. Raita and Oulasvirta (2011) tested how product reviews affect subjective usability evaluations with 36 participants and found that this basic hypothesis holds true. When compared to those in the negative-prime and no-prime groups, those who had read a good product review before the test gave the tested mobile device substantially superior post-experiment ratings (Hussain et al., 2019c: 2019d).

Furthermore, post-use contentment has been found to occur when a product outperforms expectations on key benefit dimensions (Lindgaard & Dudek, 2003; Oliver, 1997); yet, if it falls short of expectations, the user will be unsatisfied (Oliver, 1977). As a result, in some cases, people may need to change their expectations in order to avoid future disappointment (Wright et al., 2008). Nonetheless, Karapanos et al. (2009) argue that the significance of expectations in product satisfaction judgements likely varies by circumstance, and that consumers may understand that their expectations are unreasonable if they are not satisfied. As a result, the actual felt experience with the product may become more dominating, while the perceived importance of the feature that fell short of expectations may decline. As a result, the method and precise influences of anticipation in relation to the phenomenon of UX appear to be hazy. Although a number of conceptual frameworks and hypotheses have been provided, there has been relatively little actual data reported thus far (Olsson, 2012). Dewey (1925), in looking back at the beginnings of expectations, highlighted social elements (for example, other people's ideas and experiences), traditions (for example, norms and personal preferences), and the effect of education as causes of expectations. In consumer research, Zeithaml et al. (2002) identified word-of-mouth, a consumer's own past experience, personal requirements, explicit service promises (personal and non-personal comments about the service given by the company to customers), and implicit service promises as sources of expectations (for instance, price, five-star ranking of a hotel). It is worth noting that expectations may be influenced not only by previous experiences with the product, product type, or company in question, but also by other products (which could be rival (competing) products or represent different product types) or by other people's experiences and expectations (Olsson,2012; Mkpojiogu et al., 2022a; 2022b; 2022c).

In general, the aforementioned hypotheses show that expectations might be complex, targeted to multiple parts of product use, and related with numerous components of UX that have already been discovered (Olsson, 2012). The type of experience might influence expectations (that results from interaction with an interactive product). Expectations, on the other hand, may not have as many different features as real experiences. For example, predicting the overall experience over time, how various contextual circumstances would influence the encounter, or what the sensory experience from the interaction might feel like could be difficult (Olsson, 2012). Despite this, product or service expectations have not been thoroughly researched in the field of UX or HCI in general (Olsson, 2012). When there is a high risk of failing development expenditure and a large design area that would benefit from focusing, a research based on expectations method can be effective even with non-existent items. According to Yogasara et al. (2011), understanding consumers' predicted good experiences makes it easier to evaluate what product attributes might contribute to those experiences and how they do so. Similarly, examining negative expected experiences might aid in identifying undesired product characteristics that prohibit users from having positive experiences (Olsson, 2012).

Within the UX and HCI areas, there has been a rising willingness in recent years to examine the experiential side of product use, as well as the design and evaluation of interactive products (Hassenzahl et al., 2010). Emotions have become an important aspect of UX as a result of this tendency, and their assessment has become critical in UX research (Agarwal & Meyer, 2009). In the realm of human-computer interaction, research on emotions has mostly concentrated on psychological characteristics for analyzing affective interactions of interactive products (Picard, 1997; Partala & Surakka, 2003, 2004; Partala et al., 2006). Participants' facial expressions in affective HCI are an example (Rezaei, 2015). Emotions' social and experiential elements have recently received increased attention (Boehner et al., 2005). Furthermore, in recent years, evaluating subjective emotional experience has become a key task in user experience research and evaluation (Partala & Kallinen, 2012; Mkpojiogu et al., 2021).

According to Law et al. (2009), user experience is dynamic, context-dependent, and subjective. Furthermore, the experiential aspects of interactive product design and evaluation place a strong emphasis on affects and emotions (Rezaei, 2015). Similarly, McCarthy and Wright (2004) emphasized the "emotional thread" of experience in their work, emphasizing that emotion and experience are inextricably linked. All users' actions, and believe are "shot through with values, wants, ambitions, and goals." The emotional tone of events is set by the relationship between action and ideals and needs. Accepted psychological theories are widely reinforced, with an emphasis on values, wants, aspirations, and objectives (McCarthy & Wright, 2004). (Carver & Scheier, 1989). On a tactical level, action is influenced by context and conditions, but it is also influenced by broader psychological requirements (Rezaei, 2015). McCarthy and Wright (2004), on the other hand, did not provide a precise definition of these "values, wants, and desires." According to Hassenzahl et al. (2000), Hassenzahl (2001), Hassenzahl (2003), and Hassenzahl and Tractinsky (2006), the perceived qualities of an interactive product can be divided into the pragmatic dimension (which is closely associated with behavioral goals) and the hedonic dimension (which is closely associated with the individual's self and psychological wellbeing). These factors account for users' pragmatic and hedonistic requirements. Hedonic dimensions include, among other things, requirements for stimulation (satisfaction of stimulation, novelty, and challenge, which are all necessary for personal growth), identification (self-expression, engagement with important persons), and evocation (self-maintenance, memories) (Rezaei, 2015). As a result, the appeal of an interactive software program in the eyes of users is highly dependent on the users' perceptions of quality characteristics (Hassenzahl et al., 2000). Psychological needs, according to Hassenzahl and Tractinsky (2006), are a significant component of UX (Hussain et al., 2019a).

The most interesting questions, according to Hassenzahl and Tractinsky (2006), will be: what are these needs? and how are these needs prioritized? Sheldon et al. (2001) proposed a list of ten (10) broad psychological demands. Autonomy, competence, relatedness, physical well-being, security, self-esteem, self-actualization, pleasure-stimulation, money-luxury, and popularity-influence are only a few of these requirements. Each of the demands was defined as such and derived from well-known psychological theories, including: 1) self-determination theory (Ryan & Deci, 2000), 2) Maslow's theory of personality (1954), and 3) Epstein's cognitive-experiential self-theory (1990), among others. Three investigations were conducted by Sheldon et al. (2001) to determine the importance of these ten (10) psychological demands. Participants reported one recent most gratifying life event, and scores were recorded and computed for each of the 10 candidate requirements within the context of the experience using a questionnaire with 30 descriptive statements (three items for each need on a scale of 1 to 5). The study's findings revealed that competence, autonomy, and relatedness are the three most prominent demands that are most rewarding and are missing in unsatisfactory life situations (Hussain et al., 2019b; Nadzir et al., 2019a; 2019b; Rezaei, 2015).

UX and emotion are inextricably linked, just as they are for need-related aspects. An experience's emotional quality tends to describe people's or users' experiences; for example, joyful, exciting, or aggravating (Rezaei, 2015). This is how individuals are most likely to recall a once-in-a-lifetime event (McCarthy & Wright, 2004). As a result, Sheldon et al. (2001) used the Positive Affect Negative Affect Schedule (PANAS) questionnaire (Watson et al., 1988) to analyze the affects in a reported life event and found a distinct link between need fulfillment and affects (positive, negative). As a result, they discovered that the degree of need satisfaction was proportional to the intensity of pleasant emotion. All other demands, with the exception of luxury, showed positive affect connections. Later, Hassenzahl (2008) conducted research on the structure of pleasant technological experiences. He used the PANAS model to investigate emotions and satisfaction levels for self-determination demands such as autonomy, competence, and relatedness. According to the findings of his study, competence was the most important psychological need in pleasant user experiences with technology, followed by autonomy, and finally relatedness. Hassenzahl et al. (2010) followed up with a larger investigation on the same subject. They found that the most important psychological needs in positive UXs with technology were relatedness, stimulation, and competence.

Autonomy and self-esteem, however, were left out of their analysis. They also showed that the perceived hedonic quality of interactive items was influenced by need fulfillment and happy feelings (Rezaei, 2015).

Furthermore, Partala and Kallinen (2012) used a holistic approach to investigate the relative importance of various emotions and psychological demands in the most fulfilling and unsatisfied UXs, as well as the impact of various contextual aspects on those experiences. They investigated psychological requirements, emotions, and context using a three-part questionnaire. They also studied 10 candidate psychological needs in the context of UXs using Sheldon et al.'s (2001) questionnaire. In addition, the PANAS instrument (Watson et al., 1988) was utilized to analyze emotions related to user experiences, containing 10 positive and 10 negative emotions. Partala and Kallinen (2012) focused on unsatisfying experiences and unpleasant emotions, in contrast to many previous UX studies, in order to include the whole spectrum of emotions on the emotional valence scale. Finally, a set of ten contextual questions was created using Jumisko-Pyykkö and Vainio (2010)'s context framework to incorporate the most prevalent contextual variables in the existing literature: physical context, temporal context, task context, social context, and technical and information context (Rezaei, 2015). Aesthetics, usability, content, and brand all influence user judgment of interactive technologies, and this is dependent on context, task framing, and user background, according to previous study (De Angeli, Hartmann, & Sutcliffe, 2009; Hartmann et al., 2008). Although hedonics (emotion), pragmatics (usability), and beauty have been shown to influence users' perceptions of product goodness (Hassenzahl, 2004; Hussain et al., 2016a; 2016b; Mkpojiogu et al., 2016; 2018), the link between aesthetics and usability is still unclear (Hassenzahl, 2004; Hussain et al., 2016a; 2016b; Mkpojiogu e (Tuch et al., 2012). Hart (2014) investigated these dimensions in terms of their affective responses both before and during interaction with technology in order to better understand what motivates people to use, and continue to use, interactive digital technologies. Hart (2014) also looked at user involvement with various types of interactive design features using affect, flow, and presence measurements (Hart, 2014).

On the subject of needs, there are various theories. Herzberg et al. (1959) proposed the motivator-hygiene hypothesis, a two-factor requirements theory. They used the critical incident technique to analyze the impact of motivational and hygienic elements on workers' experiences in the context of job satisfaction. Motivators are factors that contribute to a positive experience and keep people motivated to improve it. Hygienes, on the other hand, are elements that are not related to a specific profession but are related to the conditions of that job (work environment). Motivators are aspects of the job's content, whereas hygienes are aspects of the job's context (Vargo et al., 2007; Soliman, 1970; Zhang & Dran, 2000). Swan and Combs (1976), on the other hand, added to the Herzberg et al. (1959) motivator-hygiene paradigm. They proposed a link between motivators and hygienes, as well as expressive and instrumental aspects. The psychological features of a product are known as expressive factors, whereas the physical (physiological) aspects are known as instrumental factors. Herzberg's theory is translated into two-factor UX models such as Hassenzahl's (2003) model, which includes pragmatic and hedonic qualities (needs), and Mahlke's (2008) model, which includes instrumental and non-instrumental qualities (needs) (Abdulkhudhur et al., 2020; Hashim et al., 2021).

Closely associated to the Herzberg theory is the Maslow's theory of hierarchy of needs. Abraham Maslow (1954) categorized human needs into five. These needs follow Herzberg propositions as lower order needs are hygiene (physiological) needs while the higher order needs are motivator (psychological) needs. However, in addition to the Herzberg's two factor categorization, Maslow included sociological needs, a third category in between the physiological and psychological needs. Maslow posits that people generally desire for lower other needs/qualities (that are basic, foundational and fundamental) and when these needs/qualities are fulfilled, their desires are pushed further up for higher other needs. Lower needs must be satisfied in order to achieve a sustained move to higher needs. A lower-level need/quality would be a motivator until it is satisfied. Once the need is satisfied, the user will be motivated by the level of needs in the hierarchy. This continues up the hierarchy. The Maslow's five-level model (consisting of: physiological, safety, love/belongingness, pride/self-esteem, and self-actualizing/fulfillment/transcendent needs) can be broken into three hierarchical levels, namely, physiological (existential/survival/maintenance), sociological, and psychological needs. Maslow's basic (physiological) needs match or map unto the pragmatic/ non-instrumental needs of users, while his sociological and psychological needs maps unto the expected and unexpected hedonic needs of users. The fulfillment or non-fulfillment of these needs defines the users' experiences. The basic level needs are objective, concrete and tangible in nature while the sociological and psychological level needs are subjective and affective (visceral). The level of motivation at the first level is more permanent and stable than at the second and third levels of the hierarchy. The first level describes what users need, the second, their wants, and the third, their dreams.

According to Maslow, the basic needs at the lowest rung of the ladder are survival needs, these when met are followed by social needs, and then the sensational (transcendent/transformation/growth) needs. Fulfilling users' survival/success needs, meets their expectation, and creates satisfaction in them, fulfilling social needs, meets their desires and creates loyalty in users, while fulfilling sensational (self-actualization/transformation) needs, meets users' unrecognized/unexpected/unspoken needs, and create evangelism, and propel users' word-of-mouth promotion of software application. These needs when met or unmet are translated into or perceived as experiences. Maslow's model can be further classified into three level: i) deficiency, ii) growth, and iii) self-actualization growth needs (Maslow, 1954). Alderfer's E-R-G model collapsed the Maslow's five-level model into three and defines three user needs or expectations that translate to their experience when met or unmet, these factors are hierarchical in nature: Existence needs are at the base, relatedness (social) needs follows, while growth needs are at the top of the hierarchy. As users get satisfied, there is progression in their motivation, however, as they experience frustration; there is regression or decline in their motivation. Access to the higher levels requires satisfaction in the lower level needs. However, if a higher level need remains unfulfilled, the user might resign to fate and regress to lower needs that appear easier to satisfy. However, Herzberg's model classifies users' needs into two: hygiene and motivator needs. Hygiene needs are extrinsic while motivator needs are intrinsic. The hygiene needs are the users' basic needs (dissatisfiers/pragmatic/ instrumental) that extrinsically motivate users in their interaction with a product. These needs are maintenance needs as well that maintain and sustain the product in use and in the market. However, the motivator needs on the other hand are the stimulator needs (non-instrumental/hedonic) that intrinsically motivate users in their interaction with software products and that give users self-functioning and self-fulfillment perceptions (Hussain et al., 2020).

Self-determination theory is a psychological theory developed by Ryan and Deci (2017) that deals with or rather explains the intrinsic motivation of users of interactive products. It explains the motivation of users to interact with a product independently without external help or support. Certain factors give users such self-motivation, they are inter alia: connectedness, user control, autonomy, competence, stimulation, etc. This theory is closely related to the self-efficacy theory that explains a users' belief in themselves that they are capable of using or interacting with a product to achieve their goals.

The dimensions of the UX needs model are theoretically supported. The pragmatic and hedonic dimensions are supported by the Herzberg 2-factor theory (Herzberg et al., 1959). This theory classified human motivational needs into intrinsic and extrinsic (the motivator-hygiene factors). These represent the hedonic and pragmatic dimensions respectively. In addition, trust, aesthetics, affectivity, ubiquity and sociability dimension are supported by the Maslow's needs theory. This theory supports human higher order transcendent needs that cater for or explains these needs dimensions (Maslow, 1954). Also, the interactivity, engageability, and self-determination dimensions are supported by the self-determination theory. Though the flow and presence theories explain user engagement at a narrower perspective, the self-determination theory is better suited as it explains a broader spectrum of UX needs dimensions, namely: interactivity, engageability, and self-determination. The self-determination theory supports users' intrinsic motivation to use or interact with technology without external support (Ryan & Deci, 2017). Hitherto, most researchers in UX are not adequately informed about the strong theoretical tie between psychological theories and UX needs. This study is geared towards establishing from extant literature such strong tie.

2. METHODOLOGY

A literature review protocol was employed to support this study. In this study, relevant articles were downloaded for review. Then, these downloaded papers were synthesized and analyzed and relevant information regarding the theoretical support for user experience needs was extracted. In sum, the following protocol was observed (Figure 1): 1) download articles relating to the psychological theories supporting user experience needs; 2) synthesize and analyze the downloaded articles; 3) extract the suitable information pertaining to the psychological theoretical support for UX needs; 4) establish a strong theoretical foundation for UX needs.

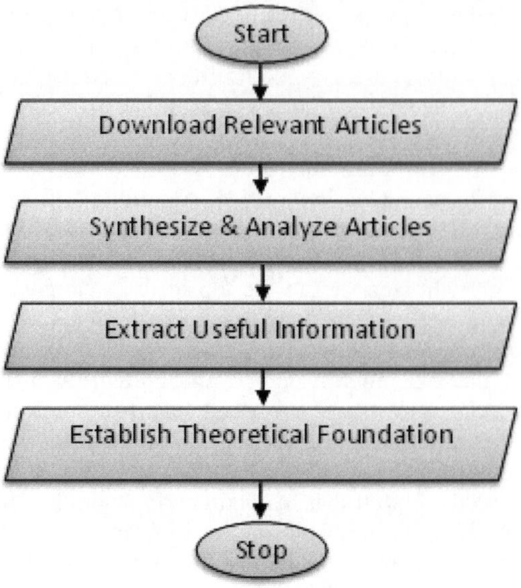

Figure 1. Research Protocol

3. RESULTS

In this study, a literature analysis is made concerning the association between psychological theories and user experience needs. The outcome revealed that there is a strong psychological theoretical support for UX needs. Table 1 shows some UX needs and the psychological theories supporting them. It is evident from an examination of literature that UX needs connected to either users' expectations or their actual felt experiences are well founded in extant literature. Sequel to this analysis and findings, the psychological supportive theories are well established. This implies that these needs as psychological needs can be fulfilled by psychological needs fulfillment methods.

Table 1. Theoretical Support for UX Needs

Theory	UX Needs	Source
Herzberg's 2-factor theory	Pragmatic	Herzberg et al., 1959
Herzberg's 2-factor theory	Hedonic	Herzberg et al., 1959
Maslow's theory	Aesthetics	Maslow, 1954
Maslow's theory	Affectivity	Maslow, 1954
Self-determination theory	Interactivity	Ryan & Deci, 2017
Self-determination theory	Engageability	Ryan & Deci, 2017
Maslow's theory	Sociability	Maslow, 1954
Maslow's theory	Trust	Maslow, 1954
Self-determination theory	Self-determination	Ryan & Deci, 2017
Maslow's theory	Ubiquity	Maslow, 1954

4. CONCLUSION

In this paper, a literature review procedure was used to elicit information that will help establish a relationship between UX needs and psychological theories. In the study, relevant literature sources were consulted and an analysis on the literature sources reveals the psychological theoretical support for user experience needs. UX needs as psychological needs are fully anchored on psychological theories. This leads to ways of meeting these needs using psychological needs fulfillment strategies. Further studies will investigate ways of fulfilling these UX needs and how these needs can be modeled for UX design and evaluation.

ACKNOWLEDGEMENT

The authors acknowledge the Durban University of Technology in South Africa for supporting this study.

REFERENCES

Abdulkhudhur, H.N., Habeeb, I.Q., Mkpojiogu, E.O.C., & Hussain, A. (2020). An interactive games experience model (GXM) for the design and evaluation of the UX of gamified apps over time. Journal of Critical Reviews (JCR), 7(8), 1281-1287

Agarwal, A., & Meyer, A. (2009). Beyond usability: evaluating emotional response as an integral part of the user experience. In CHI'09 Extended Abstracts on Human Factors in Computing Systems (pp. 2919-2930). ACM.

Arhippainen, L. (2009). Studying user experience: issues and problems of mobile service – Case Adamos: user experience (im)possible to catch? Doctoral dissertation, University of Oulu.

Baumeister, R.F., Vohs, K.D., DeWall, C.N., Zhang, L. (2007). How emotion shapes behavior: feedback, anticipation, and reflection, rather than direct causation. Personality and Social Psychology Review, 11(2), 167-203.

Bhattacherjee, A. (2001). Understanding information systems continuance: an expectation–confirmation model. MIS Quarterly, 25(3),351-370.

Boehner, K., DePaula, R., Dourish, P., & Sengers, P. (2005). Affect: from information to interaction. In Proc. of the 4th decennial conference on Critical computing: between sense and sensibility (pp. 59-68). ACM.

Carver, C. S., & Scheier, M. F. (1989). On the self-regulation of behavior. Cambridge University Press.

De Angeli, A., Hartmann, J., & Sutcliffe, A. (2009). The effect of brand on the evaluation of websites. In Human-Computer Interaction-¬INTERACT 2009 (pp. 638–651). Berlin, Heidelberg: Springer.

Demir, E., Desmet, P., Hekkert, P.P.M. (2009). Appraisal patterns of emotions in user-product interaction. Int'l Journal of Design, 3(2), 41-51.

Dewey, J. (1925). Experience and nature. McCutchen Press p.480.

Epstein, S. (1990). Cognitive-experiential self-theory. In L. A. Pervin (Ed.), Handbook of personality: Theory and research (pp. 165-192).

Hartmann, J., Sutcliffe, A., & de Angeli, A. (2008). Towards a theory of user judgment of aesthetics and user interface quality. ACM Transactions on Computer-¬Human Interaction (TOCHI), 15(4), 1–30.

Hassenzahl, M. (2001). The effect of perceived hedonic quality on product appealingness. International Journal of Human-Computer Interaction, 13(4), 481–499.

Hassenzahl, M. (2003). The thing and I: understanding the relationship between user and product. In Blythe, M., Monk, A.F., Overbeeke, K., Wright, P. (eds.), Funology: from usability to enjoyment, (pp. 31-42), Kluwer.

Hassenzahl, M. (2004). The interplay of beauty, goodness, and usability in interactive products. Human-Comp. Interaction, 19(4), 319–349.

Hassenzahl, M. (2008). User experience (UX): towards an experiential perspective on product quality. In the Proceedings of the 20th International Conference of the Association Francophone d'Interaction Homme-Machine, Metz, France.

Hassenzahl, M., Diefenbach, S., & Göritz, A. (2010). Needs, affect, and interactive products–facets of user experience. Interacting with computers,22(5), 353-362.

Hassenzahl, M., Platz, A., Burmester, M., & Lehner, K. (2000). Hedonic and ergonomic quality aspects determine a software's appeal. In Proceedings of the SIGCHI conference on Human Factors in Computing Systems (pp. 201-208).

Hassenzahl, M., & Tractinsky, N. (2006). User experience–a research agenda. Behav. & Infor. Technology 25(2), 91–97.

Hashim, W., Mkpojiogu, E.O.C., Hussain, A., & Abdul-Aziz, S.N. (2021). A Product Pain-Pleasure Framework for Software Product Design in the Usability and User Experience Domains. Webology, 18(SI), 1-31.

Herzberg, F., Snyderman, B.B., & Mausner, B. (1959). The motivation to work, 2nd Ed., New York: John Wiley & Sons.

Hiltunen, M., Laukka, M., & Luomala, J. (2002). Professional mobile user experience, (p. 300), Finland: IT Press.

Hussein, I, Hussain, A., Mkpojiogu, E.O.C., Nathan, S.S., & Zaaba, Z.F. (2019a). The knowledge of human-computer interaction (HCI) and user experience design (UXD) in Malaysia: an analysis of the characteristics of an HCI-focused conference. International Journal of Innovative Technology and Exploring Engineering, 8(8S), 483-490.

Hussein, I., Mkpojiogu, E.O.C., & Hussain, A. (2019b). A focus group assessment of participants' UX knowledge and their motivations for participating in a UXD community of practice. Journal of Advanced Research in Dynamical and Control Systems (JARDCS), 11(05-SI), 1496-1499.

Hussein, I., Hussain, A., Mkpojiogu, E.O.C., & Mahmud, M. (2019c). A UX community of practice: design goals, practice motivations and values. Test Engineering and Management, 81 (11-12), 3144-3156

Hussain, A., Mkpojiogu, E.O.C., & Kamal, F.M. (2016a). Antecedents to user adoption of interactive mobile maps. Journal of Telecommunication, Electronic & Computer Engineering (JTEC). 8(10), 41-45.

Hussain, A., Mkpojiogu, E.O.C. & Yusof, M.M. (2016b). The effects of proposed software product's features on the satisfaction and dissatisfaction of potential customers. Proceedings of the 1st International Conference on Applied Science and Technology (ICAST'16), Kedah, Malaysia, AIP Conf. Proc.1761 (1), 020052, http://dx.doi.org/10.1063/1.4960892.

Hussain, A., Mkpojiogu, E.O.C., Kamal, F.M., Wahab, R.B., & Meh, N.H.C. (2021a). An instrumental assessment of Touch'n Go eWallet mobile app. International Journal of Interactive Mobile Technologies, 15(6), 4-17.

Hussain, A., Mkpojiogu, E.O.C., & Ezekwudo, C.C. (2021b). Improving the academic self-efficacy of students using mobile educational apps in virtual learning: a review. Inter. J. of Interactive Mobile Technologies, 15(6), 149-160.

Hussain, A., Mkpojiogu, E.O.C., & Okoroafor, P.C. (2021c). Assisting children with autism spectrum disorder with educational mobile apps to acquire language and communication skills: a review. International Journal of Interactive Mobile Technologies, 15(6), 161-170.

Hussain, A., Mkpojiogu, E.O.C., & Babalola, E.T. (2020). Using mobile educational apps to foster work and play in learning: a systematic review. International Journal of Interactive Mobile Technologies, 14 (18), 178-194.

Hussain, A., Mkpojiogu, E.O.C., Ishak, N., Mokhtar, N., & Ani, Z.C. (2019a). An interview report on users' perception about the usability performance of a mobile e-government application. Inter. J. of Inter. Mob. Tech. 13 (10), 169-178.

Hussain, A., Mkpojiogu, E.O.C., & Suleiman, K. (2019b). A heuristic evaluation of Achik.biz mobile shopping app. International Journal of Recent Technology and Engineering (IJRTE), 8(2S2), 123-126.

Hussain, A., Hussein, I., & Mkpojiogu, E.O.C. (2019c). Assessing the frustrations of practicing user experience design (UXD) among the UXD community of practice in Malaysia: a netnographic approach. Compusoft: An International Journal of Advanced Computer Technology (IJACT), 8(8), 3345-3355

Hussain, A., Hussein, I., Mahmud, M., & Mkpojiogu, E.O.C. (2019d). Understanding the characteristics of UX Malaysia UXD community of practice (CoP): a participants' observation. Test Engin. and Management, 81 (11-12), 3157-3171

ISO. (2010). FDIS 9241-210: Ergonomics of human-system interaction - Part 210: Human-centered design for interactive systems (formerly known as 13407). Switzerland: Int'l Organization for Standardization (ISO).

Jumisko-Pyykkö, S., & Vainio, T., (2010). Framing the context of use for mobile HCI. Int'l J. of Mobile Human–Computer Interaction 2 (4), 1–28

Kankainen, A. (2003). UCPCD: user-centered product concept design. Proceedings of DUX'03, (pp. 1-13), ACM Press.

Karapanos, E., Martens, J.-¬B., & Hassenzahl, M. (2009). Accounting for diversity in subjective judgments. In Proceedings of the SIGCHI Conference on Human Factors in Computing Systems (pp. 639–648). ACM.

Law, E.L., Roto, V., Hassenzahl, M., Vermeeren, A., & Kort, J. (2009). Understanding, scoping and defining user experience: a survey approach. In Proc of the SIGCHI Conf on Human Factors in Computing Systems, (pp.719-728).

Lindgaard, G. & Dudek, K. (2003). What is this evasive beast we call user satisfaction? Interacting with Computers, 15(3), 429-452.

Mahlke, S. (2008). User experience of interaction with technical systems: theories, methods, empirical results, and their application to the development of interactive systems. Doctoral dissertation, Belin: Berlin University of Techn.

Maslow, A. (1954). Motivation and personality. New York: Harper &Row.

McCarthy, J., & Wright, P. (2004). Technology as experience. Interactions,11(5), 42-43.

Mkpojiogu, E.O.C., Hashim, N.L., & Adamu, R. (2016). Observed demographic differentials in user perceived satisfaction on the usability of mobile banking applications. Proceedings of the 8th Knowledge Management International Conference (KMICe'16), Chiang Mai, Thailand, 29-30 August 2016, pp. 263-268.

Mkpojiogu, E.O.C., & Hussain, A. (2018). Assessing the influence of self-reported requirements importance on the perceived quality of proposed software products. ICAST 2018, AIP Conf. Proc. 2016, 020091

Mkpojiogu, E.O.C., Okeke-Uzodike, O.E., Emmanuel, E.I. & Eze, C. (2022a). Methods for the evaluation of UX over time. IHCI 2022.

Mkpojiogu, E. O., Okeke-Uzodike, O. E., Eze, C., & Emmanuel, E. I. (2022b, March). A conceptual UX model for the design and evaluation of interactive digital artifacts over time. In 2022 Conference on Information Communications Technology and Society (ICTAS) (pp. 1-6). IEEE.

Mkpojiogu, E. O., Okeke-Uzodike, O. E., Eze, C., & Emmanuel, E. I. (2022c, January). A UX 3-Factor Hierarchical Model for Understanding, Designing and Evaluating the UX of Software Products. In 2022 30th Southern African Universities Power Engineering Conference (SAUPEC) (pp. 1-7). IEEE.

Mkpojiogu, E.O.C, Hussain, A., & Agbudu, M.O. (2021). Security issues in the use of mobile educational apps: a review. International Journal of Interactive Mobile Technologies, 15(6), 124-137.

Nadzir, M., Hussain, A., Mkpojiogu, E.O.C., Faromiki, J.O., & Abdusalam, E.M.A. (2019a). The effectiveness and efficiency of a GPS route and voice navigation app, Inter. J. of Innov. Techn. and Explor. Engin., 8 (8S), 425-427.

Nadzir, M., Hussain, A., Mkpojiogu, E.O.C., Adetunmbi, S., & Hassooni, M.N. (2019b). Assessing the comfort in use of a flipboard mobile news magazine app. International Journal of Innov Techno and Explor. Engin., 8(8S), 428-430.

Oliver, R. (1997). Satisfaction: a behavioral perspective on the consumer. McGraw-Hill Series in Marketing, New York, USA: McGraw-Hill.

Oliver, R.L. (1977). Effect of expectation and disconfirmation on post-exposure product evaluations – an alternative interpretation. Journal of Applied Psychology 62(4), 480.

Olsson, T. (2012). User expectations and experiences of mobile augmented reality services. Tampere University of Technology, Tampere.

Partala, T., & Kallinen, A. (2012). Understanding the most satisfying and unsatisfying user experiences: Emotions, psychological needs, and context. Interacting with computers, 24(1), 25-34.

Partala, T., & Surakka, V. (2003). Pupil size variation as an indication of affective processing. International journal of human-computer studies, 59(1), 185-198.

Partala, T., & Surakka, V. (2004). The effects of affective interventions in human–computer interaction. Interacting with computers, 16(2), 295-309.

Partala, T., Surakka, V., & Vanhala, T. (2006). Real-time estimation of emotional experiences from facial expressions. Interacting with Computers,18(2), 208-226.

Picard, R.W. (1997). Affective Computing. MIT Press.

Raita, E., & Oulasvirta, A. (2011.). Too good to be bad: Favorable product expectations boost subjective usability ratings. Interacting with Computers 23, 363-371.

Rezaei, P.P. (2015). User experience studies of personal cloud storage services. Masters Thesis, Tampere University of Technology, Tampere.

Ryan, R. M., & Deci, E. L. (2000). Self-determination theory and the facilitation of intrinsic motivation, social development, and well-being. American psychologist, 55(1), 68.

Ryan, R.M. & Deci, E.L. (2017). Self-Determination Theory: Basic Psychological Needs in Motivation, Development, and Wellness. New York: Guilford Publishing

Sheldon, K. M., Elliot, A. J., Kim, Y., & Kasser, T. (2001). What is satisfying about satisfying events? Testing 10 candidate psychological needs. Journal of personality and social psychology, 80(2), 325.

Soliman, H.M. (1970). Motivation-hygiene theory of job attitudes: an empirical investigation and an attempt to reconcile both the one- and two-factor theories of job attitudes. Journal of Applied Psychology, 54, 452- 461.

Swan, J.E., & Combs, L.J. (1976). Product performance and consumer satisfaction: a new concept. J. Market, 40, 25-33.

Tuch, A. N., Roth, S. P., Hornbæk, K., Opwis, K., & Bargas-¬-Avila, J. A. (2012). Is beautiful really usable? Toward understanding the relation between usability, aesthetics, and affect in HCI. Comp in Hum. Behav., 28(5), 1596–1607.

Vargo, S.L., Nagao, K., He, Y., & Morgan, F.W. (2007). Satisfiers, dissatisfiers, criticals and neutrals: a review of their relative effects on customer (dis)satisfaction. Academy of Marketing Science Review, 11(2).

Wright, P., Wallace, J., McCarthy, J. (2008). Aesthetics and experience-centered design. Trans on CHI, 15(4), 21.

Watson, D., Clark, L. A., & Tellegen, A. (1988). Development and validation of brief measures of positive and negative affect: the PANAS scales. Journal of personality and social psychology, 54(6), 1063.

Yogasara, T., Popovic, V., Kraal, B., Camorro-Koc, M. (2011). General characteristics of anticipated user experience (AUX) with interactive products, Proceedings of IASDR'11, (pp. 1-11)

Zeithaml, V.A., Bitner, M.J., Gremler, D.D. (2002). Services marketing, integrating customer focus across the firm, (p. 688), McGraw-Hill

Zhang, P. & von Dran, G.M. (2000). Satisfiers and dissatisfiers: a two-factor model for website design and evaluation. Journal of the American Society for Information Science 51(14), 1253-1268.

A FRAMEWORK FOR ETHICS EDUCATION IN PERSUASIVE UX DESIGN

Sanju Ahuja and Jyoti Kumar
Indian Institute of Technology Delhi, India

ABSTRACT

The use of persuasion has become ubiquitous in interactive systems with the intent of increasing revenue, gathering user information and maximizing user engagement. However, it has been argued that users' autonomy is an ethical concern within persuasive UX design. This paper argues that there is a need to integrate ethics education within UX pedagogy and practice. Focusing on the topic of 'persuasive UX design', the authors test a framework to educate design students about the ethics of persuasion from a user autonomy perspective. We introduced autonomy related ethical considerations to a graduate user experience class of 22 students. Through a pre/post activity, we show that the introduction of these ethical considerations increased students' critical attitudes towards persuasive designs. We also conducted in-depth qualitative interviews with five students to understand students' experiences of ethics education and its impact on their ethics understanding. Through these interviews, we identified the needs and gaps in ethics education, including the difficulties which design students face to understand and incorporate ethics in their design process. Based on the findings from this study, we discuss future directions for integrating ethics education in user experience design.

KEYWORDS

Persuasive Technology, User Experience Design, Ethics, Autonomy, Design Education, Ethics Education

1. INTRODUCTION

Persuasive technologies refer to interactive computing systems designed to influence people's attitudes and behavior (Fogg 2002). Recent years have seen the emergence of 'dark' persuasive strategies, also known as 'dark patterns' (Brignull 2010). The term dark patterns refers to interface designs which intend to manipulate or coerce users into acting in ways not desired by them or not in their best interests. Dark patterns are widely used in interaction design and have been systematically identified in different contexts such as e-commerce, games and privacy management (Mathur et al. 2021). The widespread use of dark patterns and their potential harms have led to significant criticism. Brignull (2010) created a 'Hall of Shame' to criticize the use of dark patterns by various technology companies. On social media forums, dark patterns have been met with public condemnation (Gray et al. 2020). Dark patterns have also received the attention of policymakers, especially in privacy contexts, with several ongoing attempts to regulate them (Warner & Fischer 2019). In addition, it been argued that there is a need to better educate designers about the ethical aspects of persuasive design. Gray et al. (2018) argued that to address the problem of dark patterns, there is a need to integrate ethics education within UX pedagogy and practice. However, there are few reports of integrating persuasive design ethics within design education courses in literature.

To address this gap, we tested an educational framework for persuasive UX design ethics at our university. We introduced an autonomy centric ethics framework within a graduate user experience class. We investigated the impact of this framework on students' critical attitudes towards persuasive designs through an in-class pre/post activity. We then conducted in-depth qualitative interviews with five students to understand the impact of ethics education, and to identify needs and gaps which further need to be addressed. Our findings suggest that this ethics framework may enhance students' criticality of persuasive UX design. The findings from the interviews suggest that ethics education is necessary to create a space of awareness and articulation of ethical concerns. It also promotes ethics understanding as well as ethical reflection. However, we observed tensions between students' needs as 'designers' to create the most effective designs, and their developing ethical inclinations provoked by the class. Through these observations, we provide future directions for integrating ethics education in university-level interaction design curriculums.

2. ETHICS OF PERSUASIVE UX DESIGN

Persuasive design is an important aspect of UX design, and is often taught within interaction design courses. Various theories of persuasion aid designers in influencing user decision making and affecting behavior change (Fogg 2009; Oinas-Kukkonen & Harjumaa 2009). However, ethical concerns have also emerged. Berdichevsky and Neuenschwander (1999) argued that persuasion should only be used to promote ethical outcomes, and should respect the autonomy of the individual. Fogg (2002) raised concerns about persuasive strategies such as using emotions, deception, coercion, conditioning and surveillance. Verbeek (2009) argued that ambient intelligence creates radically new experiences of persuasive design, which can encroach greatly on our everyday activities and our choice processes. Ahuja and Kumar (2020) outlined the possible degrees of autonomy harms inherent within the design of surveillance based persuasive technologies.

However, even though autonomy has been identified as an important lens with which to evaluate persuasive designs, it is not always clear how each persuasive design impacts (enhances or undermines) the autonomy of users. Such an assessment requires a careful normative consideration of the context, the users the methods, the intentions and the outcomes of persuasion (Fogg 2002). Therefore, there is a need to sensitize designers towards ethical concerns as a part of their education, and guide them to be more adept at making such normative evaluations. In educational contexts, Fiesler et al. (2020) report university courses which introduce students to ethics in technology design and to topics such as ethical theories, value-sensitive design and dark patterns. However, these courses do not include in-depth ethical perspectives on 'persuasive UX design' from the perspective of users' autonomy. The considerations of autonomy have not been sufficiently developed in design literature and therefore have not yet been integrated within design education.

3. AUTONOMY CENTRIC ETHICS FRAMEWORK

Individual autonomy is understood in philosophical literature as an individual's right to self-governance (Buss & Westlund 2018). It is constituted by the freedom to be the person one wants to be and to pursue one's goals without unjustifiable hindrances or interferences (Roskies 2021). Mathur et al. (2021) argued that within interaction design, the autonomy perspective is underdeveloped, appearing to label all interventions into decision making as dark. On the other hand, within the field of behavioral economics, there is significant literature which has developed this perspective. In a recent review, Vugts et al. (2020) identified that within nudge literature, at least three distinct conceptualizations of autonomy were at play within the ethics debate: agency, freedom of choice and self-constitution. The authors argued that these conceptualizations were distinct not only in their interpretations, but also their normative implications in different contexts.

Ahuja and Kumar (2022) expanded upon the work of Vugts et al. (2020) and proposed five distinct conceptualizations of autonomy for the normative evaluation of human computer interactions. These are *agency, freedom of choice, control, independence* and *authenticity*. The conceptualization of *agency* concerns an individual's psychological capacity or competence to choose and decide (Friedrich et al. 2018; Vugts et al. 2020). It involves the ability to reason based on information, in accordance with one's preferences and goals. Agency is threatened by deceptive and manipulative persuasive designs. The conceptualization of *freedom* concerns the availability of choices or options (Vugts et al. 2020). Freedom of a user is violated when their choices are restricted, however, freedom also means that the user has practical, and not just a theoretical accessibility of relevant choices (Hansen & Jespersen 2013). Threats to freedom also emerge from pressure tactics such as fear, pressure and coercion (Brehm 1966). The conceptualization of *control* signifies that a user has the opportunity to consent to an interactive system's actions or system behaviors. Loss of control often manifests in the form of non-transparent automatic behaviors of the system, such as automatic updates or background data processing (Gray et al. 2020). Autonomy in the sense of *independence* is grounded in the notion of non-reliance. This conceptualization of autonomy represents that a user is able to self-regulate. Independence implies absence of any compulsions and dependencies, such as those created by games (Lewis 2014). The conceptualization of *authenticity* requires a person to act for reasons grounded in her authentic self, reasons which can be considered her 'own' (Betzler 2009). Ethical concerns about authenticity have been discussed significantly in relation to neurotechnology, however other non-invasive technologies such as marketing have also been argued to pose threats to authenticity (Burwell et al. 2017).

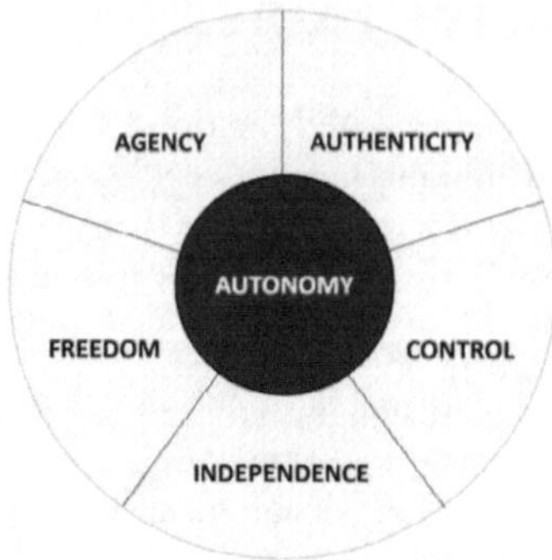

Figure 1. Ethical Considerations from the Perspective of Users' Autonomy (Ahuja and Kumar 2022)

Within persuasive UX design literature, the perspective of autonomy has not been developed and the theoretical underpinnings of ethical concerns have not been articulated. Wherever autonomy concerns have been discussed, they have been raised under the terminology of 'manipulation', 'deception' and 'coercion' (Mathur et al. 2021; Susser et al. 2019). These terminologies often accurately describe ethical concerns with dark patterns, however, ethical concerns such as technology addiction, and continued reliance on technology (the *independence* conceptualization), or *authenticity* concerns, are not very well captured. The aim of this framework is to inculcate in students a holistic understanding of autonomy as an ethical consideration, and to broaden the sphere of design responsibility. This framework can situate within a normative lens a wide range of ethical concerns which have previously not received sufficient attention within the autonomy perspective.

4. PEDAGOGICAL APPROACH

This study was conducted within a virtually running user experience design course at our university. The course is primarily taken by graduate students in Design, however it is open for other students as an elective. As part of the course curriculum, the students are exposed to the persuasive design process within UX design. Concepts of persuasion are introduced through Cialdini's (2007) six principles of persuasion. This is followed by an introduction to cognitive biases, and a detailed discussion on biases such as framing, priming and anchoring (Tversky & Kahneman 1974). The students are encouraged to look up the several documented biases in literature. The course is evaluated only through assignments, activities, and a reflective journal, without any formal exams. The course overview is presented in Figure 2.

For this study, ethical considerations were explicitly introduced into this course after the students were introduced to persuasive design and had already completed an assignment to design a persuasive e-commerce website. The ethics discussions were introduced within two sessions of 1.5 hours each. We first introduced the students to the term dark patterns and familiarized them with some dark pattern terminologies in e-commerce, games and privacy management. We also introduced students to examples of persuasive designs which could not be intuitively construed as 'dark' such as search order effects, one-click shopping and step counting features in m-health apps. The purpose of these examples was to introduce a balanced perspective on persuasive design, and indicate that several applications lied in a gray zone which could not be immediately dismissed as dark. Then we introduced the concept of macrosuasion or macro-persuasion (Fogg 2002; Rogers et al. 2020). We wanted to help students understand how persuasive designs may work cumulatively to serve an underlying intent geared towards a particular form of behavior change (Westin & Chiasson 2021). We then introduced individual autonomy as an ethical consideration. At this stage, we only introduced students to the broad definition of autonomy (Buss & Westlund 2018; Roskies 2021).

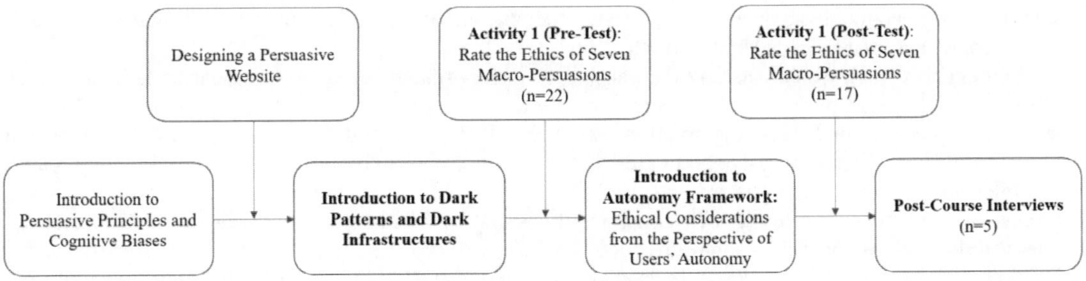

Figure 2. Course Overview of Relevant Contents

4.1 Activity 1: Evaluation of Ethics

Before the introduction of autonomy conceptualizations from within the framework, we sought to capture students' evaluations of ethics. Therefore, we conducted an activity in which we asked students to evaluate seven different examples of macro-persuasions. We chose macro-persuasions for this study because they each capture a wide range of autonomy concerns. We first discussed in class the potential persuasive designs which facilitated each of these macro-persuasions (Table 1). Then the students were asked to evaluate how ethical these macro-persuasions were on a scale of 1 (Not at all) to 5 (Very much) in a Google form.

Table 1. Macro-Persuasions Evaluated in Activity 1

Macro-Persuasion	Persuasive Designs which Facilitate the Macro-Persuasion
Digital Privacy Decision Making	Features designed to maximize data collection, such as cookie banner design, privacy unfriendly defaults, restricted access to websites, forced registrations, timing of consent
E-Commerce Discounting	Features designed to drive up the perception of value in e-commerce, such as deals, flash sales, offers, cashbacks, limited discounts, heavy discounts, urgency and scarcity
Digital Content Algorithms	Presence of fake and exaggerated news, amplification of polarized content, likes / shares driven amplification of content, personalized targeting of vulnerable populations
User Engagement Through Interruptions	Nagging, pestering or interruptive features such as advertisements, popups, notifications, spam messages, emails and robocalls
Asymmetric User Effort	Digital choice architectures with disbalanced effort to access choices, such as flight booking vs. cancellations, payments vs. refunds, ordering vs. returning, subscription vs. cancellation, complicated IVRs, chatbot or customer complaint processes
Digital Addiction	Features designed to drive or exploit obsessive / compulsive engagement in games or social media, such as grinding, streaks, likes, shares, rewards and punishments
Health Monitoring	Step counting, heart rate monitoring, activity logging, sleep monitoring, weight and calorie management, linking of health monitoring to authoritative databases (school, employer, insurance, government)

This activity was followed by an introduction to the autonomy framework. We introduced students to autonomy as an ethical consideration and to the concept of 'conceptualizations', i.e., how autonomy can have different meanings and be experienced in its different 'senses'. We showed how different persuasive strategies impacted autonomy in a different 'sense', such as the difference between having limited choices and being manipulated into making certain choices. The purpose of this framework was to broaden students' understanding of autonomy as an ethical value, and introduce relatively novel perspectives such as control, independence and authenticity. After this introduction to the framework, students were again asked to evaluate the ethics of the macro-persuasions in Table 1. We hypothesized that the students would become more critical of the same macro-persuasions after being exposed to a broadened perspective on autonomy.

4.2 Student Interviews

Post the course, we interviewed five students on a voluntary basis to understand their experience of the class and their takeaways. Three of the interview participants identified as male and two identified as female. The mean age of the participants was 26. The interviews were audio recorded with the participants' consent. Four interviews were conducted in-person and one was conducted virtually. The interviews lasted an average of 1 hour each, with a total recorded audio of 4 h 54 m.

We began the interview by asking the participant if they remembered anything particular from the class. We asked if they had previously been aware of the dark designs that were discussed. We asked about the examples of persuasions which they found most unethical. We probed the participants on their perspective of ethics, by asking which persuasive strategies they would not personally design. We occasionally brought up examples of persuasive designs such as infinite scroll, cookie banner, games, and interruptive ads, to understand how students came to their ethics judgments. We probed the participants on their sense of design responsibility, gathering their perspective on how ethical responsibility should be shared between the designer and the user. Then, we sought feedback on the class itself, and probed their understanding of and perspective on the autonomy framework that was introduced in the class.

5. FINDINGS

5.1 Activity 1: Enhanced Critical Attitude

Through the analysis of Activity 1, we investigated the change in students' critical attitudes of seven macro-persuasions after being introduced to the autonomy centric framework. The activity was completed by 22 students in the pre-condition and 17 students in the post-condition, hence 5 students were excluded from the analysis. The mean age of the 17 students was 24.5 years (13 males and 4 females). The mean rating given by students to each macro-persuasion in the pre and post conditions is presented in Table 2. We found significant overall reduction in the mean rating ($p<0.05$, one-tailed paired t-test). Among individual scores of seven macro-persuasions, we found significant reduction in the mean for two cases (*). In the other five cases, a statistically non-significant reduction of the mean was observed.

Table 2. Activity 1: Pre/Post Results

Macro-Persuasion	Pre-Score	Post-Score	P-value
Digital Privacy Decision Making	2.29	1.71	0.038*
E-Commerce Discounting	2.71	2.18	0.104
Digital Content Algorithms	2.12	1.29	0.024*
User Engagement Through Interruptions	2.18	1.94	0.281
Asymmetric User Effort	2.18	1.88	0.166
Digital Addiction	2.00	1.59	0.131
Health Monitoring	2.53	2.35	0.296
Overall Average	**2.29**	**1.85**	**0.047***

5.2 Student Experiences: Needs, Gaps and Outcomes

Figure 3 summarizes the findings from the interviews. We open coded the interview transcripts and identified the emerging themes in the discussion. We observed that students' experiences of the sessions belonged into three broad themes: *Need for Ethics Education, Expected Outcomes,* and *Gaps in Ethics Education.*

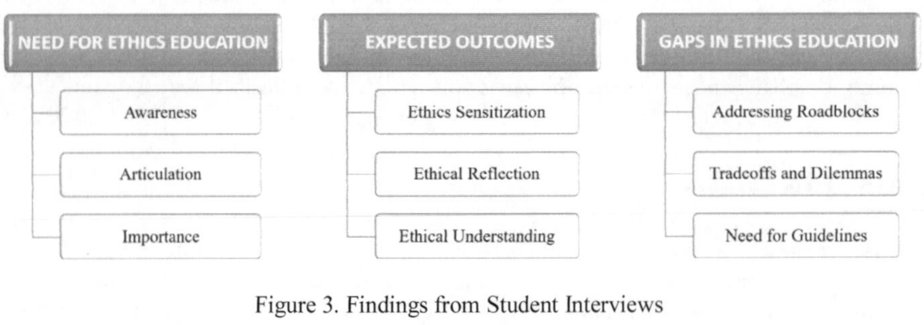

Figure 3. Findings from Student Interviews

5.2.1 Need for Ethics Education

Awareness: The introduction of ethical considerations served the purpose of creating awareness. Several participants remarked that they were not previously aware of these ethical issues. For instance, P1 said that 'many things were very new to me, I was aware about few things before, but I didn't know the science or the actual strategy'. P2 mentioned that he was aware of ethical issues in AI and neuroscience but not in interface design. P4 and P5 found the knowledge about dark patterns novel. P5 also remarked that earlier she used to ignore things like terms and conditions, but now she realizes that it's 'purposely designed like this'.

Articulation: The discussion on ethics created a space for students to articulate their concerns. P2 mentioned that he earlier had doubts such as 'why are we persuading people' and 'why do we want to get more people if they don't want'. P3 said that 'we all know but never discuss, sometimes you don't even bother, because these are things that are so frequently happening'. The students were often passively aware of ethical issues but did not ponder over them. P4 mentioned that the examples discussed in the class were 'very much in tandem with what I see in real life'. Students also discovered a frame to describe their own experiences. P2 discussed his past game addiction and P5 mentioned her sister's Snapchat streak addiction. P5 also described how in the past she felt addicted to Instagram, where her finger automatically kept going to the app location on her phone screen, even when the app was no longer there. She described the realization as scary.

Importance: We also observed that students perceived value in ethics education. P1 said that teaching ethics in the UX class 'made a lot of sense' and he thought that 'ethics must be taught in every design course'. P4 said that the course can act as a 'bible' for ethics. P5 said, 'I feel as students we should be taught about the other aspects, like we are doing certain things, okay the industry is demanding certain things, but is it ethical, I mean that thought provoking at least should be there'. She felt that 'if collectively there are students learning this thing in education system, because these students go in industry, and they build careers or they start companies, and I'm sure they would kind of implement it, so the change can start from there where it is taught to us, and not just persuading people to perform in a certain way, that can be a start'.

5.2.2 Expected Outcomes

Ethics Sensitization: Students appeared to develop a sense of responsibility after the session. P1 said that 'now I have to think a lot and plan a lot to implement any persuasion technique, I need to be more holistic in a way, basically I really don't want to violate the fundamental rights of people'. P2 said that he wants his design to be inclusive. P3 believed that design responsibility is shared. She said, 'being a designer I would definitely want that my app is used, that means it has great experience and great UI, but then it's harming the user, so it is the designer's responsibility to understand that the user is being harmed and then you provide those limitations, and for the user it is to use those features which are there.' P5 said that after the sessions, she tried to incorporate concepts from the class into her final project as part of the course.

Ethical Reflection: The interviews indicated that the session introduced ethical reflection within the design process of students. P1 said that the session 'was not just knowledge, it was good reflection' and it 'took away that excitement' about persuading people. P3 said that 'every decision, every click that I would make in that application, there would be a constant reflection on what would it do, is it asking for data, is it asking for something which is not required, every decision every click would be conscious'. P5 said that when ethical concerns come into play, she needs to be able to take a step back. With regards to her final project, she said 'after the session a lot of questioning started happening that what I am doing, is it okay if I'm doing like this, will it be overwhelming for the user or will the user not even realize that they are being taken somewhere'.

Ethical Understanding: The session helped students develop their own perspectives and understanding of ethics. Several students indicated examples for the kinds of designs they find unethical, and they would personally not use in their design activity, such as fake discounts (P3), non-consensual data extraction (P3, P5), dishonest information (P4), mindlessly addictive streak features (P5) and decoy effects (P5). Students also discussed their strategic approach towards ethical design. P1 said that he would 'respect people's boundaries', P3 said that she would try to make persuasion beneficial for users, and persuade with transparency. P4 said that he would use 'consensual roadblocks' in his design.

5.2.3 Gaps in Ethics Education

Addressing Roadblocks: We observed that several students imagined themselves in future corporate roles where they may not have complete control over their design outcomes. Therefore, they might not always find it practically possible to be as ethical as possible. P1 said, 'if I'll be working for a company then I believe things won't be in my hand completely'. P4 said that ethics is a 'guilty pleasure', and might be incompatible with working in a company. He also said that in some cases design responsibility is 'not the role of the designer because this decision would have come from somewhere else' and the designers 'would have some brief'. P5 was worried, 'when I'll be in the industry, then these corporations, they'll be asking me to do stuff and how much of a say will I have and it is scary that ultimately it might cost me my job if I say no to it'.

Tradeoffs and Dilemmas: The students expressed conflict in several situations about how to identify the boundaries between ethical and unethical design, how to make tradeoffs of ethics against profit, how to balance autonomy in relation to other values and how to prioritize different conceptualizations of autonomy when they diverged. P3 expressed that she was conflicted about health monitoring systems, because they help her but at the same time make her dependent. P4 expressed a form of empathy with designers or businesspersons trying to grow their companies and be profitable.

Need for Guidelines: Students expressed a desire for explicit guidelines, detailing how ethical design should be approached. P1's suggestion for guidelines stemmed from a difficulty to resolve ethical tradeoffs. However, the need for guidelines was also echoed by P4 who felt persuasion was essential to profit, and that guidelines and/or regulation was essential for fair play in the market.

6. DISCUSSION AND CONCLUSIONS

In Activity 1, we observed that introducing a detailed perspective on users' autonomy enhanced students' critical attitudes towards macro-persuasions. Since this study was conducted with a small sample size and with a limited time to introduce the framework, the effects were significant only for certain examples, even when the overall effects were significant. However, partial results are encouraging towards the usefulness of introducing a detailed perspective of autonomy for the normative evaluation of persuasive designs. The framework introduces conceptualizations of autonomy which are not intuitively compatible with the current understanding of design ethics and design responsibility, such as the conceptualizations of authenticity and independence. We argue that due to the inevitable impact of persuasive design on users' autonomy in these diverse 'senses', there is a need to expand the sphere of design responsibility. The framework integrates a broader and more holistic range of autonomy concerns within design education.

In student interviews, we observed a perception that being ethical is too idealized, that it is not compatible with profit making. Students appeared to perceive their future selves as not being in control of their design activity. They referred to being treated as a 'tool' to fulfill the ends of business stakeholders. One of the participants also sympathized with designers' need to make profit in a competitive business. Therefore, we observed a false dichotomy between ethics and profit, where students come to believe that ethical design is incompatible with profit. We argue that there is a strong need to address this conflict, for ethics education to be effective. We also observed a call for guidelines. In several cases, students were genuinely unable to make ethical tradeoffs, such as in the case of infinite scroll. In this case, students were conflicted on whether such a feature is ethical, because it is enjoyable to a portion of users, whereas a portion of users also tend to lose self-control, and hence it leads to compulsive or obsessive engagement in some cases. The students also desired some guidelines so that all companies have to play by the same rules, and this observation was related to the earlier observation of students perceiving some incompatibility between ethics and profit.

Overall, the results of this study were encouraging. The introduction of ethics content within an interaction design class fulfills a number of students' needs. It creates much needed pragmatic awareness about dark designs, and creates a space to articulate ethical concerns rooted in existing ethical intuitions and personal experiences. The students themselves acknowledge the need and find value in such education. The paper suggests that with further improvement based on the feedback, this autonomy framework can be used to sensitize students towards ethical concerns in persuasive UX design in educational contexts.

REFERENCES

Ahuja, S. and Kumar, J., 2020. Surveillance based Persuasion: The Good, The Bad and The Ugly. *In Proceedings of the 4th International Conference on Computer-Human Interaction Research and Applications (CHIRA '20).* Budapest (online), Hungary, pp. 120-127.

Ahuja, S. and Kumar, J., 2022. Assistant or Master: Envisioning the User Autonomy Implications of Virtual Assistants. *In 4th Conference on Conversational User Interfaces (CUI '22).* Glasgow, United Kingdom.

Berdichevsky, D. and Neuenschwander, E., 1999. Toward an ethics of persuasive technology. *Communications of the ACM,* Vol. 42, No. 5, pp. 51-58.

Betzler, M., 2009. Authenticity and self-governance. *In Emotions, ethics, and authenticity*, ed. Mikko Salmela and Verena Mayer, pp. 51–68. John Benjamins Publishing Company.

Brehm, J.W., 1966. *A theory of psychological reactance.* Academic Press.

Brignull, H., 2010. 'What are dark patterns?', viewed 20 May, 2022, <https://www.darkpatterns.org/>.

Burwell, S. et al, 2017. Ethical aspects of brain computer interfaces: a scoping review. *BMC Medical Ethics*, Vol. 18, Art. 60, pp. 1-11.

Buss, S. and Westlund, A., 2018. Personal Autonomy. *The Stanford Encyclopedia of Philosophy (Spring 2018 Edition)*, Edward N. Zalta (ed.). <https://plato.stanford.edu/archives/spr2018/entries/personal-autonomy/>

Cialdini, R.B., 2007. *Influence: The Psychology of Persuasion.* Collins, New York.

Fiesler, C. et al, 2020. What Do We Teach When We Teach Tech Ethics? A Syllabi Analysis. *In Proceedings of the 51st ACM Technical Symposium on Computer Science Education.* ACM, New York, pp. 289–295.

Fogg, B.J., 2002. *Persuasive technology: using computers to change what we think and do.* Morgan Kaufmann Publishers.

Fogg, B.J., 2009. A Behavior Model for Persuasive Design. *In Proceedings of the 4th International Conference on Persuasive Technology (Persuasive '09).* ACM, New York, Art. 40, pp. 1–7.

Friedrich, O. et al, 2018. An analysis of the impact of brain-computer interfaces on autonomy. *Neuroethics*, Vol. 14, pp. 17-29.

Gray, C.M. et al, 2018. The Dark (Patterns) Side of UX Design. *In CHI Conference on Human Factors in Computing Systems (CHI '18).* Montreal, QC, Canada.

Gray, C.M. et al, 2020. What Kind of Work Do "Asshole Designers" Create? Describing Properties of Ethical Concern on Reddit. *In ACM Designing Interactive Systems Conference (DIS '20).* Eindhoven, Netherlands.

Hansen, P.G. and Jespersen, A.M., 2013. Nudge and the manipulation of choice: A framework for the responsible use of the nudge approach to behaviour change in public policy. *European Journal of Risk Regulation*, Vol. 1, pp. 3-28.

Lewis, C., 2014. *Irresistible Apps: Motivational Design Patterns for Apps, Games, and Web-based Communities.* Apress.

Mathur, A. et al, 2021. What Makes a Dark Pattern...Dark?: Design Attributes, Normative Considerations, and Measurement Methods. *In CHI Conference on Human Factors in Computing Systems (CHI '21).* Yokohama, Japan.

Oinas-Kukkonen, H. and Harjumaa, M., 2009. Persuasive Systems Design: Key Issues, Process Model, and System Features. *Communications of the Association for Information Systems*, Vol. 24, Art. 28, pp. 485-500.

Rogers et al, 2020. The Dark Side of Interaction Design. *In CHI Conference on Human Factors in Computing Systems (CHI '20).* Honululu, USA.

Roskies, A., 2021. Neuroethics. *The Stanford Encyclopedia of Philosophy (Spring 2021 Edition)*, Edward N. Zalta (ed.). <https://plato.stanford.edu/archives/spr2021/entries/neuroethics/>

Susser, D. et al, 2019. Technology, autonomy and manipulation. *Internet Policy Review*, Vol. 8, No. 2, pp. 1–22.

Tversky, A. and Kahneman, D., 1974. Judgment under uncertainty: heuristics and biases. *Science*, Vol. 185, No. 4157, pp. 1124-1131.

Warner, M. and Fischer, D., 2019. 'Senators Introduce Bipartisan Legislation to Ban Manipulative Dark Patterns', viewed 20 May, 2022, <https://www.fischer.senate.gov/public/index.cfm/2019/4/senators-introduce-bipartisan-legislation-to-ban-manipulative-dark-patterns>

Verbeek, P.P., 2009. Ambient Intelligence and Persuasive Technology: The Blurring Boundaries Between Human and Technology. *Nanoethics*, Vol 3, No. 3, pp. 231-242.

Vugts, A. et al, 2020. How autonomy is understood in discussions on the ethics of nudging. *Behavioural Public Policy*, Vol. 4, No. 1, pp. 108-123.

Westin, F. and Chiasson, S., 2021. "It's So Difficult to Sever that Connection": The Role of FoMO in Users' Reluctant Privacy Behaviours. *In CHI Conference on Human Factors in Computing Systems (CHI '21).* Yokohama, Japan.

CORPORATE DIGITAL RESPONSIBILITY AND ACCESSIBILITY IN DIGITAL SERVICES

Terhi Kärpänen
Laurea University of Applied Sciences, Ratatie 22, Vantaa, Finland
Estonian Business School, A.Lauteri 3, Tallinn, Estonia

ABSTRACT

Digitalisation and new digital services have brought new challenges for entrepreneurs. On the one hand, digital services must be accessible to all users, and on the other hand, in the near future, new legislation will bring new requirements to this field. The purpose of this paper was to understand the current state of knowledge on both accessibility requirements and legislation, and its position in the corporate digital responsibility (CDR) framework. This paper's topic is the multi-step approach. First, this paper reviews CDR from an accessibility perspective, gaining information on the previous CDR framework definitions. Second, it reports the results of an interview with Finnish micro-entrepreneurs on web accessibility in digital services' requirements. Finally, the results were discussed and an understanding was obtained regarding the role of accessibility in digital services in the CDR framework, and topics for further research were identified.

KEYWORDS

Accessibility, Digital Services, Accessibility Directives, CDR

1. INTRODUCTION

Digitalisation rapidly changes the services in a digital environment. At the same time importance of accessible digital services arise. Accessible digital services means that all people can use digital services properly and can understand them. In providing technology that supports accessibility elements, people can choose how to interact with the content and the process or they can choose how to access information (e.g. how to navigate through content with different strategies, access information in many ways and how to personalise the content properly) (Ali, AlBalushi & AlBadi 2017). On the other hand, corporate digital responsibility (CDR) plays a significant role in digi-tal services. Recently there has been discussion related to corporate digital trust and CDR, but there are very few definitions of the term (Herden et al. 2021; Albinson et al. 2019). CDR is defined as the set of shared values and norms that guides an organisation's operations with respect to the creation and operation of digital technology and data (Herden et al. 2021).

However, accessible digital services and their role in the CDR framework have not been investigated enough from the perspective of entrepreneurs. The research gap results from an insufficient understanding about entrepreneurs' knowledge about accessibility, its current and future legislation requirements and how entrepreneurs consider CDR in the decision-making process. New technologies and digital services offer many opportunities to utilise services 24/7. Digital solutions and services should be designed to work for all people whatever their hardware, software, language, location or ability (they should be accessible to people with a diverse range of hearing, movement, sight and cognitive ability). Digital service developers can avoid barriers by taking into account accessibility requirements, thus optimising the user experience (Ali et al. 2017). Accessibility can be viewed as the 'ability to access' and benefit from some system or entity. It supports social inclusion for people with disabilities as well as others, such as older people, people in rural areas and people in developing countries.

Recent studies have investigated CDR's role in artificial intelligence (AI) and data privacy fields (Ashok et al. 2021; Ayling & Chapman 2021; Liyanaarachchi et al. 2021; Elliott et al. 2021) but not its role regarding the requirements for accessible digital services. Only one survey, the Global Digital Inclusion survey (2017), explored by Christopher Joynson revealed important CDR factors regarding digital inclusion. One result pointed out the importance of digital accessibility, and the importance of designing digital services and goods accessible to all people. Different qualitative research studies have been conducted based on the accessibility of websites – in particular the challenges faced by senior users of websites (Burmeister 2010) web practitioners' thoughts about web accessibility (Farrelly 2011) and the web accessibility of CSR communications (Adelopo et al. 2012) – but more up-to-date research in terms of combining and understanding accessible digital services, CDR and decision-making challenges from the perspective of entrepreneurs. CDR has been investigated from the perspective of large companies (Jones & Comfort 2021). CDR research from the perspective of' SMEs' and micro-entrepreneurs' perspectives is missing. It should consider that SMEs and micro-entrepreneurs have digital services that are available for customers, and it would be interesting to understand how SME's and micro-entrepreneurs consider digital responsibility in digital service decision-making process.

The purpose of this paper was to understand the current state of knowledge on accessibility requirements, legislation and accessibility's position in the CDR framework. To increase understanding of this context, in-depth interviews were conducted with micro-entrepreneurs. Microenterprises are companies with fewer than ten employees and an annual turnover of not more than two million euros (European Commission 2021). Micro-entrepreneurs have many different roles in their business, and thus, they are usually holistically responsible for the decision-making process.

This paper's topic is the multi-step approach. First, I present the results from the existing framework of CDR, accessibility in digital services and legislation. Second, I present the results of qualitative research, based on in-depth interviews. Third, I discuss the results related to the theoretical contribution and provide future research suggestions.

2. ACCESSIBILITY'S ROLE IN THE CDR FRAMEWORK

Accessibility, part of digital services, and especially cognitive accessibility in this context means that digital services are simple, consistent and clear to use, providing understandable content, taking into account all users – not only people who have some disabilities or problems in using digital services (Ali et al. 2017). Nowadays, digital service creation includes many accessibility requirements that need to be considered in digital service design and creation. Some of the accessibility requirements are defined by country legislation. The UN Convention on the Rights of Persons with Disabilities (CRPD) recognises access to information and communication technologies, including the web, as a basic human right. The CRPD is a comprehensive human rights document that includes a direct reference to the rights of all people to have equal access to communications technology (CRPD 2016; W3C 2018). Currently, the Web Accessibility Directive of 2016 requires all public sector websites and applications in EU member states to implement, enforce and maintain a uniform set of accessibility standards. The rules laid down in the directive reflect the commission's ongoing work towards building a social and inclusive European 'Union of equality', wherein all Europeans can take a full and active part in the digital economy and society. The directive obliges websites and applications of public sector bodies (with a limited number of exceptions) to meet specific technical accessibility standards (WCAG 2.1.) (EU 2020). Each European country has formed its own legislation based on the directive.

In addition to this directive, there is a newer directive, the European Accessibility Act 2019 (EAA), which aims to improve the functioning of the internal market for accessible products and services by removing accessibility barriers from digital services. The EAA covers a wide range of products, services and functionalities which need to meet the specific technical and non-technical accessibility standards (Ministry of Social Affairs and Health 2021). The EAA requires that both the public and private sector actors guarantee the accessibility of certain products and services. In particular, this new legislation affects the digital services of SMEs. In Finland, the accessibility requirements will enter into legislation on 28 June 2022 (Ministry of Social Affairs and Health 2021). Thus, it is not yet explicit whether or not the coming national regulation will only cover SMEs or also micro-entrepreneurs' digital services in Finland. On the other hand, when legislation requirements are not definite for entrepreneurs, the question of social responsibility arises. How entrepreneurs – especially SMEs and micro-entrepreneurs – involve social and digital responsibility in decision-making and are aware of future legislation and accessibility requirements.

Corporate social responsibility (CSR) and digital transformation are the most important factors of global competitiveness in the modern world (Orbik & Zozuľaková 2019). Definitions of CSR cover various dimensions including economic development, ethical practices, environmental protection, stakeholder involvement, transparency, accountability, responsible behaviour, moral obligation, corporate responsiveness and CSR. CSR encompasses the economic, legal and ethical expectations that society has of organisations at a given point in time. In the digital environment, there is a growing demand to understand corporate responsibility towards digital services (Rahman 2011; Schwartz & Carroll 2003; Hayat & Orsagh 2015). CSR is a broad concept. It can be seen and formulated in different ways depending on the size of the company and industry.

According to Lobschat et al. (2021) CDR is a subset of CSR, that relates to 'companies' responsibilities in the digital environment. CDR provides organizations with a set of shared values and norms to guide their operations with respect to the creation and use of technology and data. In the digital environment, there can be different processes which need companies' digital responsibility (e.g. the creation of technology and data capture, operation and decision-making, inspection and impact assessment, and the refinement of technology and data) (Lobschat et al. 2021). One definition of CDR is that is an extension of a firm's responsibilities that considers the ethical opportunities and challenges of digitalisation (Herdet et al. 2021). CDR becomes a new way for companies to achieve global competitiveness (Schwartz & Carroll 2003). Based on the study by Lobschat et al. 2021, CDR should be seen as a separate field from CSR, also by stakeholders (i.e. organisations, individual actors and different actors from the government, legal or institutional sides and technological actors) and four life cycles linked to data, technology and digital services. CDR culture exists in three different layers: shared values, specific norms, artefacts and behaviours. Many factors can influence CDR culture, such as public opinions, legal requirements and customer factors (Lobschat et al. 2021). Herden et al. 2021, stated different criteria and they use the ESG model as framework for CDR topics. The ESG model is divided into three categories or domains: the environmental, social and governance domains. The CDR topics have been categorised according to the ESG framework, for example, the environmental domain includes digital waste, the social domain includes digital cohesion and the governance domain includes data privacy related topics (Herden et al. 2021). Digital inclusion involves aspects as digital literacy, access to public and privacy services, participation, involves public policies and other social aspects, beyond accessibility to resources and services, is part of ESG's social category. Other topics in this category are, for example, digital cohesion, digital influence and digital freedom. The provision of digital services should not discriminate in regard to the users and should offer accessible services for all users. The governance domain also includes topics which can be seen as enhancing accessibility in digital services, such as data responsibility and data usage (Herden et al. 2021).

New technologies bring a new set of responsibilities for companies. At the same time, new regulations and legislations will be legislated for digital services. Many regulations have an impact on entrepreneurs' decision-making in the digital service environment. For example, the European Union's General Data Protection Regulation (GDPR) is an important legal framework for designing corporation-specific norms for CDR (Lobschat et al. 2021). Accessibility directives and regulations also bring requirements for digital service design. Organisations should include ethical considerations as criteria for their software selection when taking new digital services into use. Legal frameworks provide important guidelines (e.g. the GDPR), but a corporation needs specific engagement with CDR to develop a culture and norms that guide corporate behaviour across levels (Lobschat et al. 2021). Although legislation would define the digital service usage and design, and set the requirements, how much effort entrepreneurs will put into following the legislation has not been investigated enough and it is not known how they get the knowledge of how to implement the legislation requirements. The WCAG 2.1 requirements (W3C 2018) improve not only web accessibility but also other important functionalities of digital services, such as search engine optimisation, which is a competitive advantage for entrepreneurs.

3. METHODS

It is important to tailor knowledge about how entrepreneurs are designing digital services and how they consider accessibility in their decision-making. This qualitative research was designed to explore micro-entrepreneurs' perceptions and understanding of issues related to accessibility in digital services.

The qualitative research focused on the field of accessible digital services and the decision-making process from micro-entrepreneurs' perspective in Finland. The qualitative study aimed to

- describe the current state of knowledge and practices regarding the accessible digital services,
- examine the challenges they face when applying accessible digital services
- identify their understanding about current accessibility legislation

I conducted eight in-depth interviews with micro-entrepreneurs in order to solicit their experience and opinions regarding aspects of accessibility in digital services. I assured the participants of the confidentiality of the interviews to enable them to discuss sensitive or private information. All the interviewed entrepreneurs were locating in Finland.

The criteria for participating was that an interviewee needed to have digital services in use in his or her company and that the entrepreneurs should be responsible for digital service decision-making. The participants represented a variety of business types and they had different level of experiences with digital services. The interviews were semi-structured to allow for capturing comparison data. Demographic data were not collected from the participants. Instead of demographic data, data on experience as an entrepreneur in years, a description of the business area, business size and the current set of digital services were collected. The interviews were conducted between September and December 2021. The participants reported a range of types of digital services that they had in use (see Table 1).

Table 1. The participants' digital services

Participant	Business size (number of people)	Digital services in use
1	9	Website, Instagram
2	1	Website, webstore, Facebook, LinkedIn, YouTube, Instagram
3	1	Website, LinkedIn, Twitter, Facebook,
4	1	Instagram
5	1	Website, Facebook, Instagram
6	1	Webstore, Facebook
7	2	Website, Facebook, LinkedIn
8	1	Website, Facebook
		Website, LinkedIn

After the interview sessions, all the interviews were transcribed and analysed by using common themes. Each transcript was coded for different themes based upon the questions asked in the semi-structured interviews.

Two themes of interest found from interviews were:

1. the current state of knowledge and practices regarding accessible digital services and challenges
2. understanding current accessibility legislation

4. RESULTS

These sections present the results by themes and the characteristics of the research.

4.1 Knowledge about Accessibility in Digital Services and Challenges

Most of the interviewees understood that accessibility relates to finding information from digital services. Two interviewees (P2, P5) associated the term *accessibility* with clear and understandable digital services. Two interviewees (P5, P8) had the knowledge that accessibility in digital services is related to offering better services for people who has limitations in regard to using digital services (e.g. people with visual impairments). One interviewee (P1) stated that accessibility means having contact information available on a website. After the interviewee responses, I explained the meaning of web accessibility in the context of digital services in order for them to be able to understand the concepts.

When the interviewees gained an understanding of the accessibility concepts, they had to think how they considered accessibility elements in their digital services. All the interviewees mentioned that they have tried to build clear and simple websites, e-commerce stores and other digital services without knowing that these functions (being clear, understandable and easy to use) are part of accessible digital services. Five interviewees (P3, P5, P6, P7, P8) mentioned that they have focused on using more understandable language in the digital content. None of interviewees thought that people with visual limitations or other limitations would use their services by themselves or that they should consider these people when designing digital services.

The challenges in creating accessible digital services were diverse, but the main challenges were the lack of knowledge and resources, proper testing with users and the feeling that they do not need to have accessible digital services. One interviewee (P2) mentioned that he wanted to create simple digital services, but he was not sure if he has managed to do it so he was looking for help in evaluating the current digital services. Five of the interviewees (P1, P2, P5, P6, P7) mentioned that their digital services have been tested by family member, colleague or friend. Four of the interviewees (P4, P6, P7, P8) also tested the digital services themselves.

4.2 Understanding the Legislation

The knowledge about the legislations and directives in the digital environment was partial. During the interview, I asked about the interviewees' knowledge about the current legislation related to digital services, as well the factors that they need to consider when taking new digital services into use or updating the content to digital services. All the participants were familiar with the GDPR and what requirements it brings to entrepreneurs' digital services. Four interviewees (P2, P3, P6, P7) were complying with the requirements of the GDPR in their digital services, in terms of respecting the rights of consumers and informing customers about data usage in their digital services. Two interviewees (P2, P8) mentioned that they do not consider or apply any legal requirements in their digital services.

None of interviewees were familiar with the current Web Accessibility Directive or Finland's national legislation based on this directive. Some of the interviewees (P2, P4) had noticed that, in particular, the parties of public sector have done website renewal projects recently, but they did not understand why the renewals had been done. None of the interviewees were familiar with future preparation for legislation based on the EAA, and its requirements for SMEs.

5. DISCUSSIONS

The purpose of this paper was to understand the current state of knowledge of the accessibility requirements and legislation, and its position in the CDR framework. The other part of this paper revealed the results of qualitative research which aims to understand micro-entrepreneurs' knowledge about accessible digital services and the legislation based on digital services.

Based on the existing definitions and frameworks of CDR, accessibility in digital services can be seen as part of this framework. Using the ESG framework, accessibility's position falls under the 'social' category and under the 'governance' domain. Accessibility in digital services can be seen part of digital inclusion, which includes the availability and accessibility of digital technologies. It can be seen as part of fairness as all humans should be treated equally; it can also be seen as part of human–computer interaction in which people use digital services and interact with them. Companies should understand their responsibility to produce understandable digital services. If log-in or registration processes are not understandable, people do not know how companies are going to use their information.

The group of entrepreneurs who participated to interview were not aware of the accessibility requirements of digital services, the legislation or directives which are valid for the public sector and a specific group of private companies nor the EAA, which is based on the coming legislation for SMEs in the near future. However, the interviewees had sought to make their digital services simple and easy to use, and to use understandable language in their digital services without knowing that the above features are the features of accessible digital services. The most common reason for implementing and maintaining digital services is a lack of knowledge of how to make services accessible. In previous studies this lack of knowledge has been reported as one reason to not implement accessible services (Kärpänen 2021).

All of the interviewees were familiar with the GDPR, but some of them not followed the legislation requirements or thought them mandatory in their digital services. When legislation does not exist, its importance is not seen relevant in digital services' daily activities. The new European GDPR strengthens the rights of data subjects and enhances the obligations and responsibilities of those who collect, process and store personal data (Parlov et al. 2018). Based on ESG classification, the GDPR can be seen to belong to the 'governance' category in which there are most of the data privacy issues. To be able to understand GDPR requirements, the digital services should provide understandable instructions or clarifications for people. This is part of being accessible and especially part of cognitive accessibility features.

Future research should examine SMEs' awareness and corporate awareness of accessibility features and decision-making features. There is a need for a deeper understanding of accessibility in the planning of digital services and accessibility relation to CDR. Some country-specific research has conducted related to the GDPR (Parlov et al. 2018). Accessibility in digital services is not understand as well as the GDPR. It is recommended that more research by country level is conducted, especially now when the legislation based on the EAA is coming into effect for entrepreneurs. Another future research topic would be managerial decision-making features related to CDR. Digital services are changing rapidly, new technologies and services are popping up for customers and customer behaviour is changing constantly in the digital environment. CDR is wide framework and new CDR topics arise when new digital solutions come to the market.

6. CONCLUSIONS

As a conclusion, it should be emphasised that entrepreneurs should consider accessibility directives and legislation when designing digital services. Based on the results of the interviews, an understanding of the existing research was obtained, as well as an understanding of topics for further research on accessibility in digital services. The findings of this study lead to the following conclusions:

1) Accessibility in digital services should be seen as a part of the CDR framework. Legal requirements (e.g. the GDPR) influence CDR culture (e.g. the GDPR) (Lobschat et al. 2021). Accessibility directives and country-specific legislation are already valid in the public sector's digital services, and in the near future, the legislation will affect entrepreneurs.
2) There should be more information available for micro-entrepreneurs about how *accessibility in digital services* means can enhance their digital services. When they understand the benefits, more support is needed in order to be able to implement the requirements for a digital service's content and platform. This viewpoint must be taken into consideration when planning more research in this context.
3) There is a need for further research in this field among SMEs because the SMEs are part of the national legislation in EU countries. Digitalisation is shaping our digital services and providing more digital platforms, application and services. At the same time, we need to understand how to support companies of all sizes in understanding how to create accessible digital services and how digital responsibility in their decision-making can be a competitive advantage in their business. When they understand the benefits, more support is needed in order for them to be able to implement the requirements for digital services.

The roles of CDR and accessibility should be seen as the factors of corporate reputation, customer satisfaction and trust. Some studies related to this field have been conducted, and the results have revealed that customer satisfaction, trust and corporate reputation mediated the relationship between CSR and customer loyalty (Pitafi et al. 2020). Digital trust, digital responsibility and accessibility in digital services should be seen as companies' competitive advantage and just factors that need to be implemented based on legislation requirements.

REFERENCES

Adelopo, I. et al, 2012. *Determinants of web-accessibility of corporate social responsibility communications.* Journal of Global Responsibility, Vol. 3, Iss. 2, pp. 235-247.

Albinson, N. et al, 2019. *Building digital trust: technology can lead the way.* Deloitte, available at: www2.deloitte.com/content/dam/insights/us/articles/6320_Building-digital-trust/DI_Buildingdigital-trust.pdf (accessed 26 October 2021)

Ali, S., AlBalushi, T. and AlBadi, A. 2017. *Guidelines and deployment of accessibility-aware framework approach.* International Journal of Web Information Systems, 13(2), 114139.

Ashok, M. 2021. *Ethical framework for artificial intelligence and digital technologies.* International Journal of Information Management, 62, 102433. ISSN 0268-4012.

Ayling, J. and Chapman, A. 2021. *Putting AI ethics to work: are the tools fit for purpose?* AI Ethics.

Burmeister, O.K. 2010. *Websites for seniors: Cognitive accessibility*. International Journal of Emerging Technologies and Society, 8(2), pp. 99–113.

Council of the European Union 2010. Council Decision 2010/48/EC of 26 November 2009 concerning the conclusion, by the European Community, of the United Nations Convention on the Rights of Persons with Disabilities.

CRPD 2016. *Convention on the Rights of Persons with Disabilities.* Available at: https://www.un.org/development/desa/disabilities/convention-on-the-rights-of-persons-with-disabilities.html (accessed 24 October 2021).

Elliott, K. et al, 2021. *Towards an equitable digital society: Artificial intelligence (AI) and corporate digital responsibility (CDR).* Society, 14, pp. 1–10.

European commission. 2021.*Employment, Social Affairs & Inclusion. Supporting entrepreneurs and the self-employed – Microfinance.* Available at: https://ec.europa.eu/social/main.jsp?catId=952&intPageId=3510&langId=en (Accessed 11 November 2021).

European Commission 2020. Web accessibility. Available at: https://ec.europa.eu/digital-single-market/en/ web- accessibility (accessed 6 November 2021).

Farrelly, G. 2011. *Practitioner barriers to diffusion and implementation of web accessibility.* Technology and Disability, 23, 223-232.

Hayat, U. and Orsagh, M. 2015. *Environmental, Social and Governance Issues in Investing: A Guide for Investment Professionals*. CFA Institute, Charlottesville, VA, USA.

Herden, C. et al, 2021. *Corporate Digital Responsibility: New corporate responsibilities in the digital age.* Sustainability Management Forum Nachhaltigkeits Management Forum.

Jones, P. and Comfort, D. 2021. *Cameo corporate cases of digital technologies and digital responsibility.* International Journal of Management Cases. (In press.)

Joynson, C.H. 2018. *Corporate Digital Responsibility: Principles to Guide Progress.* Available at https://atos.net/en/blog /corporate-digital-responsibility-principles-guide-progress (accessed 11 November 2021).

Kärpänen, T. 2021. *A literature review on cognitive accessibility.* Stud Health Technol Inform, 282, pp. 259–270.

Liyanaarachchi, G. et al, 2021. *"Market-oriented corporate digital responsibility to manage data vulnerability in online banking"*, International Journal of Bank Marketing, Vol. 39 No. 4, pp. 571-591.

Lobschat, L. et al, 2021. *Corporate digital responsibility.* Journal of Business Research, 122(C), pp. 875–888.

Ministry of Social Affairs and Health 2021. *The European Accessibility Act*. Available at: https://stm.fi/en/the-european-accessibility-act (accessed 6 November 2021).

Orbik, Z. and Zozuľaková, V. 2019. *Corporate social and digital responsibility.* Management Systems in Production Engineering, 2(27), pp. 79–83.

Parlov, N. et al, 2018. *GDPR – impact of general data protection regulation on digital marketing.* ADRS Ann. Disaster Risk Sci., 2, pp. 105–116.

Pitafi, H. et al, 2020. *The impact of corporate social responsibility on customer loya*lty: The mediating role of corporate reputation, customer satisfaction, and trust. Sustainable Production and Consumption.

Rahman, S. 2011. *Evaluation of definitions: ten dimensions of corporate social responsibility.* Review of Business Research, pp. 166–176.

Schwartz, M. and Carroll, A.B. 2003. *Corporate social responsibility: A three-domain approach.* Business Ethics Quarterly, 13(4), pp. 503–530.

W3C 2018. *Web Content Accessibility Guidelines.* Available at: https://www.w3.org/standards/webdesign/accessibility (accessed 24 October 2021).

GENDER CLASSIFICATION USING SINGLE IMAGE PER PERSON

Rubata Riasat[1], Abdul Hannan Sadiq[2] and Faizan Ahmad[3]
[1]*Women University Swabi, Pakistan*
[2]*Comsats University Islamabad, Lahore, Pakistan*
[3]*Cardiff Metropolitan University, UK*

ABSTRACT

This paper presents a framework based on object appearance and shape based features to address gender classification problem through face image. Histogram of Oriented Gradients (HOG) based scheme is presented for gender classification having one frame/object for training. In presented scheme nearest neighbor based classifier Euclidean distance method is used for classification. Presented scheme's results have been compared in cross dataset environment with state-of-the-art various algebraic (PCA, LDA), geometric (Gabor Wavelets) and texture (LBP) based features. Experiments have been performed in two folds using FEI face dataset consisting of 99 objects each (Male and Female) having one frame/object. Experiment's results based on fold-2 are promising, indicating that HOG and the proposed ensemble framework have sufficient discriminative power for the gender classification problem with the accuracy of 91.41%. Current research findings include a claim that forehead, hair style, chin, ears and outer boundary of face having information about face shapes has significant importance in gender classification task.

KEYWORDS

Gender Classification, Cross Gender Effect, Gender Categorization

1. INTRODUCTION

Biometric identification has become a better method for classifying humans based on their physical appearance with a particular identity. In this field face processing and recognition is a key technology with a wide range of potential applications related to security and safety. As anti-terrorism has become a global issue so that surveillance is becoming more and more popular. That is why it is the most common system deployed in places under keen vigilance like elevators, banks, casinos, trade centers, and stadiums which performs passive identification unnoticed by the suspect. (Zhao et al., 2003; Abate et al., 2007) There exists significant cognitive evidence supporting that humans utilize information from various visual cues for face recognition. (Brigham, 1986; O'Toole et al., 1996) Other studies have shown that humans judge the gender of adults and children using feature sets derived from the appropriate face age category, rather than applying features derived from another age category or from a combination of age categories.

Current research efforts in this field involve developing more accurate and robust algorithms for face detection and recognition as well as to classify faces with respect to their gender, race, and age. That is non-intrusive and accurate because human facial images provide the demographic information, such as race, age and gender. Classifying people based on their gender would be sometimes complex and cannot be strategically standardized. If a prior knowledge of the gender of suspect is available then identification will be more efficient, and essentially narrow down the search space. There are certainly few statistically significant studies those have addressed this problem.

Figure-1 illustrates the general steps involved in proposed gender classification framework. It is been assume that, in fold-2, the faces have already been detected by some prior step. Initially pre-processing is applied to normalize the input face with respect to size, location, orientation, and lighting. Then, feature extraction is performed to represent the face by a compact and more discriminative set of features. Finally, a decision mechanism is employed (e.g., classifier) to identify the gender of the input face. The focus of current research is to investigate and compare the performance of proposed framework based on object appearance and shape based features for gender classification with others.

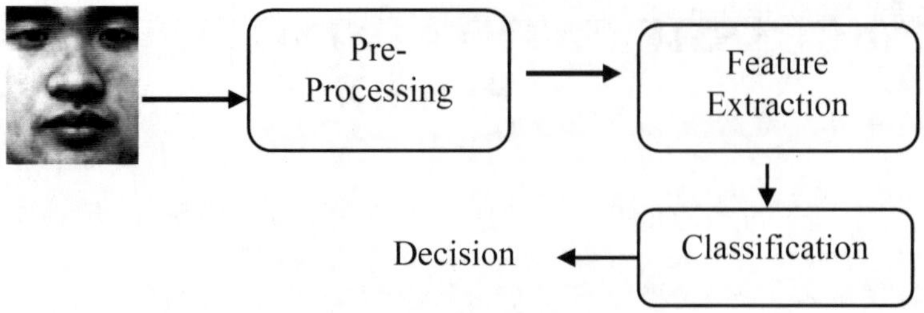

Figure 1. General steps in gender classification

Object appearance and shape based methods have gained much attention over holistic based methods in face based recognition community for their upholding invariance to geometric and photometric transformations. Histogram of Oriented Gradients (HOG) (Dalal & Triggs, 2005) is feature descriptors that count occurrences of gradient orientation in localized portions of an image. This method differs from other similar methods because computation is based on a dense grid of uniformly spaced cells and uses overlapping local contrast normalization to improve accuracy.

Gender recognition using face images is not fully discovered. Majority attempts have made for more than one training image per object. Another research (Canavan et al., 2007) reported recognition rate increased from 91% using a single frame to 100% using 7-frame fusion, under regular indoor lighting conditions and recognition rate increased from 63% using a single frame to 85% using 7-frame fusion, under strong shadow conditions.

Based on above reasons current research used object appearance and shape based features to perform face-base gender classification. Current research used holistic method for the same purpose to compare the results as a baseline with proposed HOG based scheme. In total five different features stated as Principle Component Analysis (PCA), Histogram of Oriented Gradients (HOG), Fisher Linear Discriminant Analysis (FLDA), Gabor Wavelet and Local Binary Pattern (LBP) are used. Finally an improved gender classification method that involves object appearance and shape based features called HOG with nearest neighbor classification method while having one frame/object for training has been proposed. Experimental results of fold-2 elaborated that HOG outperformed for face-based gender classification with 91.92% accuracy for male and 90.91% for female faces so that average accuracy is reported as 91.41%. Current research mainly claimed that forehead, hair style, chin, ears and outer boundary of face having information about face shapes (oval, long, round, square and triangular) have significant importance in gender classification task. Feature selection techniques by applying different number of bins and windows per bound box of HOG; radius of LBP; lambda of Gabor Wavelets are investigated as well, which showed significant improvement in results as well as performance. Another novel part of current research that provides analysis based on cross dataset experiments that which feature extraction method performs well for addressed problem.

2. PROPOSED METHOD

The block diagram of the HOG based scheme for gender classification using face images are shown in Figure 2. HOG features are extracted from the normalized input face images. Based on the number of bins and windows per bound box effect on features, best suited features have been selected. These optimized HOG features act as an input to the classifier. In the classification part, Euclidean distance is calculated using training and testing face image. The minimum distance is used to take the final decision.

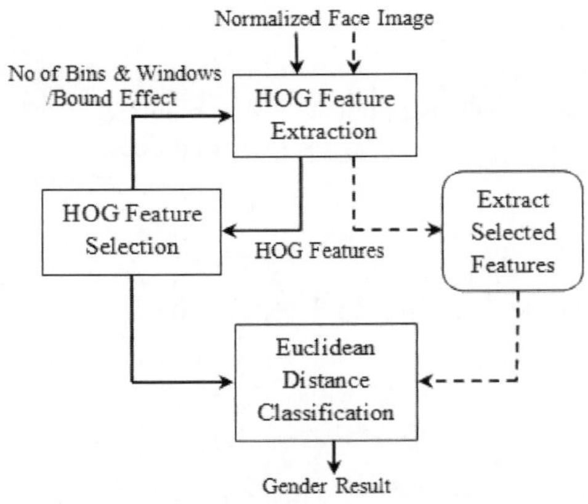

Figure 2. Block diagram presentation of HOG based scheme for gender classification

3. FEATURE EXTRACTION

In pattern recognition and image processing, feature extraction is a special form of dimensionality reduction. When the input data to an algorithm is too large to be processed and it is suspected to be notoriously redundant then the input data will be transformed into a reduced representation set of features known as features vector. Transforming the input data into the set of features is called feature extraction. If the features extraction is carefully done then it is expected that the features set will be the relevant information from the input data in order to perform the desired task using this reduced representation instead of the full size input. For that purpose, we have used five different methods, to compare and achieve high accuracy in later classification stage.

3.1 Histogram of Oriented Gradients (HOG)

Histogram of Oriented Gradients (HOG) (Dalal & Triggs, 2005) is feature descriptors which counts occurrences of gradient orientation in localized portions of an image. This method differs from other similar methods because it is computed on a dense grid of uniformly spaced cells and uses overlapping local contrast normalization for improved accuracy in terms of invariance to illumination and shadowing. It can be achieve by dividing the image into small interconnected regions called cells which can be either rectangle or radial and compiling a histogram of gradient directions or edge orientations for the pixels for each cell within itself, accumulating a weighted local 1-D histogram of gradient directions over the pixels of the cell which represents the descriptor. A local object appearance and shape within an image can be described by the distribution of intensity gradients or edge directions in Histogram of Oriented Gradients (HOG). To improve accuracy, local histograms can be contrast-normalized by calculating a measure of the intensity across a larger region of the image, called a block. Later this value can be used to normalize all cells within the block. This normalization results in better invariance to changes in illumination or shadowing. The HOG descriptor has some major advantages over other descriptor methods. The method upholds invariance to geometric and photometric transformations, except for object orientation as it operates on localized cells, which would only appear in larger spatial regions. The first step in image pre-processing is to ensure normalized color and gamma values. The second step is to creating the cell histograms. Each pixel of a cell casts a weighted vote for an orientation-based histogram channel which based on the values found in the gradient computation.

The cell's, depending on the gradient "unsigned" or "signed" value, histogram channels are evenly spread over 0-180 degrees or 0-360 degrees. The gradient strengths must be locally normalized in order to account for changes in illumination and contrast, which requires grouping the cells together into larger, spatially connected blocks. HOG descriptor is the vector of the components of the normalized cell histograms from all of the block regions. These blocks typically overlap in the final descriptor. There are two main block geometries exist, rectangular R-HOG blocks and circular C-HOG blocks. R-HOG blocks are generally square grids, represented by three parameters: the number of cells per block, the number of pixels per cell, and the number of channels per cell histogram. Block normalization is the last step to get the job done.

4. CLASSIFICATION

To analyze the performance of above mentioned feature methods, we have experimented with the basic minimum distance classifier called Euclidean distance which defined as:

$$\text{Euclidean distance} = \sqrt{\sum_{j=1}^{n} (x_{rj} - x_{sj})r^2}$$

Here r and s are two images, n is the dimension of the feature vector, and x_{rj} is the jth feature of image r.

5. EXPERIMENTS

5.1 Dataset

Experiments have been performed on FEI face dataset consisting of 99 objects each (Male and Female), having one frame/object. Dataset varies in-terms of shadow, head scale, light variation, expression, pose, emotion and face position. There is also a huge variation in head turn, tilt and slant.

Experiments have been performed in two folds. In first fold FEI cropped face dataset is used which doesn't have forehead, hair style, chin, ears as well as outer boundary of face which omits the information about face shape (oval, long, round, square and triangular); whereas in the second fold we took FEI face dataset and later extracted whole face, which had all the information that FEI cropped face dataset doesn't have, with the dimensions of 120x180. Experimental results showed that forehead, hair style, chin, ears and outer boundary of face having information about face shape (oval, long, round, square and triangular) have significant importance in gender classification task. Either fold's dataset is shown in figure 3 below.

Figure 3(a). Fold-1: Gender classification dataset

Figure 3(b). Fold-2: Gender classification dataset

5.2 Environment

Experiments have been performed in a cross dataset environment. Even though we were unable to make separate datasets for both training and testing because of the less number of objects in dataset, but to get the job done same dataset for both training and testing were used in following manner.

Dataset = [99 Male, 99 Female] Whereas
99 Male = {Image1, Image2, Image3, … , Image99} and
99 Female = {Image100, Image101, Image102, … , Image198}
So that: Dataset= [Image1, Image2, Image3, … , Image198]
To calculate the classification result for Image1 the training dataset was:
Dataset= [Image2, Image3, Image4, … , Image198]
And, to calculate the classification result for Image2 the training dataset was:
Dataset= [Image1, Image3, Image4, … , Image198]
So on and so forth
Up to calculate the classification result for Image198 the training dataset was:
Dataset= [Image1, Image2, Image3, … , Image197]

5.3 Results

Four features (LBP, PCA, FLDA and Gabor Wavelets) have been used to provide analysis, based on experimental results, with respect to the performance of proposed HOG feature based method. A concluded result summary is given below in figure.4 and table.1.

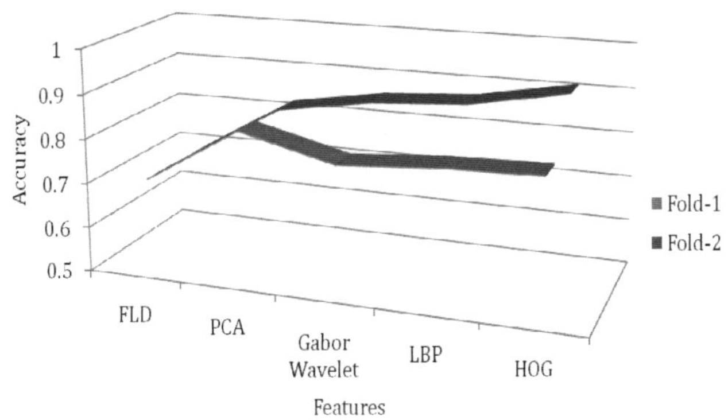

Figure 4. Summary of Classification of (LBP, PCA, FLDA and Gabor Wavelets) features

Table 1. Classification summary

		FLD	*PCA*	*Gabor Wavelets*	*LBP*	**HOG*
Fold-1	*Male*	70.00%	80.85%	79.79%	62.77%	79.79%
	Female	70.00%	85.11%	75.53%	95.74%	79.79%
	Average	***70.00%***	***82.98%***	***77.66%***	***79.26%***	***79.79%***
Fold-2	*Male*	*64.65%*	*80.81%*	*87.88%*	*74.75%*	*91.92%*
	Female	*74.75%*	*83.84%*	*83.84%*	*100.00%*	*90.91%*
	Average	***69.70%***	***82.32%***	***85.86%***	***87.37%***	****91.41%***

For Histogram of Oriented Gradients (HOG) experiments, researcher investigated results for N: 2, 3, 4, ..., 13 representing number of bins; M: 3x3 and 4x3 representing windows per bound box. Based on experiments it is concluded that for male classification; 4x3 windows per bound box with 4 number of bins have provided maximum accuracy in fold-1 and 4x3 windows per bound box with 10 and 12 number of bins have provided maximum accuracy in fold-2 whereas for female classification; 4x3 windows per bound box with 10 and 13 number of bins have provided maximum accuracy in fold-1 and 4x3 windows per bound box with 11 and 12 number of bins have provided maximum accuracy in fold -2. Details are given below in figure.5:

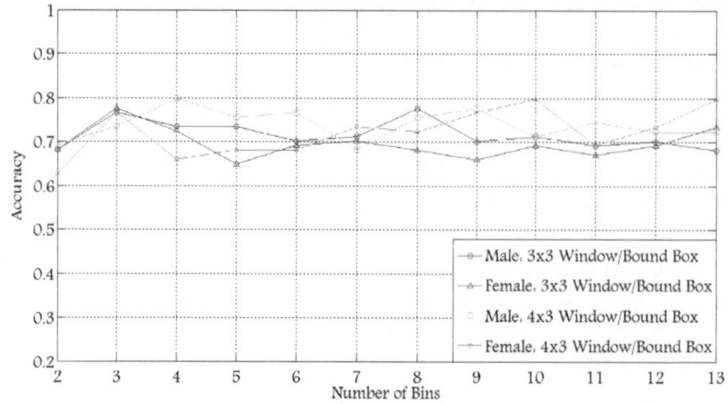

Figure 5 (a). Fold-1 Histogram of oriented gradients (HOG) classification result

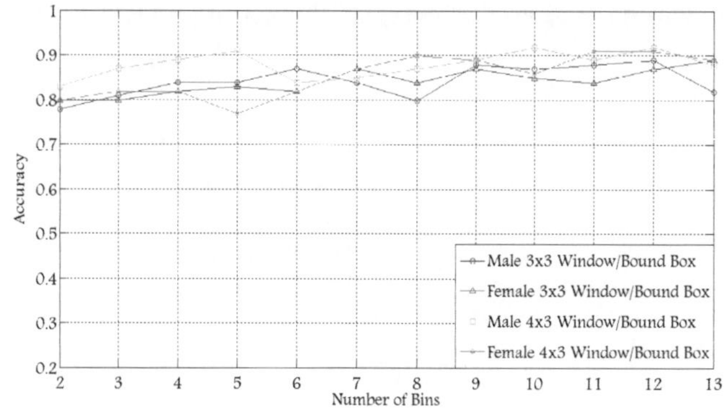

Figure 5 (b). Fold-2 Histogram of oriented gradients (HOG) classification result

For Gabor wavelets experiments, researchers investigated results for N: 2, 3, 4, ..., 16 representing lambda. Based on experiments it is concluded that for Male classification; N: 2 has provided maximum accuracy in fold-1 and N: 11 has provided maximum accuracy in fold-2 whereas for Female classification; N: 9, 12 have provided maximum accuracy in fold-1 and N: 4, 7 have provided maximum accuracy in fold-2. Details are given below in figure.6:

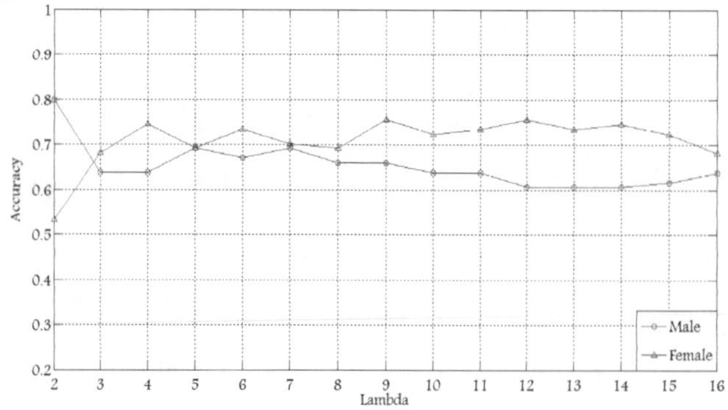

Figure 6 (a). Fold-1 Gabor wavelets classification result

For Local Binary Pattern (LBP) experiments, researchers investigated results for N: 1, 2, 3, 4,…, 16 representing radius. Based on experiments it is concluded that for Male classification; N: 10 has provided maximum accuracy in fold-1 and N: 11 has provided maximum accuracy in fold-2 whereas for Female classification; N: 1, 2 have provided maximum accuracy in fold-1 and N: 1 has provided maximum accuracy in fold-2. Details are given below in figure.7:

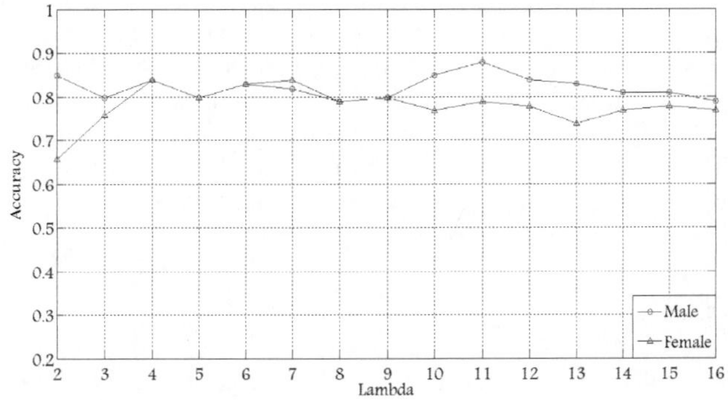

Figure 6 (b). Fold-2 Gabor wavelets classification result

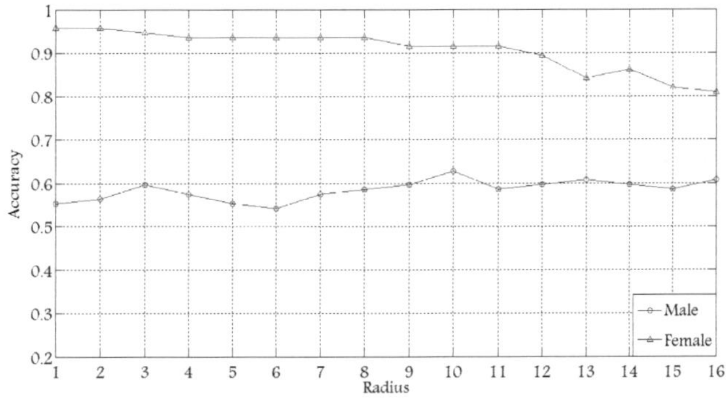

Figure 7 (a). Fold-1 Local binary pattern (LBP) classification result

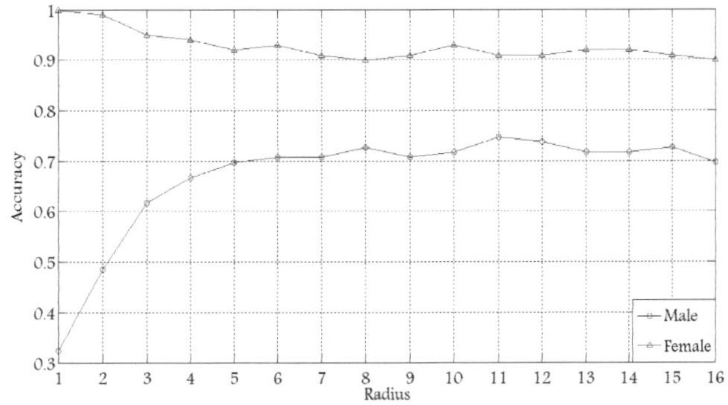

Figure 7 (b). Fold-2 Local binary pattern (LBP) classification result

6. CONCLUSION

A very popular problem of soft biometric analysis of face called gender classification has been investigated in this paper. HOG based framework is presented for gender classification. Various features have been used to analyze and conclude relatively best suited technique. According to experimental results Histogram Oriented Gradient (HOG) features outperformed LBP, PCA, FLDA and Gabor Wavelets with 91.92% accuracy for male and 90.91% for female faces by using nearest neighbor classification method called Euclidean distance. Experiments showed that forehead, hair style, chin, ears and outer boundary of face, which own information about face shapes (oval, long, round, square and triangular), have significant importance in gender classification task. Feature selection technique were investigated as well by applying different radius of LBP; lambda of Gabor Wavelets; number of bins and windows per bound box of HOG which showed significant improvement in results as well as performance.

7. FUTURE WORK

Although experimental results are quite satisfactory and accuracy is relatively high but there is still room for improvement. 1). Other feature can be considered like Haar, ICA, LCP and Weber Local Descriptors (WLD) for current study. 2). Features performance can be evaluated through different classification techniques like Support Vector Machines (SVM), KNN and C5.0 or other nearest neighbor methods like City block distance or Chi-square distance. 3). Fusion of best suited features can be performed at feature level, score level or decision level. 4). Rather than considering whole face's features; to illuminate the performance dependency on expression (to some extent); sub-parts of face can be considered like eyes, nose, forehead etc. Based on each sub-part of face, classification accuracy can be calculated separately to analyze which part of face has more impact on gender classification. Later quantization can be performed on results by assigning weight to each classification result and conclude how sub-parts of face effects gender classification as a whole. 5). Experiments can be performed by using more than one frame/object to improve the performance in-terms of accuracy by trading off with system execution speed. 6). Feature selection technique can be applied to improve the results and the performance.

REFERENCES

Abate, A., Nappi, N., Riccio, D., and Sabatino, G. (2007) "2D and 3D face recognition: A survey," *Pattern Recognition Letters* Vol. 28, No.14, pp. 1885–1906.

Brigham, J. C. (1986) "The influence of race on face recognition," *Aspects of Face Processing*, NATO ASI Series Vol. 28, pp. 170-177.

Canavan, S. J., Kozak, M. P., Zhang, Y., Sullins, J. R., Shreve, M. A., Goldgof, D. B. (2007) "Face Recognition by Multi-Frame Fusion of Rotating Heads in Videos," *First IEEE International Conference on Biometrics: Theory, Applications, and Systems (BTAS)*, E-ISBN: 978-1-4244-1597-7 Print ISBN: 978-1-4244-1597-7.

Dalal, N., and Triggs, B. (2005) "Histogram of oriented gradient for human detection," *In Proc. Computer Vision and Pattern Recognition (CVPR)*, pp. 886–893.

O'Toole, A. J., Peterson, J., and K.A, (1996) Deffenbacher; "An 'other-race effect' for categorizing faces by sex," *Perception 25*, pp. 669–676.

Zhao, W., Chellappa, R., Rosenfeld, A. and Phillips, P.J. (2003) Face Recognition: A Literature Survey. *ACM Computing Surveys*, 35, 399-458.

USING INFORMATION VISUALIZATION TO SUPPORT THE SELF-MANAGEMENT OF TYPE 2 DIABETES MELLITUS

Janet Wesson[1] and Meggan Naude
Nelson Mandela University, South Africa
[1]Prof.

ABSTRACT

The increasing number of individuals suffering from Type 2 Diabetes Mellitus highlights the need for an effective tool for users to understand the relationship between their behaviors and the effect that those behaviors have on their blood glucose levels (BGLs). There are few Information Visualization tools available that can be used to reduce the cognition required to understand correlations between behavior and BGLs. Existing tools provide simple visualizations that do not show correlations. Suitable Information Visualization techniques were identified and used to visualize Type 2 Diabetes Mellitus data to aid in the self-management of the disease. A prototype, named MedicMetric, was created as an IV tool for visualizing T2DM data. MedicMetric incorporated three charts, namely the change rate view, the radial progress view, and the annotated line view. A usability evaluation was conducted to compare these techniques, and to determine which technique is most suitable for visualizing T2DM data. The results leaned significantly in favor of the annotated line view. The MedicMetric application was compared to the MySygr and Diabetes:M applications. MedicMetric and MySugr obtained almost identical results for effectiveness and efficiency. However, participants indicated that MedicMetric provided the best support best overall, with 100 per cent of participants stating that they would prefer to use the MedicMetric application in future.

KEYWORDS

Diabetes Mellitus, Information Visualization, Self-Management, Usability Evaluation

1. INTRODUCTION

Diabetes mellitus (DM) is a long-lasting chronic disease that affects approximately 422 million people worldwide (World Health Organization, 2016). Many diabetes cases are preventable through lifestyle change (Health Information, 2017), but most of those who struggle with the condition lack the correct tools to understand and track their insulin intake. The most prominent cause of death for people with Type-2 DM (T2DM) is cardiovascular disease (Tancredi et al, 2015). This is an indicator that patients do not understand how their behavior affects their health. By not understanding the relationship between their insulin intake, blood sugar levels (BGLs), exercise, food intake, heart disease, and blood pressure (BP) (Delahanty & McCulloch, 2017), individuals with DM are less likely to make good decisions, which can negatively affect their health.

DM cannot be cured, but it can be controlled with insulin supplements, oral medication and lifestyle changes such as increasing exercise, decreasing fat and carbohydrate consumption, and monitoring BGLs (Schiffrin & Belmonte, 1982). Glucose meters allow patients to monitor their BGLs and facilitate a dramatic increase in the lifespan of DM patients by giving them immediate feedback on how they are managing their BGLs (Smith, 2002).

Information Visualization (IV) is a method for representing data in a nontraditional, interactive, graphical form (Gelman & Unwin, 2012). IV is utilized in many fields, and can be customized for various applications (Shneiderman, 2013). Interactive IV and visual analytics methods could bring profound changes to personal health programs, healthcare delivery and self-management for DM patients through effective presentation of health information (Institute of Medicine, 2011).

This paper will investigate how IV techniques can be applied to create an effective tool to aid in the self-management of DM. The aim of this research is to improve the presentation of variables associated with DM to support DM patients, and assist in the process of health-pattern identification. This could, in turn, lead to a cause-and-effect awareness for DM patients, and allow them to self-manage their DM more effectively.

2. RELATED WORK

The current methods of self-management for diabetes do not include management systems that make use of IV. While IV has previously been used for visualization of medical data, systems that are currently in use are limited (Yordanov, 2016). For this reason, mobile IV systems that are used to visualize T2DM data, such as BGLs, were reviewed.

2.1 DEXCOM G5 Mobile Continuous Glucose Monitoring System

This system is the closest existing system to the proposed IV tool. It makes use of Continuous Glucose Monitoring (CGM) to keep track of DM patients' glucose levels throughout the day. The system is comprised of three parts (Dexcom G5® Mobile App, 2015):

- A small sensor that measures glucose levels just underneath the skin.
- An element that is fastened on top of the sensor and sends data wirelessly to a compatible smart device or receiver.
- A compatible smart device with the Dexcom G5 Mobile app.

BGLs can then be viewed in different colors to identify when they are high, low or within range. With the Dexcom G5 Mobile CGM System, users are alerted on their compatible smart device when their BGLs are too high or too low. Alerts and alarm sounds can also be customized to appear as a text message, allowing for additional discretion and privacy.

The system allows users to keep track of events that affect their glucose levels on their compatible smart device. The Dexcom G5 Mobile CGM System provides a platform to enter customizable events, giving users the ability to track how their daily activities influence their glucose trends. Customized reports can also be shared with physicians. Shortfalls of this system include a lack of automated input systems for diet or exercise plans, a lack of existing health pattern identification, and a lack of analysis within the mobile system.

2.2 MySugr

MySugr (mySugr GmbH, 2012) is a free cellular application available on both the iStore and Google PlayStore. MySugr (mySugr GmbH, 2012) has the direct purpose of aiding individuals with the self-management of their condition. It does so by taking recorded information from the user and representing it as a report summarizing their BGLs over time. Food intake, medicine intake and BGLs are all represented in a calendar with time stamps and line graphs (Johnson, 2016).

The entry of this data becomes time consuming for users and was thus made optional. Whichever data the user chooses to track will be represented. Any data, which the user does not track, is discarded and not forecast.

Two features of the application that deserve attention are reminders and tags. Tags are the notable events, which occur and influence BGLs, and reminders can be set manually by the user so that an alarm can sound when medication is required (Johnson, 2016). The reminder is typically set for 15 minutes to 3 hours to remind users about a post meal medication intake. Shortfalls of this system include a lack of CGM, a lack of alerts for abnormally high/low blood glucose levels, a lack of an automated input system for BGLs, exercise or diet plan, and a lack of existing health pattern identifications.

2.3 Diabetes:M

Diabetes:M (Sirma Medical Systems, 2021) is an award-winning diabetes logbook app that was first published in Google Play in April 2013. It was developed by diabetics to meet the needs of people who want to manage all aspects of their condition. Users can track, analyze, review and export data. The main features of the application include (Yordanov, 2016): Logbook, Food Database, Bolus Calculator, Extended bolus calculator mode, Detailed Graph, and Analytical Charts.

Shortfalls of this system include a lack of CGM, a lack of alerts for abnormally high/low blood glucose levels, a lack of an automated input system for BGLs, exercise or diet plan, and a lack of existing health pattern identifications.

3. DESIGN OF IV TOOL: MEDICMETRIC

This section includes the design of the prototype visualization system, called MedicMetric. The IV techniques that were used for the prototype are described. To develop a prototype to determine to what extent IV can be used to support the self-management of T2DM, a collection of accurate, the authors used real-life DM data as a test set for implementation. The authors selected the Dexcom sandbox diabetes data, and Fitbit test data sets as sample data for the prototype.

3.1 Data Collection

The metrics that must be self-managed by DM patients include BGLs, oral medication, exercise, diet and sleep (Deacon et al, 2005). These factors were identified during the research phase as prominent behavioral factors, which a FitBit is capable of tracking, that can also affect BGLs. The analysis of DM data was based on the idea that the accumulation of the effects of lifestyle events should be represented by a summation of energy supply or expenditure data (kilojoules) due to ingestion or exercise. The accumulation of these effects may cause a variation in health data such as BMI, BGLs, BP and body-fat percentage. A dataset of BGLs, obtained from the DEXCOM and FitBit sandbox data was used as the initial data for visual representation and testing.

3.2 Visualization Techniques

Temporal visualizations are visualizations that track time-series data, i.e., the performance of an indicator over a period. To represent DM data in a manner that supports effective self-management and cognition, the techniques used to visualize this information should adhere to certain requirements.

One frequently cited guideline is the "Visual information-seeking mantra" (VISM), proposed by Shneiderman: *"Overview first, zoom and filter, then details-on-demand"* (Shneiderman et al, 2003). The taxonomy divides general VISM into seven data types and seven tasks: Overview, Zoom, Filter, Details-on-Demand, Relate, History, and Extract.

3.3 Prototype Design

Several design iterations were conducted before the design was finalized. All designs were evaluated by experts in the IV design domain, but user-driven design was difficult to implement during the design phase due to COVID-19 restrictions. Three visualizations, capable of providing users with the ability to view and correlate behaviors with BGLs, were implemented using the HighCharts (Usman, M., 2022) library in MedicMetric. These charts were implemented for comparison purposes, and all three charts support the tasks listed in Section 3.2. Users can navigate between the views by using a chart navigation screen. The chart data is a combination of sandbox data and purposefully generated data, used to highlight aspects of the IV techniques more clearly.

The **radial progress view** was implemented using the HighCharts (Usman, M., 2022) radial bar chart. The chart contains all tracked variables (Figure 1). The radial line meets the end of the track when participants have fully met their goal for the day. For instance, if a participant sets a reminder to take their medication, and selects that they have completed the task when the reminder is sent, then they have met their goal for medicine intake.

The **weekly overview** shows the same information that is shown in the day view, but it is represented using stacked bars. This way, the user performance can be compared to the other days in the current week, to determine on which days they performed their worst. For a participant to meet their goal for the BGL category, their BGL must remain within the acceptable range for the day (between 4 and 8 mmo/L). If the participant does not achieve this goal, then it is calculated as the percentage of the day for which they were outside the acceptable range.

Users are also able to filter the chart down to one criterion and then compare their individual goals throughout the week. For example, users can click on the legend at the bottom and remove all factors except water. Now they will see a radial progress view with only water, and they can compare their progress throughout the week.

Figure 1. The Radial Progress Daily and Weekly View

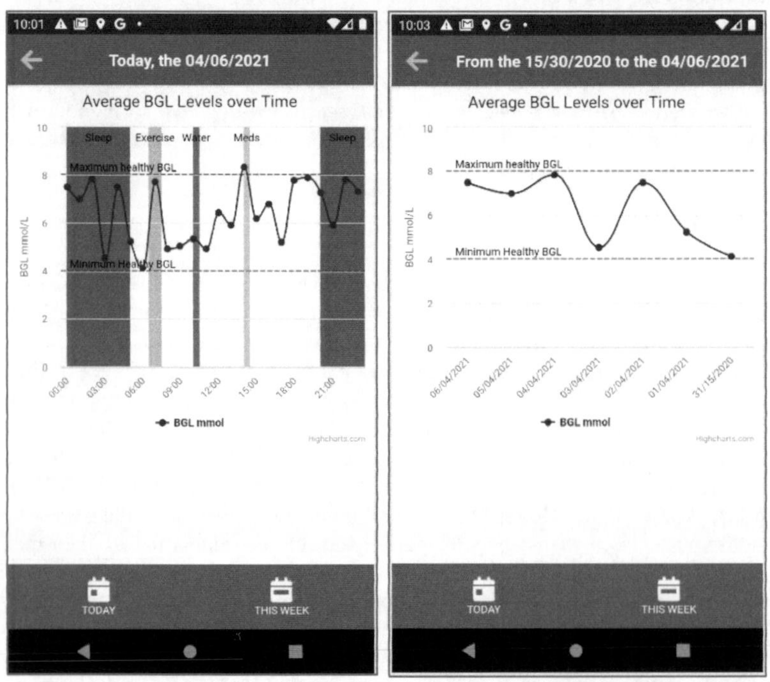

Figure 2. Annotated Line Daily and Weekly View

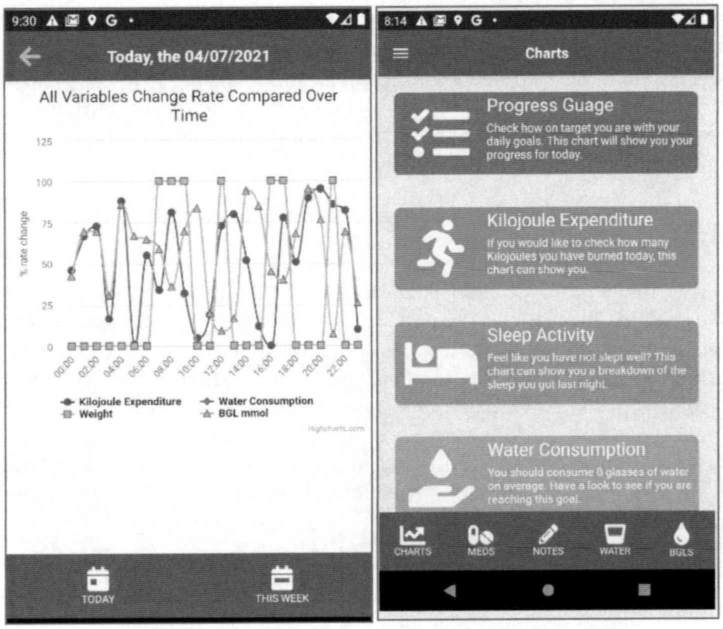

Figure 3. Change Rate Filtered View and Navigation Screen

The HighCharts (Usman, M., 2022) annotated line view was edited to display events as zones on the line chart. This process produced the **annotated line view**. The title of the event is shown, and upper and lower limits of BGLs can be seen on the chart. By showing events as zones, it becomes easier to associate the event to the BGL and, therefore, to associate a behavior to the BGL. The daily and weekly view of this chart can be seen in Figure 2.

To highlight trends in the data, a ROC line for different variables was calculated. The calculation for ROC was simple in that it takes the current value for a variable and divides it by the value from an earlier period. One is then subtracted from this amount and the remainder is multiplied by 100 to generate a percentage. This results in the chart in Figure 3. This chart would be useful in determining if one factor has an effect on another, but it would be difficult to tell if that effect was negative or positive, as ROC does not relay that kind of information

Navigation within the application can be performed using a side drawer menu, which is activated by the hamburger menu displayed on the top left of the screen. Navigation can also be done using the tabs at the bottom of the screen. Navigation between charts must be done by selecting the card on the screen with the name of the chart that the user would like to view (Figure 3).

4. EVALUATION: USER STUDY

The usability study required participants to complete a series of tasks while using the prototype application to view the visualizations. To avoid participants learning the system, the study was done before they were asked to make use of the prototype for a prolonged period. Three participants completed the evaluation using MedicMetric and were asked to make use of the entire system, including the Fitbit Charge 2 and Aria Scale for one week afterwards to identify any problems with the system as a whole. Twelve other participants were asked to evaluate the system without prolonged in-home use. In total, fifteen participants evaluated the system.

4.1 Research Objectives

MedicMetric has seven core charts, including kilojoule expenditure, BGLs, medicine intake, water intake, weight and sleep patterns. There are three charts capable of highlighting patterns or behaviors, which can have a direct impact on BGLs. The aim of the evaluation was to determine if the information was easily interpretable by the user, and to determine which of the three charts was preferred.

The radial progress view was initially not designed as an IV technique for recognizing health patterns, but its weekly overview shows a large amount of information about which goals participants met during the week. It is possible, from looking at this view of the chart, to infer a few health patterns, and thus it was evaluated with the two other charts intended for that purpose.

4.2 Participants

A sample of fifteen participants (eight male and seven females, with an average age of 34.8 years) were asked to participate in the usability evaluation. The participants either had T2DM, worked in a medical field, or lived with close relatives affected by T2DM, and could make use of a self-management tool to aid their relatives. Participants' ages ranged from 26 to 64 years. Participants were asked if they had any prior experience with IV tools, and 86 percent of the participants indicated that they had used an IV tool previously. Participants were asked to provide consent that they were willing, without coercion, to participate in the study on the premise that their DM data would be secure and that their participation could be withdrawn at any time. Participants were not evaluated on their ability to interpret graphics, and the small participant pool means that this could influence the results.

4.3 Evaluation Metrics

The following performance metrics for each task were measured:

- Effectiveness: Whether the task was completed correctly or not, and
- Efficiency: Time taken to complete the task.

User satisfaction, cognitive load, and ease-of-use were measured after the tasks were completed using standard usability questionnaires.

4.4 Experimental Setup

Two versions of the usability evaluations were developed to cater for Covid19 safety regulations and to minimize the risk for individuals with T2DM. Participants could either do an evaluation at home, or online. In the at-home environment, the evaluator was positioned out of eye-line, but within the hearing range of the participant. The participant and the evaluator communicated verbally during the evaluation. If the participant opted to do an online evaluation, the participant would communicate verbally through a video chat with the evaluator. Screen sharing was used when a participant evaluated the emulated application to minimize the amount of software they would need to download or install.

The participants completed the evaluation of the three main charts, while being asked to identify health patterns in the chart data. Participant task times were manually recorded by the evaluator, as well as the answers to questions in the task lists. Participants were given written and verbal instructions for each task, and questionnaires were administered verbally.

4.5 Procedure

Each participant completed one evaluation and all evaluations were done one at a time. The participants were asked to complete the initial set of tasks and usability, cognitive load and user experience questionnaires were administered. The participants were then asked to complete tasks for each of the main three charts and alternative IV tools. Participants were not informed that the MedicMetric application was the proposed alternative IV tool. After completing the tasks for each chart and performing similar tasks on alternative applications, namely MySugr (mySugr GmbH, 2012) and Diabetes:M (Sirma Medical Systems, 2021), the participants were asked to identify which of the three systems best supported their tasks.

4.6 Results

Tasks designed to directly compare the three main IV techniques received varying success rates. Participants had a 71.11 per cent success rate when using the change rate line view, an 80 per cent success rate when using the radial progress view, and a 96 per cent success rate when using the annotated line view. Thus, it can be concluded that the most effective chart was the annotated line view, and the least effective was the change rate line view.

Tasks were designed to compare MedicMetric in terms of efficiency with MySugr and Diabetes:M. Identical success rates were recorded for MySugr and MedicMetric. Participants correctly answered the tasks using MySugr 86.67 per cent of the time, but only answered correctly using Diabetes:M 42.22 per cent of the time. This is possibly due to the navigation mechanisms used in Diabetes:M, that multiple participants noted were confusing.

Participants felt that the MedicMetric tool best supported their tasks according to the VISM. A Shapiro-Wilk test was run between MySugr and MedicMetric, and results were statistically significant in favor of MedicMetric, apart from Extract, which was in favor of MySugr. It is worth noting that the final question asked was '*If you were to choose one of the IV tools evaluated here to use daily, which would it be?*'. One hundred percent of the participants stated that they would make use of MedicMetric in future.

Participants correctly identified the effects that water consumption, kilojoule expenditure and medication and weight have on BGLs 100 per cent of the time using the annotated line view, but could only correctly interpret the data concerning sleep 80 per cent of the time. Participants could correctly identify health patterns 71.11 per cent of the time using the change rate view, and 80 per cent of the time using the radial progress view.

Satisfaction results were captured on these questionnaires using a seven-point semantic differential scale, and a seven-point Likert scale. The satisfaction in the post-task questionnaire was broken down into three sections, namely, cognitive load, overall satisfaction, and usability.

On average, the annotated line view was evaluated to create the least cognitive load with the lowest average mental demand of 1.06. It was also estimated by the participants to increase their performance, with the highest average performance rating of 6.4.

The usability ratings were also all in favor of the annotated line view. For this reason, the Wilcoxon Matched Pairs Test (MacFarland & Yates, 2018) for Usability was performed comparing the results for the annotated line view against the other two IV techniques. The difference between the question rankings for the annotated line view and the radial progress view were statistically significant for 7 of the 15 questions.

4.7 Discussion

From the results, it can be concluded that the annotated line view was the preferred method used to visualize the effect that variables, such as water consumption and exercise, have on BGLs. The satisfaction scores were also relatively high for all three charts, but the change rate view had the worst satisfaction review overall.

For effectiveness and efficiency, MedicMetric and MySugr obtained almost identical results. However, participants estimated that MedicMetric supported their VISM tasks the best overall, allowing them to zoom and filter, search and acquire details-on-demand and generally get a better overview. One hundred percent of participants stated that they would prefer to use the MedicMetric application in the future, especially considering the MySugr results.

The following usability problems were identified by the participants and addressed shortly after the study:

- Chart coloring is not conducive to clear data interpretation as it can distract from more important information.
- Formatting issues discovered in the x-axis timeline.
- Crowded charts are difficult to read and filters should be applied initially to reduce the amount of data shown.

5. CONCLUSIONS

This research has shown that IV can be used successfully to support the self-management of T2DM through positive change affecting data interpretation. The participants of the usability study showed that the developed

IV tool is effective at reducing the cognition required to interpret their BGL data, and showed that they would prefer using such an IV tool to better manage their T2DM and personal goals.

The practical contribution of this research includes the three IV techniques, which were designed and implemented in MedicMetric. Most of the participants in the usability evaluation preferred using the advanced timeline view in all categories in which it was evaluated.

Due to the ubiquitous nature of computing today, it may be possible that an alternative to the Dexcom API or Medtronic CGM may soon become available, and it would be possible to integrate them into MedicMetric. This would generate a real-time application, capable of constantly displaying BGL data to the user. It could be possible to conduct a further study in collaboration with the health industry to evaluate this system in such an environment.

MedicMetric could be extended to enhance the features that it currently supports. With new advancements in machine learning predictions, it could be possible to incorporate prediction trend analysis so that individuals are capable of understanding how their BGLs may continue to rise or fall based on their current behavior patterns. MedicMetric could also be repurposed and used to represent more than BGL information.

REFERENCES

Committee on Patient Safety and Health Information Technology; Institute of Medicine. *Health IT and Patient Safety: Building Safer Systems for Better Care*. Washington (DC): National Academies Press (US); 2011 Nov 10. PMID: 24600741.

Deakin, T.A., McShane, C.E., Cade, J.E. and Williams, R., 2005. Group based training for self-management strategies in people with type 2 diabetes mellitus. Cochrane database of systematic reviews, (2).

Delahanty, M., & McCulloch, K. (2017, March 20). *Patient education: Type 1 diabetes mellitus and diet (Beyond the Basics)*. Retrieved from www.uptodate.com: https://www.uptodate.com/contents/type-1-diabetes-mellitus-and-diet-beyond-the-basics

Dexcom G5® Mobile App. (2015, September 12) *Dexcom G5 Mobile mmol/L DXCM5* (Version 1.7.10.0) [Mobile App]. Available at: Google Play (Downloaded: 15 March 2019)

Health Information. (2017). Retrieved from National Institute of Diabetes and Digestive Kidney Disease Retrieved from https://www.niddk.nih.gov/health-information/health-communicationprograms/ndep/am-i-at-risk/diabetes-preventable/Pages/diabetesispreventable.aspx [Last Accessed 6 January 2022].

Johnson, S. (2016, November 7*). How much does continuous glucose monitoring cost?* Retrieved from https://mysugr.com/ : https://mysugr.com/continuous-glucose-monitoring-cost/ [Last Accessed 6 January 2022].

mySugr GmbH (2012) *mySugr - Diabetes Tracker Log* (Version 3.92.22) [Mobile app]. Available at: Google Play (Downloaded: 15 March 2019)

Schiffrin A, Belmonte M. *Multiple daily self-glucose monitoring: its essential role in long-term glucose control in insulin-dependent diabetic patients treated with pump and multiple subcutaneous injections*. Diabetes Care. 1982 Sep-Oct;5(5): pp. 479-484. doi: 10.2337/diacare.5.5.479. PMID: 6765224.

Shneiderman B, Kaufmann M. (2003), *The Eyes Have It: A Task by Data Type Taxonomy for Information Visualizations*, The Craft of Information Visualization, pp. 364-371, ISBN 9781558609150

Shneiderman, Ben & Plaisant, Catherine & Hesse, Bradford. (2013). Improving Healthcare with Interactive Visualization. Computer. 46, pp. 58-66. 10.1109/MC.2013.38.

Sirma Medical Systems (2021) *Diabetes:M - Management & Blood Sugar Tracker App* (Version 8.0.12) [Mobile app]. Available at: Google Play (Downloaded: 15 March 2019)

Smith, B. K. (2002). You prick your finger we do the rest: Glucose meters evolution: User experience. Magazine of the Usability Professional Association, pp. 31-34.

Tancredi, M., Rosengren, A., Svensson, A.-M., Kosiborod, M., Pivodic, A., Gudbjörnsdottir, S., Wedel, H., Clements, M., Dahlqvist, S., & Lind, M. (2015). Excess Mortality among Persons with Type 2 Diabetes. *New England Journal of Medicine*, 373(18), pp. 1720–1732. https://doi.org/10.1056/nejmoa1504347

Usman, M., 2022. *Interactive javascript charts library*. [online] Highcharts. Available at: https://www.highcharts.com/ [Last Accessed 6 January 2022].

World Health Organization (2016). Global report on diabetes. Who.int. [online] Available at: https://apps.who.int/iris/handle/10665/204871.

Yordanov, I. (2016, December 12). *The ultimate way to understand and manage your diabetes*. Retrieved from https://www.diabetes-m.com/: https://www.diabetes-m.com/ [Last Accessed 6 January 2022].

TELEINCLUSIVE LEARNING: AN EXPLORATORY STUDY ON STUDENTS' EXPECTATIONS OF USING TELEPRESENCE ROBOT FOR ATTENDING CLASSES

Luciano Gamberini[1], Gabriella Francesca Amalia Pernice[2], Valeria Orso[3] and Daniela Mapelli[1]
[1]*Departments of General Psychology, Human Inspired Technology Research Center University of Padova, Padova, Italy*
[2]*Departments of General Psychology, University of Padova, Padova, Italy*
[3]*Human Inspired Technology Research Center, University of Padova, Padova, Italy*

ABSTRACT

Telepresence robots allow the user to attend events remotely and actively participate by controlling the robot's movement and directly addressing bystanders. Moreover, these robots proved an effective means for students with serious health issues to continue their learning process. Most of the previous studies investigated the impact of this technology on the user experience, failing to address their expectations before the adoption. The present work explored what undergraduate students with special motoric needs expect by employing a telepresence robot for attending classes. We found that respondents were concerned about their ability to control the robot, not to bother bystanders proficiently. Additionally, they were uncertain about how the look of the robot would have made them appear to their peers.
Despite the potential of the telepresence robot to enhance social interactions, we found that students did not have specific expectations.

KEYWORDS

Telepresence Robots, Technology Acceptance, Accessibility, Inclusion

1. INTRODUCTION

Robots are increasingly becoming powerful allies for humans in several different domains. For instance, they are successfully employed in Industry 4.0 (Rossato et al., 2021), in warehouses (Bolu & Korçak, 2021), to welcome guests in hotel halls (Fitter, Strait, Bisbee, Mataric & Takayama, 2021), and as companions (Cooper, Di Fava, Vivas, Marchionni & Ferro, 2020), depending on their very features. Telepresence robots allow the user not only to connect remotely, but also to participate to events by enabling her/him to independently move the device in the space, and listen, and speak with attendants. As such, telepresence robots can foster inclusion by enabling individuals with special motoric needs or severe health issues to overcome the movement limitations imposed by their condition and not have to depend on others to negotiate their social or academic experiences (Yousif, 2021).

Universities are places where the learning process is not limited to the transfer of knowledge from the lecturer to the students, rather a significant component of education is the discussion with lecturers and peers. The restrictions brought about by the COVID-19 pandemic have normalized the usage of video-conference systems to run classes (Serhan, 2020). Even after the restrictions have been loosened, the practice to run lectures both in presence and at the same time using video-conferencing tools has become widespread. While these platforms proved to be effective teaching tools, they typically lack the features to enable spontaneous social interactions in class (Yates, Starkey, Egerton & Flueggen, 2021).

At the University of Padova telepresence robots are being experimented as tools to enhance the inclusion of students who are not able to physically attend classes because of their health condition. The deployment of telepresence robots to allow students with severe diseases is not new, previous studies mainly investigated the impact that this technology has on the experience of the piloting users (e.g., Jouppi, 2002), the teachers (e.g., Bloss, 2011) and the class (e.g., Fels, Waalen, Zhai & Weiss, 2001). Less attention has been devoted to understanding what the students who will benefit from the telepresence robot expect from the technology. In the present work, we aim to fill this gap by reporting a qualitative investigation on students' expectations before the technology is introduced as part of their learning routine.

1.1 Related Work

Over the past 20 years, the introduction of increasingly advanced technology in education has made it possible to provide a link between school and home, or hospital, for those students who must be absent due to their chronic illness (Newhart & Olson, 2017; Fels et al., 2001). The telepresence robots that are available today have been designed and built to meet needs of end-users, that is to improve their sense of being *really* present in the classroom and their opportunity to learn (Page, Charteris & Berman, 2021).

Cha, Chen and Mataric (2017) investigated the features that telepresence robots should have in co-design sessions with middle-school students. They found that the quality of the audio and video technology embedded in the robot are of primary importance to enable interaction. Moreover, they suggested to provide the student attending remotely with the physical learning materials in advance to further improve their experience. The robot should be able to adjust the height and pan the display to better adapt to the situation.

Fitter et al. (2021) addressed how the personalization of the telepresence robot affects the relationship between the user and the interlocutor. They highlighted that personalization of the telepresence robot has humanizing effects, thereby facilitating the interaction.

Han and Conti (2021) devised a survey to specifically assess the acceptance of telepresence robots in the educational context. Notably, they only addressed the point of view of teachers. Differently, Khojasteh, Liu and Fussell (2019) investigated the perspective of undergraduate students using telepresence robots to navigate inside the campus. More specifically, they devise a 'search and find task', which able-bodied participants had to carry out with the telepresence robot. Participants judged their experience positively, considering the robot easy to maneuver. Still, it emerged that most participants were hesitant to start a conversation through the telepresence robot.

Newhart, Warschauer, and Sender (2016) introduced telepresence robots in classrooms to allow homebound children (ranging between 6- and 16-year-old). They explored the point of view not only of homebound children but also of the parents, the teachers, and schoolmates. They found that the anthropomorphic appearance of the robot was a key factor in making it part of the daily activities for teachers and schoolmates. Importantly, homebound students stressed the fact that the telepresence robot enabled them to see and talk with their friends. Finally, the robots were seen by both teachers and parents as tools to ensure continuity in the student's academic career. Similarly, Weibel et al. (2020) investigated the impact of telepresence on children suffering from severe diseases. They found that the robots facilitated social interaction with peers and inclusion in the learning activities. Still, some challenges also emerged, amounting to the location of the telepresence robot in the classroom, which affected the student's feeling of being present in the class. Finally, the technological capability of the device was considered a limiting factor.

Kwon, Koo, Kim and Kwon (2010) experienced minor technical issues during the unfolding of their study. Still they reported that the telepresence robot was able to deliver an experience almost as vivid as the in-person experience, for both teacher and students.

Velinov, Koceska and Koceski (2021) reflect on the need to complement the research on telepresence robots in learning environments with qualitative data, in order to provide indications for the effective introduction of these devices.

2. MATERIALS AND METHODS

2.1 Equipment

For the present study, the Ohmni telepresence robot is deployed (Figure 1). It is equipped with a touch-screen display (10.1″ HD), a camera (13 MP in High Definition), an input microphone, and a speaker to enable remote interactions between users in different locations.

The touch-screen display, with which the user can show her/him face, is supported by a rod that allows to adjust its inclination (130-degree).

Thanks to three large wheels mounted on its base, the robot can move around the space. The telepresence robot features an anti-collision sensor. More specifically, a led projects a light that changes color depending on the robot's proximity to the obstacle (either other people or objects). In safe conditions the light is blue, it turns yellow when it approaches an obstacle, and it becomes red when the robot stops because it is too close to the obstacle.

Figure 1. The telepresence robot

The telepresence robot is paired with a web app (Figure 2), to allow the user to connect with the device. Using the Internet, users can access and log in to the web app (using any device; Figure 2-A). Through the web app, they can change various parameters in the settings (such as adjusting the screen contrast, the volume of audio input and output, and the robot's movement speed). They can turn the camera on or off on their devices to show their faces (Figure 1). The webcam preview of the user's device is displayed in the lower right corner of the web platform (Figure 2-B).

Users can control the movement of the robot synchronously in the surrounding space using the keyboard of their device. As mentioned above, the robot has an anti-collision sensor that stops it when it is too close to an obstacle, preventing it from colliding. To increase safety in user movements, the wide-angle view of the robot's webcam allows a view of the environment in which it is moving and the robot's body (as shown in Figure 2-B).

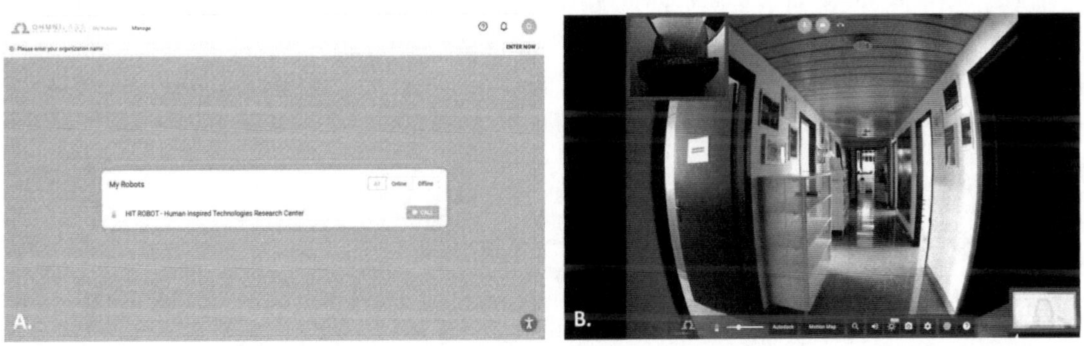

Figure 2. The login in the web platform (A). The user view from the web platform (B)

2.2 Recruitment and Contacts

Students were recruited through the University Inclusion Service. They were reached out from their database. In order to be eligible to participate in the study, students' fine motor skills had to be preserved to allow them to maneuver the robot by pressing the keys.

Once they agreed to participate in the study, a researcher called them and briefly explained the aim of the project and how the study would unfold. Next, students received an email with the informed consent form reporting the full details of the research. Participants had to send back a copy of the signed informed consent to the researcher.

The study was approved by the ethical committee board.

2.3 Participants

A total of 6 students of the University of Padova were involved (F=3; M=3). The sample had an average age of 31.16 years (ranging from 20 to 54 years). Two students attended master's degree courses, while the other attended bachelor's degree.

All participants had special motoric needs. Only one participant reported being in the habit of attending classes in person. This student is the only one who started in the current degree program prior to the onset of the Sars-CoV-2 pandemic. Others have always relied on video conferencing tools to pursue their current degree program. Finally, the sample includes only one experienced user who had already used the robot before.

2.4 Procedure

The first contact with the researchers was by telephone a few days after the students signed the informed consent. After explaining the project in detail, individual arrangements were scheduled to carry out the initial trails with the robot during the following days to train them at using the technology and increase their confidence

On an appointed day, researchers and the student met each other on the platform zoom.us. The researchers welcomed the participant and briefly explained how the meeting would be conducted.

Researchers shared a visual presentation of the robot to illustrate its functionalities. When the presentation ended, and the student felt finally ready to try out the robot, the researchers shared login credentials via email. Then they were invited to connect to the telepresence robot. At this point, the students were free to move around during the training, exploring the environment and the robot's functionalities.

Afterward, following, Rossato, Orso, Pluchino and Gamberini (2021) participants' expectations regarding the telepresence robots were investigated using a semi-structured interview. This kind of interview is well suited to investigating an experience that has just ended, for example, investigating problems the user may have had during the interaction, exploring their causes together, and clarifying their concerns (Chen, 2018).

The interview was conducted using the robot (robot-mediated interview; Lei, Clemente, Liu & Bell, 2022), and the audio was recorded using an external device. If participants had no further questions, the interview was concluded.

Finally, arrangements were made for sharing the needed information for the future connections of the student in the class.

2.5 Analysis

On average, interviews lasted 12 minutes (interviews were intentionally kept short not to stress participants). A total of 74 minutes of interviews were transcribed verbatim to enable subsequent analysis. Two independent researchers read the transcripts and looked for emerging themes. These themes were coded and then grouped into categories, following Edwards, Sainfort, Kongnakorn, and Jacko (2006).

3. RESULTS

From the analysis of the transcripts, six themes emerged: (1) motivations to participate in the project (2) hardware capabilities; (3) social acceptance; (4) pioneering the technology; (5) proficiency at maneuvering the robot; and (6) social interactions.

Motivations to participate in the study. In this category, fall all the motivations participants reported for partaking in the project. They were willing to participate, mainly because they expect that the telepresence robot will enable them to freely move around the environment and socialize with their classmates (n=4).

'I was never able to socialize with my classmates. Of course, sometimes we talked on Whatsapp to exchange information about exams but nothing more. I hope the robot will help me get to know them better.' P05

Indeed, a participant is constrained to the area in the classroom where she can move the wheelchair.

'The part I was most interested in was being able to move around the space. The classrooms do not allow me to move around and decide whom to sit next to. I can't choose the seat I want. I have a reserved seat and it's very difficult for me to move around.' P01

Hardware capabilities. This category covers all the technology-related aspects praised by respondents. Participants had the opportunity to directly try out the telepresence robot. During the interview they reported to be impressed by the short time lag between their issuing of the commands and the actual response of the robot (n=3).

'I work in the IT world, and I know about video conferencing systems. I've seen that there's an impressive ease of response of video, audio and movement.' P05

Furthermore, they appreciated how easy it was to control the movements of the robot, and the fact that it embeds anti-collision system (n=4).

'This can be useful. I have difficulty orienting myself in my surroundings.' P01

Social acceptance. This theme deals with the expectations of the interlocutors' perceptions of the user. Participants reported to be concerned about how their peers and the lecturers would look at them (n=3).

More specifically, one student feared that the robot would grab his peers' attention, thereby directing on his undesired gazes.

'Using this robot, I bring my disability into the classroom in front of everyone.' P06

Pioneering the technology. Participants were aware that it was the first time that this project was activated at their University. They felt responsible to give their contribution in order to facilitate the inclusion of other students with challenged mobility in the future. They showed to value their participation not only for the benefits they could have from the technology, but also for the benefits it will bring to other students (n=4).

'I do it with pleasure, not so much for myself, but because I know I can help others who have the same problem as me in the future. If this worked, do you know how different it could be?' P02

Proficiency at maneuvering the robot. This category collects all the instances in which respondents mentioned their concerns regarding their ability to control the robot. More specifically, they were afraid of making errors in controlling the robot that could result in damages to the objects and harming bystanders. Furthermore, they were concerned that their lack of proficiency at maneuvering the robot could negatively impact on their peers or on the lecturer, for instance by making unwanted noise or because of slow movements (n=3).

'I have a bit of a fear that I won't be able to move well, that I'll be clumsy and crash near things or worse people' P01

Social interactions. Participants did not seem to have clear expectations regarding which role the telepresence robot could play for supporting socialization. Respondents reported that they were in the habit of interacting with their colleagues only using WhatsApp, because the video-conferencing system does not support peer interactions during breaks or right after the end of the lecture (during breaks students typically leave the classroom or the call, and after the lecture the call is terminated immediately by the lecturer).

Furthermore, when asked whether they had any expectations about their peers' reactions to the robot, they mostly replied that they did not have even considered this aspect (n=3).

'I wouldn't know how to answer that question. I communicate with my colleagues only with classic messaging tools as Whatsapp. The lectures, in my experience, are not set up for socialization. I don't know how that would work. I'm leaving the possibilities open, not sure what to expect.' P03

4. DISCUSSION AND CONCLUSIONS

Telepresence robots have a high inclusive potential, as they enable students not only to attend classes, but also to participate in them. Previous research has mainly addressed the impact of adopting this technology, and the investigation of users' expectations have received little attention so far. In the present study, we have explored the expectations that users with special motoric needs hold before the adoption of telepresence robots to attend classes. To this end we interviewed a group of students before they began to employ the telepresence robot to attend classes. We found that one of their main concerns amounted to how they would be perceived through the telepresence robot by their peers and by the lecturer. This finding can be explained by the importance that is actually attributed to the appearance of the telepresence robot in easing the conversation (Fitter et al. 2021), and in helping to establish and maintain daily routines (Neuhart, 2021).

Moreover, it emerged that students struggled to figure out how the robot would be received by their peers and that they could not imagine how they would interact with them. This concern is echoed by the findings by Khojasteh, Liu & Fussell (2019), who reported that participants were not at ease at starting a conversation when using the robot. Even though it may seem obvious, the technological capabilities of the robot were praised and deemed relevant. Indeed, Weibel et al. (2020) reported that the technological limitations of the device can negatively influence the experience.

The present work contributes to the field by bringing to the foreground what users with special motoric needs expect when they have the opportunity to employ telepresence robots. The analysis of the expectations is particularly valuable to adjust the process of introduction and deployment of the robot, thereby enhancing the benefits that the technology can bring.

Next development in the research will involve the evaluation of the user experience with telepresence robots, to assess whether participants' expectations will be met.

REFERENCES

Bloss, R. (2011). High school student goes to class robotically. *Industrial Robot: An International Journal*.

Bolu, A., & Korçak, Ö. (2021). Adaptive task planning for multi-robot smart warehouse. IEEE Access, 9, 27346-27358.

Cha, E., Chen, S., & Mataric, M. J. (2017, August). Designing telepresence robots for K-12 education. In 2017 26th IEEE international symposium on robot and human interactive communication (RO-MAN) (pp. 683-688). IEEE.

Cooper, S., Di Fava, A., Vivas, C., Marchionni, L., & Ferro, F. (2020). ARI: The social assistive robot and companion. In 2020 29th IEEE International Conference on Robot and Human Interactive Communication (RO-MAN) (pp. 745-751). IEEE.

Edwards, P. J., Sainfort, F., Kongnakorn, T., & Jacko, J. (2006). Methods of evaluating outcomes. Handbook of Human Factors and Ergonomics, (G. Salvendy, ed.), 1150-1187.

Fels, D. I., Waalen, J. K., Zhai, S., & Weiss, P. L. (2001). Telepresence under exceptional circumstances: enriching the connection to school for sick children. In *Interact* (pp. 617-624).

Fitter, N. T., Strait, M., Bisbee, E., Mataric, M. J., & Takayama, L. (2021, March). You're Wigging Me Out! Is personalization of Telepresence Robots Strictly Positive?. In Proceedings of the 2021 ACM/IEEE International Conference on Human-Robot Interaction (pp. 168-176).

Han, J., & Conti, D. (2020). The use of UTAUT and post acceptance models to investigate the attitude towards a telepresence robot in an educational setting. Robotics, 9(2), 34.

Jouppi, N. P. (2002). First steps towards mutually-immersive mobile telepresence. In *Proceedings of the 2002 ACM conference on Computer supported cooperative work* (pp. 354-363).

Khojasteh, N., Liu, C., & Fussell, S. R. (2019). Understanding Undergraduate Students' Experiences of Telepresence Robots on Campus. In Conference Companion Publication of the 2019 on Computer Supported Cooperative Work and Social Computing (pp. 241-246).

Kwon, O. H., Koo, S. Y., Kim, Y. G., & Kwon, D. S. (2010). Telepresence robot system for English tutoring. In *2010 IEEE workshop on advanced robotics and its social impacts* (pp. 152-155). IEEE.

Lau, S. H., & Woods, P. C. (2009). Understanding the behavior changes in belief and attitude among experienced and inexperienced learning object users. Computers & Education, 52(2), 333-342.

Lei, M., Clemente, I. M., Liu, H., & Bell, J. (2022). The Acceptance of Telepresence Robots in Higher Education. International Journal of Social Robotics, 1-18.

Newhart, V. A., Warschauer, M., & Sender, L. (2016). Virtual inclusion via telepresence robots in the classroom: An exploratory case study. The International Journal of Technologies in Learning, 23(4), 9-25.

Newhart, V. A., & Olson, J. S. (2017). My student is a robot: How schools manage telepresence experiences for students. In *Proceedings of the 2017 CHI conference on human factors in computing systems* (pp. 342-347).7

Page, A., Charteris, J., & Berman, J. (2021). Telepresence robot use for children with chronic illness in Australian schools: a scoping review and thematic analysis. *International Journal of Social Robotics*, *13*(6), 1281-1293.

Rossato, C., Orso, V., Pluchino, P., & Gamberini, L. (2021). Adaptive Assembly Workstations and cobots: a qualitative assessment involving senior and adult workers. In European Conference on Cognitive Ergonomics 2021 (pp. 1-5).

Rossato, C., Pluchino, P., Cellini, N., Jacucci, G., Spagnolli, A., & Gamberini, L. (2021). Facing with Collaborative Robots: The Subjective Experience in Senior and Younger Workers. Cyberpsychology, Behavior, and Social Networking, 24(5), 349-356.

Serhan, D. (2020). Transitioning from face-to-face to remote learning: Students' attitudes and perceptions of using Zoom during COVID-19 pandemic. International Journal of Technology in Education and Science (IJTES), 4(4), 335-342.

Velinov, A., Koceska, N., & Koceski, S. (2021). Application of the MQTT protocol in telepresence robots.

Weibel, M., Nielsen, M. K. F., Topperzer, M. K., Hammer, N. M., Møller, S. W., Schmiegelow, K., & Bækgaard Larsen, H. (2020). Back to school with telepresence robot technology: A qualitative pilot study about how telepresence robots help school-aged children and adolescents with cancer to remain socially and academically connected with their school classes during treatment. Nursing open, 7(4), 988-997.

Yates, A., Starkey, L., Egerton, B., & Flueggen, F. (2021). High school students' experience of online learning during Covid-19: the influence of technology and pedagogy. *Technology, Pedagogy and Education*, *30*(1), 59-73.

Yousif, J. H. (2021). Social and Telepresence Robots a future of teaching. *Artificial Intelligence & Robotics Development Journal*, *1*(1), 58-65.

COMBINED UX/UXI TAXONOMY FOR PROSUMER COMMONS IN SMART SUSTAINABLE CITIES

Aleksi Kajander and Maria Claudia Solarte-Vasquez
Tallinn University of Technology
Ehitajate tee 5, 12616, Tallinn, Estonia

ABSTRACT

The transformation to renewable energy sources is becoming increasingly urgent, not only due to climate change, but additionally world events such as the COVID-19 pandemic, the 2021-22 Energy crisis, and the Russian 2022 invasion of Ukraine. The concept of prosumer microgrid commons in sustainable smart cities, consisting of peer-to-peer exchanges of renewable energy between prosumers, enabled through smart contracts promises a potential means of effectuating the energy transformation. However, the shift from consumers to prosumers brings with it legal challenges, such as the need to balance the growing dependence on standard terms in smart contracts and reduced private autonomy with a higher competency threshold for informed consent. The implementation of legal Usability and User Experience requirements represents a potential means of balancing this equation by improving the likelihood of the successful conveyance of key information. Consequently, this paper will seek to identify the factors from the combined UX/UXI taxonomy for transactional design that fit in the context of the prosumer microgrid commons and their applicability and implications for addressing the legal challenges of the consumer to prosumer shift.

KEYWORDS

Prosumer, Commons, Usability, Legal Usability (UX), Energy, Smart Contracts

1. INTRODUCTION

A smart sustainable city (SSC) is defined by the International Telecommunications union as a city that utilizes ICT technologies to improve the quality of life, efficiency of urban operations, and services in a manner that ensures the economic, social, and environmental needs of present and future generations are met (Knieps, 2017). To attain these sustainability objectives, prosumer commons have been proposed as a solution to improve, for example, the energy efficiency of a smart city (Melville, 2017).

Under such conditions, citizens of a smart city are to make a transformation from solely a consumer to that of both a producer and a consumer called a prosumer (Rao, 2019)[1]. In such a smart sustainable city, resources such as electricity would be bought and sold between the citizens based upon their needs to avoid waste. In practice, this will require a method of conducting automated transactions quickly and efficiently at all times, through Smart Contracts (SCs).

Nevertheless, as world events have demonstrated during the 'energy crisis' of Europe during the winter of 2021-22 (Euronews, 2022), the price of energy in particular can considerably shift even in the course of one day. Consequently, an individual who is not a professional, that relies on automated transactions through smart contracting for their energy needs, as may be the case in the smart city commons, is arguably at considerable risk of entering into contracts that may be severely disadvantageous, or even ruinous. Therefore, for a future smart city commons to function, prosumers must be adequately aware of the transactions they will enter, the risks they entail, and have a meaningful way of expressing their private autonomy in relation to such transactions.

[1] Very few authors have studied the role of prosumers, among these, see: Ritzer G., & Jurgenson N. (2010). Production, consumption, prosumption: the nature of capitalism in the age of the digital 'prosumer.' J. Consum. Cult., 10(1), 13–36, and Sung, E., Kim, H., & Lee, D. (2018). Why do people consume and provide sharing economy accommodation?—A sustainability perspective. *Sustainability*, *10*(6), 2072.

Among the most significant legal challenges that SCs bring, according to Mik's description of the concept (Mik, 2020), is precisely the degradation of private autonomy. The application of Usability (UX) and User Experience (UXI) factors for the design of legal transactions as proposed in the taxonomy developed by Solarte-Vasquez & Hietanen-Kunwald (2020) may represent a means of alleviating at this issue associated with the widespread utilization of SCs in a smart city. The authors updated the original taxonomy that integrated essential legal requirements and Human Computer Interaction (HCI) standards incorporating procedural justice considerations and argued that transaction design could smooth the transitional pathway to legal automation (Solarte-Vasquez & Hietanen-Kunwald, 2020). This work on combining legal and technology standards that was proposed as a methodological innovation, has become a regulatory imperative in order to get closer to the robust and trustworthy socio technical (smart) environment that the extant supranational policy demands (European Commission, 2020).

This paper aims to transfer the HCI usability heuristics and legal factors classified under the three classical usability dimensions of *effectiveness, efficiency, and satisfaction* in the Taxonomy of UX/UXI factors for transaction design to the context of the prosumer commons of a sustainable smart city and explore their applications and implications. It will focus on their relevance to the challenges related to the private autonomy of prosumers in SSCs.

2. TOWARDS SUSTAINABLE SMART CITY COMMONS

2.1 The Sustainable Smart City Electricity Commons

The successive crises of COVID-19, the 2022 energy crisis, and the Russian 2022 invasion of Ukraine have within a short-period of time created a dire need for Europe to reduce its dependency on fossil fuels, especially those supplied by Russia. While an energy transition was ongoing within the EU Member States, with states phasing out coal, natural gas production, and even nuclear plants, the effects of Russia's illegal invasion of Ukraine have caused further pressure to complete the transition quickly. Therefore, while 2050 is the EU's target for a climate-neutral continent (European Commission, 2022), the culmination of crises in 2022 have arguably added an additional objective of urgent re-structuring the EU's energy market to address the current circumstances and speedily reduce dependence on Russian fossil fuels.

In this vein, the idea of a 'prosumer' commons consisting of microgrids within a smart energy grid of an SSC, which has been proposed before (European Parliament, 2016, Knieps, 2018, Lavrijssen & Parra, 2017), conceivably appears even more attractive in Europe under the current circumstances. The prosumer commons promise an end to scarcity by both reducing the cost of electricity and increasing the incorporation and usage of renewable energy resources (Knieps 2018). The electrical prosumers commons as a concept relies on the transition of consumers to 'prosumers', who besides using electricity additionally provide it for the system through their own production, thereby decentralizing, optimizing, and reducing dependency on non-renewable energy sources (Knieps 2018). The resulting local microgrid of prosumers that produce, and exchange electricity can therefore be called a commons, as the electricity is a shared resource that is produced and consumed within that commons.

At the heart of the prosumer commons is a continuous stream of peer-to-peer (P2P) transactions, whereby individual households buy and sell electricity based on their current needs. The individual behaviour of each prosumer in the microgrid is suggested to be such that the immediate priority the production of a sufficient amount of energy, such through photovoltaic means, for their own needs and storing the leftover energy to an energy storage solution (Winter *et al*, 2021). Once a sufficient amount of charge is attained in the energy storage solution, the additional production can be introduced to the community grid (Winter *et al*, 2021). As a result, the microgrid is intended to exchange energy between the different prosumers based on their individual needs through the sharing of real-time data of each prosumer's energy status and then making appropriate exchanges.

Therefore, such a prosumer commons will be significantly less reliant on a centralized power supply that would generate the energy for them, as the prosumers are able to generate energy both for themselves as well as others in the local grid. However, this does not necessarily imply that there would be no need for a centralized power generation, rather that the amount and dependency on it would be reduced. Considering that prosumers are largely reliant on renewable energy sources, such as solar energy, for their own generated electricity, while centralized power generation often relies on coal or natural gas, the overall effect in a state would be a transformation towards renewable energies.

The transformation from consumers to prosumers represents itself a monumental shift in the role of the smart citizens, who would need to assume the risks associated to smart contracting. They will be interacting based on real-time smart city data, detailing the respective energy needs and desires of other prosumers in the grid. Due to the numerous transactions, automatic transactions are necessary, such as through the use of SCs, which will be discussed below. Moreover, the prosumer must decide for themselves what type of strategy they would like to pursue with the electricity that they produce, either to sell as much as possible as quickly as possible, or to maximize profit by selling at more opportune times (Baez-Gonzalez *et al*, 2020). Consequently, many individuals must act in a context that is outside of their profession when making these important decisions that are vital for the prosumer commons to function.

2.2 Consumers, Prosumers, and SCs

Swiftly executable P2P transactions are required for a prosumer commons microgrid to function, therefore, transactions must be streamlined and perfected for its effective operation and the uninterrupted exchange of electricity. SCs appear to be the most viable solution as they provide a means of executing transactions quickly, at low-cost, and without a need for each party to trust each other (Borgogno, 2018). SCs utilize a blockchain, which is a publicly distributed ledger, that records a long-chain of transactions, each adding a new 'block', that uses a P2P network rather than a centralized server to verify the transaction (Liczano *et al*, 2020). The verification, or 'mining', requires the usage of computation to solve a mathematical problem that validates the block and by extension the transaction, which once complete then adds the block to the existing blocks and validates the transaction (Liczano *et al*, 2020).

Therefore, the execution of SCs through blockchain requires the physical expenditure of electricity for the third parties to verify the transaction through their computers, meaning the transactions are not actually free, but rather low-cost. For example, Bitcoin transactions are notoriously energy heavy (Corbet *et al*, 2021), which is obviously undesirable for a prosumer electricity commons that is intended to, among other things, fight climate change. Nevertheless, the energy usage problem related to executing blockchain transactions is dependent on the cryptocurrency in question, and as such the carbon footprints are varied (Corbet *et al*, 2021), and as such cryptocurrencies that aim for sustainability such as Ethereum 2.0 or other more efficient mining solutions may be able to overcome the issue in the future (Kohli *et al*, 2022).

However, this highlights the importance of understanding the nature of SCs and how they are executed, as it may result otherwise in unexpected fees, especially for consumers that are operating outside of their profession. SCs themselves provide concerns from a general user and particularly from a consumer protection point of view, as the terms which can be included in a SC are severely limited as they must be expressed in software code, and SCs are not flexible in adjusting to new or unexpected circumstances (Borgogno, 2019). Considering that consumer rights are based on the notion that the both parties are imperfect, with the consumer being at a further disadvantage operating outside their own profession in a Business-to-Consumer (B2C) transaction, and therefore there is an inherent need for flexibility to address those imperfections (D'onfro, 2022). Hence, while a SC can reduce the role of humans in the relationship, they are incapable of making consumers any less human (D'onfro, 2022). Consequently, while consumers are protected by consumer protection legislation, prosumers are generally outside the scope of such protections, which exacerbates the concerns about such a widespread utilization of automated SC as a prosumer electricity commons would require.

What protection a prosumer would receive, for example in the EU, is uncertain, as the legal category of a 'prosumer' does not effectively exist, in the absence of a proper definition (Van Soest, 2018). However, the definition found in Article 2 (14) of Directive 2018/2001 utilizes the term 'renewables self-consumer' which corresponds roughly to that of a prosumer, albeit with the addition that the activities do not constitute 'its primary commercial or professional activity' (Energy Community Regulatory Board, 2020). The latter reference seeming to imply a connection to the definition of a consumer, and therefore it may imply eligibility for consumer protection. Moreover, Article 2 (14) makes reference to a 'jointly acting renewables self-consumers', which effectively describes a prosumer commons, albeit on a much smaller scale as the definition restricts it to a single household or apartment block, rather than a whole residential area, which in turn suggests that the scale of such commons in EU legislation is not envisioned to apply on a larger scale.

However, the question of whether prosumers qualify for consumer protection in the electricity prosumer commons is beyond the scope of this paper. Here what is relevant, is that the natural person whose home forms a node in the prosumer commons, is unlikely to be acting within their profession and knowledge, which means that from a purely knowledge point of view, they are acting as consumers. Consequently, if they are to enter into numerous automated transactions, the terms of which are likely to be inflexible and the financial consequences potentially significant, adequate requirements for entering into such a transaction are a significant legal challenge. In this context, focus is placed on the conveyance of information regarding the nature of transactions and their implications for the prosumer, and on how to truly acquire their informed consent (Bix, 2018).

The energy crisis of 2022 has highlighted the importance of consumers understanding the legal transactions they enter into. As the energy prices fluctuated significantly, the bills greeting consumers were a surprise to many (Canepa, 2022). While not only did consumers arguably become increasingly aware of whether they opted to a fixed or variable rate contract, on the other side, energy companies have used sneakily worded clauses to justify terminating existing fixed-term contracts due to their rising costs (Balkan Green Energy News, 2022). Consumers, who may have not appreciated the risks associated with a variable rate contract, have in some cases resorted to paying electricity bills with loans as they are otherwise unable to cover the fees (Yle, 2022).

Consequently, to put this into perspective and the context of this paper, if consumers lack understanding of a single contract for electricity, the results of which on occasion have been personally ruinous, arguably the consequences of a series of transactions as may conducted automatically by a prosumer in an electricity commons could therefore logically be even more catastrophic. As such, it is reasonable to suggest that it is imperative that the interfaces of the transactions are enhanced to ensure prosumers enter into the SCs of a prosumer commons with informed consent. Therefore, the effective communication enabled through interaction design for transactions is crucial in enabling prosumers to fairly enter into the SCs necessary in a prosumer commons efficiently, effectively and satisfactorily.

3. USABILITY (UX) AND USER EXPERIENCE (UXI) FOR SMART CONTRACTS

3.1 Self-Regulation in the Age of Smart Contracts

Smart contracts, among other digital tools, have decreased the amount of private autonomy consumers, as well as other parties, have in regard to their transactions (Hoffman, 2020). Private autonomy can be considered in the context of contracts as the ability to influence the contents of a contract (Hoffman, 2020). However, with online commerce, consumers are effectively limited to the standard contract terms offered to them with limited abilities to influence the contents therein (Hoffman, 2020). Therefore, as a general trend the amount of private autonomy enjoyed by consumers general is arguably decreasing with the popularization of online commerce and other digital tools for executing transactions.

Whether or not this a desirable development is beyond of the scope of this paper, however, it is significant in the sense that it represents the prevalent reality that is facing consumers. Hence, as this transition has been caused in part due to the depersonalization of transactions online, the utilization of SCs will progress this trend further, as the contents of a SC must be definable in software terms. In practice, this will effectively mean relying on pre-made standard terms of contracts. There may be ways to improve the private autonomy of prosumer in a microgrid commons, such as through the incorporation of Ostrom's eight principles of commons management (Ostrom, 1990). Of the eight principles, the participatory decision-making within the microgrid commons to create rules that fit the microgrid's local circumstances, which in practice could translate to adjusting the standard terms for that microgrid, could serve to improve the private autonomy of the individual prosumer, even if they still have to accept the standard terms.

Nevertheless, the reality is that a prosumer in a microgrid commons will have to accept standard terms whether they participated in deciding their content, due to the constraints of SCs. However, private autonomy can be considered to be a component of the larger concept of 'self-regulation', which can be defined as an expanded concept of agency and conceptualized as self-determination competence (Solarte-Vasquez *et al*, 2018). Therefore, the larger concept of 'self-regulation' involves not only the ability to influence the contents of a contract (private autonomy), but additionally the competence, as informed consent is required for a valid agreement (Solarte-Vasquez *et al*, 2018), to enter into them. As a result, if the prevalent reality is, that due to a variety of reasons, the private autonomy part of this equation is diminished, arguably that creates a need to compensate through a higher requirement of competence to enter into a valid agreement through informed consent. In other words, if the person lacks the meaningful ability to influence the contract terms, for the transaction to be valid, the person must have a heightened and adequate understanding of the contract contents, the risks involved and its consequences, for them to be able to enter into it lawfully.

Furthermore, this is of particular relevance in the context of a prosumer commons, as it is effectively something of a middle-ground between a Consumer-to-Consumer (C2C) and a B2C situation, where the person has the knowledge of a consumer, but also acts in a capacity that is not within the traditional role of a consumer. Consequently, to appropriately address the knowledge disparity as the prosumer acts outside of their profession, a heightened level of comprehension or competence is required. However, it is unrealistic to expect any person who buys a solar panel and wants to occasionally sell their surplus electricity to be required to become a professional in the energy field. Therefore, the utilization of HCI criteria and the incorporation of selected UX and UXI factors may provide tremendous benefits to the users and a potential solution, through the adequate conveyance of information regarding automated contracts and self-enforcing transactions within SCs.

The translation of HCI terminology and methodologies into the legal context, especially to measure the quality of legal products is a relatively new development (Solarte-Vasquez *et al*, 2016). Nonetheless, incorporating UX heuristics and standards for the design of SCs would be easy to incorporate and unlikely to create legal tensions. Notably, the most recent AI policy and regulatory developments in the EU underline human centredness and call for this type of cross-disciplinary collaboration. 'Terms and conditions' in agreements, have been long criticized for being ineffective means of communicating information to consumers (European Commission, 2016, Black, 1981, Zodi, (2019). This is in part why consumer protection legislation shields consumers from abusive contracting practices, considering that by default they are in a disadvantageous position due to their lack of knowledge in respect to professional businesses (European Commission, 2016). In the *Planet49* case, the CJEU highlighted the impact of the design of legal interfaces when entering into agreements and the legal consequences they may have, when establishing whether a person gave their informed consent (CJEU, C-673/17). While the collective requirements of 'active' and 'unambiguous' consent (CJEU, C-673/17) are definitely a step forward, it must be remembered that in practice the difference is only that the user has to click the box before moving forward, rather than only clicking 'agree'. In other words, there is still no guarantee the user has any idea or a better understanding of what the agreement is all about, but merely a duplication of an expression of consent, through two clicks of the mouse.

Therefore, while the *Planet49*-case demonstrated unambiguously that the manner in which information and consent is presented when entering into an agreement is not merely peripheral from a legal point of view, there is still significant progress yet to be made. For, arguably the next step would be to incorporate UX and UXI requirements that would significantly improve the likelihood that the user truly understands the information they are being presented, and therefore can truly give their informed consent. For it must be recognized that while it is always up to the end-user whether or not they take the time to examine the information presented to them, however, through the incorporation of UX and UXI the likelihood of that examination can be significantly improved.

The incorporation of UX and UXI requirements is a multi-faceted process with multiple and interdisciplinary aspects to be considered in order to achieve the desired overall effect of end-user understanding. Hence, the process goes beyond merely adjusting the readability of the text through plain language, but rather it encompasses a wide array of different aspects such as information visualization, pleasant aesthetics and understandability (Solarte-Vasquez *et al*, 2018). The combined taxonomy of usability components for transactional design by Solarte-Vasquez *et al* (2018), synthesizes these values, based upon which this paper will expand upon in the context of the prosumer microgrid commons that could be utilized to compensate for the diminishing private autonomy of prosumers apparent in SC related interactions.

3.2 Self-Regulation Competence through UX and UXI

The transformation of consumers to prosumers in a microgrid commons presents a considerable communication challenge, as the consumer may no longer be covered by consumer protection, and as such must be more familiar with the risks and consequences of their actions. Considering the continuous nature of the transactions in a prosumer commons, the risk to an individual is not just that of entering into one disadvantageous transactions, but a whole series. Therefore, the user must be made aware of the risks and potential consequences that are involved, as well as have a requisite amount of knowledge to correctly define their own boundaries that they are comfortable with.

Consequently, the prosumer-to-be in the microgrid commons must arguably be communicated a threefold message, so that the individual may provide their informed consent. Firstly, the prosumer must be made aware of the basics of the functioning of the system, the series of transactions through the blockchain in real-time through which energy is exchanged between the prosumers. Secondly, the risks involved, as the transactions are conducted in real-time, a series of disadvantageous transactions are possible, and how to mitigate them through for example limits to transactions. Thirdly, the prosumer's rights and obligations, as well as the dispute resolution methods available to him or her in the case of a dispute. Therefore, these three points arguably form the bare minimum for the informed consent of a prosumer in the context of the microgrid prosumer commons. With these considerations in mind, the role that legal UX/UXI can play to facilitate this process becomes more evident. The incorporation of UX/UXI has the potential to improve the chance of successful conveyance of the key information to the end user, who as a non-professional, is unlikely to be willing to acquire the knowledge they lack if it is locked behind an agonizingly tedious document or a system that is difficult to use. The combined taxonomy of UX/UXI Factors for transaction synthesized by Solarte-Vasquez *et al* (2018) highlights and classifies the HCI usability heuristics and several legal factors under the three classical usability dimensions (International Organization for Standardization, 2013), which provides a substantiated basis for the identification of legal criteria that may raise prosumer competence. Table 1 below provides an abridged version of the original taxonomy that represents a leaner and more appropriate classification as it focuses on general exchange transactions.

Table 1. Adapted Combined Taxonomy of UX/UXI Factors for Transaction Design from Solarte-Vasquez & Hietanen-Kunwald (2020)

UX Taxonomy components for transaction design		
Efficiency	Effectiveness	Satisfaction
-Readability-Clarity -Consistency -Organization -Information Visualization -Learnability -User Control	-Completeness -Relational and proactive logic (collaboration values) -Communication effect leading to consensus and satisfaction of needs -Pleasantly memorable – friendliness -Relational Sustainability	-Awareness (taking notice) -Understanding (knowing) -Consensus (wilful participation, *informed consent* engagement) -Compliance (action) -Overall satisfaction with the transacting experience -Sustainability of the agreement

The first dimension of *efficiency* relates to the amount of effort required to complete tasks or achieve goals (Solarte-Vasquez & Hietanen-Kunwald, 2020), and therefore in the context of the prosumer microgrid commons is of particular importance owing to the attributes of the target audience. Readability, which refers to the type of language (Solarte-Vasquez & Hietanen-Kunwald, 2020) used as well as is a crucial starting point to ensure that the system remains accessible and undaunting to an audience that is likely unfamiliar with specialized terminology and language. Moreover, the organization of information such as in its flow and placement (Solarte-Vasquez & Hietanen-Kunwald, 2020), is a reinforcing and interrelated factor, as the information ought to be organized in a manner whereby it does not presume extensive previous knowledge and as such flows neatly from simpler to more complex issues. The utilization of information visualization is arguably of heightened importance in the prosumer context, as a monotonous appearing imageless long text may be off-putting or appear too daunting, regardless of its consistency through neat organization. The prosumer context places therefore, an additional focus on learnability, as the user must able to navigate new and complex information, which is hence considerably intertwined with information visualization and readability, to increase the impact of the content on the users' engagement. Engagement in turn benefits from added interface flexibility and affordances, enhancing learnability and a sense of control, an important component in self-determination, which can be integrated in an interactive environment through moving and managing information as seamlessly as possible.

The second dimension of *effectiveness*, while completeness is clearly important in the sense of including all of the information, in the prosumer context caution should be attached to not overwhelming the user either. Hence, the amount of information conveyed through the interface should be carefully curated. Owing to the standardized nature of the SCs in a prosumer microgrid commons, the relational and proactive factors are of less importance due to the limited autonomy of the prosumer. However, ideally this deficit would be compensated through the prosumer's ability to influence the standardized terms in accordance with Ostrom's principle of participatory decision-making for the local microgrid, however for the purpose of the UX/UXI aspects, it does not bear a particularly significant role. Communication effect on the other hand, in the form of data enrichment techniques (Solarte-Vasquez & Hietanen-Kunwald, 2020), has considerable relevance as the utilization of graphic and technical layering of information with colours, shapes, and textures can serve to greatly encourage the user to not abandon their learning effort. Moreover, memorability is an important goal to bolster the transformation from a consumer to a prosumer through the retention of information, and as such should be a significant consideration for the system overall. Sustainability, the continuous relevance of the system (Solarte-Vasquez & Hietanen-Kunwald, 2020), should in the prosumer context have an emphasis on ensuring that the user would continue to consult the information provided when in doubt, which links strongly to the flexibility and user control of the system, for if the user would be forced to for example navigate numerous undesired sections, they may simply give up the attempt of locating the information they were seeking.

The third and final dimension, *satisfaction*, in the context of the microgrid prosumer commons is more focused on a positive disposition towards the commitment to the microgrid commons itself and the benefits that could be derived from its implementation, rather than the compliance, which is automated in this context. Consequently, it is imperative that the prosumer feels satisfied with the transaction(s) they have entered are legitimately executable, in particular through the giving of informed consent and as such are wilful participants. A satisfactory experience is defined as friendly and uncomplicated, which largely rests in the observance of the UX standards catalogued under the previous two dimensions and makes it acceptable. Hence, the resulting feelings of awareness and understanding experienced by the prosumer are likely the key factors in determining the level of satisfaction that a prosumer experiences. If a prosumer feels wronged by the automated system, they may quickly become unwilling to participate in the microgrid commons, which is naturally an undesirable outcome, both for the local commons and the transformation towards renewable energy resources on a societal level. Consequently, the overall satisfaction among prosumers is crucial for not only the success of the local microgrid commons, but additionally the state's energy policy as a whole. Consequently, SCs must entrench themselves as a sustainable basis in the sense of being lawful, remaining relational, and a useful option to support environments that promote independence from non-renewable energy sources.

4. CONCLUSION

The proposed prosumer commons microgrids within sustainable smart cities provides a credible pathway to a reduced dependence on non-renewable resources, and the attaining of climate goals. However, the change from consumers to prosumers brings with it considerable legal and regulatory challenges, such as the increased dependence on standard terms due to the constraints of SCs, and a resulting decrease in the private autonomy of the individual. This challenge is further exacerbated by the uncertainties attached to the status of a prosumer, who besides needing additional knowledge in a field they are likely not a professional in, may also not be able to rely on the safety net of consumer protection available to consumers.

Thus, as a sum of all these factors there must be a corresponding shift in the legal concept of the self-regulation of an individual, as autonomy in the form of the ability to influence the terms of agreements becomes increasingly constrained in a SC context, a counterbalancing increase in understanding and competence required to fairly enter into agreements must be implemented. Considering that a microgrid consists of an automated continuous series of transactions, this is a particularly serious concern, as an individual risks not only entering into one disadvantageous agreement, but a whole series.

Therefore, the utilization of legal UX/UXI requirements is arguably a viable means of alleviating this issue through the improved conveyance of important transactional information. The combined taxonomy of UX/UXI factors synthesized by Solarte-Vasquez *et al* (2018) which highlights and classifies HCI usability heuristics and legal factors under the three classical usability dimensions has significant relevance in the context of the prosumer microgrid commons. Numerous factors that were identified within the taxonomy, such as readability, memorability, and the transaction experience satisfaction, if implemented as UX/UXI based legal requirements for informed consent, could serve to improve the competency of prosumers to enter SCs and increase the likelihood of maintaining a sustainable microgrid prosumer commons. However, currently this potential for fairer prosumer SCs remains largely underutilized, as legal UX/UXI requirements as a prerequisite for being able to provide informed consent remain few and far between. Consequently, as the importance of the renewable energy transition intensifies, so too should the demand to incorporate legal UX/UXI requirements as prerequisites for informed consent and thus validity, when prosumers subscribe to SCs in microgrid commons.

REFERENCES

Baez-Gonzalez, P., Garcia-Torres, F., Ridao, M., Bordons, C. (2020). A Stochastic MPC Based Energy Management System for Simultaneous Participation in Continuous and Discrete Prosumer-to-Prosumer Energy Markets. *Energies*. Vol 13 (14), 37-51.

Balkan Green Energy. (2022). European energy crisis and how history repeats itself: Losses are borne by consumers while profits are retained by utilities. Retrieved from: https://balkangreenenergynews.com/european-energy-crisis-and-how-history-repeats-itself-losses-are-borne-by-consumers-while-profits-are-retained-by-utilities/ [Accessed 21.03.2022]

Bix, B. H. (2018). Consent and contracts 1. In *The Routledge handbook of the ethics of consent*, 222-234.

Black, B. (1981). A model plain language law. *Stanford law review*, 255-300.

Bourgogno, O., (2018). Smart Contracts as the (new) Power of the Powerless? The Stakes for Consumers. *European review of private law*, Vol 26 (6), 885-902.

Canepa, F. (2022). Euro zone consumers in for a shock as power bills soar. Retrieved from: https://www.reuters.com/business/energy/euro-zone-consumers-shock-power-bills-soar-2022-01-18/ [Accessed 21.03.2022].

CJEU. (2019). C-673/17, ECLI:EU:C:2019:801.

Corbet, S., Lucey, B., Yarovaya, L. (2021). Bitcoin-Energy Markets Interrelationships – new evidence. *Resources Policy*, Vol 70, 1-22.

Energy Community Regulatory Board. (2020). Prosumers in the Energy Community legal and regulatory framework for support and treatment of small-scale generators Special focus on photovoltaic (PV) systems connected to the distribution network, 1-60.

Euronews. (2022). Why is there an energy crisis in Europe?. Retrieved from: https://www.euronews.com/2022/02/03/europe-s-energy-crisis-why-are-natural-gas-prices-soaring-and-how-will-it-affect-europeans [Accessed 21.03.2022].

European Commission. (2022). Delivering the European Green Deal. Retrieved from: https://ec.europa.eu/info/strategy/priorities-2019-2024/european-green-deal/delivering-european-green-deal_en [Accessed 21.03.2022].

European Commission. (2016). Consumer's attitudes towards Terms and Condition (T&Cs). Retrieved from: https://ec.europa.eu/info/sites/default/files/termsconditions_factsheet_web_en_2.pdf [Accessed 21.03.2022].

European Commission. (2020). WHITE PAPER On Artificial Intelligence – A European approach to excellence and trust. Retrieved from: https://ec.europa.eu/info/sites/default/files/commission-white-paper-artificial-intelligence-feb2020_en.pdf [Accessed 19.05.2022]

European Parliament. (2016). Support for electricity prosumers in the European Union. Retrieved from: https://www.europarl.europa.eu/doceo/document/E-8-2019-000380_EN.html [Accessed 21.03.2022].

Hoffman, T., (2020). The Impact of Digital Autonomous Tools on Private Autonomy. *Baltic Yearbook of International Law Online*, Vol 18, 18-31.

International Organization for Standardization. (2013). Usability of consumer products and products for public use – Part 2: Summative test method. Retrieved from: https://www.iso.org/obp/ui/#iso:std:iso:ts:20282:-2:ed-2:v1:en [Accessed 21.03.2022].

Knieps, G. (2017). Internet of Things and the economics of smart sustainable cities. *Competition and Regulation in Network Industries*, Vol. 18, 115-131.

Kohli, V., Chakravarty, S., Chamola, V., Sangwan, K., Zeadally, S. (2022). An Analysis of Energy Consumption and Carbon Footprints of Cryptocurrencies and Possible Solutions. *Digital Communications and Networks*, 1-16.

Lavrijssen, S., Parra, A. (2017). Radical Prosumer Innovations in the Electricity Sector and the Impact on Prosumer Regulation. *Sustainability*. Vol 9(7), 1-21.

Liczano, D., Lara, J., White, B., Aljawarneh, S. (2020). Blockchain-based approach to create a model of trust in open and ubiquitous higher education. *Journal of Computing in Higher Education*, Vol 32, 109-134.

Melville, E., Christie, I., Burningham, K., Way, C. (2017). The electric commons: a qualitative study of community accountability. *Energy Policy*, Vol. 106, 12-21.

Mik, E. (2017). Smart Contracts: terminology, technical limitations and real world complexity. *Law, Innovation and Technology,* Vol 9(2), 269-300.

Ostrom, E. (1990). Governing the Commons. Cambridge University Press.

Rao, B., Arun, S., Selvan, M. (2019). An electric power trading framework for smart residential community in smart cities. *IET Smart Cities*, Vol 1(2), 40-51.

Ritzer G., & Jurgenson N. (2010). Production, consumption, prosumption: the nature of capitalism in the age of the digital 'prosumer.' J. Consum. Cult., 10(1), 13–36

Solarte-Vasquez, M., Järv, N., Nyman-Metcalf, K. (2016). Usability Factors in Transactional Design and Smart Contracting. The Future of Law and eTechnologies, Springer International Publishing, 149-176.

Solarte-Vasquez, M., Rungi, M., Nyman-Metcalf, K. (2018). Perceptions on self-regulation and transaction friendliness relevant to smart contracting. *International journal of law and management*, Vol 61 (1), 286-308.

Solarte-Vasquez, M., Hietanen-Kunwald, P. (2020). Responsibility and Responsiveness in the Design of Digital and Automated Dispute Resolution Processes. Conference: IRIS2020, 1-8.

Solarte-Vasquez, M., Hietanen-Kunwald, P. (2020). Transaction design standards for the operationalisation of fairness and empowerment in proactive contracting, International *and comparative law review*. Vol 20(1), 180-200.

Solarte-Vasquez, M.C, Nyman-Metcalf, K. (2017). Smart contracting: A multidisciplinary and proactive approach for the EU digital single market. *Taltech Journal of European Studies,* 7(2), 208-246.

Sung, E., Kim, H., Lee, D. (2018). Why do people consume and provide sharing economy accommodation? A sustainability perspective. *Sustainability*, 10(6), 2072.

van Soest, H., (2018). The Prosumer in European Energy Law. *Nordisk intutt for sjorett*.

Winter, D., Khatri, R., Schmidt, M. (2021). Decentralized prosumer-centric p2p2 electricity market coordination with grid security. *Energies*. Vol 14 (15), 45-65.

Zodi, Z. (2019). The limits of plain legal language: understanding the comprehensible style in law. *International Journal of Law in Context*, 15 (3), 246-262.

Yle. (2022). Sähköä jopa velaksi. Retrieved from: https://yle.fi/uutiset/3-12300788 [Accessed 21.03.2022].

A COMBINED APPROACH FOR USABILITY EVALUATION OF AN E-COMMERCE WEBSITE: REMOTE USABILITY TESTING, EYE-TRACKING, AND SUS TECHNIQUES

Thanaa Saad Alsalem, Maymunah Abdullatif Alismail and Majed Aadi Alshamari
Department of Information Systems, College of Computer Science and Information Technology, King Faisal University
Alhasa, Saudi Arabia

ABSTRACT

E-commerce has become a popular method to provide customers with their needs. This paper aims to evaluate the usability of an e-commerce Chamberlain Coffee website using remote usability testing, eye-tracking, and system usability scale (SUS). Then, it attempts to compare the effectiveness of these usability evaluation techniques. Ten users have been selected to perform a set of predefined tasks. This paper followed an experimental approach, in which both qualitative and quantitative approaches were employed to collect and analyse the data. Qualitative data were collected through eye-tracking, whereas quantitative data were collected through remote usability testing and SUS. The research findings have shown that several user interface design problems have impacted the user's performance and efficiency in terms of task success, task time, errors rate, heatmap, and overall satisfaction. The identified usability issues were rated according to their severity and impact on the user's performance in using the website. As a result, the usability evaluation methods revealed minor and major issues with the selected website.

KEYWORDS

E-commerce, Remote Usability Testing, Eye-Tracking, System Usability Scale (SUS)

1. INTRODUCTION

With the evolution of e-commerce, business owners and individuals can sell their products to customers worldwide. Accordingly, the feasibility of digital expenditure led to a revolution in the market. The web has become a target for store owners, and shops that were once concerned with decor and display have turned into photo galleries ready for a customer to browse on the web. Web design technologies were emerging at that time; websites were undergoing a significant transformation from plain and dull to rich and elegant. As a result, web designers strived to produce distinctive designs and sophisticated web pages. Websites, mainly online shops, started to evaluate their usability scores and re-design their user experience to better suit their customers (Cai & Xu, 2011). More than 83% of website users abandon it due to the difficult process of finding the needed content and the confusing user interface (Ravi Koggalage, 2021). The shops that survived were straightforward and fool proof. This phenomenon attracted considerable attention to the concept of usability and the suitability of a website to its target audience. In addition, to the traditional usability evaluation techniques, such as surveys and thinking aloud, other techniques emerged and evolved to fit the nature of computer software and web applications, such as remote testing, eye-tracking, and SUS. This paper aims to use different usability evaluation techniques to evaluate an e-commerce website using three different techniques: remote usability testing, eye-tracking, and SUS. Further, it compares the effectiveness of the selected techniques. The paper is organised as follows, Section 2 reviews previous studies of the utilised techniques, while Section 3 presents the followed research methodology. Section 4 analyses the study results. Finally, Section 5 concludes the research findings and presents future directions.

2. LITERATURE REVIEW

E-commerce websites usability have been invested due to its severe role in attracting customers to use the website. Therefore, several usability techniques are usually utilised to uncover as many usability problems as possible. They are also expected to offer multiple recommendations to improve the user experience. The following sections explore the used usability evaluation techniques: remote usability testing, eye-tracking, and SUS.

2.1 Remote Usability Testing

Remote usability testing is a technique in which the participant and examiner are in different locations; the participant is requested to perform several tasks, and the examiner monitors how they perform (Bosenick et al., 2007). The main advantage of remote usability testing is the vast pool of test subjects worldwide, especially with state-of-the-art technologies and fast network connections. In e-commerce websites, this is crucial to design a location-specific user experience. Furthermore, the participant can take the test in a friendly non-artificial environment which can lead to more realistic experiments and unbiased feedback. On the other hand, the participant may not be as engaged or focused as in a lab, and technical issues must be accounted for (Oztoprak & Erbug, 2008). Moreover, the user may require detailed guidance to perform the tasks, so two types of remote usability testing can be distinguished: moderated and unmoderated. Moderated tests are the online version of in-person lab tests in which the examiner accompanies the participant throughout the entire test. However, in unmoderated tests, participants perform the tasks independently (Alhadreti, 2021). The test often includes 3 to 5 tasks and lasts for 30 minutes, facilitated by screen sharing and video calls. Nonetheless, some dedicated platforms and technologies that help the researcher conduct remote usability testing (Chalil-Madathil & Greenstein, 2017).

The approach utilises video calls and screen sharing to mediate the participant and facilitator. It can be performed synchronously in real-time or asynchronously. Alhadreti (2021) compared synchronous and asynchronous usability evaluation techniques. Their experiment targeted the usability of two hospital websites in Saudi Arabia. Forty users with good internet skills participated in the experiment. Their findings indicated that asynchronous usability evaluation detected more severe issues on the website and provided more neutral feedback. Martin et al. (2014) investigated the validity of remote asynchronous testing compared to in-lab tests; they programmed their website portal and argued that remote testing yielded better results and discovered more issues while being cheaper than in-lab tests.

Recent research attempts to utilize augmented reality to make the experiment as authentic as possible. Chalil-Madathil and Greenstein (2017) introduced a novel usability evaluation technique using a three-dimensional collaborative virtual environment and comparing the findings with traditional in-lab experiments and regular remote testing using a screen sharing and conferencing tool. The experiment included 36 participants and 12 facilitators. The result indicated that using Virtual Reality (VR) offered higher engagement levels and a better immersive experience compared to screen sharing. However, in-lab tests produced the lowest overall workload for both the participants and the facilitators (Chalil-Madathil & Greenstein, 2017).

Puteri and Widyanti (2018) examined the usability of an Islamic fashion website and inspected its effectiveness, efficiency, and user satisfaction. Their tests were done remotely to maintain neutrality and provide a real-life experience for the participants. One hundred twenty participants were included in this experiment, and their screens were recorded throughout the process. Their approach measured efficiency through the task completion time, whereas effectiveness was indicated by the number of completed tasks. Finally, user satisfaction was measured using a questionnaire. Their finding indicated a favourable score for the website of interest. However, 8 redesign recommendations were provided for the website, including modifications in some icons, views, and navigation (Puteri & Widyanti, 2018).

2.2 Eye-Tracking

Eye-tracking is another popular tool in which the user's eye movements are recorded and analysed. The primary advantages of eye-tracking are identifying the user's areas of interest, detecting fixations, and examining how long it takes for a user to find what they are looking for (Manhartsberger et al., 2005). This can be essential for the re-design recommendations as it can highlight where essential elements must be located and what elements are unnecessarily stealing the user's attention (Vlachogianni & Tselios, 2021). However, despite the importance and quality of data that eye-tracking provides, it is considered quite expensive. Furthermore, the data provided by eye-tracking are challenging to interpret. For instance, a prolonged fixation on an element indicates either an attraction to it or difficulty understanding it, but the data does not reveal which (Collina et al. 2018).

Roth et al. (2013) argued that users have developed expectations regarding the design of web pages and that placing elements in their "typical" locations led to fewer fixations and facilitated a faster element detection by the user. Their experiment involved 40 participants and encompassed different websites such as online shops, business sites, and newspapers. Their findings proved that typically designed web pages led to more focused orientation and reduced task time.

Chynał et al. (2018) evaluated the usability of an e-commerce system known as SimplyTick using eye-tracking tools. Twelve participants attempted to complete six tasks; a Tobii X2-60 eye-tracker was employed to monitor the eye movements of the participants. The metrics of interest include time to the first mouse click, number of mouse clicks, and time from the first fixation to the next mouse click. They concluded that any issues facing users when trying to find a specific element were related to the element location and presentation. The attention of users on the homepage of SimplyTick was dispersed and not focused on the main objects.

Oyekunle et al. (2020) used the eye-tracking tool to investigate the usability of two websites: Jumia.ng and jamb.org.ng in the e-commerce and education domains, respectively. Thirty-five final-year students from the Faculty of Communication and Information Sciences participated in this experiment. The eye-tracking was performed using the OGAMA eye-tracking software, and fixation values for search tasks were recorded on both sites. The main finding of this work was the difference between the behavioural patterns of user interactions of e-commerce and educational web applications. The e-commerce website performed better in terms of atheism and multimedia deployment. However, the design of the site did not encourage the user purchase decision as the user's attention was dispersed by choice of colours and excessive media.

Pappas et al. (2018) examined the visual appeal of an e-commerce website. The equipment consisted of four SMI RED 250 and one TOBII mobile eye-tracker. Twenty-three participants were recruited, and the test was done in a dedicated lab. The results provided a great insight into users' perceptions based on their eye movement. For instance, short fixation and high saccade amplitude corresponded to a simple website design, and users did not linger on details during their first visit. In contrast, a high fixation duration variance (SD) and high backtrack indicated a diverse webpage, which allowed for a better focus on the details of the webpage.

2.3 System Usability Scale

SUS is a standardised questionnaire developed by John Brooke (Ehmke & Wilson, 2007). The simple yet effective survey consists of 10 items and is considered a reliable qualitative follow-up to usability testing as it can provide a subjective overview of system usability. SUS is a zero-cost tool that is quick to apply and easy for participants to answer. Its general nature fits with a wide variety of systems. However, it was criticised for its overly subjective questions. It is also biased by prior user experience with the system as well as external psychological and physical factors (Pappas et al., 2018). It is prone to the peak effect where the user's experience with the system is clouded by either the last task or the most difficult one. Nevertheless, SUS remains very popular among researchers and is being adapted into many other languages.

Purwadi et al. (2019) utilised SUS to examine the usability and acceptance of an Indonesian agriculture e-commerce website. The questionnaire was distributed among 35 participants, and the results obtained indicated that the system needed modification to satisfy its users. However, no clear recommendations were implied. This is because SUS provides quantitative data. Thus, it is rarely used alone but instead combined with other more qualitative methods or used as a follow-up usability test. Hamid et al. (2020) tested 20 Pakistani online stores using the heuristic evaluation and SUS; many violations of the website content accessibility guidelines were found. The authors provided recommendations such as more explicit labels and a better webpage structure. Wahyuningrum et al. (2020) also utilised the heuristic evaluation and SUS to evaluate the usability of an e-commerce website: shopee.com. Thus, the experiment included both experts and regular users and found issues in the flexibility and efficiency of the site.

3. METHODOLOGY

This section presents the methodology design that is followed in this research. It also explains the rationale for the selected evaluation techniques and website. In addition, it demonstrates the participants' characteristics, performed tasks, and usability measures. Moreover, this section discusses the test procedures, including the test environment and used tools, and the SUS for system usability testing.

3.1 Research Design

This paper is an experimental approach with a mixed design methodology; qualitative and quantitative data were combined into the paper methodology. Qualitative data was used in eye-tracking, while quantitative data was used in remote usability testing and SUS.

3.2 The Selected Evaluation Techniques

Recently, different usability evaluation techniques have been used in websites evaluation. However, there are two types of evaluation techniques: the expert and user techniques. Expert evaluation techniques, such as heuristic evaluation, cognitive walkthrough, and competitive research. User evaluation techniques, such as usability testing, eye-tracking, interview, questionnaire, and SUS. In this paper, the researchers focused on user evaluation techniques. The researchers selected three usability evaluation techniques that can offer more comprehensive assessments and detailed results: remote usability testing, eye-tracking, and SUS. The combination of the selected techniques permits involving the users, and quantitative data collection through using remote usability testing and SUS techniques, whereas qualitative data is automatically collected by executing eye-tracking techniques. Remote usability testing tests users in their natural workplace that allows users to behave more naturally in their work environment. Also, there is no need to gather all users at one time. While eye-tracking is an excellent tool to identify where a user is looking. Besides, the eye-tracking technique detects usability problems without disturbing users' natural behaviour. Meanwhile, the SUS technique measures user satisfaction which can be utilised on small sample sizes and provide reliable results. Thousands of coffee websites are now available over the Internet. The Chamberlain Coffee website is one example (Chamberlain Coffee, 2022). Its revenue is $9 million (ZoomInfo, 2022). This website is selected for evaluation as it is one of the most recent and used coffee websites that offer different products.

3.3 Participants

In this paper, ten users were selected: five users for remote usability testing and five users for the eye-tracking technique. Based on Nielsen (1994), more than 75% of the usability issues can be found within five users. The experiment was conducted on ten participants with different demographic characteristics such as gender, age, and education level as shown in Table 1. The participants were upper intermediate in English. Also, they have experience buying from online shopping websites, and they have already signed up for the Chamberlain Coffee website. Therefore, such characteristics are expected to reflect the actual users of the targeted website.

Table 1. Users' demographics

Category		**Number**
Gender	Male	5
	Female	5
Age	18–30 years old	5
	31–40 years old	4
	41 years and older	1
Academic level		
	School	2
	Bachelor	4
	Master	4

3.4 Tasks

Five tasks were selected based on the functionalities of the Chamberlain Coffee website, as shown in Table 2.

Table 2. Users' tasks

Task	Description
1	Sign in to the website.
2	Search about "Night Owl Blend."
3	Add the selected coffee bag to the cart.
4	Remove the selected coffee bag from the cart.
5	Sign out from the website.

3.5 Usability Measures

The four metrics used were task success, task time, errors number, and heatmap to measure the website's usability effectiveness, efficiency, and satisfaction, as shown in Table 3.

Table 3. Metrics definitions

Metrics	Explanation
Task Success	Success and failure of the task are measured in binary terms. Task success is represented by 1, whereas task failure is represented by 0.
Task Time	It records how long the user can complete the task in seconds or minutes.
Errors	It indicates the number of times a user makes a mistake while completing the task.
Heatmap	It shows the visualisations of users' attention and gaze points on the website

3.6 Test Procedures

Remote usability testing and SUS techniques were used to manually obtain quantitative data, while the eye-tracking technique was used to automatically collect qualitative data about the participants' performance during the test. All participants received an introduction and instruction sheets in addition to a consent and withdrawal form. The following subsections present the procedures for remote usability testing, eye-tracking, and SUS techniques on the selected website.

3.6.1 Environment

Two human-computer interaction (HCI) experts have facilitated the experiment on the selected website. For remote usability testing, the experiment was managed remotely, and every user did the experiment individually via Zoom by using their own laptop. After that, the data was recorded and collected manually. For the eye-tracking tool, a small usability lab was conducted in a peaceful environment where users could easily focus on the assigned tasks. In addition, high-speed internet was required with no external interruptions such as disturbing noise conditions or changing lighting.

3.6.2 Tools

1. Laptop: The participants conducted the experiment by using their laptops.
2. Zoom: This app was used to monitor the participants remotely and record the session to observe the participant when doing the task while estimating the time taken in every task.
3. Google Forms: This was used to design the SUS survey and collect data from participants.
4. Microsoft Excel: Microsoft Excel was used to analyse and visualise the data.
5. RealEye: RealEye is an online platform with webcam eye-tracking.

3.7 System Usability Testing

The SUS is a 10-item questionnaire that assesses how easy a product is to use. SUS was created in the 1980s by John Brooke as a fast and easy-to-use metric. In using a post-test survey, SUS metrics are often employed (Holden, 2020). The SUS is calculated by multiplying the sum of all score contributions for the ten items by 2.5. SUS score interpretation is as follows: if the SUS score is less than 50, the result is not acceptable; if the score is between 50 and 70, the result is marginal; and if the score is more than 70, the result is acceptable. SUS supports the user with the usability test categorised from strongly disagree (1) to strongly agree (5).

4. DATA ANALYSIS AND RESULTS

This section explores the data analysis and results. It starts with analyses of the task success rate, task time, error number rate, and heatmap metrics. Then, it displays the SUS outcome. Finally, it discusses the comparison of the effectiveness between the selected techniques.

4.1 Usability Metrics

The users could complete tasks 1, 2, 3, and 4 without any help, while four users failed to complete task 5. Figure 1 shows the task success rate; it is worth mentioning that task 5 resulted in the lowest success rate accomplishing 20%. The overall effectiveness of the Chamberlain Coffee website is 80% indicating that it requires improving the website interface. In addition, the users demonstrated short time on tasks 3, 4, 1, and 2, respectively. Figure 2 shows task 5 took a long time compared to other tasks with the highest average task time approximately 63.6 seconds. Further, each task's error rate was calculated after observing the users and analysing their performance while performing the tasks. Figure 3 shows the most frequent errors that occurred during task 5 with an average errors number of 0.8 followed by tasks 4, 2, and 3, respectively. As concluded from the aforementioned results, users were noticed to face difficulties finding the "Sign out" button due to its location on the website. Also, the designers might put the button in a difficult location to keep users signed in to collect more precise data about the users each time they visit the website. These results provide insightful information on the user interface design issues as users could not accomplish task 5. The study outcomes are similar to another study that reported the findings of interface issues by measuring the effectiveness and efficiency of a website using the success rate and task time metrics (Ritthiron & Jiamsanguanwong, 2017).

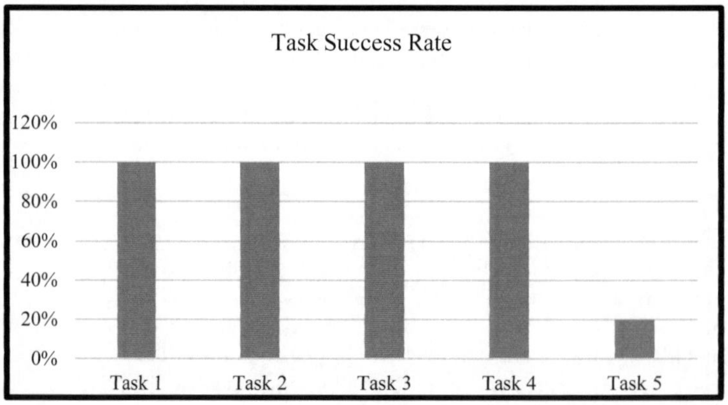

Figure 1. Task success rate

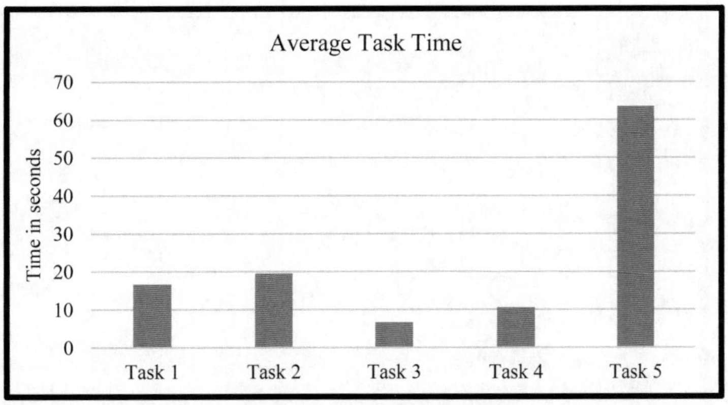

Figure 2. Average task time

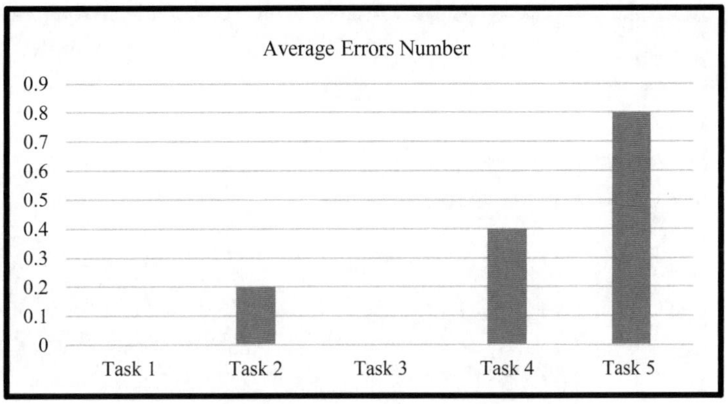

Figure 3. Average errors number

4.2 Heatmap Metrics

It is noticed from the hotspot data in the heatmap that the users focused on distributed areas on the left-side menu of the webpage, which is not the area to complete the sign-in/sign-out tasks shown in Figure 4. It is worth mentioning that this observation is in line with a previous study's findings that users view the page from a left-to-right manner (Knogler, 2020; Forsström, 2019). It is worth noticing that the Arab users in this study viewed the webpage from left-to-right, which contradicts other study observations that Arab users view the screen from right-to-left (Alsswey et al., 2018). Additionally, it is notable that users neglected the right side of the webpage, which is aligned with another study outcome that elements on the right side are ignored by Arab users (Alsaffar et al., 2018). The aforementioned observations highlighted that Arab users' view the webpage from left-to-right instead of viewing it from right-to-left might be because the website is in English. Moreover, the Arab users in this study focused on distributed areas on the drop-down list at the header of the webpage, which is not the area to complete the search for the "Night Owl Blend" task, as shown in Figure 5. The users' behaviour is aligned with other study outcomes that emphasise Arab users' focus on the top area of the webpage (Alsaffar et al., 2018).

Figure 4. Heatmap for finding sign-in/sign-out tasks

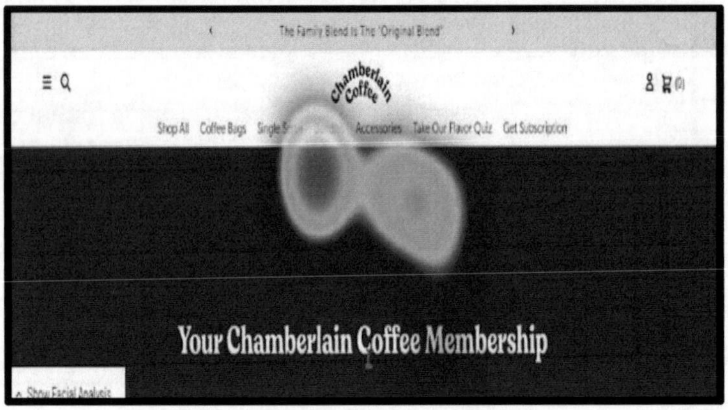

Figure 5. Heatmap for search task

It is noticed from the hotspot data in the heatmap that the users focused on quantity increment/decrement buttons and faced difficulty in finding the "Remove" button; due to the similarity between the buttons and the text as well as the poor colouring selection, which contradicts with the affordance design principle (Mikhail Mitra, 2016). This design issue is in line with another study that highlighted the importance of selecting the colours to not distract the user's attention on the screen (Oyekunle et al., 2020).

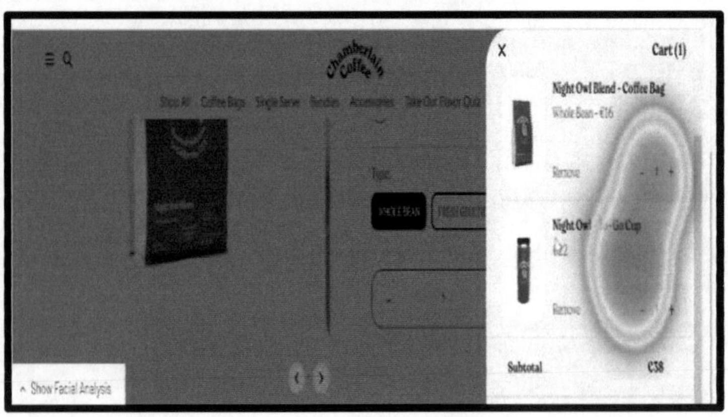

Figure 6. Heatmap for remove task

4.3 SUS Calculation and Results

The average SUS score of the website is collected, calculated, and presented in this section as shown in Table 4.

Table 4. Average SUS score

#	Chamberlain Coffee Website SUS Score	Interpretation
P1	65	Marginal
P2	75	Acceptable
P3	35	Not Acceptable
P4	82.5	Acceptable
P5	97.5	Acceptable
P6	42.5	Not Acceptable
P7	55	Marginal
P8	90	Acceptable
P9	42.5	Not Acceptable
P10	27.5	Not Acceptable
Average Score	61.25	Marginal

Users' SUS was measured through a five-point Likert scale. Four users declared that the usability of the Chamberlain Coffee website is not acceptable, while two users found the website to be marginal. In addition, four users stated that the usability of the Chamberlain Coffee website is acceptable. However, the average SUS score is 61.25, which corresponds to marginal. Consequently, based on the analysis and results, the website contains several usability issues that make users face difficulties. Hence, the website needs improvements to reach the "acceptable" level according to the SUS scale, which is equivalent to more than 70. The SUS score of this website is similar to the average satisfaction level of Shopee website users, where the SUS score reached 67.08 (Sembodo et al., 2021).

4.4 Comparison of the Effectiveness between the Selected Techniques

The comparison based on the number of issues detected is in favour of the eye-tracking tool as it revealed four usability issues, whereas remote usability testing detected three usability issues, as shown in Table 5. Both techniques have unearthed similar usability issues, but they did so differently. Remote usability testing results are based on task success, how many errors the users made, and how much time it took them to perform the task. On the other hand, the failure or difficulty of a user to complete a task combined with heatmaps obtained from eye-tracking helped uncover more in-depth usability issues of the website and provided insights into the user behaviour while interacting with the interface elements.

Table 5. Comparison of the effectiveness between the selected techniques

Technique	Number of Problems	Task Number	Usability Problems	Severity Rating
Remote Usability Testing	3	Task 2	The small size of "Search" icon.	2: Minor problem
		Task 4	The "Remove" button is similar to the text.	2: Minor problem
		Task 5	The "Sign out" button is not found in a conspicuous location.	3: Major problem
Eye-Tracking	4	Task 1	The "Sign in" button is small, making it difficult for the users to find it. Also, the users tend to focus on the left side and the web page's footer.	2: Minor problem
		Task 2	The small size of "Search" icon.	2: Minor problem
		Task 4	The "Remove" button is similar to the text.	2: Minor problem
		Task 5	The "Sign out" button is not found in a conspicuous location.	3: Major problem

From Table 5 above, it can be noticed that users faced some issues with the icons. This finding is in line with other research in e-commerce carried out by (Puteri & Widyanti, 2018). As a result, the authors provided eight re-design recommendations for the website, including modifications to some icons, views, and navigation (Puteri & Widyanti, 2018). In addition, some issues faced a few users who did not find the buttons in a conspicuous location and took a long time to find them. These results agree with (Wahyuningrum et al., 2020) findings, who uncovered some issues in the flexibility and efficiency of the website. Furthermore, the authors of this study stated that issues facing users when trying to find a specific element were related to the element's location, and presentation (Chynał et al., 2018), which is endorsed with the findings of this study as some elements are not found in the proper location. Consequently, it can be stated that these findings could help developers in overcoming such issues and addressing them in designing any e-commerce website.

5. CONCLUSION

In this paper, the usability of the Chamberlain Coffee website was examined. Three techniques were utilised to evaluate the usability of the website: remote usability testing, eye-tracking, and SUS. The evaluation methods revealed minor and major issues with the Chamberlain Coffee website. The eye-tracking tool revealed four usability issues, whereas remote usability testing detected three usability issues. This work was hindered by time constraints and limited access to hardware and equipment, especially for eye-tracking. Thus, the software version was used as a less accurate alternative with a limited user session and fewer metrics. Future research should consider using high-quality equipment to achieve the highest level of accuracy. Furthermore, Furthermore, more participants of different age groups and computer skill levels should be included to establish an inclusive population that reflects the website's potential users. Moreover, this area of research requires more studies to compare websites and a comprehensive study to examine and compare different websites to give an insight and detailed results that can be generalised.

REFERENCES

Alhadreti, O., 2022. A Comparison of Synchronous and Asynchronous Remote Usability Testing Methods. In *International Journal of Human–Computer Interaction*, vol. 38, no. 4, pp. 289-297.

Alsaffar, M., Pemberton, L., & Echavarria, K. R. (2018). An eye tracking study of viewing behaviour and preferences of Arabic, English and Chinese users. Electronic Workshops in Computing. https://doi.org/10.14236/ewic/hci2018.51

Alsswey, A., Naufal, I., & Bervell, B. (2018). Investigating the acceptance of Mobile Health Application User Interface Cultural-based design to assist Arab elderly users. International Journal of Advanced Computer Science and Applications, 9(8). https://doi.org/10.14569/ijacsa.2018.090819

Bosenick, T., Kehr, S., Kühn, M. and Nufer, S., 2007. Remote usability tests - An extension of the usability toolbox for online-shops. In *Lecture Notes in Computer Science (including subseries Lecture Notes in Artificial Intelligence and Lecture Notes in Bioinformatics),* vol. 4554 LNCS, no. PART 1, pp. 392–398.

Cai, S.and Xu, Y., 2011. Designing not just for pleasure: Effects of web site aesthetics on consumer shopping value. In *International Journal of Electronic Commerce*, vol. 15, no. 4, pp. 159–188.

Chalil-Madathil, K., and Greenstein, J. S., 2017. An investigation of the efficacy of collaborative virtual reality systems for moderated remote usability testing. In *Applied Ergonomics*, vol. 65, pp. 501–514.

Chamberlain Coffee. https://chamberlaincoffee.com/, accessed Nov. 22, 2022.

Chamberlain Coffee - Overview, News & Competitors | ZoomInfo.com. (2022). Retrieved March 16, 2022, from https://www.zoominfo.com/c/chamberlain-coffee-llc/480015623

Chynał, P., Falkowska, J. and Sobecki, J., 2018. Web Page Graphic Design Usability Testing Enhanced with Eye-Tracking. In *International Conference on Intelligent Human Systems Integration*, vol. 722, pp. 515–520. Springer, Cham.

Collina, L., Di Sabatino, P., Galluzzo, L., Mastrantoni, C. and Mazzocchi, M., 2018. What Does the System Usability Scale (SUS) Measure? Validation Using Think Aloud Verbalization and Behavioral Metrics. vol. 10918, pp. 14–26.

Ehmke, C. and Wilson, S., 2007. Identifying web usability problems from eyetracking data.

Forsström, P. (2019). An analysis of online attraction and user experience on an e-commerce website.

Hamid, S., Bawany, N. Z. and Zahoor, K., 2020. Assessing ecommerce websites: Usability and accessibility study. In *2020 International Conference on Advanced Computer Science and Information Systems (ICACSIS)*, pp. 199–204. IEEE.

Holden, R. J., 2020. A simplified system usability scale (SUS) for cognitively impaired and older adults. In *Proceedings of the International Symposium on Human Factors and Ergonomics in Health Care*, vol. 9, no. 1, pp. 180-182. SAGE Publications.

Knogler, V. (2020). Viewing Behaviour and Task Performance on Austrian Destination Websites: Comparing Generation Y and the Baby Boomers. In Eye Tracking in Tourism (pp. 225-241). Springer, Cham.

Kuruppuge Tharindu, P., & Koggalage, R. (2021). USABILITY OF E-COMMERCE WEBSITES: STATE OF THE ART AND FUTURE DIRECTIONS. In International Research Journal of Modernization in Engineering Technology and Science. www.irjmets.com

Manhartsberger, M. and Zellhofer, N., 2005. Eye tracking in usability research: What users really see. In *Usability Symposium,* vol. 198, no. 2, pp. 141-152.

Martin, R., Shamari, M. A., Seliaman, M. E. and Mayhew, P., 2014. Remote asynchronous testing: A cost-effective alternative for website usability evaluation. In *International Journal of Computer and Information Technology*, vol. 3, no. 1, pp. 99-104.

Mitra, M. (2016, March 16). 10 Most Important Interaction Design Principles. Mantra Labs. Retrieved March 23, 2022, from https://www.mantralabsglobal.com/blog/10-basic-principles-of-interaction-design/

Nielsen, J., 1994. Guerrilla HCI: using discount usability engineering to penetrate the intimidation barrier. In *Cost-justifying usability*, pp. 245-272.

Oyekunle, R., Bello, O., Jubril, Q., Sikiru, I. and Balogun, A., 2020. Usability Evaluation using Eye-Tracking on E-Commerce and Education Domains. In *Journal of Information Technology and Computing*, vol. 1, no. 1, pp. 1–13.

Oztoprak, A. and Erbug, C., 2008. Field versus laboratory usability testing: a first comparison.

Pappas, I. O., Sharma, K., Mikalef, P. and Giannakos, M. N., 2018. Visual aesthetics of e-commerce websites: An eye-tracking approach. In *Proceedings of the 51st Hawaii International Conference on System Sciences*, pp. 255–264.

Purwadi, J., Delima, R., Indrayono, N., Toding, R., Wibowo, A. and Santoso, H. B., 2019. System Usability Scale for Usability Testing of Agriculture E-Commerce Website. In *Researchers World*, vol. 10, no. 4, pp. 43-57.

Puteri, R. N. and Widyanti, A., 2018. E-commerce of Islamic fashion product: Usability and user acceptance. In *2018 International Conference on Information Technology Systems and Innovation (ICITSI)*, pp. 143–147. IEEE.

Ritthiron, S., & Jiamsanguanwong, A. (2017). Usability evaluation of the university library network's website using an eye-tracking device. *ACM International Conference Proceeding Series*, *Part F131200*, 184–188. https://doi.org/10.1145/3133264.3133294

Roth, S. P., Tuch, A. N., Mekler, E. D., Bargas-Avila, J. A. and Opwis, K., 2013. Location matters, especially for non-salient features-An eye-tracking study on the effects of web object placement on different types of websites. In *International journal of human-computer studies*, vol. 71, no. 3, pp. 228–235.

Sembodo, F. G., Fitriana, G. F., & Prasetyo, N. A. (2021). Evaluasi usability website Shopee Menggunakan system usability scale (SUS). Journal of Applied Informatics and Computing, 5(2), 146–150. https://doi.org/10.30871/jaic.v5i2.3293

Vlachogianni, P. and Tselios, N., 2021. Perceived usability evaluation of educational technology using the System Usability Scale (SUS): A systematic review. In *Journal of Research on Technology in Education*, pp. 1-18.

Wahyuningrum, T., Kartiko, C. and Wardhana, A. C., 2020. Exploring e-Commerce Usability by Heuristic Evaluation as a Compelement of System Usability Scale. In *2020 International Conference on Advancement in Data Science, E-learning and Information Systems (ICADEIS)*, pp. 1–5. IEEE.

RETHINKING THE SHOPPING EXPERIENCE: A QUALITATIVE EXPLORATIVE STUDY ON 3D WEB AND AR FOR DISPLAYING AND SELLING GOODS

Valeria Orso[1], Giovanni Portello[1], Leonardo Pierobon[1], Alice Bettelli[2], Merylin Monaro[1] and Luciano Gamberini[1,2]
[1]*Human Inspired Technologies Research Centre, University of Padova*
[2]*Department of General Psychology, University of Padova*
via Venezia 8, Padova, Italy

ABSTRACT

The restrictions brought about by the COVID-19 pandemic have challenged not only small businesses, such as local shops, but also large companies, such as those involved in the organization of trade shows. Much of the trade and the majority of events moved to online spaces, e.g., e-commerce and digital trade fairs. Still, these situations fail to convey the experience to the fullest. Technologies such as 3D Web and AR can compensate for the lack of sensorial stimulation but have not found widespread application yet in the retail and trade fairs sectors. In the present work we explored the factors that motivate small businesses to launch and manage online shops, along with the obstacles that they find in this activity. Moreover, we investigated whether and how they perceive that 3D Web could be helpful for them. Secondly, we explored the motivation of trade fairs operators into adopting AR technology to improve product display and to maintain continuity during lockdown periods. The outcomes of the study have been translated into operative guidelines, to inform the design of interfaces to support small businesses maintaining their own e-commerce site. Finally, we provide indications on how to integrate AR technology into trade fairs.

KEYWORDS

Mixed Reality, 3D Web, Augmented Reality, Marketing, Retail, Covid-19

1. INTRODUCTION

Online retail shows continually growing numbers. From 2017 to 2021, the profits generated by online retail worldwide increased from 2.2 trillion to approximately 3.8 trillion of US dollars. Moreover, the percentage of online purchases has increased from 12.2% to 22%, indicating a significant change in consumer purchasing habits. Likewise, in Europe from 2017 to 2021, the sales revenue from e-commerce increased from 370 billion to 670 billion euro, and the percentage of online purchases from 9% to 15% (Statista, 2021). The restrictions imposed by the COVID-19 pandemics have additionally emphasized these trends (Dumanska et al., 2021; Jílková & Králová, 2021).

However, purchasing online lacks many sensorial stimuli (e.g., touching the fabric of a shirt) that makes the shopping experience so rewarding. Technologies such as 3D Web and Augmented Reality (AR) have the potential to overcome these limitations by compensating the lack of sensory stimulation with high-fidelity simulations. In this perspective, the project "Hybrid Sustainable Worlds" aims to realize an e-commerce platform that leverages the strengths of 3D Web and AR to enhance the experience, not only of the consumer but also of the seller. The platform is meant to encompass both Business to Consumer (B2C) and the Business to Business (B2B) branches. To this end, it is crucial to understand end-users' needs.

The present paper reports the factors that either facilitate or hinder shop owners to launch and manage their own e-shop. Moreover, we also report the perspectives of trade fairs operators to integrate AR in trade shows.

1.1 Related Work

Previous studies have investigated the factors that encourage or hinder the adoption and use of e-commerce for different business sectors. Wymer and Regan (2005) addressed the factors favoring or inhibiting the adoption of e-commerce by small and medium-sized enterprises (SMEs). Specifically, they identified the following as the most significant antecedents of adoption: need, innovativeness, competitive pressure, value, government, reliability, e-commerce technology, models, prior experience, executive experience, cost, priority, security, capital, market, partners/vendors. Hong and Zhu (2006) reframed these factors in a study regarding the adoption of e-commerce systems by companies. They found that for companies the main predictors of adoption were technology integration, web functionalities and web spending, while firm size, partner usage, electronic data interchange usage, and perceived obstacles were found to negatively influence the migration to e-commerce. Concerning B2B, Sila (2013) found that scalability was the biggest contributor to B2B e-commerce usage.

Nowadays, 3D web, VR, and AR technologies provide retailers with new opportunities to enhance their online sales channels and are likely to represent the next step in the development of online shopping. Several studies investigated the effects of these new technologies on consumers' online purchasing habits. For instance, 3D virtual worlds have been shown to lead to a greater sense of telepresence and social presence, and a greater perception of authenticity, factors that increase users' online trust and purchase intent (Peng & Ke, 2015). Moreover, virtual and immersive worlds are perceived as more attractive and appealing (Pantano & Servidio, 2012), and evaluation of user experience within these virtual environments revealed increased engagement and enjoyment. These factors are positively correlated with user satisfaction, leading to increased intention to purchase the product (Papagiannidis et al., 2013). Thanks to the evolution of 3D web and AR technologies, virtual and immersive stores can therefore represent a starting point for further advances in online retailing, offering both sellers and consumers new opportunities for interaction (Farshid et al., 2018).

2. MATERIALS AND METHODS

2.1 Definition of User Categories and Requirement

Two groups of stakeholders were involved, namely: retailers and trade fair operators (exhibitors and organizers). Eligible participants in the retailer group had to be shop owner or employed as shop assistant. Similarly, for the trade fair group, candidates had to have professional experience as exhibitors or as organizers of trade fairs.

Participants were reached through the researchers' network of acquaintances and search on professional social networks and on the websites of the Chambers of Commerce. The initial approach was made by telephone and consisted of explaining the purpose and modalities of the meeting, and finally inviting them to the interview. Afterwards, participants received an email with the details of the activity, data collection and storage. They also received an informed consent form, which the participant was invited to sign and return. Finally, an appointment for the interview was arranged.

2.2 Participants

A total of 26 people operating in the retail sector. Only 12 of them (two women) agreed to partake in the study, with a response rate of about 46%. The final sample had an average age of 31.3 years (ranging from 24 to 43 years). They dealt with diverse products, including, hi-fi, food, flowers, ironmongery, body care, books, furniture, jewelry, clothing, household appliances and telephony.

For the recruitment of trade operators, a total of 27 people were contacted with a 22% response rate. The final sample consisted of 6 fair operators (one female), whose average age was 44 years (with a range between 27 and 65 years). Participants dealt with professional cooking machinery, professional sous-vis machinery, the production of automation systems and the production of pieces of furniture (chairs). One participant was responsible for the organization of trade fairs in the field of tourism promotion (organizing about two fairs a year) and, finally, one dealt with the organization of trade fairs events in the jewelry sector (organizing about 50 fairs a year). In addition, a stand designer and fitter were interviewed.

2.3 Materials

To deeply explore participants' experience, semi-structured interviews were conducted (McIntosh & Morse, 2015). Two different scripts were devised, one for each group of participants. In addition, two short videos (prompts) were prepared for illustrating the technologies of interest, namely 3D Web and AR. By doing this, it was possible to introduce and explain the technologies to all participants in the same way, thereby ensuring that they all had the same level of knowledge.

The interview script addressed to retailers the topics to be explored were their professional experience (i.e., type of business, goods handled), their experience with online selling, the presentation style of the products in their online shop (i.e., what kind of information was used when a product is placed in the online shop) and the frequency with which the online shop was updated (if any). Finally, the researcher showed the video and explored with the participant the interest and willingness to invest resources in the 3D web.

Similarly, for trade fair operators, the script covered the following topics: professional experience (i.e., years of activity, number of trade fairs attended), the way in which products were typically displayed on the stand and the way in which the stand was organized, the decision-making process for the selection of products to be exhibited during events, the meaning of the fair and the measures taken to maintain the continuity of fairs during lockdowns, the general differences before and after the outbreak of COVID-19 and whether there was any intention to continue with digital fairs after lockdown. Finally, after watching the clip, the participants were asked about their impressions of AR applied to the display of products in trade fairs.

Additionally, an *ad hoc* questionnaire was devised to investigate the participants' technological experience and was administered via the Google Modules platform. The questionnaire consisted of 14 items in total (to be answered on a 5-point Likert scale) and investigated the following dimensions: *personal innovativeness*, reflecting individual readiness and willingness to adopt new information technologies (Elie-Dit-Cosaque, Pallud and Kalika, 2012); *technology anxiety*, which refers to the feeling of concern related to the use of a technology (Spagnolli et al., 2014); *perceived relative advantages*, the extent to which a technology is perceived to bring benefits (Van Ittersum & Feinberg, 2010); *perceived compatibility*, which is the extent to which a technology is perceived as consistent and compatible with experiences and needs (Van Ittersum & Feinberg, 2010); p*erceived complexity*, which is the extent to which a technology is perceived as complex to understand and use (Van Ittersum & Feinberg, 2010); *perceived trialability*, the degree to which users are willing to try a new technology (Van Ittersum & Feinberg, 2010).

2.4 Procedure

To meet both the COVID-19 restraints measures and the professionals' agendas, the interviews were carried out via a teleconferencing system at day and time scheduled with participants. On the day of the interview the participant was welcomed, then the researcher introduced himself and presented the project. Then the interview started following the script (section 2.3). During the interview, the participant was shown the video (prompt) introducing the topic of 3D Web (in the case of retailers) or AR (for trade fairs operators). At the end of the interview the researcher shared the link to answer a short questionnaire about the technological experience (section 2.2.1). The interviews lasted at most about one hour. To allow subsequent data analysis, the interviews were video recorded. The recordings (approximately 11 hours) were then transcribed *verbatim*, for a total of 125 pages analyzed (Halcomb & Davidson, 2006); specifically, the researchers initially read the transcripts carefully noting possible emerging themes, subsequently, they compared the identified themes and agreed on shared categories and their titles.

3. RESULTS

We first report the findings from the technology experience questionnaire (Table 1). Subsequently, we report the findings emerging from the interviews run with retailers. Then, results from the interviews with fair trade operators are presented.

Table 1. Technology Experience Questionnaire

	Mean (M)	Standard Deviation (SD)
Personal innovativeness	3,917	0,865
Technology anxiety	4,042	0,797
Perceived relative advantages	3,594	0,712
Perceived compatibility	3,938	0,479
Perceived complexity	3,406	0,554
Perceived trialability	4,406	0,861

3.1 Retailers' Experience with e-Retail

With regard to 3D web technology, the four main topics explored were: the experience and issues with e-commerce, e-commerce features and management, time required to upload and update product-related information and the importance of direct contact with customers.

Experience and issues with e-commerce. Half of the retailers interviewed (N=6) owned and still use their own website for e-commerce, while one retailer (N=1), in addition to having its own e-commerce, also employs services by third parties (e.g., Subito.it, eBay). These retailers trade in furniture, bookshops, jewelry, food retailing, hi-fi, clothing, electronics, and household appliances. One retailer (N=1) working in the gastronomy sector reported not to have a proprietary e-commerce but relies on third-party service to deliver products. On the contrary, 34% of the retailers (N=4) reported that they had a negative experience in the management of their e-commerce sites. As a result, they closed the online shop. In detail, these retailers deal with flowers, ironware, and beauty. The main issues that emerged were different from case to case. For the flower shop, the main problem was the difficulty in meeting the customer's expectations due to the differences between the images published online and the physical product (especially the size). The ironware shop reported that the main concerns were logistical issues in warehouse management and shipment. In the case of the beauty, the main issues were the poor interaction with customers and the difficulty to regularly update it. Lastly, in the case of the jewelry shop, the issue amounted to a highly negative experience with the company responsible for managing the website.

Almost half of the e-commerce owners (N=3) reported that they had a website for the purpose of showcasing and not selling. In addition, all retailers (N=12) are on social media such as Instagram and Facebook, in an attempt to establish and maintain a direct interaction with their customers and to increase their visibility.

E-commerce features and management. With the aim of understanding which attributes of the product are more relevant when uploading a product online, retailers were asked what attributes they entered for their products. What can be observed is that all retailers emphasize the importance of the descriptive and visual aspects (images) of the product. Some focus only on these two aspects, others report that they also focus on aspects such as uploading videos or video tutorials, conveying the values of the company, the price, and the availability of additional services. The answers collected related to participants' current or past experience with their e-commerce website.

Moreover, four respondents (N=4) reported that they also uploaded emotional contents, such as images or videos. Three retailers (N=3) reported that they include (or, in one case, intended to include) video tutorials in the attempt to provide a better description of their products. One trader (N=1) reported inserting a textual description of the product with the purpose to index some keywords on search engines. Finally, two retailers (N=2) reported that the type of information varies according to the type of product on sale, and which of the attributes they decide to pay more attention to (especially in the case of the book shop).

Time required for uploading and updating product-related information. Only two retailers (N=2) managed autonomously the upload of product-related information, and they reported that this activity takes them a little time. Regarding the frequency of updates, four (N=4) reported that they spend approximately a few hours per week on this activity. Only one participant (N=1) reported dedicating a few hours monthly to this activity.

Direct contact with the customer. Overall, 82% (N=9) of retailers reported that they consider it necessary for the customer to physically visit the shop. Indeed, only by visiting the shop, the customer can try the products (i.e., hi-fi, clothing, floristry) or can receive full advice on the product. On the contrary, 18% of retailers (N = 2) do not consider physical contact with the customer to be necessary (i.e., ironware and food shops).

In addition, all retailers (N=12) have stated that they also use social media in order to maintain contact with their customers or to create a new direct sales channel. In fact, some of them reported that the use of social media has been important during the lockdown periods because it allowed direct communication with customers for issues related to product shipment and sales advice. After watching the video illustrating the 3D Web, the majority of respondents (N=7) could not contextualize the technology for their shops. In two cases (N=2) retailers reported distrust towards this technology. More generally, respondents expressed concern on the management of the technology.

3.2 Trade Fairs Operators' Experiences

Respondents reported that today the main functions of the fair continue to be to establish and maintain contacts with their clients, and to keep updated on the trends in a specific sector.

Participants reported that the COVID-19 has changed the shape of trade fairs. Indeed, they have been attending digital trade shows for two years.

Managing the stand. Overall, 75% of the exhibitors (N = 3) stated that they use modular stands, which are convenient because they can be adapted according to the space allocated by the event. On the other hand, the remaining exhibitor reported using stands made *ad hoc* by third parties, which are easy to replicate in the different events attended by the company. Moreover, exhibitors reported to use several technological devices such as computers, monitors and backlit panels to better display the products. According to respondents, it takes between one day and one week to set up these complex structures.

Exhibitors were asked whether the current arrangement of the stand allowed them to reach all interested visitors. In general, exhibitors (N=3) feel that their display method allows them to reach all interested parties, although this requires additional work to schedule purposeful visits.

Selection of the products. Exhibitors were asked about their strategy for selecting the products to be shown at the fair. In general, from the interviews it emerged that it is not possible to exhibit in the stand all the products and, therefore, it is fundamental to make a careful selection. More specifically, the respondents reported that the basic strategy is to prioritize the top of the range products (regardless of the selling volumes). Additional drivers for the choice of the products are the market trends of the country where the fair will be held and the characteristics of the customers attending the event. However, as mentioned above, emerges the importance along with the difficulty, of being able to show as many products as possible.

Integration of AR. In general, four operators (N=4) and the stand designer were interested in the adoption of AR for product display at the fair. Still, they all reckoned that the technology needed in-depth studies to understand how to fully exploit it and make it meaningful for their products. In any case, they believe that AR could give them the possibility to display a greater number of products at low costs, avoiding transport costs and the risks it entails.

One of the exhibitors (N=1) even suggests that this technology could be useful in illustrating product components in more detail. In addition, the designer expressed interest in applying augmented reality in the context of booth design as well, particularly in reference to product measurements to be included in the booths and the graphic aspect.

Although the impressions are generally positive, for the two remaining operators (N=2), the application of AR as an exhibition medium is not interesting because they consider it still immature and not equal to physical reality. While for the designer, the problem linked to the adoption of AR is due to the fact that in most cases company managers are lagging behind technological evolution.

4. DESIGN GUIDELINES

The findings from the interviews were translated into design guidelines, meant to inform the design of the interfaces to be developed within the project "Hybrid Sustainable Worlds".

First, we report on the user requirements for 3D web interfaces extracted from the interviews with retailers:

- Intuitive content upload: the interface should be simple and immediately understandable interface, to allow retailers to manage the shop autonomously and with little effort;
- Multi-modal product information input: the interface should support the upload of various media (technical description, emotional description, images, emotional photographs, video clips, video tutorials) to describe the products;
- Modularity management of product-related information: the interface should enable retailers to emphasize specific pieces of information;
- Customer care: the interface should feature a function to establish and maintain direct contact with the customers.

Secondly, guidelines for the design of augmented reality interfaces for the trade fair context are presented below, extracted from the investigation of trade fairs operators. In detail:

- Seamless integration: currently, trade fairs are composed of content and events that take place in-person and some content that is accessible online. Augmented content should integrate with the exhibition at the stand, not replace it;
- AR catalog: thanks to AR, exhibitors should be able to demonstrate to visitors all the products that they cannot display on their stand, for reasons of space, logistics and costs. In other words, AR should allow exhibitors to have a virtual catalog of their products that can be explored in full size;
- Contextualization of product features: products offered in AR should highlight product features that are normally not very visible;
- Customization: unlike the products physically displayed on the stand, products in AR must be able to be customized according to the customer's needs, compatible with the characteristics of the product.

5. DISCUSSION

The present work investigated the factors supporting and hindering the adoption of e-commerce by small businesses. Furthermore, it addressed how professionals think 3D Web could be integrated into their businesses. The findings emerged from the interviews confirmed the obstacles identified by previous research, mainly concerning organizational and technological factors (Hong & Zhu, 2006; Wymer & Regan, 2005). We also translated those findings into operative guidelines that can inform the design of interfaces meant to enable small businesses to launch and manage their own e-commerce. The guidelines emphasize the importance of an easy and effortless information input and management to smoothly integrate with all the other work activities retailers have to carry out. Additionally, we investigated how operators in the sector of trade fairs consider the application of AR technology. To the best of our knowledge, this is the first work addressing this topic. Interestingly, we found that professionals were generally open to the introduction of AR, because it would allow them to bring to the events a significantly larger number of products without increasing the costs related to the organization and transportation. Moreover, it opens possibilities to explore the products from novel perspectives. Still, it is reckoned that AR could bring an added value to trade fairs when it is employed as an addition to the traditional stand, and not as a replacement to it.

6. CONCLUSION

The impact of online retail is ever increasing, and the restrictions brought about by COVID-19 have even emphasized this trend (Jílková & Králová, 2021). Still small businesses struggle to keep up by launching and maintaining their own shop online. The B2B sector was also seriously damaged by the pandemic, with all the events and exhibitions suspended for more than two years. In the present paper, we describe the barriers encountered by small retailers in administering their own e-commerce. Additionally, we also report the design guidelines for the developments of e-commerce platforms addressed to small-sized businesses, thereby extending previous research. We further considered the deployment of AR technology in the trade fair environment, finding a substantial openness.

ACKNOWLEDGEMENT

The work was partially funded by the POR-FESR Project Hybrid Sustainable Worlds (ID. 10290827).

REFERENCES

Alcañiz, M. et al., 2019. Virtual reality in marketing: a framework, review, and research agenda. *Frontiers in psychology*, 1530.

Dumanska, I. et al., 2021. E-commerce and M-commerce as Global Trends of International Trade Caused by the Covid-19 Pandemic. WSEAS Transactions on Environment and Development, Vol. 17, pp 386-397.

Elie-Dit-Cosaque, C. et al., 2011. The influence of individual, contextual, and social factors on perceived behavioral control of information technology: A field theory approach. *Journal of Management Information Systems*, Vol. 28, No. 3, pp. 201-234.

Farshid, M. et al., 2018. Go boldly!: Explore augmented reality (AR), virtual reality (VR), and mixed reality (MR) for business. *Business Horizons*, Vol. 61, No. 5, pp. 657-663.

Halcomb, E.J. & Davidson, P.M., 2006. Is verbatim transcription of interview data always necessary? *Applied Nursing Research.* Vol. 19, No. 1, pp. 38-42.

Hong, W. & Zhu, K., 2006. Migrating to internet-based e-commerce: Factors affecting e-commerce adoption and migration at the firm level. *Information & management*, Vol. 43, No. 2, pp. 204-221.

Jílková, P. & Králová, P., 2021. Digital consumer behaviour and ecommerce trends during the COVID-19 crisis. *International Advances in Economic Research*, Vol. 27, No. 1, pp. 83-85.

McIntosh, M.J. & Morse, J.M., 2015. Situating and Constructing Diversity in Semi-Structured Interviews. *Global Qualitative Nursing Research*, Vol. 2.

Pantano, E. & Servidio, R., 2012. Modeling innovative points of sales through virtual and immersive technologies. *Journal of Retailing and Consumer Services*, Vol. 19, No. 3, pp. 279-286.

Papagiannidis, S. et al., 2013. Modelling the determinants of a simulated experience in a virtual retail store and users' product purchasing intentions. *Journal of Marketing Management*, Vol. 29, No. 13-14, pp. 1462-1492.

Peng, Y. & Ke, D., 2015. Consumer trust in 3D virtual worlds and its impact on real world purchase intention. *Nankai Business Review International.*

Sila, I., 2013. Factors affecting the adoption of B2B e-commerce technologies. *Electronic commerce research*, Vol. 13, No. 2, pp. 199-236.

Spagnolli, A. et al., 2015. Measuring user acceptance of wearable symbiotic devices: validation study across application scenarios. In *International Workshop on Symbiotic Interaction*, pp. 87-98.

Statista 2021, *eCommerce - Europe*, Statista, retrieved April 19, 2022, from www.statista.com/outlook/dmo/ecommerce/europe

Statista 2021, *eCommerce - Worldwide*, Statista, retrieved April 19, 2022, from www.statista.com/outlook/dmo/ecommerce/worldwide

Van Ittersum, K. & Feinberg, F.M., 2010. Cumulative Timed Intent: A New Predictive Tool for Technology Adoption. *Journal of Marketing Research*. Vol. 47, No. 5, pp. 808-822.

Wedel, M. et al., 2020. Virtual and augmented reality: Advancing research in consumer marketing. *International Journal of Research in Marketing*, Vol. 37, No. 3, pp. 443-465.

Wymer, S. A. & Regan, E. A., 2005. Factors influencing e-commerce adoption and use by small and medium businesses. *Electronic markets*, Vol. 15. No. 4, pp. 438-453.

ON THE IMPACT OF THE USER CONTEXT CRITERIA IN THE DETECTION OF MOBILE USER INTERFACES DEFECTS

Mabrouka Chouchane[1]and Makram Soui[2]
[1]*National School of Computer Sciences, University of Manouba, Manouba, Tunisia*
[2]*College of Computing and Informatics Saudi Electronic University, Riyadh, Saudi Arabia*

ABSTRACT

The evaluation of the mobile user interfaces remains one of the most challenging issues in order to improve the interaction between the user and the mobile applications. In this context, many methods and tools have been proposed to evaluate the quality of Graphical Mobile User Interface (GMUI), like heuristic evaluation and field-testing. However, these available techniques tend to be time consuming and error-prone. An evident solution is to define a set of rules as a combination of metrics quality, context criteria and a list of possible defect types. In fact, the preferences of users are different and heterogeneous. Indeed, the users don't have the same profiles and to satisfy all users' preferences, we can highly decrease the accuracy of the detection rules. In this paper, we consider the generation of the GMUI quality evaluation rules as a multi-objective problem where the goal is to find the best rules maximizing the number of detected aesthetic quality issues and minimizing the complexity of the rules. In addition, we studied the impact of the context criteria in the detection of mobileuser defects by applying same feature selection techniques in order to select the most pertinent features of context criteria and to increase the detection rules process.

KEYWORDS

Mobile User Interfaces, Evaluation, Feature Selection

1. INTRODUCTION

Nowadays, the mobile phone has rapidly evolved from a simple device for making or receiving phone callsto a complex multimedia interactive system (Schaffer et al., 2015). The shift towards mobile devices involvesthe daily massive interactions with mobile user interfaces in different contexts for use: gaming, editing, messaging, etc. According to statistics, there are 4.77 billion mobile subscribers in 2017 worldwide, which is estimated to climb to 7.69 billion in 2027 (Statista, 2022). As the technological sophistication of mobile devices has grown, the user interfaces of mobile applications are becoming more and more complex. Most researchers in HCI are interested in developing new design methodologies, experimenting with new hardware devices, prototyping new software systems (Alnanih and Ormandjieva, 2016).

The evaluation of visual aesthetic requires not only measurement of a set metrics of user interface characteristics, but also consideration of the characteristics of the users themselves, their goals, and contextual information such as user location, date and time, the resources available, the characteristics of the target platform, ambientconditions, etc. (Schmidt et al., 2016). In fact, evaluation of mobile user interfaces is a crucial phase in their development. It becomes a necessity phase to enhance the user's satisfaction. Different works (Baldwin and Chai, 2012; Ghiani et al., 2015) have underlined the difficulties and the importance of this task. According to (Forrester, 2011), recent mobile researches show that developers neglected the mobile user interface quality aspect like aesthetic.

Therefore, detecting and fixing up these quality defects help users to interact easily with the GMUI. In this work, we focus on the detection of defects related to the aesthetic quality of the mobile user interfaces. Most of the existing works on defects detection of MUI rely on manual declarative rules definition(Alemerien and Magel, 2015). In fact, rules are manually defined to identify problems using combinations of quantitative metrics and context criteria (user experience, user motivation, age, etc.). These evaluation metrics are based on a set of interface attributes (number of interface components, number of the alignment point, number of colors, etc.). In this context, in an exhaustive scenario, the number of possible quality issues and the number of context criteria, used to manually define rules, can be various. For each quality defect, rules that are expressed in terms of evaluation metric and context criteria combinations need efforts to find the right threshold value for each metric. In fact, this task is complex, time-consuming and error-prone. Thus, we need to define an automatic process to generate these rules automatically instead of the manual process. To address these issues, we propose in this paper an automatic approach based on a multi-objective evolutionary algorithm, namely the NSGA-II proposed by (Deb et al., 2002). Our multi-objective approach aims to find the best trade- off between maximizing the number of detected aesthetic defects and minimizing rules-complexity. In addition, we studied the impact of the context criteria in the detection of mobile user defects by applying same feature selection techniques in order to select the most pertinent features of context criteria and to increase the detectionrules process.

The remainder of this paper is structured as follows: Section 2 presents the related works. However, section 3 explains how we adapted the NSGA-II algorithm to find the best rules, maximizing the number of detected aesthetic defects and minimizing rules- complexity. Section 4 discusses the results of evaluating our approach. Section 5 deals with some trends related to future work.

2. RELATED WORK

Several works (Reinecke et al., 2013; Sonderegger, 2014) drawn attention to evaluate aesthetic dimension of mobile user interfaces. (Seckler et al., 2015) classified the existing evaluation approaches of visual aesthetic of MUI into two categories:

The subjective evaluation approaches, known as qualitative methods, can be used to measure the visual aesthetic dimensions of mobile user interfaces. Dahlgaard (Zaframand et al., 2006) presented a quantitative and qualitative research design including three types of data collection instruments (direct observations, rating scales, and interviews) to discuss the impact of the aesthetic design of smart phones on users emotional reactions and preferences towards the product. Their study explored the emotional reactions of males to varying aesthetic designs of the BlackBerry and empirically evaluated their degree of satisfaction about the BlackBerry with different colors and patterns. In this context, (Dahlgaard et al., 2008) showed that the generation of optimal mobile phones design can effectively enhance the overall aesthetic performance and customers satisfaction. In addition, Li (Hou and Ho, 2013) investigated mobile phone' s interfaces style as a combination of content and forms, proposing a qualitative method that can assess these interfaces. But, these techniques have several limits. They present a time consuming process and requires a great human expertise. They are still also subjective inspections and error-prone strategies.

The second method used is an objective evaluation approach also known as quantitative measurement which uses specific features such as structure and color factors in order to assess the visual aesthetics of Mobile User Interface (MUI). For instance, (Nathan-Roberts and Liu, 2015) used the computational aesthetic quantification algorithms based on symmetry, balance and quantity of elements that relate to aesthetic ratings. (Miniukovich and De Angeli, 2016) assessed the complexity based on visual dimensions from the aesthetics model to study the popularity of mobile apps on Google Play. These works assess the aesthetic of MUI based on a set of metrics without detecting aesthetic defects. However, the aesthetic metrics measures can be interpreted as certain symptoms of one or more defects. In the defects detection process, we need to compare these measures with an adequate thresholds values. In this context, our contribution aims to detect automatically defects of MUIs based on an automatic tool that facilitates the detection of aesthetic quality defects. In this way, we define a generic evaluation rules for MUIs based on multi-objective evolutionary algorithm that allows the coverage of context criteria.

3. APPROACH OVERVIEW

This section shows how the generation of the evaluation rules can be seen as an optimization problem. Wealso show why the size of the corresponding search space makes heuristic search necessary in order to exploreit. The goal of our approach is to generate the best evaluation rules among all possible rules that maximize the number of detected defects and also minimizes the number of rules by the solution. We use a multi-objective optimization algorithm to find the best tradeoff between these two conflicting objectives. Figure 1 shows the approach overview steps.

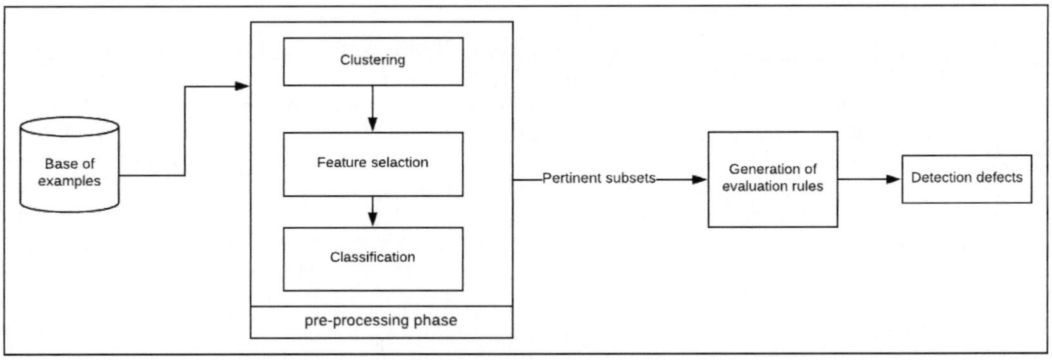

Figure 1. Approach overview

3.1 The Prepossessing Phase

3.1.1 Clustering Step

This step aims to divide the used data set which contains the context criteria, into a number of groups. Each group includes similar elements. In this step, we performed KMeans technique.

Input :

k: the number of the clusters.

D: the dataset containing *n* context criteria.

Output: a set of *k* clusters.

Method:

1) Randomly choose *k* context criteria in D as an initial representative cases ;
2) **Repeat**
3) Assign each remaining case to the cluster with the nearest representative case ;
4) Randomly select a non-representative case o_{random} ;
5) Compute the total cost S, of swopping representative case, o_j with o_{random} ;
6) If S<0 then swap o_j with o_{random} to form the new set of k representative cases ;
7) **Until** no change was observed.

Figure 2. K-means algorithm

In our work, k-Means clustering algorithm is used to divide the dataset into k clusters in which each context criterion belongs to the cluster with the nearest mean, serving as a prototype of the cluster. The basic operation of K-Means clustering algorithms is relatively simple: Given a fixed numberof k clusters, assign observations to those clusters so that the means across clusters (for all variables) are as different from each other as possible. After the application of K-Means clustering, we divided the used dataset intwo clusters. (0,1). Figure 3 shows our dataset structure after clustering.

	A	B	C	D	E	F	G	H	I	J	K
1	Age	User Experie	Motivation	Education le	Interest	sex	competence	user knowled	location	luminosity	Cluster
2	0	1	1	2	2	3	2	2	2	1	cluster0
3	0	1	1	2	2	3	2	2	2	1	cluster0
4	0	1	1	2	2	3	2	2	2	1	cluster0
5	0	1	1	2	2	3	0	2	0	1	cluster1
6	0	1	1	2	2	3	0	2	0	1	cluster1
7	0	1	1	2	2	3	0	2	0	1	cluster1
8	0	1	1	2	2	3	0	2	0	1	cluster1
9	0	1	1	2	2	3	0	2	0	1	cluster1
10	0	0	2	0	0	3	0	2	0	1	cluster1
11	0	0	2	0	0	3	0	2	0	1	cluster1
12	0	0	2	0	0	3	0	2	0	1	cluster1
13	0	0	2	0	0	3	0	2	0	1	cluster1
14	0	0	2	0	0	3	0	2	0	1	cluster1
15	0	0	2	0	0	3	1	1	2	2	cluster0
16	0	0	2	0	0	3	1	1	2	2	cluster0
17	0	0	2	0	0	3	1	1	2	2	cluster0
18	1	1	2	2	2	3	1	1	2	2	cluster0
19	1	1	2	2	2	3	0	2	0	0	cluster1
20	1	1	2	2	2	3	0	2	0	0	cluster1
21	1	1	2	2	2	3	2	2	2	1	cluster0
22	1	1	2	2	2	4	2	2	2	1	cluster0
23	1	1	2	2	2	4	2	2	2	1	cluster0
24	1	1	2	2	2	4	2	2	2	1	cluster0
25	1	1	2	2	2	4	2	2	2	1	cluster0

Figure 3. The dataset after clustering step

3.1.2 Feature Selection Step

According to the literature, there are three approaches for feature selection (Kumar and Minz, 2014). The first approach called Filter approach. It aims to take advantage of the general characteristics of training data with independent of the mining algorithm. The second approach called Wrapper approach. It looks for the relationship between relevance and optimal feature subset. It tries to find an optimal subset suited the used mining algorithm. The third approach named Embedded approach. It uses learning algorithm to perform feature selection process. In This step, we used the second approach which aims to filter the features from the dataset using Gain ration filter (Nagpal and Gaur, 2015). Gain ratio (GR) is a modification of the information gain that reduces its bias. Gain ratio takes number and size of branches into account when choosing an attribute. It corrects the information gain by taking the intrinsic information of a split into account. Intrinsic information is entropy of distribution of instances into branches (i.e., how much info do we need to tell which branch an instance belongs to) (Mitra et al., 2002).

Table 1. The evaluation of dataset using GR

Attribute name	Gain ratio	Rank
Age	0.0571	5
User experience	0	8
Motivation	0	9
Education level	0	10
Interest	0.0483	6
sex	0.0294	7
Competence	1	1
User knowledge	0.238	4
Location	1	2
Luminosity	0.3602	3

As showing in table 1, we used ranking method to select subset of 7 attributes from 10 attributes. The attributes: competence, location, luminosity, user knowledge, age, interest and sex are the selected feature of the subset. However, the attributes: user experience, motivation and education level are the removed features.

3.1.3 Classification Step

In this step, we classify the best features of the subset into the k clusters using a classifier. In the literature,there are different classifiers such as K-Nearest Neighbors (KNN) (Fallahpour et al., 2017), Support Vector Machine (SVM)(Maldonado et al. , 2017), Neural Network (Lai et al. , 2015), etc. In this work, we use SupportVector Machine (SVM). They are a set of supervised learning algorithms that supports both regression and classification tasks. However, it's mostly used for classification problems. SVMs seek for the best separating hyperplane in order to minimize the total of the distances among two classes by mapping the pattern points into high dimensional feature space using a set of mathematical functions knows as Kernels. Support Vector Machine generates a linear decision boundary with the largest distance to test called maximum margin and experiments sequences are classified by either they belong to the positive or negative edge.

3.2 Generation of Evaluation Rules

We will generate evaluation rules as an optimization problem using a mono-objective genetic algorithm. The generated rules are likely to be near-optimal rules in detecting aesthetic defects of MUI. Their quality is determined by a fitness function that compares the list of detected defects in the rules and the expected ones from the base of examples. To this end, a heuristic search is conducted over the base to make the best set of combinations between the metrics and context criteria that accurately detects most defects. Our proposed approach has 4 steps: (1) generation of the initial population, (2) individual's selection, (3) reproduction operators, and (4) new individuals' generation. The high-level pseudo code for the algorithm is given in Figure below. From line 1 to 3, the algorithm generates an initial population (solutions), where each of these solutions contains set of evaluation rules. In lines 4-13, the GP will perform his repeated iterations in which it searches for the fittest evaluation rule (the best). During each iteration, a fitness function will evaluate each individual, and the solution having the best fitness is saved (line 9). Then, the GP will start its optimization. Once the crossover and mutation are applied, a new population is produced for the next generation. The algorithm ceases when it completes the maximum iteration number and returns the best set of evaluation rules.

```
Input: Set of context criteria, structural metrics and usability
defects type
Input: Base of examples.
Process:
  S: =set-of-rules (R)
  P: =set-of (S)
  generate-initial-population (P, Max-size)
  repeat
  for all S in P do
  Detected-defect: = execute-rules(R)
  fitness (S): = Compare (detected-defects, expected-defects)
  end for
  best-solution: = best-fitness(S);
  P: =generate-new-population(P)
  it: =it+1;
  until it=max-it
  return best-solution
Output: best-solution
```

Figure 4. The pseudo-code of used algorithm

• **Generation of initial population:** This phase takes in input context criteria (user experience, age, sex, and education level), 8 structural metrics, and 8 aesthetic defects. This step generates an initial set of rules representing random combinations of metrics and context criteria.

• **Encoding of solution:** We need to define how to represent the solution of our problem. In our method, an individual is a set of IF-THEN rules. The IF part defines the combination between a metric and context criterion using the logical operator (AND). Each context criterion is a triplet of (context, operator, value), and each metric is a triplet of (metric, operator, value). The THEN part informs on the detected defect type. An evaluation rule has the following structure: IF (context, operator, value) AND (metric, operator, value) THEN detected usability problem.

• **Individuals evaluation:** At this level, we select the best individuals from the initial population in order to estimate and discover the interesting rules. This selection is based on the calculation of the fitness function by reaching the two following objectives of the problem:

- **Maximizing the number of defects in each solution:** we consider the best solution that which contains rules that maximize the number of defects.

- **Minimizing the number of rules in each population:** we consider the best solution is the solution that which has a smaller number of rules per solution. This objective aims to minimize the size of an individual in the population having the maximum number of defects and calculated using the following equation:

$$F(x)\begin{cases}\text{Minimize } f1(x) = \min(nb1, nb2, ..., nbn) & (1)\\ \text{Maximize } f2(x) = Q(P)\end{cases}$$

Where x is the decision variables of the problem. N: number of solutions by population. nbi: number of rules by solution i. Q(P): is the rate of problem by solution and it is calculated as follows:

$$Q(P)= \sum R(Pi)/ n \quad (2)$$

Where R(Pi) is the Number of occurrence of problem i in solution j divided by the number of occurrence of problem i in the base of examples.

• **Phase 2: Individuals selection:** The selection operator will give preference to good individuals and discard the bad individuals, allowing them to pass on to the next generation of the population.

• **Phase 3: Reproduction operators**: This step is based on two fundamental genetic operators: crossover and mutation.

• *Crossover*: During crossover, we create new individuals (offspring) by combining portions from the selected individuals (parents) by the selection operator. The algorithm will select the cut-point of the parents and recombine these four portions into two new children. Afterwards, both parents and offspring will pass on to the next generation of the population.

• *Mutation:* Mutation consists of making some modification over the children to maintain the diversity within the population. In our setting, the mutation operator will change the value of metrics, context criteria, and the arithmetic operators.

• **Phase 4: New individuals' generation:** Once the reproduction operators are applied, the selected individuals and the newly generated offspring will convey to the next generation of the population. Then a fitness function will be measured again to each individual.

4. VALIDATION

In order to assess the feasibility and the efficiency of our approach for generating correct evaluation rules while minimizing the rules complexity and maximizing the number of detected mobile interface defects, we start by presenting our research questions. Then, we describe and discuss the obtained results. This section addresses three main research questions and explains how our experiments are designed to address them.

4.1 Research Questions

We designed our experiment to answer the following three research questions:

RQ1: To what extent can the proposed approach enhance the mobile user interface aesthetic quality by thedetection of defects?

- **RQ1.1:** Are all the context criteria have the same importance when detecting mobile defects?
- **RQ1.2:** How do the generated rules can change from one category of user than others?

RQ2: How accurate is the proposed NSGA-II-based algorithm for aesthetic defects detection?

To answer RQ1, we evaluate the performance of our algorithm adaptation on the detection of five different types of problems on several projects implemented by different developers coming from heterogeneous backgrounds (students, developers, etc.). Four of the tested systems are senior design projects while the fifth one is an open source system.

To answer RQ1.1, we classify users into n category (N number of context criteria persist after feature selectionstep).

To answer RQ1.2, we use machine learning techniques (3 differents algorithms) to calculate the weight assignment of each user criteria in order to provide the importance of each one.

To assess the accuracy of our approach, we answer RQ2 by computing two measures, precision and recall thatare originally defined in the domain of information retrieval and widely used when comparing search algorithms' results.

In general, the precision calculates the probability that a detected defect is correct, and the recall is the probability that an expected defect is detected. Thus, both values are between 0 and 1, and the higher value the better it is. The expected rules were reported by the manual inspection of the interfaces. To answer RQ03, we compare our algorithm to the mono-objective genetic algorithm and we report a comparison in terms of number of needed rules to detect the defects.

4.2 Studied Projects

The validation is being conducted over the evolution of different open source mobile applications: Duolingo, AccuWeather, loan calculator and HandicraftWomen (see table 2). The corpus used includes releases of Duolingo which is a great application for learning a different language. It customizes the course according to the users goal (casual, regular, serious) and experience (beginner or medium). Accuweather is an application that provides a prediction about the current and future weather. It has adynamic user interface that changes depending on the location, time of day and weather conditions. This application allows users to personalize the number of displayed information according to their needs. loan calculator is one of the best simulation credit applications that help users to simulate their personal loan. And, Handcraft Women that aims to support handcraft women in their business activities. We have chosen these projects because of their medium to large size; they considered the most popular used application and can be used as inputs to our tool. We also extracted from theGoogle Play Store the user rating of each application.

Table 2. The studied projects

Application	Release	Interface	Solution length limit
AccuWeather	v3.21.0	11	[50, 200]
Duolingo	v4.1.0	6	[20, 100]
Loan Calculator	v1.7.2	5	[20, 80]
handcraft women	v1.0	10	[50, 200]

4.3 Results of Research Questions

4.3.1 Results of Research Questions 1

In this research question, we show how the generated rules are different among different types of users. In this context, we classify users into 15 groups according to the different values of their context criteria (C1: Users with low age, C2: users with medium age, C3: users with high age, C4 users with low motivation, C5: Users with medium motivation, C6: users with high motivation, C7: users with low interest, C8: users with medium interest, C9: Users with high interest, C10: Users with low education level, C11: users with medium education level, C12: Users with high education level, C13: Users with low user experience, C14: Users with medium user experience, C15: Users with high user experience). After this classification we calculate the number of rules in the solution which have 'if clause' contains the value of each category. Figure 3 present the distribution of the different rules which cover all type of users.

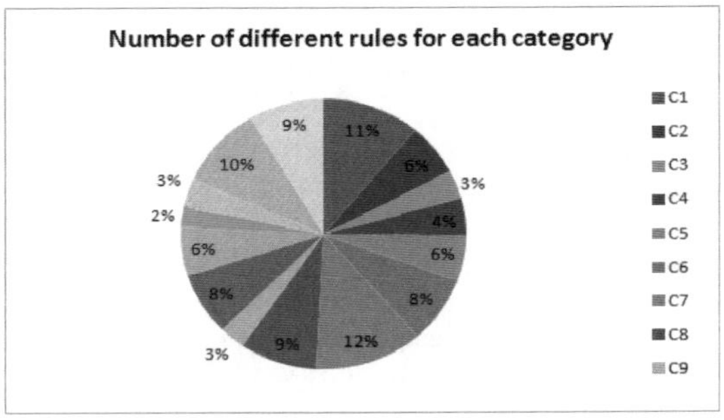

Figure 5. The distribution of the evaluation rules in relation

4.3.2 Results of Research Questions 2

The expected defects were detected with an average of more than 90% of precision and recall on the five tested systems. The highest precision for systems was found in Duolingo where 95% of defects were detected. The lowest precision was found in Easy loan calculator with a median of 78% of detected defects. This is can confirm that the list of returned defects did not contain a high number of false positives and so our reported defects can be trusted by the developers and they can include it in their manual inspection process. We found similar observation when analyzing the recall scores on the different interfaces where an average ofmore than 91% of expected defects was detected. The highest and lowest median recalls ratios for the defectswere respectively 97% for the difficult navigation and 80% for the Incorrect data presentation. The PR and REscores of Duolingo (largest system) are among the highest ones with more than 90%, which are better than thedetection results of the smaller system such as Easy loan calculator.

5. CONCLUSION

As a conclusion, we have noticed that there has been no consensus about the evaluation of the aesthetic quality of MUI. We propose a genetic algorithm (NSGA-II) using a by-example technique to automatically evaluate the aesthetic of mobile user interfaces. We have introduced a new bi-objective evolutionary optimization approach for generating detection rules. Our approach differs from rule-based definition methods as it does not require writing manually rules. To our best knowledge, our proposal represents the first work that uses multi-objective approach to the generation of detection rules. We have tested our approach on four open-sourceprojects. The experimental results have indicated that the quality of the derived detection rules is comparable,close and sometimes better than those defined manually by experts. As a part of future work, we plan to compare our results with other existing evaluation approaches with the objective to refine our approach. In addition, future directions for this research will deal with extending the proposed approach to consider other evaluation metrics and dealing with larger mobile apps.

REFERENCES

Adipat, B., D. Zhang, and L. Zhou, The effects of tree-view based presentation adaptation on mobile web browsing. Mis Quarterly, 2011: p. 99-121.

Alemerien, K. and K. Magel. GUIEvaluator: A Metric-tool for Evaluating the Complexity of Graphical User Interfaces. In SEKE. 2014. Sears, A., Layout appropriateness: A metric for evaluating user interface widget layout. IEEE Transactions on Software Engineering, 1993. 19(7): p. 707-719.

Alemerien, K. and K. Magel. SLC: a visual cohesion metric to predict the usability of graphical user interfaces. In Proceedings of the 30th Annual ACM Symposium on Applied Computing. 2015. ACM.

Alnanih, R. and O. Ormandjieva, Mapping HCI Principles to Design Quality of Mobile User Interfaces in Healthcare Applications. Procedia Computer Science, 2016. 94: p. 75- 82.

Baldwin, T. and J. Chai. Towards online adaptation and personalization of key-target resizing for mobile devices. In Proceedings of the 2012 ACM international conference on Intelligent User Interfaces. 2012. ACM.

Computers and Graphics 23 (6) (1999) 893âĂŞ901 X.

Deb, K., et al., A fast and elitist multiobjective genetic algorithm: NSGA-II. IEEE Transactions on Evolutionary Computation, 2002. 6(2): p. 182-197.

Fallahpour, S., Lakvan, E. N., and Zadeh, M. H. (2017). Using an ensemble classifier based on sequential floating forward selection for financial distress prediction problem. Journal of Retailing and Consumer Services, 34, 159-167. Maldonado, S., PÃľrez, J., and Bravo, C. (2017).

Ghiani, G., et al., Evaluating context-aware user interface migration in multi-device environments. Journal of Ambient Intelligence and Humanized Computing, 2015. 6(2): p. 259- 277.

Hoehle, H., R. Aljafari, and V. Venkatesh, Leveraging MicrosoftŒş s mobile usability guidelines: Conceptualizing and developing scales for mobile application usability. International Journal of Human-Computer Studies, 2016. 89: p. 35-53.

Hu, W., et al. Smartphone software development course design based on android. in Computer and Information Technology (CIT), 2010 IEEE 10th International Conference on. 2010. IEEE.

International Journal of Human-Computer Studies, 2015. 75: p. 21-34.

Kobsa, A., Privacy-enhanced personalization. Communications of the ACM, 2007. 50(8): p. 24-33.

Lai, S., Xu, L., Liu, K., and Zhao, J. (2015, February). Recurrent convolutional neural networks for text classification. In Twenty-ninth AAAI conference on artificial intelligence.

Lelli, V., A. Blouin, and B. Baudry. Classifying and qualifying GUI defects. in 2015 IEEE 8th International Conference on Software Testing, Verification and Validation (ICST). 2015.

Mach. Intell. 24, 301âĂŞ302 (2002)

Mitra, P., Murthy, C.A., Pal, S.K.: Unsupervised feature selection using feature similarity. IEEE Trans. Pattern Anal.

Moshagen, M. and M. Thielsch, A short version of the visual aesthetics of websites inventory. Behaviour and Information Technology, 2013. 32(12): p. 1305-1311.

Nagpal, A., and Gaur, D. (2015). A New Proposed Feature Subset Selection Algorithm Based on Maximization of Gain Ratio. In International Conference on Big Data Analytics (pp. 181-197). Springer, Cham.

Schaffer, S., R. Schleicher, and S. MÃűller, Modeling input modality choice in mobile graphical and speech interfaces.

Schmidt, B., D. Galar, and L. Wang, Context Awareness in Predictive Maintenance, in Current Trends in Reliability, Availability, Maintainability and Safety. 2016, Springer. p. 197-211.

Soui, M. Chouchane, I. Gasmi, M. W. Mkaouer, Plain: Plugin for predicting the usability of mobile user interface., in: VISIGRAPP (1:860GRAPP), 2017, pp. 127âĂŞ136.

Zen, M., and Vanderdonckt, J. (2014). Towards an evaluation of graphical user interfaces aesthetics based on metrics. In2014 IEEE Eighth International Conference on Research Challenges in Information Science (RCIS) (pp. 1- 12). IEEE. Miniukovich, A., De Angeli, A. (2016). Webpage aesthetics: One size doesn't fit all. In Proceedings of the 9th Nordic Conference on Human-Computer Interaction (p. 70). ACM.

GAMIFICATION OF DISCUSSOO: AN ONLINE AI-BASED FORUM FOR SERIOUS DISCUSSIONS

Elena Bakhanova[1], Madiha Anjum[2], Jaime A. Garcia[1], William L. Raffe[1] and Alexey Voinov[3]
[1]*UTS Games Studio, Faculty of Engineering and Information Technology, University of Technology Sydney*
81-113 Broadway, Ultimo NSW 2007, Australia
[2]*School of Computer Science, Faculty of Engineering and Information Technology, University of Technology Sydney*
81-113 Broadway, Ultimo NSW 2007, Australia
[3]*Faculty of Engineering Technology, University of Twente*
Drienerlolaan 5, 7522 NB Enschede, Netherlands

ABSTRACT

Engagement in the discussion process is one of the common challenges of asynchronous online forums. It becomes especially crucial if the discussion is organized over a serious topic about a complex problem with a group of diverse stakeholders. Gamification gives much promise in addressing this challenge. In this paper, we propose possible game design solutions to the engagement challenge for an existing online AI-based platform Discussoo and reflect on the results from the expert interviews and an experiment with students.

KEYWORDS

Asynchronous Discussion, Game Design, Stakeholder Engagement, Participatory Modeling

1. INTRODUCTION

Today effective science-based policy-making assumes transparency and trust from the stakeholders involved and affected. Stakeholder engagement usually means that there is an educational component in the exchange of knowledge between the parties. Participatory modeling (PM) is one of the methods that imply 'a purposeful learning process for action that engages the implicit and explicit knowledge of stakeholders to create formalized and shared representations of reality' (Jordan *et al.*, 2018, p. 3). PM organizes stakeholder engagement around the process of building models of the systems of interest. Models offer a unique opportunity to study human reasoning and elucidate the way in which one thinks and makes decisions regarding the system at stake (Voinov *et al.*, 2016). Building explicit and shared models using the PM approach can greatly increase the applicability and robustness of the results.

However, the PM method has several challenges associated with its implementation. Modeling workshops are usually restricted in time (between 2 and 5 hours) and these workshops can accommodate only a limited number of participants (normally up to 30 people) (Van den Belt, 2004). It would be challenging to conduct a constructive discussion by inviting many more stakeholders and it will be hard to get all of them to join a workshop at a particular time in one place. One of the possible solutions to overcome these limitations is to use online discussion forums. Still, there are two difficulties associated with this solution in the PM context. Firstly, to our best knowledge, there is no discussion forum that holds modeling functionality or can mimic the modeling process. Secondly, it is challenging to sustain participants' engagement in such an asynchronous discussion setting.

In this paper, we focus on suggesting possible game design solutions to the engagement challenge for an existing online AI-based platform Discussoo that is designed to use in modeling context for the involvement of stakeholders in discussions on complex problems.

2. ONLINE DISCUSSIONS: ENGAGEMENT CHALLENGES AND EXISTING SOLUTIONS

Despite the anticipated value of using online forums for stakeholder involvement in problem analysis and decision-making, in the existing literature, such a format of asynchronous discussions appeared to be mostly used in formal and informal educational settings. In formal education discussion forums often serve as a complementary tool to promote peer-to-peer interaction and learning as well as critical thinking and stronger involvement in the topics of the subject (Huang *et al.*, 2019; Ding, Kim and Orey, 2020). This is due to the freedom of choosing the time and extent of interaction with other students and the ability to adjust the speed of learning and self-reflection (Hewitt, 2005; Huang *et al.*, 2019).

However, a range of researchers mentions that the positive outcomes of using online discussion forums largely depend on the level of engagement and motivation of the students (Tsai *et al.*, 2018; Ding, Kim and Orey, 2020). Hewitt (2005) explored the dynamics behind the growth and death of forum threads. Among the reasons for thread death were exhaustion of the discussion, a high degree of confrontation, loss of interest, lack of moderation, and use of 'clunkers' (phrases such as 'I agree' that prevent further elaboration on the topic).

There are multiple ways of how engagement challenges have been addressed in education literature. Following the principles of self-determination theory, Ding et al. (Ding, Kim and Orey, 2020) focus on the motivational drivers of the students such as the need for clear expectations and free expression along with the need for a sense of competence and relatedness. In an earlier study, Ding et al. (Ding, Er and Orey, 2018) explored the use of gamification in the context of online education and concluded that it worked efficiently in increasing the number of comments and performance but did not contribute to the sense of community. Overall, online education has been significantly exposed to game design use. Hansch et al. (Hansch, Newman and Schildhauer, 2015) reviewed gamification use at MOOC platforms and summarized the most commonly used game mechanics (badges & certificates, levels & goals, unlock content, progress bar and so forth) and social elements (peer-to-peer grading, profile, followers and so forth). As for non-gamified solutions, Rovai (Rovai, 2007) suggested a set of principles for the design and facilitation of online discussions such as grading that encourages participation, setting clear rules, promoting the feeling of social presence, creating space for informal communication for building the sense of community and others.

There are also a few examples of using online discussion forums for learning in informal settings, for example, helping a group of stakeholders to initiate a discussion about some problem (and improve their learning about the problem), collecting opinions of citizens, building joint actions of a community, or expanding citizen science. Bista et al. (2012) described the case of creating an online community to discuss and facilitate the acceptance of a legislative change on welfare payments among citizens. All the three challenges for organizing such an online interaction were associated with engagement: how to attract new members and motivate them to participate, how to monitor activities and how to sustain long-term engagement. In the context of citizen science, the engagement challenge is also a significant one for involving citizens' skills and time into research tasks that could be initially perceived as tiresome (Ponti, Hillman and Stankovic, 2015). In both examples, gamification has been used as a tool to increase engagement. Points and badges introduced to the online community appeared to be a useful tool to monitor engagement (S. K. Bista *et al.*, 2012). The outcome of using gamified features in citizen science projects is more controversial since playful experiences might be misinterpreted by the participants and make them perceive real scientific work as unserious (Ponti, Hillman and Stankovic, 2015).

The above-mentioned literature on using gamification to improve engagement in online discussions suggests that this approach can be useful. However, the suggested gamified interventions for formal education are not fully compatible with the context of discussions on serious topics with a group of stakeholders. For example, Ding et al. (Ding, Kim and Orey, 2020) discussed higher effectiveness of skill-related badges (the more skills acquired, the quicker a person progresses with receiving badges) as opposed to participatory badges (the more tasks completed, the quicker a person progresses with receiving badges). In online discussions there is no explicit goal to teach the participants, it is rather an intention to build an environment where they can get to a shared understanding of the problem while learning the perspectives of each other. Therefore, skill-based points or badges will unlikely work. At the same time, using participatory badges is also tricky because they promote active posting of comments without any attention to their quality, and in case of serious discussions quality of ideas is an important factor of the overall effectiveness. Several other suggested solutions such as the higher presence of a moderator support (Rovai, 2007) and points (S. K. Bista *et al.*, 2012) should be considered with caution since they might prevent free expression of opinions (if a moderator guides a discussion more tightly) and create undesired group dynamics (for example, if the most active participants in the forum get even more opportunities to express their opinions through the benefits of having particular badges). Both of these risks are undesirable in the context of organizing deliberative discussions with stakeholders because of its overall focus on equality in participation and democratization of decision-making. Hence, in our research, we elaborate further on existing solutions for increasing engagement in online discussion forums such as Discussoo.

3. INTRODUCTION TO DISCUSSOO PLATFORM

We can rely on some of the existing experience from the educational and gaming domains mentioned earlier, if we are to move a part or even the whole PM workshop process to the Internet, offering stakeholders an easy and asynchronous way to learn from each other and express their opinions about the problem at stake.

One could also refer to the existing online platforms (like Facebook or Twitter) to mimic some parts of the discussions that are normally occurring during the PM workshops. However, there are several limitations associated with such social media platforms: (1) limited access to the information collected in the comments, which makes it hard to process the comments and extract any knowledge from them; (2) absence of a facilitator who could guide the discussion; (3) absence of the functionality of translating discussions into more formal models (qualitative or quantitative). These considerations and challenges convinced us that instead of relying on existing platforms, we should develop a designated online tool, Discussoo, that can be deployed in the PM process (*Figure 1 (1)*) (Anjum *et al.*, 2021). This tool provides a platform for stakeholders where they can share their opinions by submitting comments. The recorded comments are immediately processed, and with help of artificial intelligence (AI) algorithms, information is extracted from available texts to generate on the fly the conceptual model (mind map), which can be instantly fed back into the discussion for stakeholder checking and validation. As with all AI methods, they require training and learning to improve their performance. It might take some time for us to make sure that the methods that are being used always produce meaningful and useful conceptual models automatically or in real-time. At this stage we also allow the moderator to play a role in validating and improving the conceptual model.

While involving multiple stakeholders in a discussion provides an opportunity for groups and organizations to improve the quality of their decisions, they inevitably face a new set of challenges about engaging people and managing conversations. Overall, people are time-poor and overloaded with information and it's difficult to sustain a high level of participation, especially if the topic of discussion is not a top priority for a particular group of stakeholders. The anticipated challenges can be the following:

(1) *Retention of stakeholders at the platform.* A better understanding of the problem is happening where the opinions are shared and discussed. Additionally, the output of AI algorithms (the conceptual model) will be more accurate if there is enough data to analyze. Therefore, there is a need to create mechanisms that motivate participants to come back to the platform and keep on participating in the discussion.

(2) *Too many comments that need to be read by the participants.* Since Discussoo is targeting serious discussions on complex problems, it's likely that comments of the participants will be long explaining the reasoning behind opinions. In addition to that, considering that there is no limitation on the number of participants, the quantity of comments can also be significant. Hence, there is a need to avoid single-pass practices when a participant scans all the new comments (Hewitt, 2005). On the contrary, the process should provoke the participants to read, understand and respond to the comments of others (either elaborating on the opinions that they agree with or arguing about the opinions that are opposite to their own).

(3) *No feeling of community or social presence.* Asynchronous discussions and the anonymity of users provide very different experiences in terms of human-like connections as compared to face-to-face traditional workshops with stakeholders. However, most complex problems require joint actions to be solved, all these require trust and a sense of community. Although it's hard to claim that such online discussion tools can substitute actual participation in decision-making, still a certain level of community support would be desired and can be a motivational driver for extended conversations and debates on the platform. A range of researchers suggests that a feeling of community helps to sustain engagement in online discussions (Hansch, Newman and Schildhauer, 2015; Ding, Kim and Orey, 2020).

(4) *Validating the concepts extracted by AI algorithms for improving the conceptual model (mind map).* As mentioned earlier, at the initial stage of using algorithms there is a need for additional validation of the extracted concepts by the participants. If this task of sorting concepts into valid or invalid is suggested in a straightforward way, it could be perceived as a tiresome and uninteresting activity for the participants. Therefore, there is a need to make this process of concepts validation more entertaining but still meaningful.

4. GAMIFICATION OF DISCUSSOO PLATFORM

Considering the existing research about the positive effects of gamification on engagement, motivation, and enjoyment of a process (e.g., Sailer *et al.*, 2017; Sailer and Homner, 2019; Bakhanova *et al.*, 2020), we suggest incorporating gamified features into Discussoo platform with aim of solving the above-mentioned engagement challenges.

Retention of stakeholders at the platform. Often the challenge with user retention in online discussions is solved by using email notifications. In the case of Discussoo, there are four types of notifications that consider the context of several possible scenarios:

1. If you reply to a user comment, you get an email notification with a suggestion for action (e.g., 'Hey, others are commenting on your opinion. Have a look and let us know what you think!').
2. If several other participants rate your comment at 7 scores or above, then you get an email notification with a suggestion for action ('Hey, your comment is trending! Look at what those people who liked your comment think!').
3. If no one replies/rates your comment, you get an email notification pointing to someone else's idea ('Hey! There are some like-minded people in the discussion. Check out what their arguments are!').
4. If you do not come back to the platform for 5 days in a row, you get an email notification with a reference to someone else's comment and a suggestion to give feedback (e.g., 'Peter XX said 'Citation of comment'. Do you agree?')

Some of the notifications build on "satisfaction of the need for relatedness", others on the "need for competence" as per definitions from self-determination theory (Ryan and Deci, 2000).

Too many comments that need to be read by the participants. With the passage of time, the number of comments about particular topics will become larger. Since the participants are usually time-poor, they will hardly be willing to go through all the available comments. But one of the main purposes of using such a platform is to provide the stakeholders with an environment where they can learn about the opinions of others and debate in a constructive way, which could be hardly achieved if many of the comments are neglected. A chatbot is introduced into the platform functionality to solve this challenge (*Figure 1(2)*). The chatbot suggests the participants to read a relevant comment from any other participant. Then it encourages the participant to rate or respond to the suggested comment. Additionally, when the comment of a user is too short, the chatbot asks to elaborate more on the idea. The rationale behind it is to keep the conversation going and to get more detailed responses that could be better processed by AI algorithms. With the introduction of this chatbot into the discussion, we aim at satisfying the need for competence through giving the participants a chance to take the challenge of responding to a comment that is contradicting their opinion about the discussed topic.

No feeling of community or social presence. A system of points and badges is introduced in the platform (*Figure 1 (3)*). The higher and more a participant's comments are scored by others in the community, the more points s/he gets and, hence, progresses through three levels of 'Influencer' badges (beginner - mid-level - pro). Here we target the need for relatedness (Ryan and Deci, 2000) and direct encouragement from the peers that motivates users to keep on participating in the discussion.

Validating the concepts extracted by AI algorithms for improving the mind map. This challenge is about converting the tiresome task of sorting the concepts into a more entertaining one. This task can be implemented in a form of a mini-game similar to the classical 'bubble shooter' game (*Figure 1(4)*). In the game concepts extracted earlier from the comments are suggested one-by-one to the users. To keep a concept, they need to throw a blue bubble at it; to discard a concept they throw a red bubble. The game continues till all the irrelevant concepts are removed. Following the principles of self-determination theory, this game targets the satisfaction of the need for autonomy. On the one hand, the user can independently decide whether to keep or discard a bubble with a concept. On the other hand, the task is still challenging since one gets most of the points if hits a larger number of bubbles (similar to the standard 'bubble shooter' game).

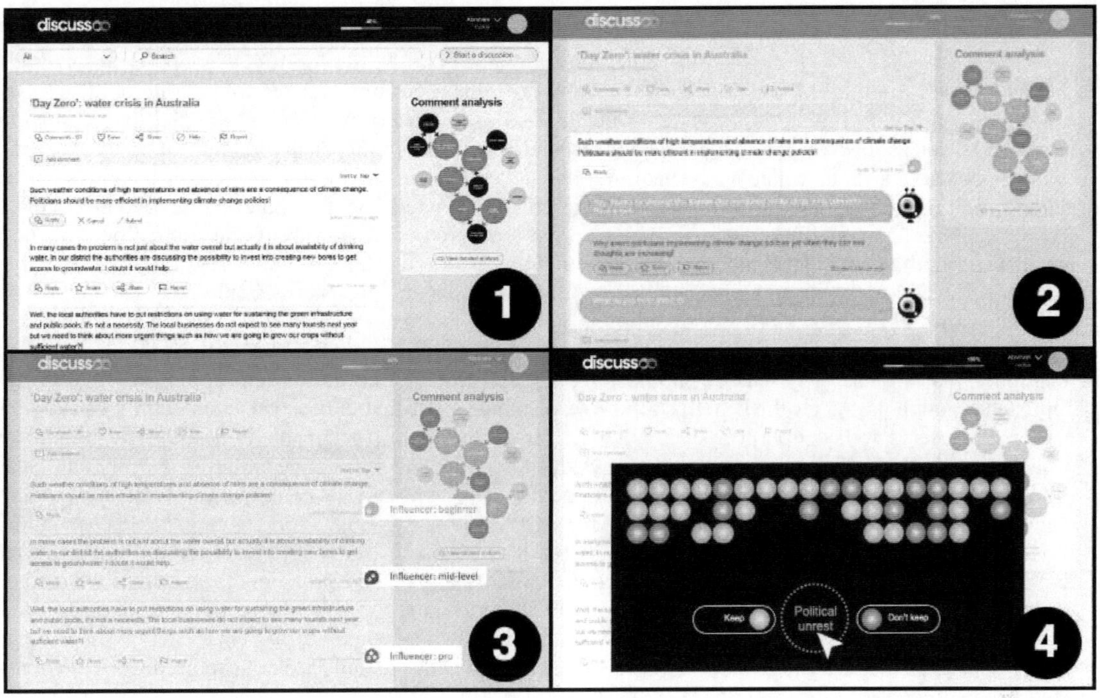

Figure 1. Discussoo platform: (1) standard discussion view, (2) chatbot for keeping conversations going, (3) 'Influencer' badges, (4) 'Concept shooter' game for validating the concepts for the model

5. METHOD

The proposed gamified features were incorporated into the Discussoo platform (Discussoo, 2020). The 'concept shooter' game and the chatbot are optional features that can be switched on once the discussion organizer sets up the topic. Notifications and 'influencer' badges are by default operating for every discussion on the platform. Once the newly registered user enters Discussoo, they are suggested to go through brief introductory slides explaining the functionality of the platform including gamified features.

We conducted a pilot study to collect feedback on the usability of the platform and the overall idea of using Discussoo in the context of stakeholder engagement. There were two target audiences: those who organize such serious discussions with stakeholders (i.e., PM practitioners) and those who directly interact with the platform (i.e., stakeholders).

As for the first group, we conducted interviews with four experts in the field of PM, social sciences, and environmental engineering who actively involve stakeholders in their research. Experts represent not only different scientific fields but also diverse geographies (Australia, India, Finland, and the USA). During the interview, we demonstrated the main features of the Discussoo platform as per descriptions in Sections 3 and 4 of this paper. The aim of the interviews was to understand what could be perceived as *successful* stakeholder engagement and to collect initial feedback on the idea of Discussoo and its implementation.

As for the second group, we conducted an experiment with 57 university students who were suggested to contribute to a discussion on learning in COVID time. They were given one week to participate in the discussion, after that they were asked to fill in a post-test questionnaire. It included questions associated with usability and level of engagement when interacting on the platform. There were eight statements to be assessed on the Likert scale; some statements referred to overall engagement during the online discussion (e.g., 'I felt like time went by quickly while I was active at the platform'), other questions were associated with specific gamified features (e.g., 'Interaction with the chatbot was interesting'). The questionnaire also included open-ended questions where the respondents could share what they liked and disliked in the Discussoo platform.

6. RESULTS

The interviews with the PM practitioners have shown two main positions related to the criteria of success in stakeholder engagement. One is focusing on the process of involvement itself and the fact that it should be intensive as well as flexible. Another position is associated with results that such engagement brings; the results could be concrete such as collaborative learning and acknowledgment of the perspectives of others or more generic such as whether the process served the initial stakeholders' needs whatever they were. As for the feedback on the functionality of Discussoo platform, there were two categories of questions: first is about the benefits and applicability of this tool; second is about drawbacks and potential challenges of its use. The experts mentioned several ways of applications of this tool: (1) for collecting perspectives/opinions of stakeholders at the early stages of the project, (2) for avoiding the bias of a facilitator (which is one of the possible risks of face-to-face workshops with stakeholders) and collecting direct responses from the participants. A few experts mentioned that the use of Discussoo should have a clear goal as well as it could be combined with other approaches and tools. As for the benefits, all the respondents agree that the current functionality of Discussoo platform can serve well the purpose of involving a large number of participants in a discussion about some problem as well as facilitate the process of knowledge elicitation. The attractive and user-friendly interface of the platform was mentioned as one of the plus points. The experts also mentioned several drawbacks or challenges associated with the use of such a tool for stakeholder engagement. Among them could be mentioned the following: (1) conceptual models that Discussoo generates with help of AI algorithms can capture only those ideas that are on the surface while for a deeper understanding of the problem other, qualitative methods, could be of more use, (2) the use of AI-algorithms could be misinterpreted by the participants of discussion as if there is lack of control over the content that is visualized in the final outcome, mind map, (3) typing comments is a slow process that is a limitation, (4) emotions associated with opinions are not captured while it could be useful if the topic is of high importance or sensitive, (5) there is an 'ambiguity related to the language' which is about the fact that the same word/concept might have a different meaning for different people while AI-algorithms so far are not able to differentiate or clear out this issue.

The results of the experiment appeared to be overall positive: all of the statements from the post-test questionnaire were scored above three on a Likert scale where one is 'Strongly Disagree' and five is 'Strongly Agree' (*Figure 2*). The interaction with the platform got an average score of 3.88 (S1). The participants enjoyed scoring the comments of others (S7) and interacting with the chatbot (S5 and S6) more as compared to other features of the platform. Interestingly, female participants on average were less satisfied with the features of the platform; this could be observed from the responses on the statements S3, S4, S5, and S8 which correspond with such features as notifications, chatbot, and badges. The participants seem to be enjoying the possibility to score the comments of others (S7), but they enjoy much less when someone scored their comments (S8). This tendency can be also seen in the responses to the question 'What did you like the most about Discussoo?'. There were multiple responses appreciating the possibility to rate the comments. However, there were also several responses where the respondents did not appreciate the rating system and badges (i.e., rating someone's *personal* view did not seem exciting for some participants).

Among other positive aspects could be mentioned the possibility of getting the views of others, new perspectives, and seeing alike ideas; while the negative comments from the respondents included repetition of ideas and the need to scroll through long threads. Although these comments were not common, still, it tells us that most likely the participants could not take advantage of the mind map developed by AI. One of the initial ideas was that a user can get a general idea about the discussion just by looking at the mind map and with no need to read all the comments. This could become one of the aspects for further improvement in terms of visibility and interaction with the mind map, so that the participants could take the most out of it.

Another aspect for further improvement is retention of users at the platform. As we can see from *Figure 5* (S4), statement S4 'I returned to the platform several times' received the lowest average score among all the other statements.

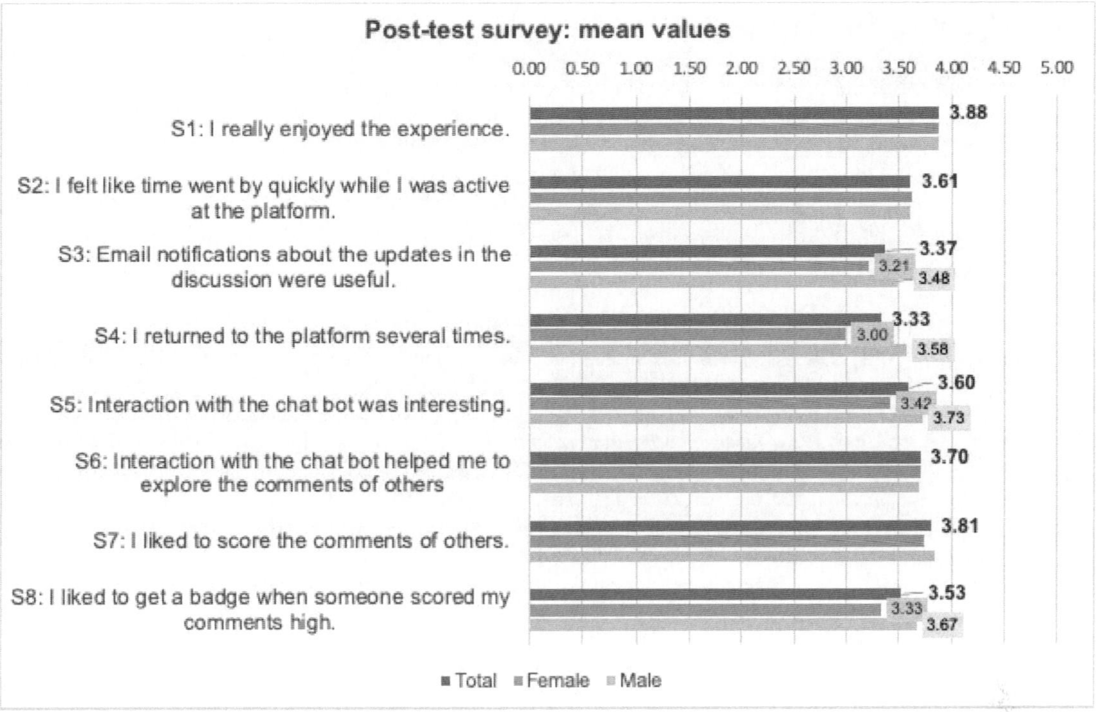

Figure 2. Results of the brief post-test survey: mean values for engagement-related statements

7. CONCLUSION

Game design offers a variety of possible applications for addressing the engagement challenges of asynchronous online discussions. The proposed gamified features for the Discussoo platform cover the most urgent challenges that are anticipated in the process of stakeholder involvement in serious discussions. In our pilot study, the respondents positively assessed the usability and gamified features of the Discussoo platform. Still, we could not achieve high scores for the retention to the platform and, therefore, there is a window of opportunities to improve the design of Discussoo. In general, with help of this experiment, we could assess the implementation of suggested game concepts. However, one could think of other ways to design the visuals of the badges or chatbot, which, in turn, can influence the overall user experience. From the methodological perspective, we managed to collect insights on the usability and usefulness of the platform from multiple angles (from PM practitioners as organizers and stakeholders as direct users). The survey gave us a general understanding; however, we still lack detailed information about what exactly the users liked about each gamified feature and why. The next step could be more in-depth usability studies with help of post-test interviews. It could be also useful to explore the perception of different gamified features from cultural perspective. For example, scoring someone else's opinion in some cultures can be perceived as a norm, in others, it could be taken personally and lead to unnecessary tensions in the group discussion.

Overall, there are many other potential directions for gamifying the process of online discussions. One could think of creating a user experience that is similar to reality (for example, an online forum as a fully developed virtual world where participants can choose avatars, enter the 'virtual' meeting rooms on diverse topics, see and interact with more visually appealing mind maps of the discussed issues). Based on the feedback from interviews with experts, one could also consider adding features of audio commenting and transcribing or introducing emoji panels to better represent emotions and make the process of discussions more human-like.

ACKNOWLEDGEMENT

The development of the prototype for the gamified version of the Discussoo platform has been done with the mentoring and financial support of the Techcelerator program of the Faculty of Engineering and IT at the University of Technology Sydney. The authors would like to thank the UTS Techcelerator team and experts who participated in the interviews for the evaluation of the Discussoo platform.

REFERENCES

Anjum, M. (2020) *Discussoo*. Available at: https://discussoo.com/ (Accessed: 2 May 2022).

Anjum, M. *et al.* (2021) 'Discussoo: Towards an intelligent tool for multi-scale participatory modeling', *Environmental Modelling & Software*, 140, p. 105044. doi:10.1016/j.envsoft.2021.105044.

Bakhanova, E. *et al.* (2020) 'Targeting social learning and engagement: What serious games and gamification can offer to participatory modeling', *Environmental Modelling & Software*, 134, p. 104846. doi:10.1016/j.envsoft.2020.104846.

Ding, L., Er, E. and Orey, M. (2018) 'An exploratory study of student engagement in gamified online discussions', *Computers & Education*, 120, pp. 213–226. doi:10.1016/j.compedu.2018.02.007.

Ding, L., Kim, C. and Orey, M. (2020) 'Design of gamified asynchronous online discussions', *Technology, Pedagogy and Education*, pp. 1–17. doi:10.1080/1475939X.2020.1801495.

Hansch, A., Newman, C. and Schildhauer, T. (2015) 'Fostering Engagement with Gamification: Review of Current Practices on Online Learning Platforms', *SSRN Electronic Journal* [Preprint]. doi:10.2139/ssrn.2694736.

Hewitt, J. (2005) 'Toward an Understanding of How Threads Die in Asynchronous Computer Conferences', *Journal of the Learning Sciences*, 14(4), pp. 567–589. doi:10.1207/s15327809jls1404_4.

Huang, B. *et al.* (2019) 'Effects of gamification on students' online interactive patterns and peer-feedback', *Distance Education*, 40(3), pp. 350–379. doi:10.1080/01587919.2019.1632168.

Jordan, R. *et al.* (2018) 'Twelve Questions for the Participatory Modeling Community', *Earth's Future* [Preprint]. doi:10.1029/2018EF000841.

Ponti, M., Hillman, T. and Stankovic, I. (2015) 'Science and Gamification: The Odd Couple?', in *Proceedings of the 2015 Annual Symposium on Computer-Human Interaction in Play - CHI PLAY '15. the 2015 Annual Symposium*, London, United Kingdom: ACM Press, pp. 679–684. doi:10.1145/2793107.2810293.

Rovai, A.P. (2007) 'Facilitating online discussions effectively', *The Internet and Higher Education*, 10(1), pp. 77–88. doi:10.1016/j.iheduc.2006.10.001.

Ryan, R.M. and Deci, E.L. (2000) 'Self-determination theory and the facilitation of intrinsic motivation, social development, and well-being.', *American Psychologist*, 55(1), pp. 68–78. doi:10.1037/0003-066X.55.1.68.

S. K. Bista *et al.* (2012) 'Using gamification in an online community', in *8th International Conference on Collaborative Computing: Networking, Applications and Worksharing (CollaborateCom). 8th International Conference on Collaborative Computing: Networking, Applications and Worksharing (CollaborateCom)*, pp. 611–618.

Sailer, M. *et al.* (2017) 'How gamification motivates: An experimental study of the effects of specific game design elements on psychological need satisfaction', *Computers in Human Behavior* [Preprint]. doi:10.1016/j.chb.2016.12.033.

Sailer, M. and Homner, L. (2019) 'The Gamification of Learning: a Meta-analysis', *Educational Psychology Review* [Preprint]. doi:10.1007/s10648-019-09498-w.

Tsai, Y. *et al.* (2018) 'The effects of metacognition on online learning interest and continuance to learn with MOOCs', *Computers & Education*, 121, pp. 18–29. doi:10.1016/j.compedu.2018.02.011.

Van den Belt, M. (2004) *Mediated modeling: a system dynamics approach to environmental consensus building*. Washington, DC: Island press.

Voinov, A. *et al.* (2016) 'Modelling with stakeholders - Next generation', *Environmental Modelling and Software* [Preprint]. doi:10.1016/j.envsoft.2015.11.016.

GAME GRAPHICS AND EFFECTIVE LEARNING: A REVIEW OF VISUAL COMMUNICATION RESEARCH IN SERIOUS GAMES

Hua Bai, Ran Zhang, Björn Berg Marklund and Ulf Wilhelmsson
School of informatics, University of Skövde
Högskolevägen, Box 408, 54128, Skövde, Sweden

ABSTRACT

The visuals of a game is a crucial element when it comes to providing good player experiences. Visuals are also an incredibly complex subject in a game context since different modes of visual representation can be more or less "appropriate" for different settings. For example, while one can look at photo-realism as an impressive feature of a game due to its technical complexity and functionally accurate representation of real-world objects, it might still not be a fitting choice for different audiences, or for different pedagogical strategies. Serious game research seldom focuses on understanding the design of these components or their applicability to different types of learning, and it more often focuses on games' mechanics and how well they manage to capture subject matter content while still being engaging. The aim of this paper is to explore the gap in visual communication research, describing what studies tend to focus on providing some valuable context. This review was conducted on papers that dealt with visual aspects of serious games. The results show that visual communication is rarely addressed in serious game development research. Future research would benefit from taking visual communication in detail to facilitate the effectiveness of serious games.

KEYWORDS

Serious Games, Literature Review, Visual Communication, Visual Design, Game Design, Learning Outcome

1. INTRODUCTION

In his book *Audio-visual Methods in Teaching*, the pedagogical researcher Edgar Dale introduced the 'cone of experience' model (Dale, 1969). The model serves to describe memory retention in relation to different types of stimuli, or modes of receiving information. For example, a person tends to easily forget information that has only been received through written text - but if the information is presented in a way that stimulates more senses it is subject to less entropy. According to the model, visual presentation of information (through images or video) is a particularly significant improvement over just reading and listening. Thus, from the perspective of learning outcomes, the ways serious games (SGs) choose to visualize subject matters - and not only their design of interactive elements - are worth some examination.

With digital games, the mere presence of visual materials as support is not really up for debate - the exact shape and purpose of the visuals, however, are. Understanding visuals in games is a multi-faceted challenge. Games themselves range from simplistic 2D single-player environments, to complex fully realized 3D massively multiplayer worlds. Games are also played through a myriad of user interfaces (e.g., PCs, phones, VR sets, AR technologies, home consoles, etc.), and these affect the way players "connect" with the visuals. The game players themselves are also complex; different players perceive visuals differently. This both comes down to demographic aspects (e.g., a player's age), but is also affected by cultural contexts and differences in peoples' visual media literacies (Buckingham and Burn, 2007). From a SGs perspective, there is even more added complexity in terms of pedagogical processes and learning goals (which are, in themselves, incredibly intricate).

With all these challenges in mind, what do we currently know about the function and effects of different visuals in SGs? Currently, research on these relationships seems to be rare in comparison to research on how game design principles might match 'serious' purposes. For SGs to progress, their visual aspects need to be understood equally well. With this purpose in mind, this paper aims to contribute to the discourse around visuals in SGs through a systematic review of published research on the topic.

2. METHOD

The literature review search was conducted in February 2022. A set of potential keywords, and keyword combinations, were used to search on the most relevant databases for the topic within the technology informatics perspective, namely Scopus and IEEE Xplore. The search was conducted over article titles, keywords, and abstracts to accommodate a wider scope. After several preliminary searches, we found out that most visual-related papers in SGs are published after 2010. We also found that some relevant papers were not part of the search result and thus we did a second search string which resulted in more relevant articles without too many false positives. The purpose for the review is not to focus on game platform. The results were restricted to articles published between the years 2010 to 2021, and non-English articles were excluded. This of course creates a strong bias in the research by the database, search time range, and language. To be included in this review, the publication had to relate to visual communication in the context of SGs. In order to expand our search results, we did not limit our search according to the type of documents, such as journals, conferences, and book chapters. No limitations on the end-users in terms of gender, age, health, or geographical location were made.

To conduct a review that met our objectives, the search term needs to accommodate two key purposes. The first purpose was to find papers relating to SGs. We expanded the term, serious games, to include educational, learning, gamification, mobile, virtual reality, artificial reality. The second purpose was to narrow it to studies of visual design. We therefore included the terms, aesthetic, graphic, informative, and complexity. The resulting search string used for the literature review is listed in Table 1.

Table 1. Concepts and composition of search string

Concepts	Keywords
Game	(gamif*) OR (serious* OR educat* OR learn* OR mobil* OR vr OR ar) W/1 (game*)
Visual	(aesthetic OR esthetics) OR ((visual* OR graphic* OR informative*) W/1 (design*) OR (language*) OR (complex*))

Reporting Items for Systematic Reviews and Meta-Analyses (PRISMA) 2020 selection process (Page MJ et al., 2020) as depicted in Figure 1.

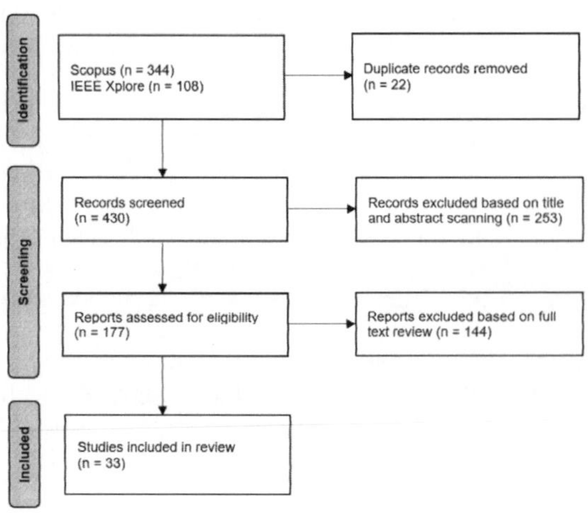

Figure 1. Selection process for literature review

The initial search resulted in 452 studies from Scopus (n=344) and IEEE Xplore (n=108). After removing duplicates (n=22), 430 articles were retained for screening. To be included in this review, the publication had to include visual communication related content in SGs. In order to look at the situation regarding visual components in the SGs community, games for entertainment were excluded. These papers were then manually filtered by title and abstract based on inclusion and exclusion criteria, resulting in the exclusion of 253 articles. The remaining 177 articles were further screened after reading their full text, which resulted in 144 articles being excluded from the study. At the conclusion of the searching and filtering processes, a total of 33 articles were identified to meet all inclusion and exclusion criteria and were fully reviewed in this paper.

3. RESULTS

After considering all qualifying studies, papers were categorized into three different categories based on what they aimed to contribute to visual communication. These are visual representation evaluation, visual design guidelines, and visual as a component. Since some studies focus on more than one of the purposes, we sorted them by their primary purpose. To better present the results, we created Table 2 that details the purposes of each visual communication related category and lists all the studies.

Table 2. Result of reviewed articles based on study context

Study Purpose	Descriptions	Total	Studies
Visual Representation Evaluation	Examining how different forms of visual representation correlate to user experiences and/or learning outcomes	19	(Alcivar et al., 2021), (Tuah et al., 2021), (Zhang et al., 2021), (Sarić et al., 2021), (Plass et al., 2020), (Pagano et al., 2020), (Gee and Dolah, 2020), (Alyami et al., 2019), (Gee and Dolah, 2018a), (Gee and Dolah, 2018b) (Javora et al., 2018), (Ontañón et al., 2017), (Gee and Dolah, 2016), (Selmbacherova et al., 2014), (Veinott et al., 2014), (Wang and Lee, 2014) , (Wattanasoontorn et al., 2013), (Bedi et al., 2011) , (Kartiko et al., 2010)
Visual Design Guidelines	Presenting models, guidelines or methods for visual design	7	(Rizvic et al., 2020) , (Gee, 2019), (Soriano et al., 2018), (Grabska, 2015), (Mahmoud amd Wloka, 2015), (Yusoff and Kamsin, 2015), (McLaughlin et al., 2010)
Visual as a Component	Examining the relationship between visual components and other game components (e.g., audio, mechanics, controllers, etc.)	7	(Alexiou et al., 2020), (Poullis et al., 2019), (Kapralos et al., 2017), (Rowe et al., 2017), (Cheng et al., 2016), (Fuchs et al., 2016), (Rojas, 2014)

In general, the most common subject of examination is ways to improve the visual representation in SGs with 19 papers, through evaluating visual representations for how to affect engagement or learning objectives better. The method to improve the visual design pipeline in SGs was also a common research topic with seven papers. The last seven papers focus on visual communication related to other game components from a game development perspective. Figure 2 shows how the found papers were distributed across the 2010-2021 timespan, as well as which topics they were covering (based on the three categories used here).

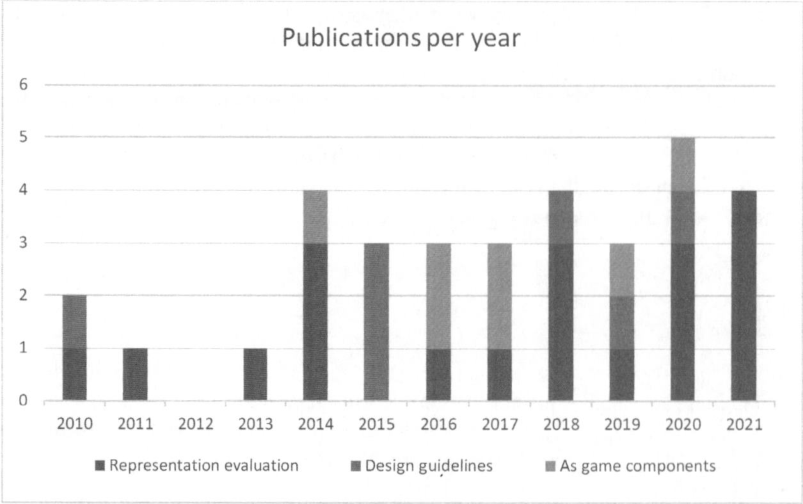

Figure 2. Publication distribution between 2010-2021

3.1 Visual Representation Evaluation

The visual representation is, by far, most frequently subject to investigation. In total, 19 papers investigate how visual representations affect the user experience or learning outcome. The main evaluation objective is between photorealistic, cartoon-like, and abstract, different visual complexity, visual fidelity, and specific visual features in detail.

Ten papers specifically discussed visuals in 2D-based SG contexts. Here, the research of Shiau Gee and Dolah (2020) focuses on how different graphic styles influence user experience in a math game. They find that the 'Abstract' version better delivers information to users. This is also ratified by Wouters and Oostendorp (2017), as they found that cartoon-like visuals are more effective than photorealistic in SGs. To break down which design features such as shape, texture, and shading contribute to graphic style visualization, Shiau Gee and Dolah (2018b) report that a combination of natural form and toon shading in abstract style is more attractive than realistic style. However, all this research is done in different markets and on different end-users, and they do not all reach the same conclusions in support of cartoon-like visual representations. For example, Czechoslovakia 38-89 (Selmbacherova et al., 2014) is a historic game for high school students, enabling them to "experience" historical events from the perspectives of different individuals. They evaluated the photorealistic version as more authentic and attractive than the cartoon-like style to tell a historical story.

Four other papers focused on 3D-based simulation contexts, and aimed to examine the effectiveness of visual realism. These studies make statements both regarding users feeling positive within photorealism environments, and that realism plays a key role in simulation SGs. For example, *The Arkae Vision* (Pagano et al., 2020) identifies positive engagement feedback through the realism of the virtual reconstructions, the atmosphere, and the sense of the past. While engagement studies were positive, studies on learning outcomes were less conclusive. Veinott (2014) finds no main effects on learning between two types of visual fidelity and cognitive fidelity. Kartiko et al. (2010) also report that no significant differences in presence and learning outcomes between different levels of visual complexity of animated-virtual actors.

Moving on from the specific dimensions/game types - the reviewed papers used a very wide variety of factors in their evaluation. User satisfaction, learning outcome, engagement, motivation, attractiveness, authenticity, immersion, and enjoyment were encountered in different papers. The majority of studies examined attractiveness or satisfaction on different visual representations, while only 6 out of 19 looked at the learning outcomes. One of those, a science game, developed by (Javora et al., 2018), examines visual representation to what extent detail will affect perceived attractiveness and learning outcomes. Children between 9 to 11 years of age preferred the high esthetic version, but this did not improve their learning outcome. Considering preference, this finding is consistent with the results of Wang and Lee (2014) that only the learners of the younger and older age groups have a special preference for pictures of very high complexity. In fact, the majority of learners prefer pictures of medium complexity, followed by slightly higher complexity pictures. Another study (Alyami et al., 2019) introduces the visual metaphor to a serious game, which presents that playing a serious game is more satisfying than reading text files. However, there are no significant differences between groups in learning outcome, self-efficacy, cognitive load, ease of use, acceptability, or examination scores.

In addition, two of the papers consider visual metaphors as a research objective. Alyami et al. (2019) reported that visual metaphors enhance memory retrieval, while Ontañón et al. (2017) show that abstract visual metaphors better support the learning process than the physical metaphor by not misguiding students in a programming game. And, another two papers presented a new tool for evaluating avatar characters. Alcivar (2021) evaluates game usability and player's avatar preferences, and connects it with motivation in educational games for learning. Tuah (2021) created a model of player and avatar attachment based on user engagement by using questionnaires and eye-tracking. Besides, Zhang et al. (2021) report that visual perception had a great influence on learning and cognition.

3.2 Visual Design Guidelines

Seven of the discovered articles provide guidelines to visual design. They are, in many cases, analyzed from established art and cognitive principles (McLaughlin et al., 2010; Soriano et al., 2018; Grabska, 2015). McLaughlin et al. (2010) create a framework intended to provide a guide through computer graphics techniques and visual style in SGs. The model is organized in a table depicting Bloom's taxonomy of the cognitive domain (Knowledge, Comprehension, Application, Analysis, Synthesis, and Evaluation) and categories of computer graphics imagery (Simplified, Stylized, Naturalistic). This model has evolved through the analysis of computer graphics in movies and games for entertainment. Soriano et al. (2018) evaluated the method for designing complex pictograms for SGs that take into account both the impact of visual complexity on memory performance and how graphical content affects player engagement. Their results suggest that the method can directly assist designers in formalizing the main intention of each learning objective. In addition, Gee's (2019) study explains visual elements in detail. They create a guideline for educational games that provide a visual design guideline to identify appropriate improvements. The concepts of the abstract and realistic style include design theory, art direction, theme, and combining shapes, texture and shading to produce positive experiences. Designers can also utilize it as a map to reduce the cost of resources, thus enabling more efficient and effective representation in educational game development. In addition, two of the papers present a guideline or approach based on visual perception, while two papers present an interaction design model.

3.3 Visual as a Component

Several papers aimed to understand visuals as components within larger game contexts. Since players don't experience game components in isolation from one another, these papers looked at the ways visuals affect, and are affected by, other game components. Some studies specifically examined the coupling between audio and visuals. For example, Rojas (2014) suggests that contextual sound cues influence visual fidelity perception and perception of visual fidelity increases with contextual sound cues. Kapralos et al. (2017) reported that sound could directly affect visual fidelity perception and task performance within a virtual environment. Other researchers, like Alexiou et al (2020), found that visual aesthetics positively affect learning outcomes when they are effectively combined with other narrative components. Besides, 4 articles mentioned visual components in general. For example, a negative user experience from the evaluation of The Seafarers (Poullis et al., 2019), game players felt that the graphics were not visually appealing. Although the main objective of the developed game is learning, it will be important to have an attractive graphics design that may engage more users and may allow for better retention of information.

4. ANALYSIS

In this section, some common challenges identified in the literature will be summarized. Games as a medium definitely provide new and powerful affordances, but it is the design within the medium to leverage those affordances that will determine the efficacy of a learning environment (Clark et al., 2016). Visual components have already become an indispensable part of teaching materials. However, the amount of research reported about visual communication within SGs was minimal in the game community, restricting the results we were able to find.

4.1 Inconsistency of Terminology and Taxonomy

One recurring issue during this review was that the terminology used in research regarding game visuals is highly inconsistent. Different terms are often used to elaborate the same idea, which is unsurprising given the interdisciplinary nature of the field of SGs. For example, visual complexity, visual sophistication, visual esthetic value, visual style and graphic style, realistic and photorealistic, etc., were all used to refer to issues of visual fidelity. This lack of unified language might be an obstacle for discussions of game visuals in the SGs community. Using our own review as an example, in our first search we found that highly relevant research (that was, for example, cited in several papers we had found) didn't show up in search results. Thus we repeated the search process a second time, where we included different synonymous terminologies we found in the literature in an attempt to avoid excluding important research due to an issue of semantics.

The taxonomy of visual style in SGs contexts is slightly different in the literature. Game scholars Aki Järvinen (2002), McLaughlin et al. (2010) as well as Egenfeldt-Nielsen, Smith and Tosca (2015) have arrived at the classification of styles as: abstract, stylized, and realistic. However, another set of concepts is more common when looking at practitioner literature (or literature specifically oriented towards game artists and developers). For example, in his book *Game feel: a game designer's guide to virtual sensation*, Swink (2008) classifies game visuals as being either realistic, iconic, or abstract (with reference to Scott McCloud (1993)). In addition, Wouters and Van (2013) provide a category based on Vogel et al. (2006) research that is photorealistic, cartoon-like, and Schematic/Basic.

4.2 The Relationship between Budget, Learning Goals, and Visual Representation

In visual design, the nature, shape, and form of the environment a serious game functions in is also a vital factor. Here, we need to make a distinction between "informal" and "formal" contexts. For games played in informal contexts (for example, at home), it is important to invest development time in a game's graphics as the game will ultimately be competing for the players' attention, where they have plenty of other entertainment options to choose from (Javora, 2018). Player retention, thus, becomes a major challenge the game has to overcome. However, in a formal schooling context, Javora points out that children are mandatorily motivated in learning. A less attractive design does not seem to harm learning if it carries all the learning needs. Developing games for learning can be very complex and costly and still provide significant challenges (Boyle, 2016). Visual complexity could be a high-cost pursuit that the typical budget for educational games cannot accommodate (McLaughlin et al., 2010). This begs the question: how can a developer, and other stakeholders, effectively balance visual representation needs, the learning/behavior/training goals, and economic factors when creating SGs?

To this point, the impact of visual representation in SGs (whether it's in 2D or 3D graphics) is still not fully understood. However, in the review, we discovered three recurring statements: (1) abstract or cartoon-like style is better than realistic style in terms of user experience (see Wouters and Van, 2013; Clark et al., 2015); (2) high visual realism will provide an immersive environment to users in 3D simulation context but might not affect learning outcome (see Pagano et al., 2020); and (3) visual complexity in SGs can obstruct information and prevent learning, "Complex art creates noise," (Sylvester, 2013). Based on these three perspectives, abstract and symbolic game visuals seem to be preferable for learning and for providing an engaging experience, but realism has a higher potential to be immersive. This echoes previous research from instructional sciences (e.g., Alesandrini, 1984; Dwyer, 1978), which posits that while complex pictures are interesting, they will also increase cognitive load and affect memory retention. People are more responsive to simple pictures than complex pictures (Pezdek and Maki, 1988). Visual perception has a great influence on learning and cognition. To grasp the potential of visual communication, it is key to understand the interplay between visual and cognitive to enhance engagement and learning outcomes.

4.3 Design Model in Different Contexts

It is important to note that the effectiveness of visual communication in SGs depends on several factors, e.g., audiences, pedagogical strategies, learning environment, visual perception, cognitive load, etc. As we mentioned before, while one can look at photo-realism as an impressive feature of a game within socio-cultural edutainment games (*The Arkae Vision*) in the museum, it is not a fitting choice for constructionism pedagogical in elementary school (Shiau Gee and Dolah, 2020). The research on SGs rarely focuses on the design of these components or their applicability to learning. Instead, the research looks more at how well they capture subject matter content while still remaining engaging. Thus visual design models should be considered more specific on different conditions.

4.4 Limitation

As in any other literature review, our work is limited by the database, search terms and search time range. For example, the literature search only included publications in English, which, naturally, creates a strong bias in the research by the database and likely excludes some relevant research. The choices of databases also affect the results. Since the paper focuses on SGs from a technology and informatics perspective, Scopus and IEEE Xplore were seen as the most relevant. Further research, including other databases - such as ERIC/EBSCO - can likely reveal research approaching SGs from a slightly different angle.

This literature review should not be considered as a comprehensive investigation or definitive quantitative analysis on visual communication research in the context of SGs. It is primarily intended to highlight how material published concerning visual aspects of SGs examines visual communication. The categorization of visual communication used in this review generally worked well, but there were still some problematic boundary decisions and ambiguities. Papers could, for example, provide a brief design guideline based on a representation evaluation study, thus relating to two of our categories - we chose to categorize these papers on what we consider to be their main focal point and stated contribution.

5. CONCLUSION

During this review, a few key challenges and patterns associated with visuals in SGs emerged. In general, research on visuals in SGs is relatively rare, and there is an issue with inconsistent terminologies and taxonomies on the topic. The studies that were found in this review focus most heavily on visual representation. Researchers seldom evaluate learning outcomes of different visual representations, and the results are widely debated. One common conclusion is that visual complexity distracts students from the intended learning content. This result implies that experts, educational researchers, and game designers need to merge together to develop SGs to keep game graphics optimally aligned with assessed learning objectives.

As covered in this review, there are no definitively "right" or "wrong" visuals - it depends on the use context and the individual players. The literature does, however, point towards some visuals potentially being more or less appropriate for different types of goals. But there is a need for more examinations of the relationship between visual communication and learning in games. Since "games" are also a constantly moving target as technologies and modes of expression evolve, this need will continue to develop.

REFERENCES

Alcivar, N. I. S., Quijije, L. I. S. & Gallego, D. a. C. 2021. Evaluations of software developed as research tools to analyze trends of educational videogames characters. *International Journal on Advanced Science, Engineering and Information Technology*, 11, 1162-1171.

Alesandrini, K.L., 1984. Pictures and adult learning. *Instructional Science*, 13(1), pp. 63-77.

Alexiou, A., Schippers, M.C., Oshri, I. and Angelopoulos, S., 2020. Narrative and aesthetics as antecedents of perceived learning in serious games. *Information Technology & People*.

Alyami, H., Alawami, M., Lyndon, M., Alyami, M., Coomarasamy, C., Henning, M., Hill, A. and Sundram, F., 2019. Impact of using a 3D visual metaphor serious game to teach history-taking content to medical students: longitudinal mixed methods pilot study. *JMIR serious games*, 7(3), p.e13748.

Bedi, K., Hrustek, N.Ž. and Ćorić, A., 2011, May. Teaching vs. 3D gaming in secondary school. In *2011 Proceedings of the 34th International Convention MIPRO* (pp. 1325-1330). IEEE.

Boyle, E.A., Hainey, T., Connolly, T.M., Gray, G., Earp, J., Ott, M., Lim, T., Ninaus, M., Ribeiro, C. and Pereira, J., 2016. An update to the systematic literature review of empirical evidence of the impacts and outcomes of computer games and serious games. *Computers & Education*, 94, pp. 178-192

Buckingham, D. & Burn, A. 2007. Game literacy in theory and practice. Journal of Educational Multimedia and Hypermedia. 16 (3), pp. 323-349. Waynesville, NC USA: *Association for the Advancement of Computing in Education (AACE).*

Chandler, T., Anthony, M. and Klinger, D., 2009. Applying high cognitive vs. high physical fidelity within serious games. In *The InterserviceIndustry Training, Simulation, and Education Conference (IITSEC).*

Cheng, M.T., Lin, Y.W., She, H.C. and Kuo, P.C., 2017. Is immersion of any value? Whether, and to what extent, game immersion experience during serious gaming affects science learning. *British Journal of Educational Technology*, 48(2), pp.246-263.

Clark, D.B., Tanner-Smith, E.E. and Killingsworth, S.S., 2016. Digital games, design, and learning: A systematic review and meta-analysis. *Review of educational research*, 86(1), pp.79-122.

Dale, E., 1969. *Audiovisual methods in teaching.*

Dwyer, F.M., 1978. *Strategies for Improving Visual Learning*, PA: State College, Learning Services

Fuchs, K.L., Huonder, V., Vuckovac, D. and Ilic, A., 2016, June. Swiss Foodquiz: Inducing Nutritional Knowledge via a Visual Learning based Serious Game. In *ECIS.*

Gee, L.L.S. and Dolah, J., 2016. Graphic styles appearance in educational games to enhance malaysian students learning: A preliminary study. In *2nd international conference on creative media, design & technology (26th to 27th September 2016) Penang*, Malaysia file:///C:/Users/sh. asadzandi/Downloads/Paper14. pdf.

Gee, L. L. S. & Dolah, J. 2018. Abstract versus realistic styles: Experience based design graphic style (ebdgs) games. *Journal of Advanced Research in Dynamical and Control Systems*, 10, 1463-1471.

Gee, L.L.S. and Dolah, J., 2018. Influence of Form, Texture and Shading on 'Abstract'and 'Realistic'Style Preferences: An Overview of Design Characteristics through Incidental Thematic Results. *Advances in Social Science, Education and Humanities Research*, 207(3), pp.38-43.

Gee, L.L.S., Dolah, J. and Pangayan, V.B., 2019. Visual Preferences for Educational Game Designs through the Graphic Style Approaches. *Jurnal Gendang Alam (GA).*

Grabska, E. 2015. Serious game graphic design based on understanding of a new model of visual perception - computer graphics. *Simulations in medicine: Pre-clinical and clinical applications.*

Järvinen, A., 2002, June. Gran Stylissimo: The Audiovisual Elements and Styles in Computer and Video Games. In *CGDC Conf.*

Javora, O., Hannemann, T., Stárková, T., Volná, K. & Brom, C. 2018. Children like it more but don't learn more: Effects of esthetic visual design in educational games. *British Journal of Educational Technology.*

Jiang, J. Y., Guo, F., Chen, J. H., Tian, X. H., & Lv, W. (2019). Applying Eye-Tracking Technology to Measure Interactive Experience Toward the Navigation Interface of Mobile Games Considering Different Visual Attention Mechanisms. *Applied Sciences-Basel*, 9(16), Article 3242. https://doi.org/10.3390/app9163242

Kapralos, B., Moussa, F., Collins, K. and Dubrowski, A., 2017. Fidelity and multimodal interactions. In *Instructional Techniques to Facilitate Learning and Motivation of Serious Games* (pp. 79-101). Springer, Cham.

Kartiko, I., Kavakli, M. and Cheng, K., 2010. Learning science in a virtual reality application: The impacts of animated-virtual actors' visual complexity. *Computers & Education*, 55(2), pp.881-891.

Mahmoud, I. & Wloka, D. Planning for non-player characters using htn and visual perception. *2015 IEEE European Modelling Symposium (EMS)*, 6-8 Oct. 2015 2015. 321-327.

McCloud, S., 1993. *Understanding comics: The invisible art*. Northampton, Mass.

Mckay, E., 1999. Exploring the effect of graphical metaphors on the performance of learning computer programming concepts in adult learners: a pilot study. *Educational Psychology*, 19(4), pp.471-487.

McLaughlin, T., Smith, D. and Brown, I.A., 2010, June. A framework for evidence based visual style development for serious games. In *Proceedings of the fifth international conference on the foundations of digital games* (pp. 132-138).

Ontañón, S., Zhu, J., Smith, B. K., Char, B., Freed, E. & Furqan, A. Designing visual metaphors for an educational game for parallel programming. *Conference on Human Factors in Computing Systems - Proceedings*, 2017. 2818-2824.

Pagano, A., Palombini, A., Bozzelli, G., De Nino, M., Cerato, I. and Ricciardi, S., 2020. Arkaevision vr game: User experience research between real and virtual paestum. *Applied Sciences*, 10(9), p.3182.

Page, M.J., McKenzie, J.E., Bossuyt, P.M., Boutron, I., Hoffmann, T.C., Mulrow, C.D., Shamseer, L., Tetzlaff, J.M., Akl, E.A., Brennan, S.E. and Chou, R., 2021. The PRISMA 2020 statement: an updated guideline for reporting systematic reviews. *International Journal of Surgery*, 88, p.105906.

Pezdek, K., Maki, R., Valencia-Laver, D., Whetstone, T., Stoeckert, J. and Dougherty, T., 1988. Picture memory: Recognizing added and deleted details. *Journal of Experimental Psychology: Learning, Memory, and Cognition*, 14(3), p.468.

Plass, J.L., Homer, B.D., MacNamara, A., Ober, T., Rose, M.C., Pawar, S., Hovey, C.M. and Olsen, A., 2020. Emotional design for digital games for learning: The effect of expression, color, shape, and dimensionality on the affective quality of game characters. *Learning and instruction*, 70, p.101194.

Rizvic, S., Okanovic, V. & Boskovic, D. 2020. *Digital storytelling*. Springer Series on Cultural Computing.

Rowe, J.P., Lobene, E.V., Mott, B.W. and Lester, J.C., 2017. Play in the museum: Design and development of a game-based learning exhibit for informal science education. *International Journal of Gaming and Computer-Mediated Simulations* (IJGCMS), 9(3), pp.96-113.

Sarić, R., Halilović, M., Bajramović, D., Raducan, G. and Čustović, E., 2021, June. Development of 3D Serious Game: Colorful Classroom to Effectively Teach Children Colors Letters and Numbers. In *International Symposium on Innovative and Interdisciplinary Applications of Advanced Technologies* (pp. 248-263). Springer, Cham.

Selmbacherova, T., Sisler, V. & Brom, C. The impact of visual realism on the authenticity of educational simulation: A comparative study. *Proceedings of the European Conference on Games-based Learning*, 2014. 520-528.

Shiau Gee, L. L. & Dolah, J. 2020. Abstract or realistic style: Inclusive designing for student experience in educational games. *ASM Science Journal*, 13, 82-88.

Soriano, D., Mueller, S., Fordham, M., Arjyal, A., Baral, S., Hearn, G. J., Le Masson, V., Boscor, A., Saville, N. M. & Kostkova, P. Engaging pictograms! A methodology for graphic design in enhancing player engagement as applied to the design of a serious game for nepalese women with low literacy. *ACM International Conference Proceeding Series*, 2018. 30-34.

Swink, S., 2008. *Game feel: a game designer's guide to virtual sensation.* CRC press.

Sylvester, T., 2013. *Designing games: A guide to engineering experiences.* " O'Reilly Media, Inc.".

Veinott, E. S., Perleman, B., Polander, E., Leonard, J., Berry, G., Catrambone, R., Whitaker, E., Eby, B., Mayell, S., Teodorescu, K., Hammack, T. & Lemaster, L. Is more information better? Examining the effects of visual and cognitive fidelity on learning in a serious video game. *2014 IEEE Games Media Entertainment*, 22-24 Oct. 2014 2014. 1-6.

Wang, L.T. and Lee, K.C., 2014. The Study of Learners' Preference for Visual Complexity on Small Screens of Mobile Computers Using Neural Networks. *Turkish Online Journal of Educational Technology-TOJET*, 13(2), pp.168-180.

Wattanasoontorn, V., Magdics, M. & Sbert, M. Visual realism in 3d serious games for learning: A case study. Proceedings of IDEE 2013: 2nd International Workshop on Interaction Design in Educational Environments - In Conjunction with the 15th Int. *Conference on Enterprise Information Systems*, ICEIS 2013, 2013. 24-33.

Wouters, P. and Van Oostendorp, H., 2013. A meta-analytic review of the role of instructional support in game-based learning. *Computers & Education*, 60(1), pp.412-425.

Wouters, P. and Oostendorp, H.V., 2017. Overview of instructional techniques to facilitate learning and motivation of serious games. In *Instructional techniques to facilitate learning and motivation of serious games* (pp. 1-16). Springer, Cham.

Yusoff, Z. and Kamsin, A., 2015, August. Game rhetoric: Interaction design model of persuasive learning for serious games. In *International Conference on Learning and Collaboration Technologies* (pp. 644-654). Springer, Cham.

Zhang, K., Zheng, F., Chen, J., Liu, X., Chen, X. & Wang, G. Application of computer games in the visual perception assessment of children with autism spectrum disorder. *2021 IEEE International Conference on Engineering, Technology & Education (TALE)*, 5-8 Dec. 2021 2021. 01-06.

THE EMERGENT ASPECT OF CLIMATE CHANGE IN VIDEO GAMES: A HISTORICAL REVIEW

Khalil Morad El Ghilali[1,2], Spiros Papadopoulos[1] and Iman Meriem Benkirane[2]
[1]*University of Thessaly (UTH), Greece*
[2]*Euromed University of Fes, Morocco*

ABSTRACT

In response to recurrent natural catastrophes and climate change, research into the use of videogames in sustainability is on the rise, and it is cementing their position as part of the contemporary digital education. The educational impact of such games rapidly becomes an important field. By retracing the history of the main climate change engaged video games, this paper describes and analyses the advantages and drawbacks of using serious games for environmental awareness, showcasing their capacity to simulate major topics in a mediated manner and to invite players to act in an unmediated way.

KEYWORDS

Serious Games, Sustainability, Alternative Education, Environmental Consciousness, Environmental Media, Gamification

1. INTRODUCTION

For the last five decades video games have prevailed as a fun diversion (Alex Kypriotakis-Weijers, 2018; Rollings and Morris, 2004), but also as a means to build connection between friends, family, and even strangers, or as a way to release stress (Hirst, 2021).

While arcade halls belong to the past, video games are still here to stay and their industry is bigger than ever. In the past years, it blossomed into one of the most profitable industries in the world with an estimated $165 billion revenue generated in 2020 (Wallach, 2020), and more than 3 billion gamers Worldwide (Hruska, 2020).

Throughout the last years, video games have been upgraded to a valuable source of knowledge and information in educational settings (Michael and Chen, 2005), especially for serious matters (Abraham and Jayemanne, 2017) such as global warming or climate change.

This paper analyses a corpus of video games in chronological order that have been used to promote environmental consciousness, education and awareness through the emergence of serious play, arguing that videogames can be seen as states of exception on two different levels. On the one hand, if we see videogames about politics as simulations of real politics, then in game rules and consequences appear as generally inefficient in regard to the external real world politics; on the other hand, videogames about politics can be seen as an exceptional space to talk about and reflect on political issues (Pfister, 2020).

2. HISTORICAL REVIEW OF ENVIROMENTAL VIDEO GAMES

2.1 'Before the Great Crash'

Even though the impact of human activity on the local climate has been identified in the early 19th century and the general rise of temperature and carbon dioxide has also been associated with climate change in the late 19th century (Weart, 2015), it was after 1983 that global warming became public knowledge. As a matter of fact, it was until Farman's discovery of a huge hole opening up in the ozone layer over Antarctica in 1983 (Pearce, 2008) followed by the hottest summer ever recorded at that point in1988 (LAT Archives, 1989) that urged media to start publishing about this issue (History, 2020). Global warming was the inevitable result of the so-called greenhouse effect. However, how did all of that translate to video games and when?

In the early 1980's, arcade halls were still living their 'golden age' (Mark J.P. Wolf, 2008), as a popular and powerful means of entertainment. Nobody would go to an arcade hall to learn about global warming, but rather to beat other player's records. It wasn't until later in the decade that people were able to have access to videogames at home, mainly because of the 1985 crash (Mark J.P. Wolf, 2008) and the release of home consoles, notably the hugely popular Nintendo entertainment system in the USA in 1986. Developers were then able to create games with a focus on storytelling.

Although strategy games would appear in the arcade games from time to time, they would eventually find their niche on home computers (Mark J.P. Wolf, 2008, p. 43) where the first signs of educational purpose of video games started to show up. For instance, **M.U.L.E.** (Ozark Softscape, 1983) is an early colony simulation game that requires players to consider ecological factors such as the proximity of their farming plots to water resources, strategical placement of solar panels to gather sunlight, and the abundance of metals and minerals on a newly colonized planet. Weather events like cosmic storms occur randomly and have unpredictable effects on the player's colonies (Barton, 2008).

SIMCITY released in 1989 was initially meant to be a satire of American consumerism (Channel4, 2013) and was far from the city builder we know nowadays. Instead of building your own city entirely, the player would get dropped as the mayor of a new municipality in an existing city with the responsibility of building and maintaining a place where his or her citizens could have happy and fulfilling lives (Roberto Dillon, 2011). In the game process, the mayor had to plan for housing, streets, factories, etc. while also balancing pollution and traffic jams. Managing taxes properly was also a fundamental aspect of improving the quality of the public services while keeping the citizens happy. To make things more unpredictable and exciting, six predefined, time-limited scenarios were added. In one of these, **RIO DE JANEIRO 2047**, the player had to save Rio from an incoming flood caused by global warming (Roberto Dillon, 2011). Earthquakes and other natural calamities were also possible, a fact that increased advance planning for storing enough resources to be used in time of need. Though very limited in its technology and educational purpose, it came out to be one of the most influential strategy games in the history of urban planning (Friedrich von Borries, Steffen P. Walz, 2007, p. 206), along with being the first video game that ever tackled climate change.

It is highly likely that SIMCITY creator, Will Wright, used his knowledge from this title as a baseline for his next project: 1990's **SIMEARTH** (Roberto Dillon, 2011, p. 141). Despite the disappointing sales performance, Maxis' SIMEARTH (1990) is perhaps the best known ecological game at that time (Barton, 2008). Whereas SimCity focused on just one scenario in one city, SIMEARTH allowed the player to alter the development of a planet. The player was able, among other things, to modify the atmosphere, the temperature and the mass of the planet that dominated, and then they could place different life forms and societies and watch them evolving while making sure that they hadn't kill each other (Michael Bremer, 1990). Namely, climate change became the main gameplay element in this game.

Whereas later strategy games would focus more on war and defeating enemies, SIMEARTH'S main goal was to maintain world peace with as less pollution as possible. By implementing climate change into its gameplay, SIMEARTH was in a lot of ways ahead of the curve. However, the solutions presented kept being very naïve: whenever a society starts generating too many emissions, the player can simply press a button to convince world leaders to start looking for cleaner energy resources. If only it was that simple in real life.

The same year will also know the rise in popularity of another sort of games: THUIS IN HET MILIEU or AT HOME AND THE ENVIRONMENT was a Dutch educational game developed by Redline Software Design and published by Malmberg that could be found on many computers at primary schools in the early 90s (Malmberg, 1990). It was one of the many games used to teach young children about certain topics. In the game, players in a role of a man have to perform tasks in and around the house. Everything has to do with the environment: You have to control the radiators, clean the house, throw out the trash, take a shower, go to the bathroom and do the laundry. At the end of the week the player is evaluated on how well he conserved energy and saved the environment (retrolorian.com, 2022). During each task you perform you are prompted with very basic questions about what he or she can do to counter pollution or littering that has to be answered correctly. Things like bringing your own bag to the grocery store, recycling and walking to school instead of letting your parents drive you there, are just some of the simple things presented in this game to fight environmental issues. Hugely outdated by today's standards and very illusive as far as solutions go, these types of games were at the vanguard of what would become serious gaming.

By the end of the 1980's efforts to raise awareness on the effects of the climate change gradually advanced. The subject became increasingly prominent in the international public debate and political agenda. World leaders started discussing the situation resulting in the very first Climate Treaty in 1992, the establishment of The United Nations Framework Convention On Climate Change in 1995 and the signing of The Kyoto Protocol by 160 nations worldwide in 1997, focusing on scaling atmospheric concentrations of "greenhouse gases" at a level that would prevent dangerous anthropogenic interference with the climate system (Jackson, 2007).

Strategy games kept up the trend of including real world problems as game mechanics: The second edition of SIMCITY released on 1994 (SimCity2000), now, lets the player decide what kind of city he wants to build (Maxis, 1994), and introduce new game strategies like ground air pollution and energy resources.

2.2 'The Golden Age'

It was actually ın 1991, when world management simulator games were taken into a whole new level, with Sid Meier's **CIVILIZATION (MicroProse)**. Becoming his most successful game and most recognizable franchise, (Roberto Dillon, 2011, p. 143) Civilization's massive scale and ambitious aims were unheard of before—to start your own nation and make it prosper from the Stone Age until the 21st century.

Pollution, now actually, can cause permanent global warming consequences: Deserts, plains, and grasslands on coasts may become swamps and coastal forests may become jungles. Plains, grasslands and forests may become deserts. These land tiles then can never be rebuilt by the player (Sid Meier, 1992). The result is much lower food, industry and trade for your civilization.

The CIVILIZATION games kept this theme of challenge in the second installment in 1996. These land plots that were permanently damaged by pollution were now indicated with a skull, just to point out the necessity of paying attention to the environment even more. On the other hand, games depicting climate change in more subtle ways, started to appear. In fact, it might be surprising that 1991 brought us environmental awareness in the form of **SONIC the hedgehog**. Most children who used to play the game wouldn't even notice that the gameplay was a condemnation of mankind's effect on the world around us (Scott Tailford, 2015).

SONIC'S creator Yuji Naka stated in a 1997 interview: "Dr. Robotnik is a slightly radical representation of all humanity and the impact humanity is having on nature. In 1991, it was a very sensitive subject to talk about the environment, and while I had my viewpoint, I did not speak of it. With sonic I was given an opportunity to express my views in a different way and did so showing Robotnik using pollution and creating machinery which desecrates the environment and it is down to sonic to change his ways" (Ray Willmott, 2010).

Because the threats of climate change started being popular, mainstream media began to reflect them as well. The serious negative impacts global warming would have on the world we know were being portrayed in movies like **WATERWORLD (1995)** (dell'Agnese, 2014). Dark dystopian futures became the most common settings in various media including video games. Therefore, it's not a surprise to see games like SID MEIER'S **ALPHA CENTAURI** and the first **FALLOUT** game depicting the future of the world in a grim fashion.

In ALPHA CENTAURI post-apocalyptic scenario, the environment was so badly damaged that the game begins by the player leaving the earth looking for alternative planets. In the other hand FALLOUT'S game, saw the realization of the futurist predictions of the 1950s ("Fallout series | Fallout Wiki | Fandom," n.d.), it depicts a scenario in which world leaders while engaging in a resource war, induce the end of the world by dropping their complete nuclear arsenal on each other; yet another way to visualize environmental issues in the world.

FALLOUT and **COMMAND AND CONQUER** (another game that came out in the same decade) worlds were heavily influenced by the ongoing conflicts of their time (the First Gulf War, and the Yugoslav Wars) (A Loyal Soldier, 2019). Given that the First Gulf War was primarily about defending Saudi & Kuwait oil fields. Both games portray world leaders fighting for the remaining resources: Tiberium as a narrative device and game mechanic in COMMAND AND CONQUER for example, stand in for fossil fuels and its deleterious effects on the environment and humanity.

Even if climate change was at this point inevitable and became a household term mainly because of documentaries like AL GORE'S **AN INCONVENIENT TRUTH** in 2004, the rise of terrorism will drastically change popular trends in media, freezing the depiction of climate change and environmentalism for quite a moment.

2.3 'Entering the Void'

While the existence of terrorism dates back to years before 2001 (IRA were active from 1969, Hamas have been active since 1987), the attacks on the world trade center on September 11th, marked a huge turning point in history and sparked an unprecedented change in worldview (Claire Parker, 2021).

Representations from popular media and digital culture started to shift from dystopian narratives as portrayed in games like **DEUS EX** and **FINAL FANTASY VII** to realistic gaming scenarios with a prevalence of inland violence. First person shooter games or what Gonzalo Frasca's calls "news gaming" (a genre that is based on actual news events) (Florencia Espel, 2015), became also more popular with franchises like **BATTLEFIELD 1942** and **CALL OF DUTY**, which in the same decade would shift from Second World War to more counter-terrorism focused stories (Galloway, 2004).

With the launch of home consoles like The PlayStation and later The Xbox video games industry reached unprecedented success and popularity (Roberto Dillon, 2011). They were now, recognized as a real part of the mainstream media. The impact all these twists had on previous video games tackling climate change, like CIVILIZATION, were that the mainstream audiences weren't really looking for the challenges that these kinds of video games had to offer. The franchise drastically dumbed down the consequences of polluting in their next CIVILIZATION game narratives (Kriston Capps, 2016). This went as far as their later games, not having any climate related mechanics at all.

Interests of the main game developers and publishers (EA games, Activision or Ubisoft) shifted into making lucrative games that were appealing to the mainstream audiences instead of risking a huge loss while focusing on more challenging topics like climate change (Author,(Mark J.P. Wolf, 2008)). However, it doesn't mean that not a single game depicting climate change was released - as a lot of video games were now story driven, they started pointing it out in a more subtle way.

For instance, 2008's **DEADSPACE** and 2009's **BORDERLANDS** are set in a world where Global warming became a primordial concern of humanity causing major shortages in earth natural resources. The crisis prompted world leaders to try to find them replacement in space (Fandom, n.d.). Of course it can be glossed over pretty easily while playing these games, but once you realize that the USG Ishimura, where DEADSPACE takes place, is an interstellar mining ship (Fandom, n.d.), and that the only reason you're on the planet Pandora in BORDERLANDS, is its abundant mineral wealth (Fandom, n.d.), you start to see the bigger picture.

In the meantime, SIMCITY kept using pollution as a gameplay mechanic in **2007 SIMCITY SOCIETIES** which is notably the first game that had specifically the most expanded way of exploring the pressing issues of pollution and global warming. Not only were greener solutions, ground and air pollution, visual indications of pollution and even waste management present in this game (Tiltfactor, n.d.), but nearby property values and the citizen's safety would drastically suffer when the player would pollute too much.

However, whenever we start talking about good environmental awareness games, SIMCITY SOCIETIES is never brought up. Mainly because publisher Electronic Arts and energy giant BP have collaborated to incorporate branded clean power sources in the game mechanics. Every single environmental or climate related problem can be fixed with wind turbines, solar panels and natural gas factories (Tiltfactor, n.d.). All made possible by BP, a company that would pay $50 million in criminal fines and "plead guilty to a felony violation of the Clean Air Act" as a result of a fatal refinery explosion in 2005 and a massive oil spill in 2006, causing one of the biggest environmental disasters in history. Needless to say, that big companies were avoiding serious subjects and discussions in the risk of losing money, yet at the same time, a new wave of video games started to emerge.

2.4 'TERRA NOVA'

The 2000's delivered a wide array of changes in animation and gaming industries (Academy Contributor, 2020). With the evolution of smartphones, computers and social media, video platforms like YouTube were starting to gain more popularity. Gamers' blogs and forums were filled with new game tips, and sites such as Macworld, Ars Technica and TouchArcade were allowing people to give their opinion on the internet (Chikhani, 2015; Mark J.P. Wolf, 2008).

Enabled by affordable and technologically accessible platforms such as Flash from Macromedia (now Adobe), independent developers or indie developers could craft simple, compact, and elegant games, creating the equivalent of short films, charcoal sketches or poetry. They were soon creating their own products and sharing them with the gaming community, enough to propel a new wave of independent creation, succinctly captured by *Newgrounds*'s slogan: ''Everything, by everyone'' (Mark J.P. Wolf, 2008) (Newgrounds, n.d.).

Most importantly this resulted in freedom of gameplay since these indie games didn't have to be molded into corporate constraints or into what sort of game was popular at that point. Gradually this also resulted in more freedom around themes and subjects that were depicted within the games, and discussions about climate change started to rise again.

The tail end of the decade saw the initial release of indie video game **MINECRAFT**, a game that started out as just a simple idea that would maybe grab some people's attention but rather would turn out to be one of the most popular games of all time with 200 million copies sold worldwide (Academy Contributor, 2020). Proving that video games didn't need a "triple A" budget, or huge publishers to become well known. MINECRAFT developers decided that because of the freedom people had in the game, it might also be a useful tool of education, which resulted in the education edition: this version was specifically meant for teachers and to use in classrooms.

In this game, these lessons are either about construction or exploration. Construction is the most common one and Minecraft is often seen as the digital version of Lego (Cotton, 2011, p. 5). Lego is not defined as a game, but as a tool and system that provide emergent gameplay. Children build whatever they want and then play with it. Just like with situations that arise when playing with Lego. For this, Minecraft is a true emergent system but also makes use of gameplay elements to support it. This specific characteristic allowed the MINECRAFT community to use the game for educational purposes. That's how **CLIMATE HOPE CITY** (Keith Stuart, 2015) came to be a special server filled with real life and fictional ideas on how to tackle environmental and climate related issues.

Universities like Oxford started to experiment with video games as an educational tool and made its own video games: something we would call serious games. The result was for instance, 2011's **FATE OF THE WORLD** from Red Redemption: a game based on climate prediction models developed by Myles Allen, head of the Climate Dynamics group at the Oxford University (Javier Yanes, 2019), in which the player has to find a way to make mankind progress while tackling some of the world's biggest problems like war, economy and climate change.

In this game the player is placed at the head of a world-spanning United Nations tasked with mitigating the worst effects of climate change while also trying to meet goals like encouraging third world development and not going bankrupt. Gameplay involves decisions about limited resources (in line with Kelly and Nardi 2014 propositions) while maintaining the delicate balance of pleasing member nations and keeping carbon emissions in check. Simply put, finding a balance between different aspects of world biggest problems and realizing you can't fix everything, is the key to win this game (Abraham, 2018). Therefore, it sufficiently models the anthropogenic nature of climate change.

Meanwhile the University of Washington through Earth Games UW, a growing community of researchers, game developers and students that designs and develops climate-centered games, started to experiment with serious gaming as well. Feeling that most games that tackle climate change, were not engaging enough for the player (Fernández Galeote and Hamari, 2021), they started a series of small mobile games, one of them being **CLIMATE QUEST** in 2016.

In this game climate disasters are occurring across the United States, the players have to choose between four scientists to prepare against the upcoming disasters: the urban planner, the ecologist, the agricultural scientist, or the climate scientist (EarthGames, 2016). Only the swiftest player will be able to prepare for all the events and earn the top score. Forecasts of climate disruptions appearing across the map are based on real impacts selected from the US National Climate Assessment.

In order to create environmental awareness, smaller game developers kept coming up with new ways of promoting active learning: **ECO** (2018), developed by Strange Loop Games and funded by the United States Department of Education (John, 2015; Strange Loop Games, 2018) and an online crowdfunding campaign (Kickstarter, 2015), shows how private and public sector groups can come together to create popular games with a real-life impact (UN Environment Programe, 2021). What at first it seems just like another MINECRAFT copy, turns out to be much more than that. In Minecraft, players can carry near-unlimited amounts of materials. In Eco, the amount of resources a player can carry is limited in order to reflect a more realistic resource gathering situation (Fjællingsdal and Klöckner, 2019). It's more than just a "survive and create" game, in that every action may affect the environment you live in: using fossil fuels will cause pollution and cutting trees will wipe out forests if you don't replant them which can result in the destruction of environments or habitats (Fernández Galeote and Hamari, 2021). With a sort of huge excel sheet you can monitor everything you do in the game and what effect it has on the environment. It can thus be described as an ambitious commercial educational simulation game, that enhances environmental knowledge through direct action, simulational aspects (those actions having consequences) and social elements (specifically cooperation).

Released by the Italian game designer **MOLLEINDUSTRIA** (Paolo Pedercini) in 2019, **'LICHENIA'** is an alternative to SIMCITY that challenges you to experiment in the post-apocalyptic unknown (Cameron Kunzelman, 2019). This indie title is about creating human habitats amidst climate chaos (Pedercini, 2019). It involves reshaping the natural and built environment, reclaiming dead cities, and growing sustainable ones.

Finding a good balance between different blocks representing water, ice and city soil etc. is the way to complete this game: for instance, cities will only thrive when the environment is livable otherwise these cities turn into ruins. Creating a livable environment can be done by using water, but using too much water will flood the earth. Playing LICHENIA is all about trial and error, forcing us to think about the power of misrecognition and the planet. Do we really ever know the full effects of our actions? (Cameron Kunzelman, 2019).

Experiencing the world through the eyes of a bee is what the game **BEE SIMULATOR** is all about (Fondation GoodPlanet, 2019). To mark the importance of bees in the ecosystem, Lukasz Rosinski imagined in 2019, an indie game in which you're assigned to accomplish multiple tasks like: collecting pollen, defeating bugs and saving your hive from workmen who threaten to cut the tree in which your hive is located, in order to keep your hive healthy.

2.5 'A Rennaissance'

In the meantime, bigger companies started to pay attention to the environment, even going as far as to come up with solutions for climate change in the real world. From August 2016, a new approach of planting trees started to emerge in China, the Ant Forest program which connects individual users, Fintech, and reforestation action, has been initiated (Zhang et al., 2021). Launched by Ant Financial Services Group, a branch of China's largest online shopping company Alibaba, **ANT FOREST** aims to encourage the users of Alipay (Alibaba's mobile payment platform), to reduce carbon footprint.

The goal of this game is to plant trees. If a user successfully plants a virtual tree in Ant Forest, then the department of Ant forest in charge of "Tree Planting" plants a tree in real world for the user (Zhang et al., 2020). This way, users can contribute to environment protection. However, in order to actually plant a tree, players need to collect enough "green energy" through conducting specific activities such as walking, sharing bikes, using electronic invoices and paying online for public transportation. As of August 2019, there are 500 million Ant Forest users. More than 122 million trees have been planted in some of the driest areas in China, covering a total of 112,000 ha of land (Rukikaire, 2019).

Simply titled **SIMCITY**, an updated release of the original classic game was released in 2013. Despite being badly received by pretty much the entire fan base in the first weeks of its release (due to the required internet connection that made the game virtually unplayable) environment wise, it was however the most complete of all the SimCity titles. Despite this one sequel that did drastically alter the single-player, off-line format of the Sims games, the massively multiplayer online role-playing game meant that your city would be part of a province shared with other people's cities. If you decided not to care about the environment and started polluting a lot, huge clouds of smog would cover your town, but would then continue to spread over the whole province also polluting your neighbor cities (Mark J. P. Wolf, 2021, p. 927). Simply put your actions also affect people around you, creating a game world where crucial decisions revolve around human relationships.

SIMCITY fans in 2015 would get exactly what they want, not in the form of a new SIM CITY game but rather in the title of **CITIES: SKYLINES** by Colossal Order. This game was quickly seen as the definitive city builder. Unlike the SimCity series it has become increasingly popular among city simulator enthusiasts for the fact that it allows a lot of room for modifications on every aspect of the game (Alex Kypriotakis-Weijers, 2018). It did pretty much everything SIMCITY did in a similar or even better way. The base game would already give the player the opportunity to make an environmental friendly city, but with the launch of the **GREEN CITIES** expansion this would get even easier (Skylines Wiki, 2018). Adding 350 assets in the form of biological supermarkets, recycling centers and self-sufficient homes to name a few, green cities let players create the most environmentally friendly city ever to be possible in video games.

CIVILIZATION VI was released in 2016, however it took Sid Meier three additional years before addressing climate change head-on again. Just like **GREEN CITIES**, **GATHERING STORM** launched a downloadable content and brought the addition of climate change into the game (Civilization Wiki, 2019). It added, among other things, a carbon-dioxide meter, ground tiles could once again be permanently destroyed by pollution and huge coastal cities would have to be protected by flood walls if climate change would result in melting ice caps (Meier, 2019).

It took the Sims 20 years to release its sustainability themed game, with a few references here and there throughout the years (Stanitsas et al., 2019), it was quite surprising that a life simulation game where the creative work can take the form of designing our homes and families didn't tackle climate change earlier. When the **ECO LIFESTYLE** came out in 2020, as an extension of **THE SIMS 4**, it included considerable new features to the game (The Sims Wiki, 2020), such as sustainable living, renewable energy, crafting and community projects. Focusing on Eco-friendly living returns, made it possible to start recycling, create a self-sufficient house, letting you make biological products like drinks and candles for whatever reason, and even allowing you to go out on the streets to convince other Sims to change to a green lifestyle as well.

It's no wonder to see these huge publishers going back to environment related subjects in their games: The Paris Climate Agreement in 2015 sparked a huge rise in interest around climate change. Meanwhile the United states exit from the agreement on November 4, 2020 and reentering in February 2021 (The Editors of Encyclopaedia Britannica, 2022), sparked a lot of outrage around the subject due to the noticeable and devastating effects of climate change.

While many of the examples above are from earlier eras of gaming, the environment-as-background is present in all games insofar as they are finite in scale. **HORIZON ZERO DAWN (2017)**, was one of the huge titles of the past few years, that pointed out how in the name of progress, human expansionism can actually be sealing our fate through substantive objects and environs, residential sites marked by techno-tribal civilizations and unexplored remnants of an ancient world, invoking the state of the Earth at the beginning of the twenty-first century (Abraham and Jayemanne, 2017). The ecological precarity stemming from the reclaimed ruins is a statement that nature will definitely move on and even thrive when humans disappear. HORIZON ZERO DAWN showcases therefore a temporally layered game environment (Aghoro et al., 2022) that alludes to a fictionalized historical past, to our contemporary present, and to possible futures through the post-apocalyptic frontier that it generates.

On the other hand, you have a game like **FROSTPUNK** 2018 by 11bit Studios that show's how nature can itself, be the cause of climate disasters. Set in 1886, after the eruption of Krakatoa, a real life event that actually happened in 1883, that caused an actual volcanic winter (John P. Rafferty, 2018). In the game, the sun is blocked out by the huge amounts of volcanic dust, leaving the world encased in ice and frequent snowstorms (Hubertova, 2021). Low temperatures are threatening the lives of the last humans escaping cities to build a new life and survive. FROSTPUNK has clear connections to climate change, in that it shows, that even if human beings decide to start living greener, nature itself can still create situations in which we're all doomed anyway. It is however, a good attempt of allowing players to put themselves in the shoes of others living through catastrophic events, in order to connect the events they witness in game to reality (Takemoto et al., 2021).

Even in the near past, you can observe these trends going strong with games like **ENDLING: Extinction is Forever**, a side scrolling 3D survival adventure where you play the role of a fox mother (the last of her kind), and her three vulnerable cubs through the dystopian future of an exploited Earth, where there is barely enough room or food for them to survive (Florian Emmerich, 2021), or even **BEYOND BLUE** an exploration game made with the sole intent to create awareness around the ethereal majesty of the underwater world (Cian Maher, 2020), but also emphasize just how ephemeral this magical world is.

3. CONCLUSIONS

In this study, we have discussed how diachronically videogames for environmental awareness have regenerated the debate about climate change. A large number of videogames address this issue by introducing new technological innovations or by creating effective awareness to lessen the effects of the climate change phenomenon. Whether this is accomplished by using the climate as an actual gameplay feature, by setting narratives around a world being destroyed by climate change or, even in a more symbolic way, by hinting to the human interference to the environment, we can argue that video games aiming at raising environmental awareness are, without a doubt, no longer a mere fun diversion.

In addition, we believe that playing games can foster environmental consciousness for two reasons: first, because the severe global environmental challenges shown up at regional and global scales have direct effects to public health, climate change and socio-economic crisis, and second, because, inherently, video games can achieve an effective visualization of intangible objects that can help players' motivation. Far from being a mere innocent medium, gaming practices can combine the dissemination of information that could engage players in particular attitudes and behaviors (Bogost, 2007), which can be harnessed towards a better future.

REFERENCES

A Loyal Soldier, 2019. Tiberium as an allegory for climate change : commandandconquer [WWW Document]. Reddit. URL https://www.reddit.com/r/commandandconquer/comments/boh0cd/tiberium_as_an_allegory_for_climate_change/ (accessed 4.14.22).

Abraham, B., 2018. Video Game Visions of Climate Futures: ARMA 3 and Implications for Games and Persuasion. Games Cult. 13, 71–91. https://doi.org/10.1177/1555412015603844

Abraham, B., Jayemanne, D., 2017. Where are all the climate change games? Locating digital games' response to climate change. Transformations 30, 74–94.

Academy Contributor, 2020. Game Development and New Media of the 2000s: A Decade of Innovation [WWW Document]. URL https://academyblog.dev.onpressidium.com/a-decade-of-game-development-major-milestones-from-2000-to-2010/ (accessed 4.15.22).

Aghoro, N., Filippaki, I., Kempshall, C., Maccallum-stewart, E., Mccall, J., Pöhlmann, S., 2022. Video Games and the Humanities Edited by Volume 5.

Alex Kypriotakis-Weijers, 2018. SPACE MODDERS Architects, Game Developers and Gamers. TU Delft.

Barton, M., 2008. How's the weather: Simulating weather in virtual environments. Game Stud. 8.

Bogost, I., 2007. Persuasive Games The Expressive Power of Videogames.

Cameron Kunzelman, 2019. This City Builder Asks You to Rebuild the World After Climate Devastation [WWW Document]. URL https://www.vice.com/en/article/qv7pyx/this-city-builder-asks-you-to-rebuild-the-world-after-climate-devastation (accessed 4.17.22).

Channel4, 2013. Charlie Brooker: How video games changed the world.

Chikhani, R., 2015. The history of gaming; An Evolving Community. TechCrunch 18.

Cian Maher, 2020. A new wave of indies are using games to explore climate change - The Verge [WWW Document]. URL https://www.theverge.com/2020/2/13/21135321/video-games-climate-change-beyond-blue-bee-simulator-temtem-endling (accessed 4.18.22).

Civilization Wiki, 2019. Civilization VI: Gathering Storm | Civilization Wiki | Fandom [WWW Document]. URL https://civilization.fandom.com/wiki/Civilization_VI:_Gathering_Storm (accessed 4.17.22).

Claire Parker, 2021. Readers share how 9/11 changed their worldviews - The Washington Post [WWW Document]. Washington Post. URL https://www.washingtonpost.com/world/2021/09/10/911-wordview-reader-responses/ (accessed 4.14.22).

Cotton, B., 2011. Minecraft: guided emergent game design. Cottonsoftdesign.Com 1–9.

dell'Agnese, E., 2014. Post-apocalypse now: Landscape and environmental values in the road and the walking dead. Geogr. Pol. 87, 327–341. https://doi.org/10.7163/GPol.2014.22

EarthGames, 2016. Climate Quest.

Fallout series | Fallout Wiki | Fandom [WWW Document], n.d. URL https://fallout.fandom.com/wiki/Fallout_series#Fallout (accessed 4.14.22).

Fandom, n.d. Global Warming Epidemic | Dead Space Wiki | Fandom [WWW Document]. Fallout Wiki. URL https://deadspace.fandom.com/wiki/Global_Warming_Epidemic#Sources (accessed 4.15.22a).

Fandom, n.d. USG Ishimura | Monster Wiki | Fandom [WWW Document]. Monster Wiki. URL https://monster.fandom.com/wiki/USG_Ishimura (accessed 4.15.22b).

Fandom, n.d. Pandora | Borderlands Wiki | Fandom [WWW Document]. Fandom. URL https://borderlands.fandom.com/wiki/Pandora (accessed 4.15.22c).

Fernández Galeote, D., Hamari, J., 2021. Game-based Climate Change Engagement: Analyzing the Potential of Entertainment and Serious Games. Proc. ACM Human-Computer Interact. 5. https://doi.org/10.1145/3474653

Fjællingsdal, K.S., Klöckner, C.A., 2019. Gaming Green: The Educational Potential of Eco – A Digital Simulated Ecosystem. Front. Psychol. 10, 1–13. https://doi.org/10.3389/fpsyg.2019.02846

Florencia Espel, 2015. September 12th: A Toy World - On Serious Games [WWW Document]. URL http://www.onseriousgames.com/september-12th-a-toy-world-newsgame/ (accessed 4.14.22).

Florian Emmerich, 2021. It's a Hard Fox Life ... [WWW Document]. URL https://press.handy-games.com/its-a-hard-fox-life (accessed 4.18.22).

Fondation GoodPlanet, 2019. Bee Simulator [WWW Document]. URL https://beesimulator.com/ (accessed 4.17.22).

Friedrich von Borries, Steffen P. Walz, M.B., 2007. Space Time Play Computer Games, Architecture and urbanism: The next level, Birkhäuser Basel _ Boston _ Berlin.

Galloway, A.R., 2004. Social realism in gaming. Game Stud. 4.

Hirst, A., 2021. "Videogames saved my life": Everyday resistance and Ludic recovery among US Military Veterans. Int. Polit. Sociol. 15, 482–503. https://doi.org/10.1093/ips/olab018

History, 2020. Discovery of Ozone Hole announced [WWW Document]. A&E Telev. Networks. URL https://www.history.com/this-day-in-history/discovery-of-antarctic-ozone-hole-announced (accessed 4.10.22).

Hruska, J., 2020. 3 Billion People Worldwide Are Gamers, and Nearly Half Play on PCs [WWW Document]. ExtremeTech. URL https://www.extremetech.com/gaming/314009-3-billion-people-worldwide-are-gamers-and-nearly-half-play-on-pcs (accessed 4.10.22).

Hubertova, B.A., 2021. Reflection on Environmental Issues in Mainstream Video Games : Asking Players.

Jackson, P., 2007. From Stockholm to Kyoto: A Brief History of Climate Change | United Nations. UN Chron. 44, 3.

Javier Yanes, 2019. Video Games Against Climate Change | OpenMind [WWW Document]. URL https://www.bbvaopenmind.com/en/science/environment/video-games-against-climate-change/ (accessed 4.16.22).

John, K., 2015. Search Funded Research Grants and Contracts -Eco: An Online Virtual World for Middle School Environmental Literacy and Collaborative Problem Solving.

John P. Rafferty, 2018. volcanic winter | Duration, Temperatures, & Facts | Britannica [WWW Document]. URL https://www.britannica.com/science/volcanic-winter (accessed 4.18.22).

keith stuart, 2015. Climate Hope City: how Minecraft can tell the story of climate change | Minecraft | The Guardian [WWW Document]. URL https://www.theguardian.com/environment/keep-it-in-the-ground-blog/2015/jun/12/climate-hope-city-how-minecraft-can-tell-the-story-of-climate-change (accessed 4.15.22).

Kelly, S., Nardi, B., 2014. Playing with sustainability: Using video games to simulate futures of scarcity. First Monday. https://doi.org/10.5210/fm.v19i5.5259

Kickstarter, 2015. Eco - Global Survival Game by John Krajewski » Eco at 202% funding, Kickstarter finished! — Kickstarter [WWW Document]. URL https://www.kickstarter.com/projects/1037798999/eco-global-survival-game/posts/1350435 (accessed 4.16.22).

Kriston Capps, 2016. What Sid Meier's Civilization VI Gets Wrong - Bloomberg [WWW Document]. URL https://www.bloomberg.com/news/articles/2016-10-20/what-sid-meier-s-civilization-vi-gets-wrong (accessed 4.15.22).

LAT Archives, 1989. 1988 Was Hottest Year on Record As Global Warming Trend Continues [WWW Document]. Los Angeles Times. URL https://www.latimes.com/archives/la-xpm-1989-02-04-mn-1524-story.html (accessed 4.10.22).

Malmberg, 1990. Thuis in het Milieu [WWW Document]. Internet Arch. Free Download, Borrow, Streaming . URL https://archive.org/details/ThuisInHetMilieu (accessed 4.11.22).

Mark J. P. Wolf, E., 2021. Encyclopedia of Video Games The Culture, Technology, and Art of Gaming Second Edition Volume, Library of Congress Cataloging-in-Publication Data.

Mark J.P. Wolf, 2008. THE VIDEO GAME EXPLOSION A History from PONG to PlayStation® and Beyond, Library of Congress Cataloging-in-Publication Data.

Maxis, 1994. Sim City 2000 - Manual, Docs - Lemon Amiga [WWW Document]. URL https://www.lemonamiga.com/games/docs.php?id=1450 (accessed 4.11.22).

Meier, S., 2019. CIVILIZATION VI GATHERING STORM. Pap. Knowl. . Towar. a Media Hist. Doc.

Michael Bremer, 1990. SIM Earth 10–12.

Michael, D.R., Chen, S.L., 2005. Serious games: Games that educate, train, and inform.

Newgrounds, n.d. Newgrounds.com - Everything, by Everyone [WWW Document]. URL https://www.newgrounds.com/ (accessed 4.15.22).

Pearce, F., 2008. Histories: {W}ho really discovered the ozone hole? New Sci. 2674, 46–47.

Pedercini, P., 2019. Lichenia Release Notes [WWW Document]. Molleindustria. URL https://www.molleindustria.org/blog/lichenia-release-notes/ (accessed 4.17.22).

Pfister, E., 2020. Special Issue Democracy Dies Playfully . (Anti-) Democratic Ideas in and Around Video Games edited by Eugen Pfister , Tobias Winnerling and Felix Zimmermann 357.

Ray Willmott, 2010. Interview: Yuji Naka - This Is My Joystick! [WWW Document]. URL http://thisismyjoystick.com/feature/interview-yuji-naka/ (accessed 4.11.22).

retrolorian.com, 2022. ▷ Download Thuis In Het Milieu 【FREE】 | Retrolorian [WWW Document]. URL https://www.retrolorian.com/en/thuis-in-het-milieu-13815#tech_info (accessed 4.11.22).

Roberto Dillon, 2011. The Golden Age of Video Games The Birth of a Multi-Billion Dollar Industry, Angewandte Chemie International Edition, 6(11), 951–952.

Rollings, A., Morris, D., 2004. Game Architecture and Design.

Rukikaire, K., 2019. US outdoor clothing brand Patagonia wins UN Champions of the Earth award. UN Environ. 5.

Scott Tailford, 2015. 15 Mind-Blowing Facts You Didn't Know About Sonic The Hedgehog – Page 12 [WWW Document]. URL https://whatculture.com/gaming/15-mind-blowing-facts-you-didnt-know-about-sonic-the-hedgehog?page=12 (accessed 4.11.22).

Sid Meier, B.S., 1992. Civilization - Manual, Docs - Lemon Amiga [WWW Document]. URL https://www.lemonamiga.com/games/docs.php?id=339 (accessed 4.11.22).

Skylines Wiki, 2018. Districts - Cities: Skylines Wiki [WWW Document]. URL https://skylines.paradoxwikis.com/Green_Cities#cite_note-1 (accessed 4.17.22).

Stanitsas, M., Kirytopoulos, K., Vareilles, E., 2019. Facilitating sustainability transition through serious games: A systematic literature review. J. Clean. Prod. 208, 924–936. https://doi.org/10.1016/j.jclepro.2018.10.157

Strange Loop Games, 2018. Eco Équipe [WWW Document]. URL https://play.eco/team (accessed 4.16.22).

Takemoto, T., Kosuke Asakura, Srivichai Nuwaree, Mayuko Mizuno, Tomoki Minami, Mahiro Muramatsu, Sota Yamamoto, Sachiyo Kamimura, Hiroko Oe, 2021. A Typology of Digital Games Focusing on Potential Contributions to Communicating United Nations Sustainable Development Goals. Econ. J. Sci. J. Accountancy, Manag. Financ. 1, 137–152. https://doi.org/10.33258/economit.v1i3.482

The Editors of Encyclopaedia Britannica, 2022. Kyoto Protocol | History, Provisions, & Facts | Britannica [WWW Document]. URL https://www.britannica.com/event/Kyoto-Protocol (accessed 4.17.22).

The Sims Wiki, 2020. The Sims 4: Eco Lifestyle | The Sims Wiki | Fandom [WWW Document]. URL https://sims.fandom.com/wiki/The_Sims_4:_Eco_Lifestyle (accessed 4.17.22).

Tiltfactor, n.d. Tiltfactor | Corporate Sponsored Values in SimCity: Societies [WWW Document]. URL https://tiltfactor.org/corporate-sponsored-values-in-simcity-societies/ (accessed 4.15.22).

UN Environment Programe, 2021. Playing for the Planet Charter.

Wallach, O., 2020. 50 Years of Gaming History , by Revenue Stream (1970-2020) [WWW Document]. Vis. Capatalist. URL https://www.visualcapitalist.com/50-years-gaming-history-revenue-stream/ (accessed 4.9.22).

Weart, S., 2015. Climate and Climate Change: History of Scientific Work on Climate Change, Encyclopedia of Atmospheric Sciences: Second Edition. Elsevier. https://doi.org/10.1016/B978-0-12-382225-3.00491-6

Zhang, Y., Chen, J., Han, Y., Qian, M., Guo, X., Chen, R., Xu, D., Chen, Y., 2021. The contribution of Fintech to sustainable development in the digital age: Ant forest and land restoration in China. Land use policy 103, 1–9. https://doi.org/10.1016/j.landusepol.2021.105306

Zhang, Y., Xiao, S., Zhou, G., 2020. User continuance of a green behavior mobile application in China: An empirical study of Ant Forest. J. Clean. Prod. 242, 118497. https://doi.org/10.1016/j.jclepro.2019.118497

GAMING SKILL DEMOGRAPHICS: AN ANALYSIS OF CONSISTENCY IN VIDEO GAME RESEARCH

Elizabeth A. Matthews[1], Irina Koleva and Sujana Basnet
Washington and Lee University, USA
[1]Dr.

ABSTRACT

Video games are a popular topic in academia, with many varied subjects of research. Often researchers investigating video game subjects partition the participants bythe participant's familiarity with video games. Unlike other demographic categories on which research subjects are divided, such as age range or income, sorting participants intogamer skill categories, such as "Expert Gamer," has no objective consensus on what the labels should be. The inconsistency in terminology makes comparison between research works impossible. This paper highlights this problem, collects demographic questions in existing research, and showcases the data collected from a user study with these questions.The results show that self-chosen categories are a statistically significant metric and is recommended as an easy-to-obtain value.

KEYWORDS

Gamer Skills, Gamer Demographics, Video Games, HCI

1. INTRODUCTION

Academic research containing human subjects requires a standardized method of categorizing study participants into demographic labels for accurate analysis of results. Standard demographics include age, gender, ethnicity, or income. One such way to categorize participants when involved in video game research is the participant's perceived gamer experience level. Categorizing participants into "Expert" or "Novice" groupings could control for the differences that arise from players' varying levels of expertise, experience, and familiarity with a gaming system. The problem arises when trying to find a consensus on the definition of what makes someone a specific gaming demographic.

One option from Adams and Ip (2002) is a 15-factor gamer classification method based on the previous work of Adams (2000) and Kim (2001). Each factor is given a different weight based on importance, and each player is given a player dedication score. These scores are then used to categorize gamers into "ultra casual," "casual," "transitional/modern," "hardcore," and "ultra hardcore." This classification method could be used as a standard and is a great starting point for defining important questions and factors, but a standardized weighting should be created that all researchers use. Adams and Ip state: "Moreover, in applying the classification procedure, weightings can be determined arbitrarily according to the importance the marketer perceives them to hold for his own purposes." Further, the authors go on to suggest ways to quantify each of the 15 factors in a vague way, but they did not provide a specific standardized set of questions. The lack of a standardization results in a body of research that cannot be compared with any accuracy, making it difficult to draw conclusions based on data from multiple studies.

A different option used by many works of research is hours per week (HPW) spent playing video games. However, expertise in a field is not directly a result of sheer quantity of hours (Ericsson et al., 1993; Ericsson et al., 2016). Even with this caveat, none of the papers showed a consensus on where the standard hours per week would be for an "Expert Gamer." In this paper, we gathered multiple academic sources which divided the participants into gaming skill demographics to examine the metrics used and provide analysis of correlations in these metrics.

2. SURVEY OF RELATED WORKS

For this study we surveyed multiple peer-reviewed academic publications for the purpose of identifying a clear metric for video game player categorization. Unlike other demographic categories on which research subjects are divided, such as age range or income, sorting participants into gamer skill categories has no objective consensus on what the labels should be. The metrics used to determine these non-standardized labels vary greatly, even within papers that agree on a demographic labeling scheme. Many papers were examined, and we selected any paper which mentioned categorization and provided the specific questionnaire metrics used to create the categorization.

2.1 Demographic Categories

The terminology used across papers is inconsistent. Some papers label the more experienced gamers as "hardcore" (Baumann et al., 2018; Paaßen et al., 2017; Poels et al., 2012) while others use the terminology "expert" (Boot et al., 2008; Liu et al., 2020; Marre et al., 2021; Shafer et al., 2011). The use of the "expert" label is on wildly differing scales between research works. A simple distinction between "video game player" (VGP) and "non-video game player" (NGVP) is a common label (Castel et al., 2005; Feng et al., 2007; Green and Bavelier, 2006). This casts a large net for the VGP category, under which even casual players can fall, and makes no distinction between VPGs who play the minimum required by the metric versus those who play far beyond the minimum.

Paaßen et al. (2017) reviewed the existing literature on gender and gaming to investigate the accuracy and effects of the gamer stereotype. They proceed to evaluate the meanings of "casual" and "hardcore gamers," looking at criteria such as time investment, gaming knowledge, playing attitudes, buying habits, game genre, and self-identification to define those terms. None of those criteria except for self-identification could be used reliably to define "hardcore" gamers. Even video game skill was not mentioned as an identifying feature. They conclude that based on their review of relevant literature the definition of "gamer" overall is varied.

2.2 Time Spent Per Week

An assumption among researchers is that the skill of a gamer has statistical significance with the time spent playing video games. This assumption is not an outlandish one but is untested and not standardized. Researchers that use play time as a gaming skill demographics have a wide range of metric cut-offs. Table 1 shows a summary of the hours per week cutoff for category of "gamer," where the labels used for these groups varied by research. There is a large discrepancy in defining what an expert gamer is among these papers, with some setting a much higher bar to cross than others.

Baumann et al. (2018) use one of the highest cutoffs, 20 hours per week, but cite Poels et al. (2012) for their reasoning; Poels et al. used at least one hour per day. The 20 hours per week from Poels et al. work comes from the average time spent of those labeled as "expert" ("hardcore") gamers. By using 20 hours per week as the cutoff, the work by Baumann et al. can't compare their data for "expert" ("hardcore") gamers with Poels et al., despite basing on Poels et al. Other papers that used hours per week as a metric to categorize gamers only defined participants as video game players (VPGs) or non-video game players (NVPGs) (Castel et al., 2005; Feng et al., 2007; Green and Bavelier, 2006).

2.3 Self-Reporting Skill

Another metric to obtain gamer categorization is a self-reported gamer label. Motivation for the use of a self-reported skill category is that a self-applied metric captures the participants self-perceived skill set. How a participant sees themselves is a quantifiable, yet subjective, metric. But if the wording of the question used by different researchers remains the same, a self-applied metric could be compared between research projects. Table 2 shows the summary of questions used in the related works to obtain a self-reported skill category.

Table 1. A summary based on the papers that used some form of hours per week as a categorization for gamers

Research Author(s)	Hours Per Week Range	Label
Marre et al. (2021)	> 4	Expert
Feng et al. (2007)	> 4	Players
Castel et al. (2005)	> 4	VGP
Boot et al. (2008)	> 7	Expert
Poels et al. (2012)	> 7	Hardcore
Baumann et al. (2018)	> 20	Hardcore
Pontes et al. (2015)	> 30	Disordered

There is evidence that a self-reported skill level does match with in-game metrics. Huang et al. (2013) and Liu et al. (2020) found that self-rated skill was a strong predictor of player performance on average. However, as Table 2 catalogs, the types of questions used across research are inconsistent and the labels chosen by researchers vary greatly (noobie vs Newbie/Non-Gamer vs None (Bracken et al., 2006; Matthews and Gilbert, 2020; Schafer et al., 2011)).

3. METHODOLOGY

Our survey was designed with the intention to collect a large amount of data using several demographic metrics based on data collected by previous research. Each of the 15-factors proposed by Adams and Ip (2002) were converted into Likert statements. For example, factor 1, "Play games over many long sessions," was changed to "I play video games over many long sessions." Any other metrics discovered in the related works were also converted to Likert statements and included in the survey. A few non-Likert scale questions were also added: a free-form question about how many years have they played video games, a multiple-choice question allowed participants to select a self-assigned label out of five categories: Expert Gamer, Intermediate Gamer, Casual Gamer, Novice Gamer, or Non-Gamer, and a follow up free-form question asked what factors they considered for choosing the label in the previous question.

The survey was posted on Prolific and among gaming communities on Discord, a messaging application. A total of 116 responses were received. Each participant was paid $5.00 upon completion of the survey. Of these participants, 67% (77) were male, 29.6% (34) were female, and 3.5% (4) were non-binary. The average age of the participants was 26, with the age range being 18 to 42.

4. ANALYSIS

Statistical analyses were performed using the R programming language. We selected a p-value significance threshold of 0.05, using contingency tables for visualization of patterns in the data. Contingency tables use proportional rectangles to represent numerical summations within a group. The chi-squared p-value was reported beneath the title of each table and the wilcoxon pairwise analysis results were represented by alphabetical labels along the bottom of the table. If two columns shared a letter, they were not significantly different; columns with different letters were statistically different.

4.1 Likert Scale Comparisons

The independent variables used for our Likert scale analyses were hours played per week and self-chosen gamer experience level ("Gamer Category" in the tables). Participants were given five options for the Gamer Category responses but only two participants labeled themselves as a "Novice Gamer" and none chose the "Non-Gamer" label. When analyzing Gamer Category as an independent or dependent variable, those labeled "Novice Gamer" were combined with "Casual" due to the relatively small number of responses. Hours per week responses were grouped into five categories (Pontes et al., 2015): <7, 8-14, 15-20, 21-30, and >30 (31-40 and >40 combined due to small number of response). For the dependent variable was the value response to the Likert questions from the questionnaire,from 1 as "strongly disagree" to 5 as "strongly agree." The Likert statement analyzed is the top title in the figures.

Table 2. A summary of the questions used by researchers for a self-reported skill metric

Author(s)	Question Used	Response Range
Bracken et al. (2006)	"I am a good video game player."	"strongly agree" to "strongly disagree"
Schrader and McCreery (2008)	Asked participants to select their gaming level	noobie, novice, proficient, expert, master
Matthews (2015)	Asked participants to assess their skill level	"well above average" to "well below average"
Matthews (2013)	Asked participants to assess their skill level	"expert" to "poor"
Matthews and Gilbert (2020)	"Which of the following describes your experiences with video games?"	Newbie/Non-Gamer, Casual Gamer, Frequent Gamer, Expert Gamer
Chesney et al. (2014)	"Do you play video games?" "Do you consider yourself a gamer (someone who plays video games frequently)?"	Yes/No
Shafer et al. (2011)	"How would you rate your skill at the game?"	"Expert" to "None"
Shafer et al. (2011)	"Rate how often you play computer games"	"Every Day" to "Never"

Figure 1 shows the contingency tables for the responses to the statement "I am a good video game player" (Bracken et al., 2006). The hours per week categories were not statistically significantly different from each other (Figure 1a) while all the self-chosen gaming labels were significant (Figure 1b). "Casual/Novice" disagreed with the statement the most, "Intermediate" was either neutral or agreed with the statement, while "Expert" had the most strongly agree responses. This analysis showed that it was not the number of hours put into a subject that makes skill. One could spend several hours each day practicing something and still not consider themselves an expert in that subject. The answers in the follow-up free-form question querying participants about which factors influenced their decision of selecting a self-chosen gamer experience label support this figure. Out of the responses, the most mentioned code was "skill." This was defined as gaming ability, how well the player can complete in-game tasks and how "good" they are compared to other players. Skill was mentioned by 33% of all respondents, 26% of casual players, 36% of intermediate players, and 35% of expert players.

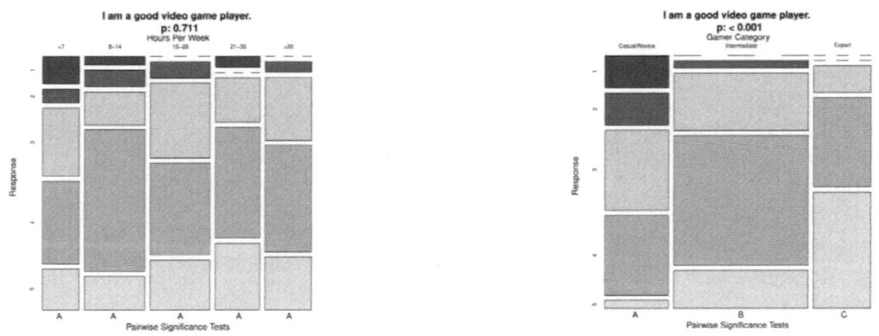

(a) Compared to hours per week

(b) Compared to self-chosen gaming label

Figure 1. Responses 1 (Strongly Disagree) to 5 (Strongly Agree) to the statement "I am a good video game player."

Figure 2 shows the contingency tables for the responses to the question "I know a lot about video games." The hours spent playing video games each week was not a significantly related to the respondents' statements about video game knowledge (Figure 2a), and again, all three categories of self-chosen gamer label were (Figure 2b). The participants who identified as "Casual/Novice" were the only ones to answer "strongly disagree" to this statement. "Expert" participants selected neutral or agreement options and did not select "disagree" or "strongly disagree."

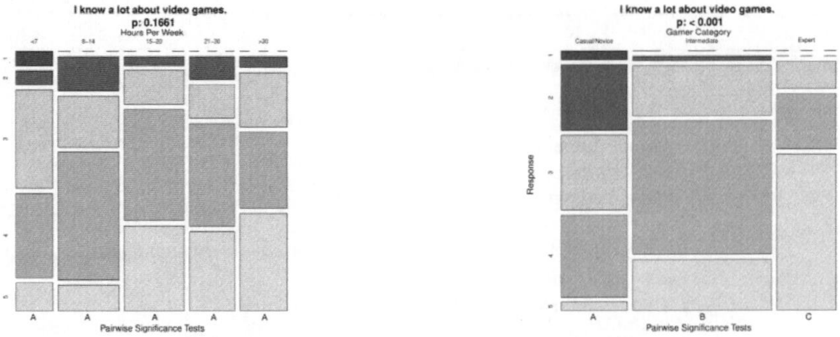

(a) Compared to hours per week

(b) Compared to self-chosen gaming label

Figure 2. Responses 1 (Strongly Disagree) to 5 (Strongly Agree) to the statement “I know a lot about video games”

Contingency tables were created for the 13 of the 15 factors that were converted to Likert response statements for this study. Table 3 shows which tables had statistical significance for hours per week and self-chosen gaming labels. It also lists the suggested weighting by Adams and Ip for each of those factors and two significance columns. An asterisk in the Sig. HPW or Sig. Labels columns indicates that we found statistically significant differences, as demonstrated in Figures 1 and 2, based on either the hours per week or self-choosing gaming labels. Factors which did not have a statistical significance with either HPW or Labels are omitted. In our study, only one of the 15 factors (“Play games over many long sessions”) was significantly associated with hours per week. The factors “Play games over many long sessions,” “Comparative knowledge of the industry,” “Technologically savvy,” “Have the latest high-end computers/consoles,” and “Hunger for gaming-related information” were significantly associated with the self-chosen gaming labels.

Table 3. Pairwise statistically significant differences between Hours Per Week (HPW) groups or Self-Chosen Gaming Labels (Labels). Presence of * in Sig. columns represent a pairwise p-value significance. Weight is from Adams and Ip (2002)

Factor	Weight	Sig. HPW	Sig. Labels
Play games over many long sessions	10	*	*
Comparative knowledge of the industry	10		*
Technologically savvy	7		*
Have the latest high-end computers/consoles	7		*
Hunger for gaming-related information	6		*

4.2 Code Book

The free form question asking, “What factors did you consider for choosing the label in the above question?”, in reference to self-chosen gaming experience labels, was converted into a code book. Twenty-four codes were created for the study. Frequencies of each code were recorded for all participants and broken into the self-defined gamer labels of Casual, Intermediate, and Expert. Novice was omitted due to the low number of participants. Table 4 shows the five most frequent codes.

Table 4. Top five codes (based on All category) discovered in free form feedback. Columns represent All participants, then participants self-labeled as Casual, Intermediate, and Expert. Items more frequent than 25% are marked with *

	All	Casual	Intermediate	Expert
Time Spent Playing	*0.371	*0.519	*0.344	*0.308
Skill	*0.328	*0.260	*0.360	*0.346
Knowledge	0.207	0.148	0.213	*0.269
Years Spent Playing	0.164	0.037	0.098	*0.462
Variety of genres played	0.112	0.074	0.131	0.115

The most common theme mentioned when considering all categories was how often participants played video games, with 37% of all participants mentioning it. However, the breakdown changed when examining "Casual" versus "Intermediate" and "Expert." Almost 52% of all casual participants cited their time spent playing, but only 34% of intermediate and 31% of expert participants. The most common code referenced by intermediate players was their skill at a game,with 36% of participants mentioning it, compared to 35% for experts and only 26% for casuals. The highest code for expert players was the number of years spent playing at 46%, compared to 10% for intermediate and only 3% of casual participants.

Figure 3 shows years spent playing as a percentage of the participant's lifespan. The "Casual/Novice" category was not statistically significantly different from the other two, but "Intermediate" and "Expert" were significantly different. Participants picking the "Expert" label overwhelmingly had spent 75% or more of their life playing video games. No one in the "Expert" category had spent less than 50% of their life playing video games. The closest of the 15 factors related to this aspect would be number 14, "Time started playing games relative to the age of the industry," for which Adams and Ip recommend the extremely low weighting of 2 out of 10.

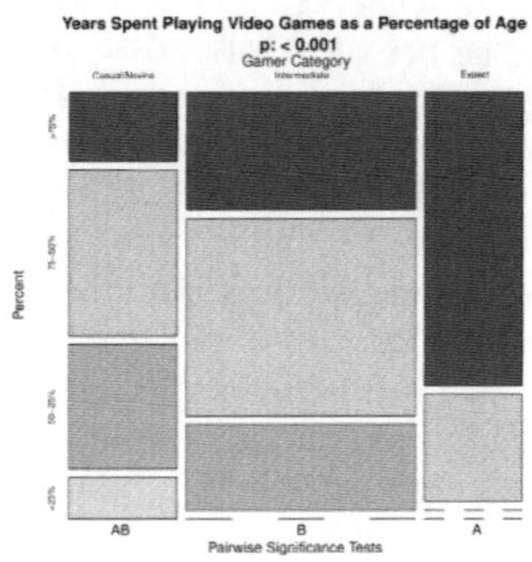

Figure 3. Years spent playing video games scaled as a percentage of the participant's reported age

5. DISCUSSION

5.1 Future Work and Limitations

Some of these factors can build to a gamer skill demographic or categorization useful for academia, but more specific testing is required. We intend to continue this work to define a binary category (gamer/not gamer) as well as a nonlinear gamer skill demographic framework for gamer archetypes. The concept labeled as "Expert" varies meaning between research, meaning anywhere from "familiarity with gaming in general" to "spends a lot of time playing video games." By applying standard HCI survey validation techniques to the 15 factors from Adams and Ip a standardized weighting and resulting demographic categories can be obtained.

The factors collected in this study creates a large multivariate data set. Contingency tables are only as powerful as how two factors interact with each other. Clustering is another statistical analysis tool for detecting associated factors. Future work will use nonparametric clustering to begin the framework for gaming demographic archetypes.

The free-form answers to hours per week spent on video games were categorized to five groups for the contingency table columns compared to just three for the self-chosen gaming label. This can reduce the power of the statistical analysis due to the further subdividing of the group, containing less participants per column. Since no other precedent could be found, future work will attempt to find hour per week cutoffs with only three columns via quantile estimates and other analysis.

Additionally, individual researchers may have specific reasoning relevant to their own research subjects for which a one-off definition for gamer skill categories is necessary. We caution against this as it leads to confusion if the common terms of "Expert," "Novice," etc. are used. It would be more beneficial if researchers make note of the context in which their definitions apply.

Finally, the suggested metric of self-chosen gaming labels is one of a subjective measurement. When using subjective self-reporting measurements, researchers should keep in mind the characteristics of the participants and how they might affect the metric. Despite the subjectivity, however, our work has shown the metric to be reliable and statistically significant with many factors.

5.2 Conclusion

Table 1 shows that there is no consensus for hours per week as a metric for defining demographics of gaming skill. While hours per week does have statistical significance with some factors, a self-chosen gaming label has more reliable significance. The 15 factors from Adams and Ip (2002) are promising, but there was no experimental data examining the validity of their factors. Adams and Ip indicated that you can weight each factor arbitrarily according to the perceived importance by the game marketer. But this did not create a standard for comparison with other studies.

Despite being a subjective label, requesting participants to provide their own evaluation of their gamer seems to capture a measurement of the participant's mindset that is significantly associated with many of the responses in our survey. Conversely, hours per week was mostly independent of the survey responses. In fact, there was no response category associated with hours per week that was not also associated with the self-chosen gaming label. Hours per week may capture the idea, but a self-chosen gaming label appears to be the stronger metric.

While clustering is intended to be utilized in future work to examine nonlinear gaming demographic categorization, self-chosen gamer level appears to be a more predictive category than hours per week. We recommend that hours per week should only be used in the context of previous familiarity with video games, not as a generalization of expert/non-expert demographics. Based on our results, the three self-chosen gamer labels (Casual/Novice, Intermediate, and Expert) can be a good choice for researchers. It not only captured the same idea across research topics but could be used to predict many other factors. Researchers, when given the choice to pick between asking one question versus 15, when both options capture the same complexity, the shorter survey should be chosen.

ACKNOWLEDGEMENT

The authors of this paper extend their appreciation to Dr. Robin A Matthews for her expertise in statistical analysis.

REFERENCES

Adams, Ernest (2000). Casual versus core. https://www.gamasutra.com/view/feature/3120/casual_versus_core.php. [Online, accessed 28-April-2022].

Adams, Ernest and Ip, Barry (2002). From casual to core: A statistical mechanism for studying gamer dedication. https://www.gamedeveloper.com/business/from-casual-to-core-a-statistical-mechanism-for-studying-gamer-dedication. [Online, accessed 28-April-2022].

Baumann, F., Emmert, D., Baumgartl, H., and Buettner, R. (2018). Hardcore gamer profiling: Results from an unsupervised learning approach to playing behavior on the steam platform. *Procedia Computer Science*, 126:1289-1297.

Boot, W. R., Kramer, A. F., Simons, D. J., Fabiani, M., and Gratton, G. (2008). The effects of video game playing on attention, memory, and executive control. *Acta psychologica*, 129(3):387-398.

Bracken, C. C. and Skalski, P. (2006). Presence and video games: The impact of image quality and skill level. In *Proceedings of the ninth annual international workshop on presence*, pages 28-29. Cleveland State University Cleveland, OH.

Castel, A. D., Pratt, J., and Drummond, E. (2005). The effects of action video game experience on the time course of inhibition of return and the efficiency of visual search. *Acta psychologica*, 119(2):217-230.

Chesney, T., Chuah, S.-H., Hoffmann, R., Hui, W., and Larner, J. (2014). A study of gamer experience and virtual world behaviour. *Interacting with Computers*, 26(1):1-11.

Ericsson, K. A. (2016). Summing up hours of any type of practice versus identifying optimal practice activities: Commentary on macnamara, moreau, & hambrick (2016). *Perspectives on Psychological Science*, 11(3):351-354.

Ericsson, K. A., Krampe, R. T., and Tesch-Römer, C. (1993). The role of deliberate practice in the acquisition of expert performance. *Psychological review*, 100(3):363.

Feng, J., Spence, I., and Pratt, J. (2007). Playing an action video game reduces gender differences in spatialcognition. *Psychological science*, 18(10):850-855.

Green, C. S. and Bavelier, D. (2006). Enumeration versus multiple object tracking: The case of action videogame players. *Cognition*, 101(1):217-245.

Huang, J., Zimmermann, T., Nagapan, N., Harrison, C., and Phillips, B. C. (2013). Mastering the art of war:how patterns of gameplay influence skill in halo. In *Proceedings of the SIGCHI Conference on Human Factorsin Computing Systems*, pages 695-704.

Kim, S. (2001). Designing web games that make business sense. In *Game Developers' Conference 2001 Proceedings*, pages 423-431.

Liu, S., Claypool, M., Devigere, B., Kuwahara, A., and Sherman, J. (2020). 'git gud!'-evaluation of self rated player skill compared to actual player performance. In *Extended Abstracts of the 2020 Annual Symposiumon Computer-Human Interaction in Play*, pages 306-310.

Marre, Q., Caroux, L., and Sakdavong, J.-C. (2021). Video game interfaces and diegesis: The impact on experts and novices' performance and experience in virtual reality. *International Journal of Human-ComputerInteraction*, pages 1-15.

Matthews, E. A. and Gilbert, J. E. (2020). Atlas chronicle: Development and verification of a system for procedural generation of story-driven games. *IADIS International Journal on Computer Science & InformationSystems*, 15(2).

Matthews, N. L. (2015). Too good to care: The effect of skill on hostility and aggression following violent video game play. *Computers in Human Behavior*, 48:219-225.

Matthews, N. L. and Weaver, A. J. (2013). Skill gap: Quantifying violent content in video game play between variably skilled users. *Mass communication and society*, 16(6):829-846.

Paaßen, B., Morgenroth, T., and Stratemeyer, M. (2017). What is a true gamer? the male gamer stereotype and the marginalization of women in video game culture. *Sex Roles*, 76(7):421-435.

Poels, Y., Annema, J. H., Verstraete, M., Zaman, B., and De Grooff, D. (2012). Are you a gamer? a qualitative study on the parameters for categorizing casual and hardcore gamers. *Iadis International Journal on www/internet*, pages 1-16.

Pontes, H. M. and Griffiths, M. D. (2015). Measuring dsm-5 internet gaming disorder: Development and validation of a short psychometric scale. *Computers in human behavior*, 45:137-143.

Schrader, P. G. and McCreery, M. (2008). The acquisition of skill and expertise in massively multiplayer online games. *Educational Technology Research and Development*, 56(5):557-574.

Shafer, D. M., Carbonara, C. P., and Popova, L. (2011). Spatial presence and perceived reality as predictorsof motion-based video game enjoyment. *Presence: Teleoperators and Virtual Environments*, 20(6):591-619.

SHORT PAPERS

USING AN INTENTION PREDICTION ALGORITHM TO DISPLAY ADAPTIVE WARNINGS OF CYCLISTS

Lisa Graichen[1], Matthias Graichen[2] and Leon Gärtner[3]
[1]*TU Berlin, 10587 Berlin, Germany*
[2]*81377 München, Germany*
[3]*TU Chemnitz, 09111 Chemnitz, Germany*

ABSTRACT

Adaptive advanced driver assistance systems may be able to adapt to the needs of the driver, thus reducing the risk of information overload and driver distraction in complex traffic situations. One way of achieving this may include the use of predictive algorithms that anticipate the driver's intention to perform a certain traffic maneuver based on vehicle data. The work in progress study that is planned and described in this paper investigates a warning system for intersections aimed at informing drivers about cyclists that are potentially crossing their anticipated trajectory. Drivers will be presented with three different warning types, differing in their level of adaptivity. To create the level of adaptivity, we base the warning system on algorithms for predicting turning maneuvers and hazard detection. Gaze data and subjective ratings will be used to assess the level of driver distraction and user experience while interacting with the warning system.

KEYWORDS

Driver Distraction, Warnings, Intersection, ADAS

1. INTRODUCTION

Modern vehicles can be equipped with an increasing number of advanced driver assistance systems (ADAS) and in-vehicle information systems (IVISs) that aim to improve driving safety, efficiency, and comfort (e.g. Bengler et al., 2018). One application for which these systems can be used is to display warnings of potential hazards. There is extensive research on the design of different warnings and their effects on users (Werneke, 2015). According to Rogers, Lamson and Rousseau (2000), the processing of a warning generally consists of three stages: a) notice (attention shifts toward the warning), b) encode (information is implemented into an internal representation), and c) comprehend (the meaning of the warning is understood) and comply (behavior changes). All stages can be assumed to be potentially affected by the characteristics of the individual person and the specific type of warning presented to the user. Therefore, it is important to anticipate those characteristics and to adaptively support the user at every stage so that adequate behavioral change can be achieved. Research on adaptive warnings has found early warning onsets to be more effective in terms of the behavioral adaptation of the driver (Werneke & Vollrath, 2013). Similarly, Puente Guillen and Gohl (2019) found warnings to be more effective when they emerge before the driver would want to break. Thereby, preferences about warning timing do not seem to differ between varying environmental scenarios (urban, rural or highway; Werneke et al., 2014). Large et al. (2019) found a time to collision of five seconds and a combination of visual and auditive warning to be most effective for behavioral changes. Studies have also found that a warning can be presented too early, resulting in drivers braking too early (Zhang et al., 2019). However, if the warning was presented after the desired moment of braking, drivers rated the warning as more disturbing (Puente Guillen & Gohl, 2019). Warnings adapted to the driver's current state, such as a distracted driver talking to a passenger, are found to be potentially more effective in terms of behavioral change (Reinmueller et al., 2018). With regard to the question of how to inform drivers about the functional principle of the system, it was shown that proper information led to longer time headways, fewer collisions, and better reactions but not higher acceptance (Koustanaï et al., 2012). When (additional) auditory warnings are used, it is important to adapt the psychoacoustic parameters according to the urgency of the hazard (see e.g. Edworthy et al., 1991).

Due to the large amount of information that could potentially be displayed at any given time, there is a risk of attention being shifted away from the primary driving task to the secondary interaction task and eventually leading to driver distraction (cf. Lee et al., 2009, Regan et al., 2009b). Driver Distraction can be divided into visual, manual and cognitive distraction (NHTSA, 2010), and visual distraction can potentially lead to very long glances off the road (e.g. Lee et al., 2012). Studies have found that driver distraction negatively affects driver behavior and driving performance (for an overview see Regan et al., 2009a, 2009b; Regan et al., 2013). Studies have found that driver distraction negatively affects driver behavior and driving performance. Official reports show that in 9% of all fatal crashes, 15% of all injury crashes, and 15% of all total crashes in 2019, driver distraction played a role (National Center for Statistics and Analysis, 2021). To minimize harmful effects, design guidelines have been developed that recommend that the total glance time for a secondary task should not exceed 20 s and a single glance should not exceed 2 s in duration (Alliance of Automobile Manufacturers, 2006; McGehee, 2001). Therefore, it is important to address the impact these systems have on driver distraction.

The upcoming study is based on an algorithm that aims to support drivers at intersections by predicting turning maneuvers. When a driver approaches an intersection, the algorithm predicts if they are likely to turn right or go straight (see Liebner et al., 2013 and Graichen, 2019). One of the applications for such an algorithm is to present drivers with a dynamic warning in situations in which they intend to turn and another traffic participant (such as a cyclist) could potentially cross the driver's anticipated trajectory. In order to evaluate the applicability of those adaptive warnings, it is necessary to analyze the user experience when interacting with such systems. The planned study addresses the following research questions:

1. How will drivers rate the usage of traditional versus adaptive warning in terms of acceptance, attractivity, and subjective workload?
2. What impact do traditional versus adaptive warnings have on driver distraction?

2. METHODS

2.1 Design and Independent Variables

A one-way repeated measure design was chosen, with three warning systems representing the factor levels. The warning systems differ in their levels of adaptivity. In this study, warnings will be only presented at intersections with the possibility to turn right. The first warning type (map-based warning [MW]) displays a warning every time the driver approaches an intersection based on map data. The second warning type (map- and intention-based warning [MIW]) only displays a warning when the algorithm detects the intention of the driver to turn right. The third warning type (map- and intention-based and hazard-related warning [MIHW]) is similar to MIW. However, it only displays a warning when a traffic hazard is detected (in this case, a cyclist that is potentially crossing the driver's trajectory). To avoid learning effects, the intersections where cyclists are present will be changing between the trips. The order of the warning types will be counterbalanced using the standard Latin square.

2.2 Participants

An opportunity sample of about 30 persons will be selected using the mailing lists of TU Chemnitz. It will mostly contain psychology students. This research will comply with the tenets of the Declaration of Helsinki, and informed consent will be obtained from each participant.

2.3 Facilities and Apparatus

A fixed-based driving simulator (STISIM Drive 100w) will be used for the study. Participants will sit in a BMW 350i driving cab with automatic transmission (see Figure 1). The projection provides a horizontal field of view of 135 degrees. Two cameras will be mounted in the car, one on the dashboard and the other on the top of the rear seat, and positioned to record the driver's interactions with the IVIS.

Instead of the built-in central information display, a 10-in tablet (Acer Iconia Tab W501P) will be mounted on the center console (see Figure 1). This screen will be used to display the navigational information using a video that is screen-shared via VNC by the examiner. At the time of the experimental trials, the examiner will be able to observe the driving simulation and driver activity with video and audio monitoring from an adjoining room.

As a driving scenario, an inner-city traffic environment will be used. The route is based on an existing route in Munich Neuperlach (see Figure 2). It consists of 16 right-turning maneuvers, four left-turning maneuvers, and four intersections where the driver goes straight.

The navigational information is based on a video of the original route that was recorded using the mobile application Here, which offers the functionality of simulating a trip on a fixed route with a fixed driving speed. The playback speed of the recorded video was adjusted according to the driving speed (the technical interface between the simulator and the video playback uses the User Diagram Protocol). Depending on the warning type and intersections, an additional layer will be displayed on top of the video showing the potential hazard.

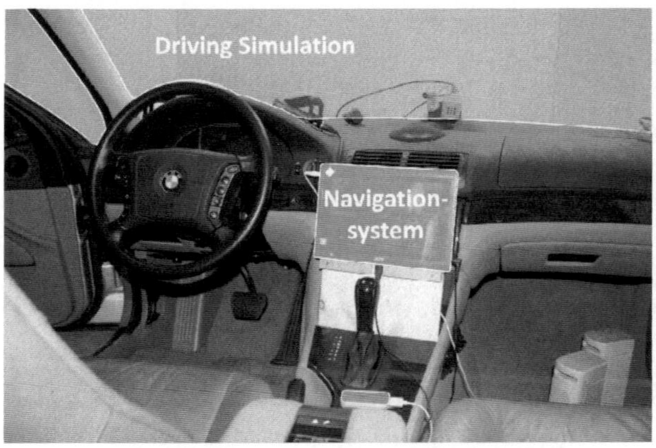

Figure 1. Driving Simulator setup

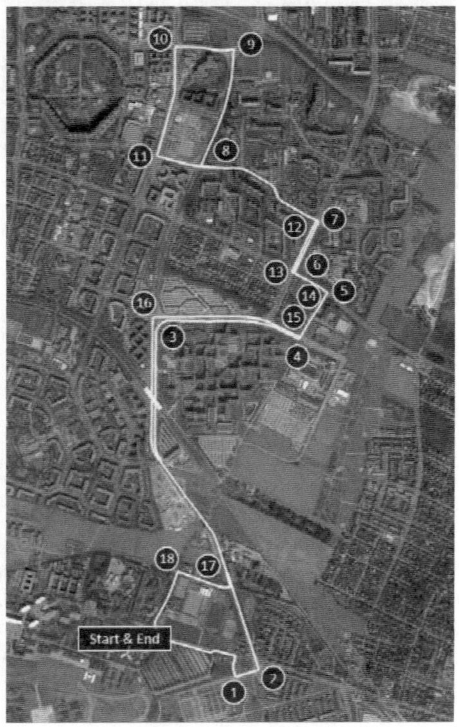

Figure 2. Driving route

Overall, participants will drive five trips: one training trip to become familiar with the simulator and the route, one baseline trip before the experimental trials, and three experimental trials using one of the warning systems. During the experimental trials, participants will perform a right-turning maneuver at five intersections and see a cyclist in the simulation. At those intersections, the warning will be displayed.

2.4 Procedure

Upon arrival, participants will be introduced to the simulator, navigation device, and warning types. Before the experiment starts, participants will be introduced to the eye-tracking device, which will then be calibrated individually. Each participant will then drive five trips and be asked to answer questionnaires pertaining to acceptance, attractivity, and workload afterward. Participants will be told to drive according to the German Road Traffic Act and keep to the standard velocity allowed in urban areas.

2.5 Dependent Variables

Gaze behavior will be assessed using metrics such as the frequency and duration that participants looked toward the display during each trip.

The subjective rating of the warning types will be measured using questionnaires. The general impression of safe driving when using the warning types in comparison to other secondary tasks will be measured using a seven-item questionnaire. We based items on the scale of "distraction engagement" in the questionnaire "Susceptibility to Driver Distraction" developed by Feng et al. (2014). The original introductory term "When driving…" was replaced with "I have the impression of safe driving when…" Items were adapted to capture the warning types by adding an item each. In addition, the last item "…you daydream" was omitted.

Acceptance will be measured using a nine-item questionnaire (with a 5-point rating scale ranging from -2 to 2) developed by Van der Laan et al. (1997). It consists of the two subscales "usefulness" (five items) and "satisfying" (four items).

Attractivity will be assessed for all warning types using the AttrakDiff questionnaire created by Hassenzahl et al. (2003). This questionnaire consists of four subscales (with seven items each ranging from 1 to 7): 1) pragmatic quality (PQ, pertaining to usability criteria), 2) stimulation (pertaining to interestingness and voluptuousness), 3) identity (pertaining to identification with the product) and 4) attractiveness (Attr.). The subscales "stimulation" and "identity" together form the general subscale of "hedonic quality" (HQ).

The workload will be assessed using the six-item NASA-TLX questionnaire crafted by Hart and Staveland (1988). This estimates levels of "mental demand," "physical demand," "temporal demand," "effort," "performance," and "frustration level," with each item using a rating scale from 0 to 20 where the maximum total score is 120.

3. IMPLICATION

This study will be conducted to address how different levels of adaptive ADASs impact user experience and driver distraction.

REFERENCES

Alliance of Automobile Manufacturers. (2006, June 26). *Statement of principles, criteria and verification Procedures on driver interactions with advanced in-vehicle information and communication systems*. Washington, D.C. http://umich.edu/~driving/publications/documents/DF-T%20with%202006%20-Updates-prot.doc

Bengler, K., Drüke, J., Hoffmann, S., Manstetten, D., & Neukum, A. (Eds.). (2018). *UR:BAN Human Factors in Traffic. Approaches for Safe, Efficient and Stressfree Urban Traffic*. Springer. https://doi.org/10.1007/978-3-658-15418-9

Edworthy, J., Loxley, S., & Dennis, I. (1991). Improving auditory warning design: Relationship between warning sound parameters and perceived urgency. *Human Factors: The Journal of the Human Factors and Ergonomics Society*, *33*(2), 205–231. https://doi.org/10.1177/001872089103300206

Feng, J., Marulanda, S., & Donmez, B. (2014). Susceptibility to Driver Distraction Questionnaire. *Transportation Research Record: Journal of the Transportation Research Board*, *2434*, 26–34. https://doi.org/10.3141/2434-04

Graichen, M. (2019). *Analyse des Fahrverhaltens bei der Annäherung an Knotenpunkte und personenspezifsiche Vorhersage von Abbiegemanövern* [Doctoral thesis]. Universität der Bundeswehr München, Neubiberg. http://athene-forschung.rz.unibw-muenchen.de/129783

Hart, S. G., & Staveland, L. E. (1988). Development of NASA-TLX (Task Load Index): Results of empirical and theoretical research. In *Advances in Psychology. Human Mental Workload* (Vol. 52, pp. 139–183). Elsevier. https://doi.org/10.1016/S0166-4115(08)62386-9

Hassenzahl, M., Burmester, M., & Koller, F. (2003). AttrakDiff: Ein Fragebogen zur Messung wahrgenommfener hedonischer und pragmatischer Qualität. In G. Szwillus & J. Ziegler (Eds.), *Berichte des German Chapter of the ACM: Vol. 57. Mensch & Computer 2003: Interaktion in Bewegung* (pp. 187–196). B.G. Teubner.

Koustanaï, A., Cavallo, V., Delhomme, P., & Mas, A. (2012). Simulator training with a forward collision warning system: Effects on driver-system interactions and driver trust. *Human Factors: The Journal of the Human Factors and Ergonomics Society*, *54*(5), 709–721. https://doi.org/10.1177/0018720812441796

Large, D. R., Kim, H., Merenda, C., Leong, S., Harvey, C., Burnett, G., & Gabbard, J. (2019). Investigating the effect of urgency and modality of pedestrian alert warnings on driver acceptance and performance. *Transportation Research Part F: Traffic Psychology and Behaviour*, *60*, 11–24. https://doi.org/10.1016/j.trf.2018.09.028

Lee, J. D., Roberts, S. C., Hoffman, J. D., & Angell, L. S. (2012). Scrolling and driving: How an MP3 player and its aftermarket controller affect driving performance and visual behavior. *Human Factors: The Journal of the Human Factors and Ergonomics Society*, *54*(2), 250–263. https://doi.org/10.1177/0018720811429562

Lee, J. D., Young, K. L., & Regan, M. A. (2009). Defining driver distraction. In M. A. Regan, J. D. Lee, & K. L. Young (Eds.), *Driver distraction. Theory, effects, and mitigation.* CRC Press.

Liebner, M., Klanner, F., Baumann, M., Ruhhammer, C., & Stiller, C. (2013). Velocity-Based Driver Intent Inference at Urban Intersections in the Presence of Preceding Vehicles. *IEEE Intelligent Transportation System Magazine*, *5*(2), 10–21. https://doi.org/10.1109/MITS.2013.2246291

McGehee, D. V. (2001). New design guidelines aim to reduce driver distraction. *Human Factors and Ergonomics Society Bulletin*, *44*(10), 1–3.

National Center for Statistics and Analysis. (2021). *Distracted driving 2019 (Research Note. Report No. DOT HS 813 111.*

NHTSA. (2010). *Overview of the national highway traffic safety administration's driver distraction program.* (DOT HS 811 299). Washington, DC: US Department of Transportation.

Puente Guillen, P., & Gohl, I. (2019). Forward collision warning based on a driver model to increase drivers' acceptance. *Traffic Injury Prevention*, *20*(sup1), S21-S26. https://doi.org/10.1080/15389588.2019.1623397

Regan, M. A., Lee, J. D., & Victor, T. W. (Eds.). (2013). *Driver distraction and inattention. Advances in research and countermeasures*. Ashgate.

Regan, M. A., Lee, J. D., & Young, K. L. (Eds.). (2009a). *Driver distraction. Theory, effects, and mitigation*. CRC Press.

Regan, M. A., Lee, J. D., & Young, K. L. (2009b). Driver distraction: Toward a common definition. In *First International Conference on Driver Diststraction and Inattention. 28-29 September 2009, Gothenburg, Sweden.*

Reinmueller, K., Koehler, L., & Steinhauser, M. (2018). Adaptive warning signals adjusted to driver passenger conversation: Impact of system awareness on behavioral adaptations. *Transportation Research Part F: Traffic Psychology and Behaviour*, *58*, 242–252. https://doi.org/10.1016/j.trf.2018.06.013

Rogers, W. A., Lamson, N., & Rousseau, G. K. (2000). Warning research: An integrative perspective. *Human Factors: The Journal of the Human Factors and Ergonomics Society*, *42*(1), 102–139. https://doi.org/10.1518/001872000779656624

Van der Laan, J. D., Heino, A., & Waard, D. de (1997). A simple procedure for the assessment of acceptance of advanced transport telematics. *Transportation Research Part C: Emerging Technologies*, *5*(1), 1–10. https://doi.org/10.1016/S0968-090X(96)00025-3

Werneke, J. (2015, June 18). *3. Meilensteinbericht (Q12): Implementierung funktionsspezifischer MMI Konzepte in Funktionsträger und Demonstatoren*. UR:BAN, Projekt MV, Teilprojekt MMI [projektintern]. Wolfsburg. UR:BAN.

Werneke, J., Kleen, A., & Vollrath, M. (2014). Perfect Timing: Urgency, Not Driving Situations, Influence the Best Timing to Activate Warnings. *Human Factors: The Journal of the Human Factors and Ergonomics Society*, *56*(2), 249–259. https://doi.org/10.1177/0018720813490728

Werneke, J., & Vollrath, M. (2013). How to present collision warnings at intersections? - A comparison of different approaches. *Accident Analysis and Prevention*, *52*, 91–99. https://doi.org/10.1016/j.aap.2012.12.001

Zhang, Y., Yan, X., Li, X., & Wu, J. (2019). Changes of drivers' visual performances when approaching a signalized intersection under different collision avoidance warning conditions. *Transportation Research Part F: Traffic Psychology and Behaviour*, *65*, 584–597. https://doi.org/10.1016/j.trf.2017.12.018

RESEARCH ON LOW CARBON DESIGN STRATEGY OF CATERING TAKEOUT FROM THE PERSPECTIVE OF "DOUBLE CARBON"

Shen Chuanyue
Wuhan University of Technology, Wuhan 430000, China

ABSTRACT

Objective to study the carbon neutralization and carbon emission reduction design strategy and specific implementation scheme of China's catering takeout industry from the international background of carbon neutralization action. Methods Based on the theories and research methods of interaction design and service design, the current situation of food delivery problems was analyzed. Based on the factors related to the impact of food delivery on the environment, the limitations and opportunities of low-carbon design in the process of food delivery service were analyzed from the perspective of the whole life cycle of food delivery. Results Low-carbon guided design and low-carbon environmental awareness education are the key factors to promote users to practice low-carbon behavior. To construct a low-carbon design strategy for food and beverage delivery, the design should be combined with the environment, and low-carbon behavior guided design should be carried out based on user behavior - system identification - incentive feedback. Conclusion This study provides useful guidance for the carbon emission reduction design strategy of food and beverage delivery products and has certain reference significance for the development of green catering and the realization of carbon neutrality in food and beverage delivery service field.

KEYWORDS

Low Carbon Design, Catering Takeout, Design Strategy, Environmental Protection

1. INTRODUCTION

On September 22, 2020, General Secretary Xi Jinping stated at the seventy-fifth Session of the United Nations General Assembly, "China will enhance its nationally determined contribution, adopt more effective policies and measures, strive to peak CO_2 emissions by 2030, and strive to achieve carbon neutrality by 2060 .At the same time, in the 2021 government work report, "doing a good job in carbon peak and carbon neutralization" is listed as one of the key tasks, and the 14th five year plan will also accelerate the promotion of green and low-carbon development. According to the "Research Report on the development of China's takeout industry from 2020 to 2021" released by hungry and China Hotel Association, by the end of 2020, the number of takeout users in China was close to 500 million, the transaction scale increased by 14.8% year-on-year, and more than 670000 takeout related enterprises were added, with a year-on-year increase of 14.87%. The O2O platform for domestic takeout has a large-scale business foundation, a multi-level distribution mode system and a habitual consumer group. The huge user scale and business system, and the environmental problems caused by takeaway catering have also caused great pressure to the society. Based on the "double carbon" perspective, discussing the low-carbon and carbon reduction design strategy of takeaway industry will help to achieve the goal of "carbon peak and carbon neutrality" as soon as possible.

2. LOW CARBON DESIGN CONCEPT

With the constant depletion of traditional energy resources on earth, people gradually realize the energy crisis, Low-carbon design arises at the historic moment. Low-carbon design refers to that enterprises and designers should start from energy conservation and environmental protection in the process of product development, fully consider the relationship between design and environment in the design process, optimize each link of the product, in order to achieve the purpose of energy conservation and carbon emission reduction. Low-carbon design requires designers to apply the low-carbon concept in the conception stage of innovative design, so that the newly developed products can not only achieve the sustainable development benefits of human beings, but also fully reflect the low-carbon ideas of energy saving, consumption reduction and material saving.

3. EXISTING PROBLEMS OF CATERING TAKEOUT

Based on the concept of product life cycle, analyze the impact of takeout food on the environment in the links of production, transportation, consumption and waste disposal. Firstly, in food production, the main sources of environmental pollution are the transportation of food materials, food processing and cooking, as well as the production of lunch boxes, tableware and packaging bags. The second is the transportation link, that is, the delivery link of takeout from merchants to consumers. The main factors affecting the environment in this link are distribution efficiency and carbon emission in the process of transportation and so on. Finally, there is the consumption and waste link. The main factors affecting the environment in this link are food scraps, lunch boxes, tableware, packaging bags and other wastes.

3.1 The Environmental Pollution

With the continuous development of online ordering in China, take-out has almost become the rigid demand of office workers and students. According to statistics, China's four major online food ordering platforms sell 20 million takeaways a day, with each order consuming two disposable lunch boxes at a total cost of more than $40 million ($14.6 billion a year). Each order consumes one plastic bag (0.06), which can cover 1.2 million bags per day. About 46 billion tea straws (30,000 tons) are used each year. More than 2 million tons of disposable meal boxes and plastic bags are produced every year, but the above data is conservative, but the waste generated by takeout is far more than that.

3.2 Takeaway Food Transportation Carbon Emissions

Takeaway delivery. That is, the rider will be delivered to the user designated location. First, the energy consumption caused using non-standard vehicles is also one of the reasons for the carbon emission pollution of food and beverage takeaway products. Secondly, the service process of the platform is not standardized, the distribution path algorithm is not good and other problems lead to the occurrence of rider's detour, resulting in the decrease of distribution efficiency. The above unreasonable phenomena all increase the carbon emission of takeaway food in the transportation process to a certain extent.

3.3 Low Carbon Design is Insufficient

With the increasing awareness of environmental protection of enterprises and designers, takeout APP has also added low-carbon environmental design measures in the design process to encourage users to practice low-carbon environmental protection and reduce the harm to the environment. For example, users are encouraged not to use disposable tableware and can obtain 16g environmental energy in Alipay. But the reality is that even after users click the button that doesn't need cutlery, they sometimes still receive disposable cutlery. In terms of APP function design, low-carbon design has low intensity, weak effect and unclear design, which needs to be improved.

4. LOW-CARBON DESIGN STRATEGY

The low-carbon behavior of residents in daily life is mainly reflected in the following two aspects: on the one hand, energy saving, and emission reduction can be achieved by purchasing low-carbon products, high-efficiency equipment and facilities or green energy products; On the other hand, carbon dioxide emissions can be reduced by actively reducing energy consumption and waste in daily life. Catering takeout low carbon design strategies should be combined with the environmental impact (pollutants) and the relationship between stakeholders, in respect of stakeholders working process, behavior habit and consumer eating habits under the premise of low carbon design analysis and design of low carbonization method is given, guide the practice of low carbon environmental stakeholders' behavior, develop good environmental behavior.

4.1 Low Carbon Guided Design

The environmental impact of the takeout industry runs through production, transportation, food, waste disposal and other links. First, before the low-carbon guidance design is carried out, the catering takeaway link to be improved should be selected first, and the link and stakeholder groups should be determined. Secondly, in the analysis and research stage, qualitative and quantitative research methods related to service design and interaction design are adopted to analyze the relationship between target groups and the environment, study the behavior habits, motivation and purpose of target groups, and dig out their pain points and low-carbon design opportunities. Thirdly, determine the low-carbon design scheme. This stage is divided into intrinsic motivation and extrinsic motivation. The reason for users' low carbon behavior intention may be the lack of environmental system knowledge such as environmental awareness, environmental attitude, environmental knowledge and environmental perception, or the lack of design functions and design plates. Therefore, the internal motivation of low-carbon design should consciously improve users' awareness of the environment, enhance users' ability to perceive the environment, and advocate the concept of low-carbon behavior in design. In terms of extrinsic motivation, various design schemes are explored. Good interactive experience design, high-quality visual experience, social needs, moral responsibility design and sense of achievement design can stimulate users to practice low-carbon behavior in terms of extrinsic motivation. Finally, the implementation effect of low-carbon design scheme is evaluated and tested, and the effect of low-carbon design strategy is analyzed through the environmental status. At the user level, we will continuously optimize interaction and visual experience and guide users to practice low-carbon and environmental protection behaviors. as shown in Figure 1.

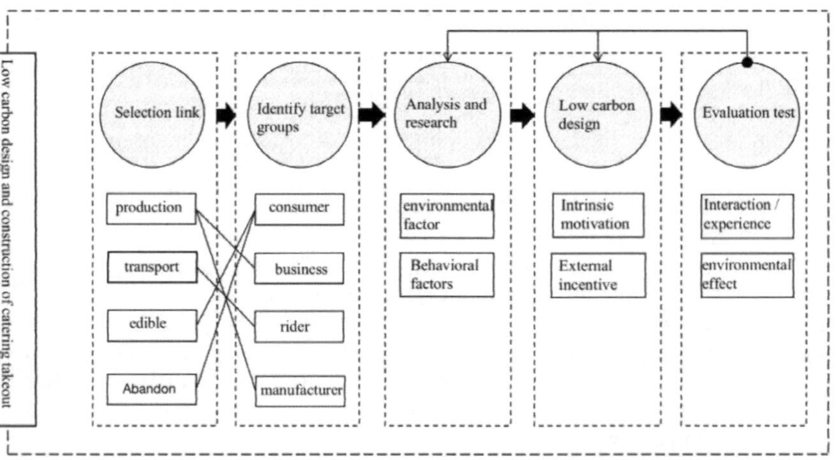

Figure 1. Low carbon design and construction flow chart of catering takeout

At the stage of low-carbon design, the low-carbon behavior guidance design is emphasized, and the low-carbon behavior guidance design is carried out around the user behavior-system identification - incentive feedback model, as shown in Figure 2. Users who have developed low-carbon and environmental protection behaviors should be given corresponding incentive feedback, and low-carbon behaviors should be cultivated into a fixed habit, to increase users' sense of recognition and social responsibility moral honor, to promote the sustainable transformation of users' low-carbon behaviors.

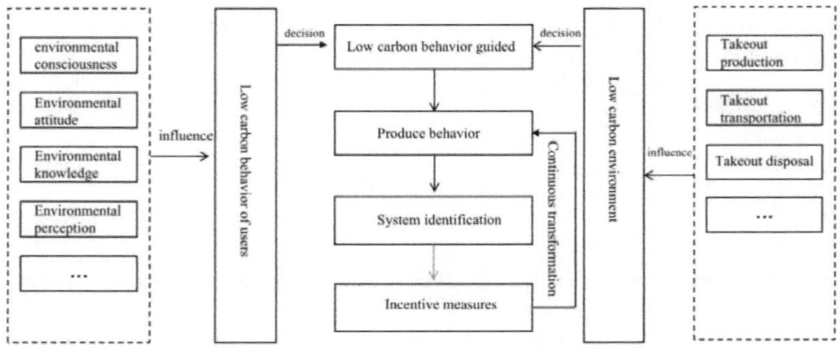

Figure 2. Takeout low-carbon behavior guidance design

4.2 Carbon Label Low-Carbon Design

As an effective tool for carbon dioxide emission reduction, carbon labeling can not only motivate enterprises or organizations to reduce carbon emissions in the product life cycle, but also encourage consumers to choose green and low-carbon consumer products, thus achieving the purpose of energy conservation and emission reduction. Carbon footprint labels allow manufacturers to display information about the environmental impact of their food production and help consumers make more sustainable choices. The whole life cycle evaluation of food components in takeout food is carried out, and the carbon coefficient generated in the production process of food is quantified by combining the amount of greenhouse gases (GHG) generated by the source, transportation, processing, cooking and production of food, so that users can choose more green and low-carbon food. With the continuous strengthening of people's knowledge of environmental system, more consumers will give priority to the low-carbon food with low carbon coefficient and good environment. The food with higher carbon coefficient and greater impact on environmental pollution will not be chosen by consumers.

4.3 Sustainable Design of Takeout Lunch Box and Packaging

Starting from the whole life cycle of boxes, carbide on food take-away packaging design patterns, a comprehensive packaging boxes in the period of products and goods, amount of carbon emissions, supplies and scrap, strictly control the market and the packaging are low carbon audit, to not meet the requirements of the low carbon take-out packaging boxes will not be able to use through the market. Secondly, in terms of material selection, manufacturers of meal boxes, tableware and packaging bags should use environmentally friendly, recyclable, easily degradable and environmentally friendly packaging materials to reduce the harm of external packaging to the environment as far as possible.

4.4 Strengthen Environmental Education

There are significant differences in the effects of system knowledge, action knowledge and effectiveness knowledge on residents' low-carbon behavior. Only action knowledge can directly drive the two types of low-carbon behaviors, while both system knowledge and effectiveness knowledge can only indirectly affect residents' low-carbon behaviors through low-carbon willingness or low-carbon ability. Consumers lack awareness of the impact of low-carbon food, low-carbon consumption and low-carbon behavior on the environment. To enhance users' awareness of low-carbon consumption and environmental protection and practice the benefits of low-carbon behavior on the environment, the government should strengthen the education and communication of low-carbon environmental protection and do a good job in the education and publicity of daily low-carbon behavior in specific actions.

ACKNOWLEDGEMENT

Takeout catering products are an unprecedented new service field formed by smart phones, passengers and catering platforms. Indeed, in many cases, it facilitates people's lives and promotes economic development, but environmental pollution caused by food and beverage takeaway products is also an unavoidable problem. Reducing environmental pollution in the takeout industry requires the joint efforts of packaging manufacturers, governments, takeout platforms, passengers, businesses, users, designers, waste treatment plants and other parties.

REFERENCES

Bao Hong, Hu Di, Zhang Cheng,et al. Innovative design method for low-carbon product based one evolution potential analysis[J]. *Computer Integrated Manufacturing Systems,* 2018, 24 (8): 8.

Ding Xiong, Zhou Wen-jie, Liu Shan.Analysis and Research on Journey Visualization Tools in Service Design [J]. *Decoration,* 2021 (3): 4.

Ganbavale G. Carbon Neutral Food Menu for Restaurants [J]. 2018.

Lan Zi-rui. Innovative Model of Carbon Labeling System in Developed Countries and Its Enlightenment to China [J]. *Environmental Protection,* 2020 (12).

Li De-xiang, Ye Lei, Zhi Zhao-hui, et al. Life Cycle Evaluation Analysis of Three Typical Disposable Plastic Tablewares.[J]. *Modern Food Science and Technology,* 2022, 38 (1): 6.]

Li Xiao-ying, Huang Chu, Zhou Da-tao,et al.Application of Product Innovation Design Method Based on User Experience Map[J]. *Packaging Engineering,* 2019, 40 (10): 6.

Liu Zong-ming, Zhao Yue-Hao. Low-carbon design of food packaging based on life circle concept of product [J]. *Food & Machinery,* 2018, 34 (4): 5.

Mi Ling -Yun, Gu Man, Yang Jie, et al. Empirical research on the psychological motivation factors of urban residents' lowcarbon oriented energy consumption behavior in Xuzhou City [J]. *Resources Science,* 2016, 38 (4): 13.

Mi Ling-Yun, Cong Jin-Qiu, Ding Chao-Qiong, Et Al. Why urban residents'deeds do not match their attitude? A dual mediation model of knowledge-behavior in low- carbon consumption [J]. *Resources Science,* 2019, 41 (5): 11.

Rondoni A, Grasso S.Consumers behaviour towards carbon footprint labels on food:A review of the literature and discussion of industry implications[J].*Journal of Cleaner Production,* 2021, 301: 1270312

Tang Mei-li, WU Jian-Xin, XIE Zhen-Zhou. WeChat Mini Program Interface Design Based on Optimized Delivery Service[J]. *Hunan Packing,* 2020 (2): 6.

Wang Jian-hua,SHEN Min-min, ZHU Dian.Research on the pro-environment behaviors of rural residents under the background of comprehensive environmental governance[J]. *China population, resources and environment,* 2020, 30 (7): 12.

Wen Zong-guo, ZHANG Yu-Ting, FU Dai-shi. The environmental impact assessment of a takeaway food delivery order based on of industry chain evaluation in China[J]. *China Environmental Science,* 2019, 39 (9): 8

Weng Zhi-xiong.Study on market-based emission reduction mechanism to achieve carbon neutrality in China [J]. *Environmental Protection,* 2021, 49 (3): 4.

Yu Yi-miao,LI Jian.Research on interactive design of environmental behavior based on situational experience[J].*Design,*2021, 34 (16): 138-140.

Zhang Ke, Chen Zhan, Dong Du-bin,et al.Strengthening legal System construction and Promoting low-carbon Development -- An exclusive interview with Shen Manhong, Deputy to THE National People's Congress and Secretary of the Party Committee of Zhejiang A&F University[J]. *Zhenjiang Forestry,* 2021 (3): 2.

Zhang Xu-fang. Based on Perceived Waiting Time of the O2O Platforms User Experience [J]. *Packaging Engineering,* 2021, 42 (16): 159-166.

FORMAL EDUCATION AND THE READINESS FOR WORK IN UX: THE RESULTS FROM A MIXED-METHODS RESEARCH STUDY

Ladislava Zbiejczuk Suchá, Jáchym Kubáček and Jitka Bartošová
Department of Information and Library Studies, Masaryk University
Arna Nováka 1/1, Brno, Czech Republic

ABSTRACT

In this short article, we focus on the topic of formal education among professionals in the UX field. The article provides some interesting insights - for example, that female UX professionals usually have higher formal education than men. The higher formal education is connected to the position of UX researcher, rather than UX designer. The higher the level of formal education our respondents have, the more prepared they feel for work in the UX industry. Based on the data, we make five recommendations for universities in the following areas: non-traditional forms of teaching, lifelong learning offerings, interdisciplinary collaboration, individual approach and mentoring and readiness of UX professionals to teach.

KEYWORDS

UX, Education, Survey, User Experience, Interaction Design Education

1. INTRODUCTION

User experience (UX) is a field that has been developing in design practice since the 1950s (Nielsen, 2017) and has been growing rapidly since the 1990s (NNG, 2016). Along with the development of the profession, educational activities have emerged - whether in the form of individual courses or comprehensive curricula for degree programs. Several authors stressed that the competencies imparted by UX courses and programs may not always match the requirements of employers (Butiurca & Zancanaro, 2021; Chang & Lu, 2021: Girouard & Kang, 2021) - while the latter emphasize the acquisition of methods and tools, universities focus on cognitive and interpersonal skills (Branch et al., 2021). There are also several barriers to the development of formal UX education in universities: the lack of expertise in key UX competencies, the risks associated with establishing any new program, and the difficulty of finding the right disciplinary background for the interdisciplinary nature of UX (Getto & Beecher, 2016). The temporality of UX knowledge is also an important factor entering into thinking about university education (Kou & Gray, 2019) - curricula aimed at imparting relevant contemporary knowledge must respond to this temporality.

In our research, we decided to focus on the topic of education professional training as part of a larger survey of UX professionals conducted in the Czech Republic and Slovakia (Bartošová et al., 2022). Our main research questions were:

1. *What areas of education do UX professionals in the Czech Republic and Slovakia come from?*
2. *How do the areas of education differ according to the type of UX profession?*
3. *How does the level of formal education differ by type of UX profession?*
4. *Does formal education increase the readiness of graduates to work in the UX field?*
5. *Does the level of formal education affect the salary of UX professionals?*

2. BODY OF PAPER

2.1 Methodology

To answer the research questions, the data was collected as part of the Humans of UX II project (Bartošová et al., 2022), which had two phases. At the turn of 2020 and 2021, we used qualitative research to gain more detailed insight into the current issues facing the UX community and to confirm the questions the whole research was designed to answer. The interviews involved 31 UX professionals from different types of organizations and at different levels of seniority. The interviews were followed by a survey conducted from July 29 to September 3, 2021. A total of 893 respondents completed the questionnaire, in Czech, Slovak, or English, at least partially. After data cleaning, responses from 598 respondents were allowed for analysis, including 400 UX professionals from the Czech Republic, 185 from Slovakia, and 13 expatriates working in the Czech or the Slovak Republic.

2.2 Results

2.2.1 Formal Education Characteristics

UX professionals in the Czech Republic and Slovakia most often have a Master's degree (52% of respondents), with Bachelor's degree (23%) and High School diploma (18%) being the second and third most common option (see Table 1). Both in the Czech Republic and Slovakia, there are currently no specialized programs focused purely on UX, but many universities offer either individual courses or study profiles close to the field of UX.

Table 1. Types of education in UX

Education (N=468)	Frequency
Postgraduate and higher	3%
University Master's degree	52%
University Bachelor's degree	23%
Practical College	2%
High School with graduation	18%
Secondary school without GCSE	1%

2.2.2 Female UX Professionals have Higher Formal Education

The highest degree of formal education differs based on the gender of respondents. Women in our survey were more likely than men to have completed a master's degree (64% and 46% for women and men, respectively). Men, on the other hand, are more likely than women to have a high school diploma as their highest formal education (23% for men, only 9% for women). In general, table 2 shows that women have a higher level of formal education than men. However, this result is not only specific to the UX profession, it is in line with the Czech Statistical Office's national survey Focus on women and men (2021). A similar result is also reported in the Swedish study The State of Design (2020), with the difference that women predominate in their sample of respondents.

Table 2. Formal education in UX by gender

Education (N=468)	Female	Male
Postgraduate and higher	6%	2%
University Master's degree	64%	46%
University Bachelor's degree	20%	25%
Practical College	0%	3%
High School with graduation	9%	23%

2.2.3 A Diploma in ICT is the Most Common Path to UX

The field of study for the UX professionals in our sample is diverse, but the most common focus is information and communication technology, which 40% of our respondents have studied. The second most common field is arts and humanities (23%) and the third is social sciences, journalism and information sciences (19%), followed by Business, Administration and Law (11%), Technology, Production and Construction (7%) and Natural Sciences, Mathematics and Statistics (6%).

Chart 1 shows that the field of study varies in our sample depending on the UX profession one works in. UX researchers (55%) studied social sciences, journalism and information sciences more often than product designers (18%) and UX designers (15%). Conversely, UX designers (52%) and product designers (52%) studied information and communication technologies more often than UX researchers (33%).

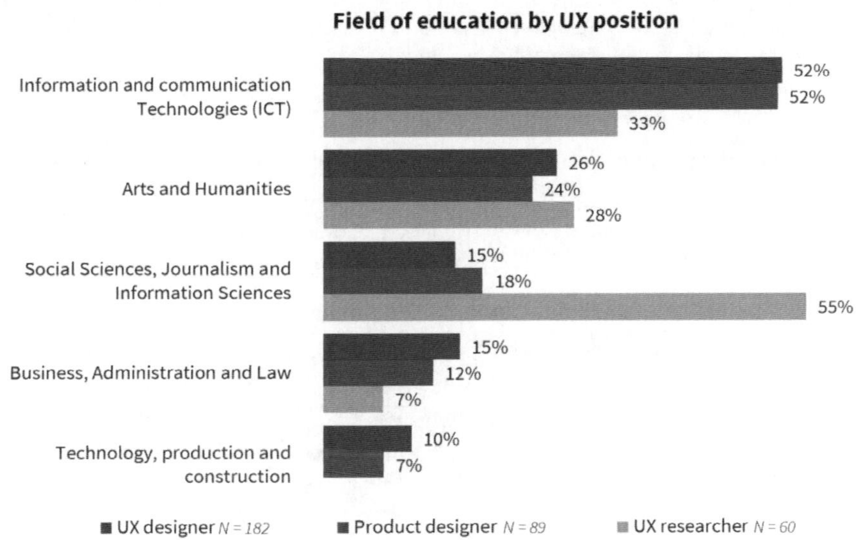

Chart 1. Field of education by UX position

These differences are described in one of the quotes from the interviews:

"User research takes a lot of inspiration from the social sciences and how they study human behavior. So I already had some background." (anonymous respondent).

2.2.4 University Degree Increases Readiness for Work in UX

"School should give a smackdown. You choose what interests you, then you finish your degree yourself. School helps in finding data and information that one should study." (anonymous respondent)

Table 3 shows how UX professionals felt prepared for work in UX. Respondents with a postgraduate degree felt the most prepared for the UX profession (mean of 3.4 on a 5-point Likert scale, where 5 corresponds to a rating of "completely prepared"), while respondents with a master's degree (mean of 2.7) and a bachelor's degree (mean of 2.6) felt slightly less prepared. Respondents with higher vocational education (mean 2.3) and secondary education with a high school diploma (mean 2.1) felt rather unprepared.

Where respondents studied had an impact on their perceived readiness for UX practice. Respondents who had studied abroad felt the most prepared (mean 3.2).

Table 3. Education and readiness to work in UX

Education	Mean (1 – not at all prepared to 5 – completely prepared)
Postgraduate (N=16)	3,4
University Master's degree (N=243)	2,7
University Bachelor's degree (N=109)	2,6
Practical College (N=10)	2,3
High School with graduation (N=85)	2,1

2.2.5 Self-Education

The UX profession requires continuous learning, which is why we decided to focus more on self-education in the survey (Bartošová et al., 2022). The most popular self-education activity among our respondents is reading UX blogs (76%) and UX books (59%). Other popular activities are attending UX conferences (46%) and taking online courses and training (45%), podcasts (30%) and community gatherings (27%).

A mentor is also seen as an important guide to a UX career. Although only 16% of UX professionals meet a mentor according to the survey data, the interview data suggests a crucial role of mentors. A larger proportion of the designers we interviewed had some experience with being mentored. Those who have a mentor find their experience with the mentor beneficial.

"If that mentor is like a top person in their field, then you're probably going to be able to learn and move a lot faster because of that mentor than you would have done without them..." (anonymous respondent).

2.2.6 UX Researchers Spend More Time at a University, Designers Self-Study

UX researchers have higher formal education than other professions (see chart 2) - most often a master's degree (70%) or postgraduate degree (13%). Higher educational attainment is also likely to be related to the representation of men and women in the UX profession (see chart 2).

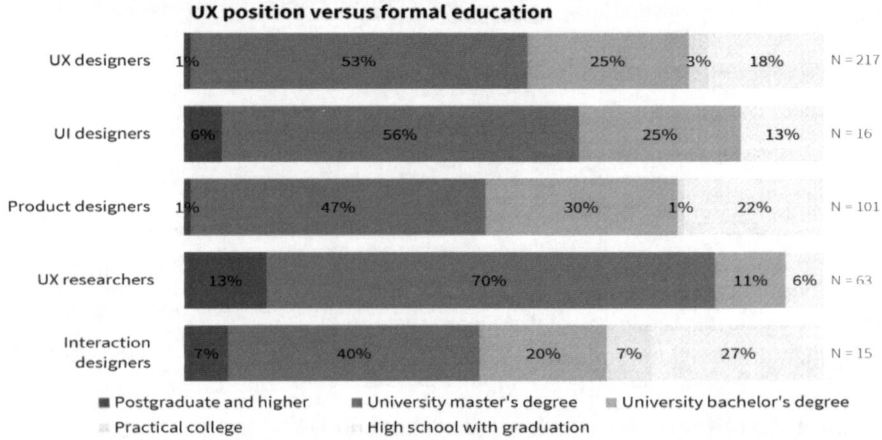

Chart 2. UX position and formal education

2.2.7 Higher Education does not Mean Higher Pay

The survey data also revealed the interesting fact that UX professionals' salaries are not influenced by the level of university education. As Table 4 shows, UX professionals with a high school degree may even have higher salaries than their colleagues with a university degree.

Table 4. Education and salary in UX

	Mean	Median
Postgraduate (N=16)	70001-77000 CZK	63001-70000 CZK
University Master's degree (N=243)	70001-77000 CZK	63001-70000 CZK
University Bachelor's degree (N=109)	70001-77000 CZK	63001-70000 CZK
High school with graduation (N=85)	77001-84000 CZK	77001-84000 CZK

3. CONCLUSION

Although the participants were a diverse sample in terms of disciplinary background, in most cases the belief in the crucial importance of self-study and self-education prevailed. In the interviews, it emerged that higher education was perceived by UX designers to be essential mainly for acquiring competencies of a universal nature that enable further (self-)education in the field of UX. This phenomenon is illustrated by two statements from our participants:

"You know, what the university will give you. That mindset and attitude, critical thinking and stuff like that." (anonymous respondent)

"So school gets you more excited and shows you the possibilities and then you have to get better at it yourself." (anonymous respondent)

Taking the data into account, we can conclude that the knowledge gained at universities serves very well as a foundation applicable to the practice of UX research. In UX design, however, the programs current Czech and Slovak universities offer tend to lag behind informal education. In both cases, continuous self-study is essential.

Based on the research results, we would like to offer some recommendations and suggestions for the future direction of professional UX education at universities:

1. **Non-traditional forms of teaching**. UX programs at universities should engage non-traditional forms of teaching that promote communication and connection to practice. Many universities are already working and experimenting with such formats (Fabus & Fabusova, 2019; Spartz & Weber, 2016; Vorvoreanu et al., 2017; Chang & Lu, 2021).
2. **Lifelong learning offerings**. In the future, universities could expand their educational offerings to meet the lifelong learning needs of UX designers. Micro-degrees, shortened programs and new forms of online learning can not only add value for designers, but also provide peer learning opportunities for educators and inspiration for "traditional" bachelor's and master's programs.
3. **Interdisciplinary collaboration**. Data shows that social science, design and ICT-based disciplines prepare very well for careers in UX. Linking them would allow for greater permeability between UX professions.
4. **Individual approach and mentoring**. Mentoring is a highly valued way of learning at the interface of formal and informal practical education. Incorporating individual mentoring into the curriculum can improve learners' practical skills.
5. **Readiness of UX professionals to teach**. Data show that graduating from university increases readiness for entering UX. We suggest paying attention to the reverse link - that is, the point at which a UX professional is ready to pass on their knowledge and offer it to learners at university.

ACKNOWLEDGEMENT

The authors would like to thank the UX Association Czech Republic and SUXA Slovakia for their cooperation in the research. We also thank to our many collaborators, namely Alexandra Jakabová, for her contribution in qualitative parts of the research.

REFERENCES

Bartošová, J., Zbiejczuk Suchá, L., Kubáček, J., & Jakabová, A. (2022). #HumansofUX: Výsledky sčítání českých a slovenských UX profesionálů. Flow. https://www.humansofux.com/cz/vysledky-scitani-2021

Branch, J., Parker, C. J., & Evans, M. (2021). Do User Experience (UX) Design Courses Meet Industry's Needs? Analysing UX Degrees and Job Adverts. The Design Journal, 24(4), 631–652. https://doi.org/10.1080/14606925.2021.1930935

Butiurca, A. D., & Zancanaro, M. (2021). What is it like to be a UX designer in Italy? An initial analysis of job advertisements to improve training and education in HCI. CHItaly 2021: 14th Biannual Conference of the Italian SIGCHI Chapter, 1–5. https://doi.org/10.1145/3464385.3464714

Chang, W.-L., & Lu, W.-H. (2021). Building Common Ground: Applying Mutual Learning in the UI/UX Education. In M. Kurosu (Ed.), Human-Computer Interaction. Theory, Methods and Tools (Vol. 12762, pp. 66–76). Springer International Publishing. https://doi.org/10.1007/978-3-030-78462-1_5

CZSO. (2021). Focus on women and men. Czech Statistical Office. https://www.czso.cz/documents/10180/120583268/30000220.pdf/45d09d6e-670e-4d7f-842d-3f2a5bfc4201?version=1.7

Design Leadership Sweden. (2020). The State of Design — Swedish Edition 2020 report. https://designleadership.se/state-of-design-the-swedish-edition/the-state-of-design-swedish-edition-2020-report/

Fabus, J., & Fabusova, V. (2019, June 26). Design of the UX Laboratory for the Department of Communications. 5th International Conference on Higher Education Advances (HEAd'19). Fifth International Conference on Higher Education Advances. https://doi.org/10.4995/HEAD19.2019.9329

Getto, G., & Beecher, F. (2016). Toward a Model of UX Education: Training UX Designers Within the Academy. IEEE Transactions on Professional Communication, 59(2), 153–164. https://doi.org/10.1109/TPC.2016.2561139

Girouard, A., & Kang, J. (2021). Reducing the UX Skill Gap Through Experiential Learning: Description and Initial Assessment of Collaborative Learning of Usability Experiences Program. In C. Ardito, R. Lanzilotti, A. Malizia, H. Petrie, A. Piccinno, G. Desolda, & K. Inkpen (Eds.), Human-Computer Interaction – INTERACT 2021 (Vol. 12933, pp. 481–500). Springer International Publishing. https://doi.org/10.1007/978-3-030-85616-8_28

Kou, Y., & Gray, C. M. (2019). A Practice-Led Account of the Conceptual Evolution of UX Knowledge. Proceedings of the 2019 CHI Conference on Human Factors in Computing Systems, 1–13. https://doi.org/10.1145/3290605.3300279

Nielsen, J. (2017). A 100-Year View of User Experience. Nielsen Norman Group. https://www.nngroup.com/articles/100-years-ux/

NNG. (2016). Don Norman: The term "UX." https://www.youtube.com/watch?v=9BdtGjoIN4E

Spartz, J. M., & Weber, R. P. (2016). User experience as a driver of entrepreneurial innovation. 2016 IEEE International Professional Communication Conference (IPCC), 1–7. https://doi.org/10.1109/IPCC.2016.7740486

Vorvoreanu, M., Gray, C. M., Parsons, P., & Rasche, N. (2017). Advancing UX Education: A Model for Integrated Studio Pedagogy. Proceedings of the 2017 CHI Conference on Human Factors in Computing Systems, 1441–1446. https://doi.org/10.1145/3025453.3025726

SPEAKING, TOUCHING OR GESTICULATING? HOW DOES IN-VEHICLE INTERACTION TYPE AFFECT DRIVER DISTRACTION?

Lisa Graichen[1], Matthias Graichen[2] and Lena Hanstein[3]
[1]TU Berlin, 10587 Berlin, Germany
[2]81377 München, Germany
[3]TU Chemnitz, 09111 Chemnitz, Germany

ABSTRACT

Driver distraction plays a major role in traffic safety. While driving, drivers often engage in different secondary tasks, including interactions with the in-vehicle information system (IVIS). Different interaction types can be implemented into these systems, such as touch-based, gesture-based, and speech-based interactions. The upcoming study described in this paper aims to clarify how these three interaction types impact driver distraction. Additionally, the preferences of drivers regarding these interaction types will be investigated.

KEYWORDS

Driver Distraction, Gesture, Touch, Speech

1. INTRODUCTION

Modern vehicles are being equipped with an increasing number of advanced driver assistance systems (ADAS) and in-vehicle information systems (IVIS) that aim to improve driving safety, efficiency, and comfort (e.g. Bengler et al., 2018). However, using these systems causes attention to be shifted away from the primary driving task and toward the secondary interaction task, resulting in driver distraction (see Lee et al., 2009, Regan et al., 2009b). Driver Distraction can be divided into visual, manual and cognitive distraction (NHTSA, 2010). Visual distraction can lead to long glances away from the road (e.g. Lee et al., 2012). Studies have found that driver distraction negatively affects driver behavior and driving performance (for an overview see (Regan et al., 2009a, 2009b; Regan et al., 2013). Official reports show that driver distraction played a role in 9% of fatal crashes in the US, 15% of injury crashes, and 15% of total crashes in 2019 (National Center for Statistics and Analysis, 2021). Nowadays, touch-based interaction (TBI) is widely used in various systems and represents the standard interaction system to which other interaction types are compared. Alternatively, gesture- and speech-based interaction (GBI, SBI) are also increasingly used and have the potential to create new ways of interaction or replace traditional systems. Therefore, it is important to clarify what impact these systems have on driver distraction.

Previous studies have shown that using gestures for interacting with IVIS provides some advantages over touch-based systems (see e.g. Geiger et al., 2002; Graichen et al., 2019, 2020), as there is no visual search required to find a haptic interaction element or button on the touchscreen (TS). The same reasoning can be applied to SBI. Therefore, the question arises of how users will perform with TBI, GBI, and SBI in direct comparison. The planned study addresses the following research questions:

1. How will the use of TBI, GBI, and SBI affect driving behavior?
2. How will the use of TBI, GBI, and SBI affect gaze behavior?
3. How will drivers rate the usage of TBI, GBI, and SBI in terms of acceptance, attractivity, and subjective workload?

2. METHODS

2.1 Design and Independent Variables

A one-way repeated measure design was chosen, with three interaction types representing the factor levels (TBI vs. GBI vs. SBI). To provide a representative variation of the interaction tasks, we implemented interaction stories with the IVIS to use basic, frequent functions as well as tasks that require more complex interactions (i.e., several steps of interaction in a TBI system). Table 1 provides task details. The order of interaction types during the experimental trials and during each trip will be counterbalanced using the standard Latin square.

2.2 Participants

An opportunity sample of about 30 persons will be selected using TU Chemnitz mailing lists and will primarily comprise psychology students. This research will comply with the tenets of the Declaration of Helsinki, and informed consent will be obtained from each participant.

2.3 Facilities and Apparatus

A fixed-based driving simulator (STISIM Drive 100w) will be used for the study. Participants will sit in a BMW 350i driving cab with automatic transmission (see Figure 1). The projection will provide a horizontal FOV of 135°. To record gaze data, an SMI eye tracker will be used.

For the driving scenario, the lane change task (LCT; Mattes, 2003) will be used. The LCT is a highly standardized driving task designed to represent a driving task with a certain cognitive demand. The driver is positioned on a three-lane road. There are signs displayed indicating to which lane the driver should change, and the task is to perform the lane change as fast as possible. In the standard LCT, the signs are displayed at a fixed distance, making the task somewhat easier for the driver, as it is predictable when a lane change is to be performed. Therefore, we made the distance between the signs variable and non-predictable (see e.g. Petzoldt et al.). See Figure 2 for an example screen of the LCT.

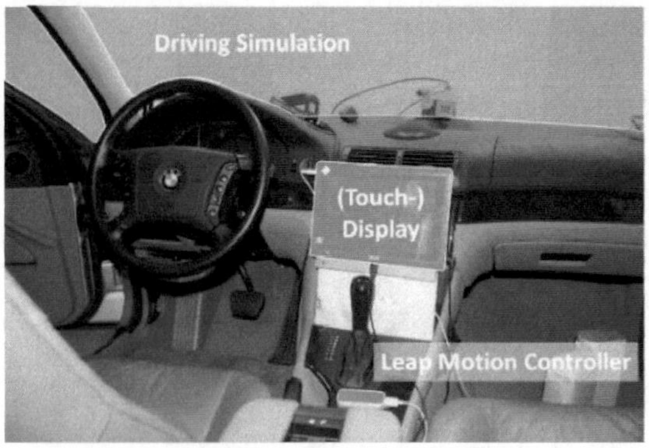

Figure 1. Driving Simulator setup

Figure 2. Example screen of the LCT

Participants will drive five trips in total: one training trip to become familiar with the simulator and the LCT, one baseline trip before the experimental trials, and three experimental trials.

Instead of the built-in central information display, a 10-inch tablet (Acer Iconia Tab W501P) will be mounted on the center console (see Figure 1). The tablet will be connected to a gesture recognition device (Leap Motion). Although the gesture detection rate of the Leap Motion is quite high, we will use the Wizard-of-Oz technique (WoO, Dahlbäck et al., 1993) for TBI, GBI, and SBI, meaning all user inputs will be operated by the examiner. This will be done to avoid sensor-related errors or long completion times of the tablet, gesture, or speech recognition device but may confound the individual evaluations of all three interaction systems. Furthermore, it will avoid any unintended interactions that could be triggered by pressing the wrong button or speaking with the examiner. This setup has also been used in Graichen et al. (2019).

The interaction display design is based on the original displays of a Seat Leon ST brand vehicle. The interaction menus will be displayed on the tablet in a slideshow format using VNC screen sharing operated by the examiner.

For all three interaction types, four interaction tasks were derived from typical IVIS tasks. Two of the tasks can be performed by operating a single control element in a conventional IVIS. The remaining tasks usually require more complex operations and several interaction steps in the interface.

To ensure the gestures fit the interaction tasks, a pretest with 73 participants was conducted. In the upcoming study participants will perform all three tasks in one driving round for each interaction type. Audio snippet acoustic feedback will be implemented in each interaction type to signal the participants that the task is finished without them having to look at the interface. The interaction tasks are similar to those used in Graichen et al. (2019) and Graichen et al. (2020).

2.4 Procedure

Upon arrival, participants will be introduced to the IVIS tasks and the general use of IVIS gesture-based, touch-based, and speech-based functionalities. Each participant will be provided as much time as needed to learn and practice all interaction types. Gesture recognition functionality will be demonstrated using an online visualization on the tablet, illustrating device tracking of the participant's fingers and palm. Before the experiment starts, participants will be introduced to the eye-tracking device, which will then be calibrated individually. Each participant will then drive five trips and be asked to complete questionnaires after each trip. Participants will be instructed to drive according to the German Road Traffic Act and perform the tasks only when they feel comfortable to do so.

2.5 Dependent Variables

To assess driving performance, lane keeping performance between the lane changes will be analyzed. Furthermore, there is an ideal trajectory of the lane change maneuver to which participants' driving behavior will be compared. Gaze behavior will be assessed using metrics such as the frequency and duration of participants looking toward the display during each trip. The response time between observing signs and initiating a lane change will also be assessed. Finally, the subjective rating of the interaction types will be measured using questionnaires on acceptance (Van der Laan et al., 1997), attractivity (Hassenzahl et al., 2003), workload (Hart & Staveland, 1988) as well as the subscales "distraction engagement" of the "Susceptibility to Driver Distraction Questionnaire" (Feng et al., 2014).

3. IMPLICATION

This study will be conducted to elucidate which interaction types are suitable for IVIS and to assess and compare their level of impact on driver distraction. All three investigated interaction types are already available; therefore, the question arises of whether users prefer one over the others in terms of perceived safety, acceptance, and attractivity.

Table 1. Tasks with corresponding gestures and procedures for completion: GBI, TBI & SBI

Task	Picture of Gesture	Initial Situation	GBI Subtasks	TBI Subtasks	SBI Subtasks	Result
Start navigation system to "Wilhelm-Raabe-Strasse" in Chemnitz		Map displayed	(1) Perform gesture (2) Voice command: destination	(1) Press button for "start navigation" on TS (2) Speak destination (3) Press button for "accept destination" on TS	(1) Voice command: Start navigation (2) Voice command: destination	Auditory feedback + Navigation map is displayed
Mute radio	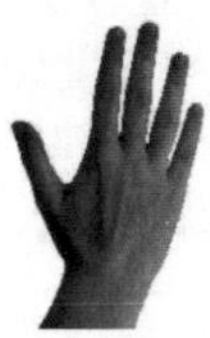	Radio menu displayed Song snippet played	(1) Perform gesture	(1) Press button for "mute" on TS	(1) Voice command: Mute Radio	Song snippet is stopped
Zoom into map		Map displayed	(1) Perform gesture	(1) Press button for "zoom" on TS	(1) Voice command: Zoom Map	Auditory feedback + more detailed map displayed
Call for traffic information		Map displayed Instruction of navigation device played	(1) Perform gesture	(1) Press button for "settings" on TS (2) Press button for "traffic information" on TS	(1) Voice command: Traffic information	Example traffic information is displayed and readout

REFERENCES

Bengler, K., Drüke, J., Hoffmann, S., Manstetten, D., & Neukum, A. (Eds.). (2018). *UR:BAN Human Factors in Traffic. Approaches for Safe, Efficient and Stressfree Urban Traffic*. Springer. https://doi.org/10.1007/978-3-658-15418-9

Dahlbäck, N., Jönsson, A., & Ahrenberg, L. (1993). Wizard of Oz studies. In W. D. Gray (Ed.), *Proceedings of the 1st international conference on Intelligent user interfaces* (pp. 193–200). ACM. https://doi.org/10.1145/169891.169968

Feng, J., Marulanda, S., & Donmez, B. (2014). Susceptibility to Driver Distraction Questionnaire. *Transportation Research Record: Journal of the Transportation Research Board*, *2434*, 26–34. https://doi.org/10.3141/2434-04

Geiger, M., Nieschulz, R., Zobl, M., & Lang, M. (2002). Bedienkonzept zur gestenbasierten Interaktion mit Geräten im Automobil (Gesture-based control concept for in-car devices). In *VDI-Berichte 1678, GMA Fachtagung USEWARE 2002. Darmstadt, Germany, June 11-12.* VDI Verlag.

Graichen, L., Graichen, M., & Krems, J. F. (2019). Evaluation of Gesture-Based In-Vehicle Interaction: User Experience and the Potential to Reduce Driver Distraction. *Human Factors: The Journal of the Human Factors and Ergonomics Society*, *61*(5), 774–792. https://doi.org/10.1177/0018720818824253

Graichen, L., Graichen, M., & Krems, J. F. (2020). Effects of Gesture-Based Interaction on Driving Behavior: A Driving Simulator Study Using the Projection-Based Vehicle-in-the-Loop. *Human Factors: The Journal of the Human Factors and Ergonomics Society*, 18720820943284. https://doi.org/10.1177/0018720820943284

Hart, S. G., & Staveland, L. E. (1988). Development of NASA-TLX (Task Load Index): Results of empirical and theoretical research. In *Advances in Psychology. Human Mental Workload* (Vol. 52, pp. 139–183). Elsevier. https://doi.org/10.1016/S0166-4115(08)62386-9

Hassenzahl, M., Burmester, M., & Koller, F. (2003). AttrakDiff: Ein Fragebogen zur Messung wahrgenommener hedonischer und pragmatischer Qualität. In G. Szwillus & J. Ziegler (Eds.), *Berichte des German Chapter of the ACM: Vol. 57. Mensch & Computer 2003: Interaktion in Bewegung* (pp. 187–196). B.G. Teubner.

Lee, J. D., Roberts, S. C., Hoffman, J. D., & Angell, L. S. (2012). Scrolling and driving: How an MP3 player and its aftermarket controller affect driving performance and visual behavior. *Human Factors: The Journal of the Human Factors and Ergonomics Society*, *54*(2), 250–263. https://doi.org/10.1177/0018720811429562

Lee, J. D., Young, K. L., & Regan, M. A. (2009). Defining driver distraction. In M. A. Regan, J. D. Lee, & K. L. Young (Eds.), *Driver distraction. Theory, effects, and mitigation.* CRC Press.

Mattes, S. (2003). The Lane-Change-Task as a tool for driver distraction evaluation. In H. Strasser, Kluth, K., Rausch, H., & H. Bubb (Eds.), *Quality of Work and Products in Enterprises of the Future* (pp. 57–60). Ergonomia.

National Center for Statistics and Analysis. (2021). *Distracted driving 2019 (Research Note. Report No. DOT HS 813 111.*

NHTSA. (2010). *Overview of the national highway traffic safety administration's driver distraction program*. (DOT HS 811 299). Washington, DC: US Department of Transportation.

Petzoldt, T., Graichen, L., & Krems, J. F. Modifying the lane change task - How does increased unpredictability of lane changes affect performance? In *3rd International Conference on Driver Diststraction and Inattention: September 4-6, 2013, Gothenburg, Sweden.*

Regan, M. A., Lee, J. D., & Victor, T. W. (Eds.). (2013). *Driver distraction and inattention. Advances in research and countermeasures*. Ashgate.

Regan, M. A., Lee, J. D., & Young, K. L. (Eds.). (2009a). *Driver distraction. Theory, effects, and mitigation*. CRC Press.

Regan, M. A., Lee, J. D., & Young, K. L. (2009b). Driver distraction: Toward a common definition. In *First International Conference on Driver Diststraction and Inattention. 28-29 September 2009, Gothenburg, Sweden.*

Van der Laan, J. D., Heino, A., & Waard, D. de (1997). A simple procedure for the assessment of acceptance of advanced transport telematics. *Transportation Research Part C: Emerging Technologies*, *5*(1), 1–10. https://doi.org/10.1016/S0968-090X(96)00025-3

A DEEP REINFORCEMENT LEARNING APPROACH TO THE ANCIENT INDIAN GAME - CHOWKA BHARA

Annapurna P. Patil, Sanjay Raghavendra, Shruthi Srinarasi and Reshma Ram
Ramaiah Institute of Technology
MSRIT Post, M S Ramaiah Nagar, MSR Nagar, Bengaluru, Karnataka, India 560054

ABSTRACT

Reinforcement Learning (RL) is the study of how Artificial Intelligence (AI) agents learn to make their own decisions in an environment to maximize the cumulative reward received. Although there has been notable progress in the application of RL for games, the category of ancient Indian games has remained almost untouched. *Chowka Bhara* is one such ancient Indian board game. This work aims at developing a Q-Learning-based RL *Chowka Bhara* player whose strategies and methodologies are obtained from three Strategic Players viz. Fast Player, Random Player, and Balanced Player. It is observed through the experimental results that the Q-Learning Player outperforms all three Strategic Players.

KEYWORDS

Reinforcement Learning, Chowka Bhara, Strategic Player, Q-Learning Player, Indian Board Game

1. INTRODUCTION

Chowka Bhara is a two to four-player board game *(Roll the Dice, 2021)* that is similar to the popular board game Ludo. This game is an example of a "fully observable" system with an element of chance introduced by the roll of cowry shells and an element of strategy. The game is controlled by tossing the four cowry shells and counting how many fall 'as it is' versus those that land 'inverted'. The game's objective is for the player to get all their four pawns to the innermost square on the board (seen in Figure 1(a)). Artificial intelligence in games *(Yildirim, S. and Stene, S.B., 2010)* involves perception and decision-making in game environments. The two main challenges of applying AI in games are: (1) The state-space of the game is very large and; (2) Learning policies to make decisions in a dynamic unknown environment is difficult. However, Reinforcement Learning (RL) *(Sutton, R.S. and Barto, A.G., 2018)* algorithms like Q-Learning (QL) *(Watkins, C.J. and Dayan, P., 1992)* help overcome these challenges to a certain extent. Being one of the three basic paradigms of Machine Learning (ML), RL is the study of how intelligent agents make decisions in an environment to maximize their cumulative reward. It is a policy-based and reward-based system. Both reinforcement learning and deep learning have been used previously and have delivered great results in gaming, computer vision, Natural Language Processing (NLP), etc.

RL and Deep Reinforcement Learning (DRL) have been observed to perform exceedingly well in games *(Mnih, V. et al., 2013) (Lample, G. and Chaplot, D.S., 2017) (Dedieu, A. and Amar, J., 2017) (Block, M. et al., 2008)*. For modern games, a lot of focus has been on very difficult competitive games like StarCraft *(Shao, K. et al., 2019)*, and they have also achieved great results from DeepMind and OpenAI. Although several categories of games have been implemented using AI, one category that has been neglected is the regional, ancient Indian board games. Through this work, a novel RL approach for a traditional Indian game such as *Chowka Bhara* is introduced that helps to bridge the gap between ancient games and modern artificial intelligence methods.

Although there has been increasing use of reinforcement learning methods in gaming, the domain of ancient Indian games *(Expedition Magazine - Penn Museum, 2021)* has not been explored enough. This work aims to design a QL player that can successfully play *Chowka Bhara* which helps highlight Indian history and culture and forms a stepping stone to more automation of other unexplored ancient Indian games like Indian Ludo *(Live History India, 2021)*. *Chowka Bhara* is partially a game of chance but it also involves critical thinking and careful planning. The game also enhances counting skills. Further, the *Chowka Bhara* game can also be extended to modeling real-life problems since the game involves stochastic components like decision-making under uncertainty, a problem most people face in the real world.

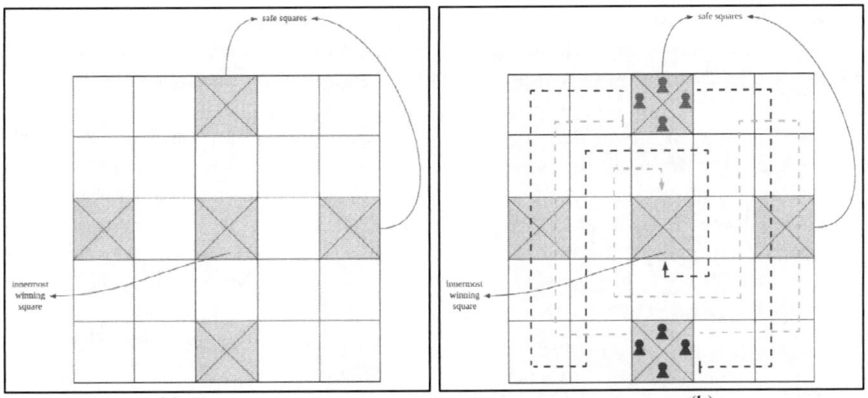

Figure 1. (a) Traditional *Chowka Bhara* board (b) Red dashed lines indicate the path taken by the red pawns, and blue dashed lines indicate the path taken by blue pawns in the game

2. RELATED WORKS

Deep Reinforcement Learning (DRL) *(Arulkumaran, K. et al., 2017)* combines reinforcement learning and artificial neural networks to design autonomous systems capable of a higher-level understanding of the environment. The training of agents to play games acts as a precursor in developing systems to adapt to the real world. Such techniques can be very beneficial in developing RL agents for games such as *Chowka Bhara* and many more. However, developing DRL methods that can adapt rapidly to new tasks is a significant challenge in RL. Previous works have shown that recurrent networks can support meta-learning in a fully supervised context, but this approach can be extended to an RL setting. Deep meta reinforcement learning *(Wang, J.X. et al., 2016)*, one of the possible solutions for the aforementioned tasks, includes the Two-Step Tasks Problem, which does not require huge training sets to develop a model and hence it is not as dependent on the past as other methods. This helps the model adapt to new tasks rapidly, leading to a robust RL agent.

The main goal of RL is to find a sequence of steps in a sequential decision problem that can obtain a maximum cumulative reward. QL is one of the most popular algorithms to achieve this goal, but QL with Deep Neural Networks often suffers from overestimations. *Double Q-Learning Algorithm (Van Hasselt, H., Guez, A. and Silver, D., 2016)* solves this to a great extent. Two value functions are learned by assigning each experience randomly to update one of the two value functions, such that there are two sets of weights. Such Deep Q Networks (DQN) are possible solutions to reduce overestimations in RL implementations of games such as *Chowka Bhara*. Due to the inherent similarities in the rules and strategies of Ludo with those of *Chowka Bhara*, concepts of Q-learning and TD-based players *(Alhajry, M., Alvi, F. and Ahmed, M., 2012)* can be closely followed in implementing the latter. TD-based players choose the next step by considering the value functions of each state, whereas Q-Learning-based players use action-value quality pairs to choose the next step from the given/current step. Each position is assigned by a real number normalized by taking an average of 4; this number indicates the number of players in that particular position.

3. RULES AND STRATEGIES OF THE GAME

Chowka Bhara is a two to four-player 5x5 board game similar to *Ludo*. Players take turns in throwing the shells with possible outcomes being 1, 2, 3, 4 and 8 with probabilities {0.243, 0.381, 0.236, 0.074, 0.066} respectively *(Davoudian, P. and Nagabhushan, P., 2019)*. If all the four shells land inverted (equals 1), it is known as *chowka*, and if they all land 'as it is' it is termed as *bhara* (equals 0). The game begins with all pawns in the players' respective 'home' squares, as seen in Figure 1(b). The player whose all four pawns move to the center square the fastest wins the game. A player can enter the inner square only after tracing the entire outer ring and defeating at least one opponent's pawn. The players navigate their pawns in an anticlockwise direction throughout the game.

Strategies in the game of *Chowka Bhara* determine which pawn should be moved next. To increase the winning probabilities of a player, various strategies can be adopted. Such strategies include fast, random, and balanced players. The fast player is a Strategic player that, given the outcome of a throw, chooses the pawn that is farthest from the starting box of the player and closest to the innermost square, given that the pawn has at least one remaining legal move. This player chooses one pawn to move and chooses it until it has reached the goal state resembling the depth-first search. The random player is a Strategic player that, given the outcome of a throw, randomly chooses one among the four pawns to move with a probability of 0.25. All the pawns of a player have equal probabilities (0.25) of being chosen. In a scenario where two pawns have reached the innermost square, one among the other two remaining pawns is chosen with a probability of 0.5 each. The balanced player is a Strategic player who chooses the pawns to move according to the breadth-first search strategy given the outcome of a throw.

4. PROPOSED Q-LEARNING PLAYER

4.1 Q-Learning Player

Q-Learning is a model-free, off-policy algorithm that aims to learn those policies that will lead to the highest cumulative reward. Rather than using greedy techniques to estimate the value function, Q-Learning is value-based and updates the value function using mathematical equations like the Bellman equation given below, where s is the current state, s' is the state after taking action a and, γ is the discount factor:

$$V(s) = max_a(R(s,a) + \gamma \sum_{s'} P(s,a,s')V(s')) \quad (1)$$

4.1.1 State Representation

Chowka Bhara uses a 5x5 board, i.e., there are 25 different squares on the board. There can be up to 4 pawns per player on each square. To reduce the computation time and make the agent's training simpler, raw representations of the states are chosen. Each square on the board is marked as a real number indicating the pawns on the given square. Further, which player's turn is also recorded, and two unary inputs are added for this. Since there are two players, the total number of states will be (25*2) + 2 = 52 states.

4.1.2 Rewards

The rewards designed to maximize the winning rate of the RL agent are as follows: -1 for moving to a non-safe square, +1 for moving to a safe square, +5 for capturing an opponent pawn, -5 for getting a pawn captured, +10 for getting one pawn to the innermost square, +100 for winning the game, i.e., getting all four pawns to the innermost square and, -100 for losing the game. The positive rewards encourage the agent to perform those actions, whereas the negative rewards penalize the agent.

4.2 Experimental Design

The QL Player is made to play against each Strategic Player viz. Random Player, Fast Player, and Balanced Player, and the performance of the players are evaluated. The players are trained for 10,000 episodes, each using a twenty hidden-layer neural network. A predominant problem in RL is the exploration-exploitation dilemma. To balance exploration and exploitation, the Epsilon-Greedy algorithm is used, taking the value of Epsilon as 0.9. This method randomly chooses either exploration or exploitation and ensures that the exploration-exploitation problem is taken care of.

5. RESULTS

To test the working of the Q-Learning (QL) Player, each of the Strategic Players - Fast Player, Random Player, and Balanced Player - are made to play against the QL Player. As seen in Figure 2, when trained using 10,000 games, the QL Player outperforms all three Strategic Players. The QL Player's winning percentage against the

Random Player, Fast Player, and Balanced Player is observed to be 88.01%, 72.64%, and 70.77% respectively. Figure 3(a) compares the winning percentages of each Strategic Player against the QL Player. The number of games the players are trained using starts at 1,000 games and increases in increments of 1,000 up to 10,000 games each. It is observed that the Balanced Player has the highest winning rate, closely followed by the Fast Player.

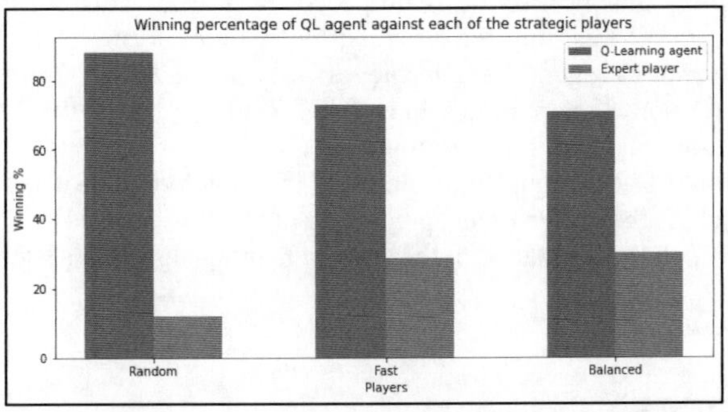

Figure 2. Winning percentage of QL Player and each Strategic Player against each other

As seen in Figure 3(b), it is observed that when the players are trained using a sufficient number of games (greater than 4,000 training games), the QL Player performs and, if not outperforms, the Fast Player. As seen in Figure 3(c), it is observed that QL Player consistently outperforms the Random Player irrespective of the number of training games. As seen in Figure 3(d), it is observed that when the players are trained using a sufficient number of games (greater than 5,000 training games), the QL Player gradually outperforms the Balanced Player.

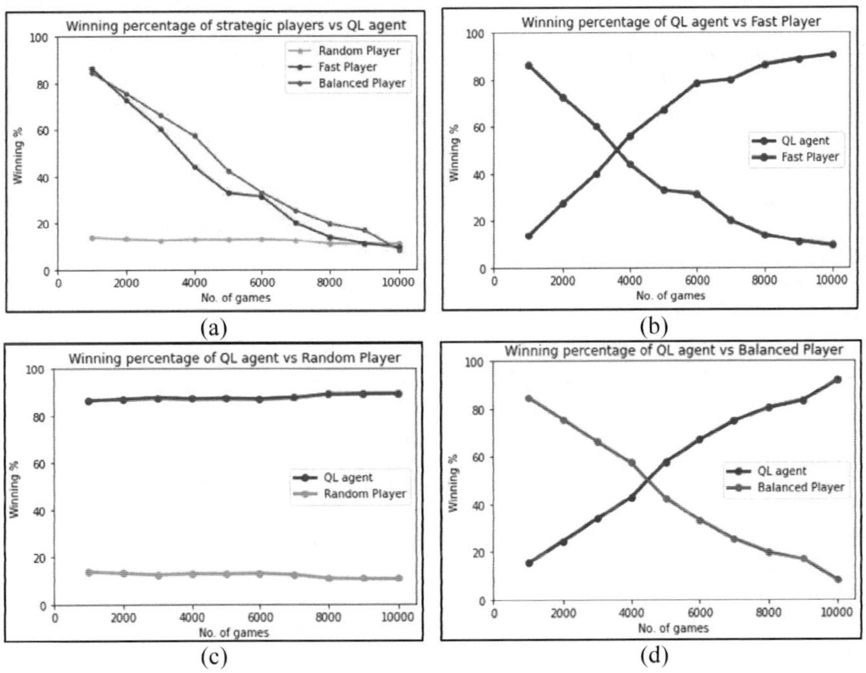

Figure 3. Winning percentages of (a) each Strategic Player against the QL Player; (b) QL Player against the Fast Player; (c) QL Player against the Random Player; (d) QL Player against the Balanced Player

6. CONCLUSION AND FUTURE WORK

The work focuses on three Strategic Players viz. Random Player, Fast Player, and Balanced Player for the traditional Indian game *Chowka Bhara*. Further, a Q-Learning Player based on the methodologies and strategies of the developed Strategic Players is proposed. It is observed from the experimental results that, when trained sufficiently, the Q-Learning Player consistently outperforms each of the three Strategic Players. Our objective of designing an RL agent that can successfully play *Chowka Bhara* can be significant in future implementations of many more Indian games like Indian Ludo. It can solve problems involving stochastic components and decision-making under uncertainty.

This work explores only Q-Learning algorithms for the development of the RL agent. However, future scope of this work can include the design of an agent using algorithms such as the Temporal Difference Lambda (TD-λ). Further, to enhance the performance of the agent, planning algorithms such as Monte Carlo Tree Search can be employed.

ACKNOWLEDGEMENT

This research was supported and funded by the M.S. Ramaiah Institute of Technology (RIT) Alumni Association. The authors would like to thank RIT for providing the facilities and means to enable the research.

REFERENCES

Alhajry, M., Alvi, F. and Ahmed, M., 2012, September. TD (λ) and Q-learning based Ludo players. In *2012 IEEE Conference on Computational Intelligence and Games (CIG)* (pp. 83-90). IEEE.

Arulkumaran, K., Deisenroth, M.P., Brundage, M. and Bharath, A.A., 2017. A brief survey of deep reinforcement learning. *arXiv preprint arXiv:1708.05866*.

Block, M., Bader, M., Tapia, E., Ramírez, M., Gunnarsson, K., Cuevas, E., Zaldivar, D. and Rojas, R., 2008. Using reinforcement learning in chess engines. *Research in Computing Science*, *35*, pp.31-40.

Davoudian, P. and Nagabhushan, P., 2019. Machine as One Player in Indian Cowry Board Game: Advanced Playing Strategies. *International Journal of Computer Engineering and Technology*, *10*(2).

Dedieu, A. and Amar, J., 2017. Deep reinforcement learning for 2048. In *Conference on Neural Information Processing Systems (NIPS), 31st, Long Beach, CA, USA*.

Lample, G. and Chaplot, D.S., 2017, February. Playing FPS games with deep reinforcement learning. In *Thirty-First AAAI Conference on Artificial Intelligence*.

Live History India. 2021. Ludo's Indian Roots. [online] Available at: <https://www.livehistoryindia.com/story/forgotten-treasures/ludos-indian-roots/> [Accessed 19 June 2021].

Mnih, V., Kavukcuoglu, K., Silver, D., Graves, A., Antonoglou, I., Wierstra, D. and Riedmiller, M., 2013. Playing Atari with deep reinforcement learning. *arXiv preprint arXiv:1312.5602*.

Penn.museum. 2021. *Expedition Magazine - Penn Museum*. [online] Available at: <https://www.penn.museum/sites/expedition/the-indian-games-of-pachisi-chaupar-and-chausar> [Accessed 19 July 2021].

Roll the Dice. 2021. Chowka Bara builds energy, strategic thinking and family bonding. [online] Available at: <https://www.rollthedice.in/chowka-bara/> [Accessed 1 July 2021].Yildirim, S. and Stene, S.B., 2010. *A survey on the need and use of AI in game agents*. InTech.

Shao, K., Tang, Z., Zhu, Y., Li, N. and Zhao, D., 2019. A survey of deep reinforcement learning in video games. *arXiv preprint arXiv:1912.10944*.

Sutton, R.S. and Barto, A.G., 2018. *Reinforcement learning: An introduction*. MIT press.

Van Hasselt, H., Guez, A. and Silver, D., 2016, March. Deep reinforcement learning with double q-learning. In *Proceedings of the AAAI conference on artificial intelligence* (Vol. 30, No. 1).

Wang, J.X., Kurth-Nelson, Z., Tirumala, D., Soyer, H., Leibo, J.Z., Munos, R., Blundell, C., Kumaran, D. and Botvinick, M., 2016. Learning to reinforcement learn. *arXiv preprint arXiv:1611.05763*.

Watkins, C.J. and Dayan, P., 1992. Q-learning. *Machine learning*, *8*(3), pp.279-292.

Yildirim, S. and Stene, S.B., 2010. *A survey on the need and use of AI in game agents*. InTech.

FLOW, ITS STRANDS AND MICROFLOW IN THE GAME DESIGN OF HORROR GAMES

Reinaldo Augusto de Oliveira Ramos[1] and Rafael Diogo Rossetti[2]
PUC – SP, Brazil
[1]Prof. Dr.
[2]Prof. Msc.

ABSTRACT

First of all, in the mission of looking for answers about how engage the player during the game we found some theories, how flow, Dynamic Difficult Adjustment and some tips how make a great game, but it is normal understand that some gaps appears when the developers must be some decisions, this difficult increase during the tests and blind the developers in time-life of development, making a hard task understood in all of perspectives which will be the behavior of the player. The micro-flow comes up to help understand this and make good decisions about game design.

KEYWORDS

Flow, Game Design, Game, Development, Design, Horror Game

1. INTRODUCTION

MicroFlow is the last tool to help others developers make great decisions to create a good game design. To explain how it is possible, was studied in details the most important theories about flow and engagement of the player in horror games.

2. MICRO-FLOW

In this study, it will be observed and evidenced the existence of the concept of Micro-Flow in Flow state, in order to validate the hypothesis that this concept, in fact, corroborate to keep the player engaged in involvement in the games.

It is known that during the game development process one of the main concerns is to ensure that the player stays immersed in the game and enjoys it as long as it is possible, as fun is subjective, that is, we sought a methodology to identify the factors that concatenate these, desires, behavior and the intensity of the relationships between the player and the game, this theory was called "Flow".

According to CSÍKSZENTMIHÁILYI, (1990) the feelings that a long-distance swimmer felt when crossing the channel was very close to that of a chess player during a tournament or a climber when faced a difficult part of his journey, that's because the reasons why they had fun or felt good was very similar, especially when we sought to understand the "how" it was to do certain activity. This is because the pleasure generated by that activity was extremely satisfactory and pleasant for the individual, thus favoring the experience.

In that way, with the continuous development of the study, it was understood that engagement was more likely to happen when a particular activity required somehow a need for skill on the part of those who would perform in this can be easily perceived when observing sports, deep down the competition is because the opponent's ability can sometimes prove more efficient than that of his team, requiring more effort to overcome that challenge. However, if comparing a game between unbalanced teams, what was supposed to be something engaging becomes frustrating, in other words, there are other premises that must exist to increase the chance of generating engagement for both players. One of the premises is pertinent to the goal, goal and rule, they must be as clear as possible, so that the participant, performer or player, perfectly understands what must be done, how it must be done and why, creating in the individual's mind a relation between challenge and ability.

Allied to this, there are facts that collaborate with the possibility of engaging, one of the main factors is what the author called the possibility of being the "Direct Feedback", which means that when the individual has constant answers about the activity that they are doing serves to assist them in understanding whether it is closer or further away from its goal, thus enhancing its own engagement.

According to the author, when engagement is reached, a mental state is created that promotes the loss of self-consciousness, the individual the individual is so immersed in the activity that he loses the notion of one and what is around him, in this way the "fluidity' of his actions becomes spontaneous and natural, that can be easily observed in professional dancers that in the apex of their presentation move as they were a part of the dance, or even dance itself, merging with the activity and perceiving only the pleasure and well-being of performing that activity. And it is from this reasoning that comes the term ***"flow".***

It can also be seen, analogously, in the game Silent Hill PT in which looping provides the players with the feeling of progress and even corroborates the generation of psychic tension since they feel stuck at the same time goes on.

Finally, as one of the man results of this, one perceives the transformation of time, the author describes as if the clock did not measure time during the activities thar generate the flow. That can be easily understood when comparing two situations, one of pain and other of pleasure, if both last for the same amount of time the perception will be changed. Therefore, a minute of pain can seem to last an eternity that won't ever end, one minute of pleasure generates short-lived perception and the feeling that remains is that it occurred very quickly.

FERRARA, (2012) also talks about this method and concept, further deepening in his gaming job, according to the author, the flow can be established when the plays dominate the interface and their attention is only on the challenges presented on the game, these challenges cannot be so hard to overcome that they become frustrating, but cannot be easy enough to be boring.

In this way, one can understand the graphs **Structure of Flow** elaborated by CSÍKSENTMIHÁLYI, validated by FERRARA and used to this day.

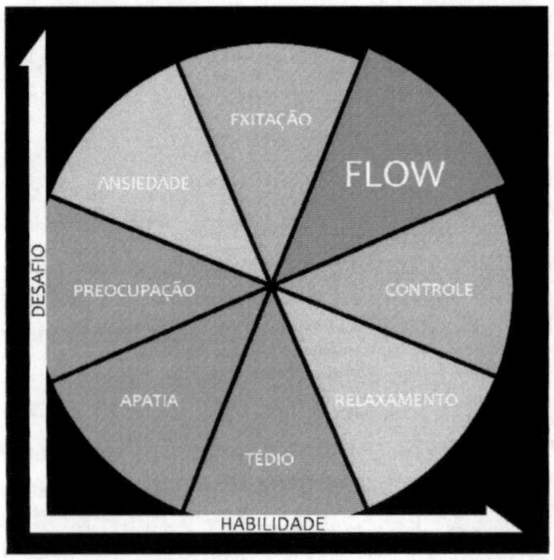

Figure 1. Structure of Flow. Source: Flow. The Psychology of Optimal Experience, 1990

This are the types of feeling that can be awakened in individuals in whatever task is to be performed, that is, according to the personal relationship between the challenge and the ability needed in each, different types of people might have different ways of relating to that determined activity.

Besides desired, the constant flow state is utopian and virtually impossible to be achieved a hundred percent of the time, what suggests us a closer relation of reality is something like the figure 2.

That is, although the goal of the game is to achieve the state of flow, it is prudent to understand that the player will approach sometimes the boredom and anxiety zone, having this feeling is important for the rescue mechanisms to be triggered, using in favor of the title, it is as if on purpose the game carried you between anxiety and boredom, therefore increasing the transition of state and enabling a longer experimentation time of it, these triggers can be considered of two types, Passive or Active.

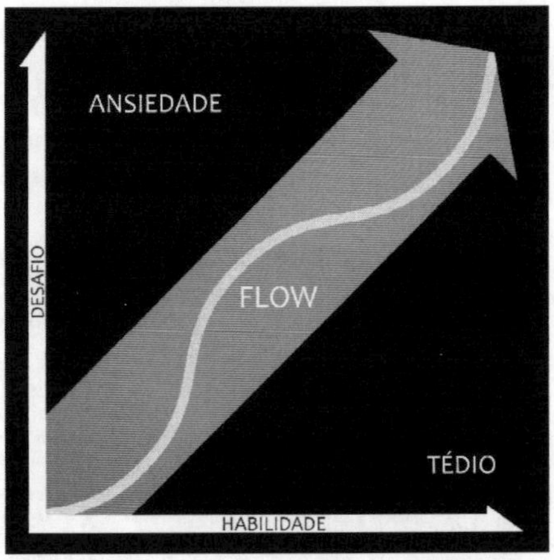

Figure 2. Understanding of Flow. Source: Flow. The Psychology of Optimal Experience, 1990

According to JENOVA, (2006) for the trigger to be understood in a passive way, the player's flow needs to have their actions monitored during the game, so that the player themself assists the game to provide the flow state. For that, the author describes de use of the method known as "**DDA**" or "**Dynamic Difficulty Adjustment**", in which the player generates data during the game play, the monitoring system collects their data, filters the data so that the transition occurs naturally, without fake understandings, generates de analysis of this results by evaluating player performance and sends new suggestions to the game's central system to adjust the challenge, both up and down.

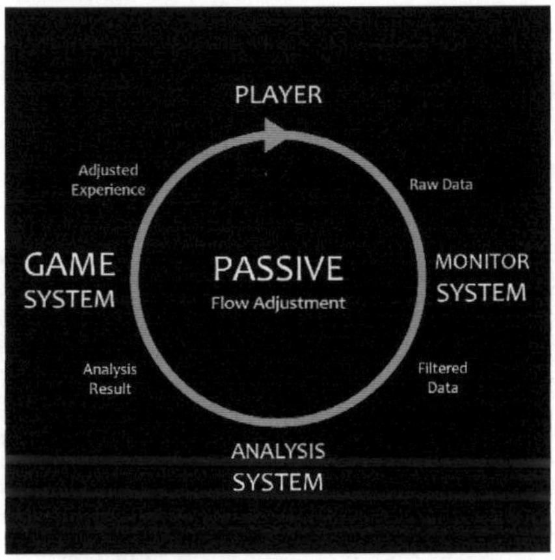

Figure 3. Dynamic Difficulty Adjustment. Source: Flow. The Psychology of Optimal Experience, 1990

This shape can regularly in online games that have a power-based character level and evolution system, such as those offered by franchises, The Elder Schools, Diablo, etc. allowing stronger opponents to introduced as the players strengthens and dominates all the functions the game provides.

This loop besides assisting in maintaining the plays in flow, allows these games to have a longer service life resembling the business models of services, in which the game never ends and allows developer updates so that larger challenges are created from player evolution.

Like passive triggers, the actives are equally important, the difference lies precisely in the way they are activated, because it will depend on the player's action. A simple example to understand these triggers is the adjust of difficulty of the challenge to be faced from de decision taken before de beginning of the game play. This moment can be considered important to begging to create the parameters needed for the flow to be generated, it can be simplistic or already seek the beginning of the relationship with the player in order to demonstrate what can be expected.

One of the percussors that exemplifies and already allows of this communication format is the game DOOM of the 90's that instead of the known format "Easy, Medium and Hard" presented the following five modes - "I am too young to die / Hey, not so violent / Hurt me a lot / Ultra-Violent / Nightmare!"

This type of choice allows the players to have an idea of what they might face in the way and already starts to create expectations that when full field, will turn into enthusiasm and consequently provide the state of the flow gradually with the **Self-Adjustment of Flow**.

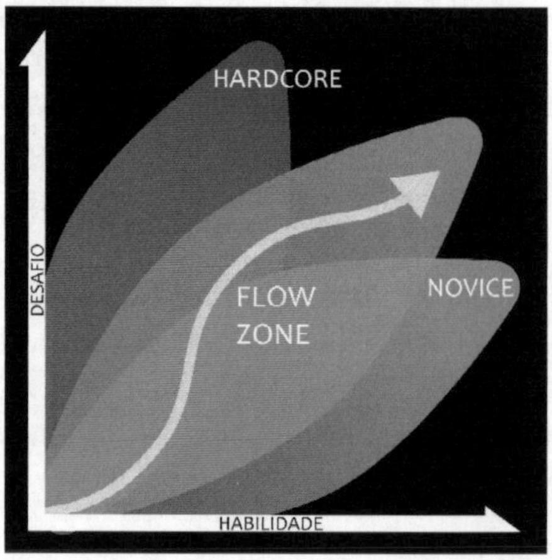

Figure 4. Self-Adjustment of Flow. Source: Flow. The Psychology of Optimal Experience, 1990

This adjustment proves to be important as different players have different skill levels, even sharing factors that determinates them as target audience, in this way, the active adjustment of difficulty guarantees the bigger capillarity so that different players have in different ways a pleasant gameplay that matches their expectation of given challenge and required ability, allowing different flows.

According to the author, there is more than one capable way of keeping the player on flow and he describes this format as it was a tree of decision in which multiple times during the gameplay the plays is questions and placed to make decisions that alter the flow of the game, allowing experimentation by the player.

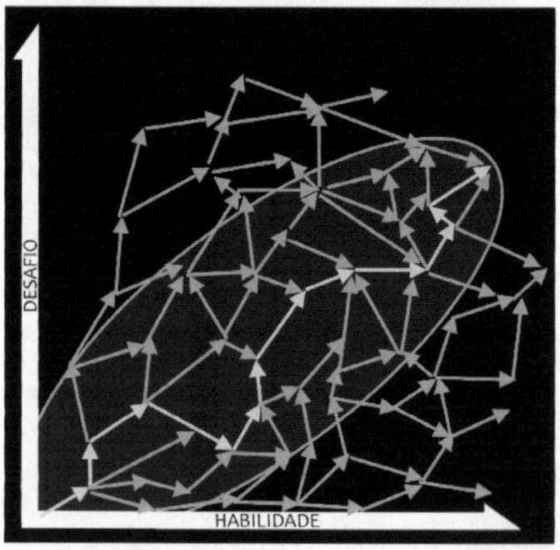

Figure 5. Tree of decision. Source: Flow. The Psychology of Optimal Experience, 1990

A good example that illustrates this type of questioning to the players is the mode used by the horror game "Until Dawn" of 2015, during the gameplay the player has to make decisions multiple times, some of the consequences strongly related to the game ending, others note so much but enable differentiated experiences during the advancement of the gameplay.

Right at the beginning, the players have a preview of how their relationship with the game will be like and must choose dropping the sister off a cliff and saving himself or dying along with her in the fall. Following this way, sometimes with decisions that put ethics in check, sometimes asking the question of survival, "Until Dawn" still makes adjustments to the phobias each particular player has.

Watching all these titles and several others that were critical success, it can be seen that there is something more, a few concepts used by the evidenced authors to describe flow, the adjustments of difficulty and its distinctions between passive and active triggers does not comprehend all aspects of current games and sometimes get mistaken, even, Mihaly Csikszentmihalyi himself says is possible to keep the flow during the whole time, especially for longer actions.

Some things happen to zoom in or out the player, reader or any other that is making a function of themself. Therefore, it comes the concept that here will be presented as micro-flow, those little moments, details, events that force people, more precisely the player for being our focus, back to the Flow state.

Imagine the situation in which you find yourself in front of a puzzle, you are really enjoying the game, but, you do not know what to do there, the feeling that before was of **excitement becomes frustration**, if we observe the excitement and engagement, we would have something similar to this:

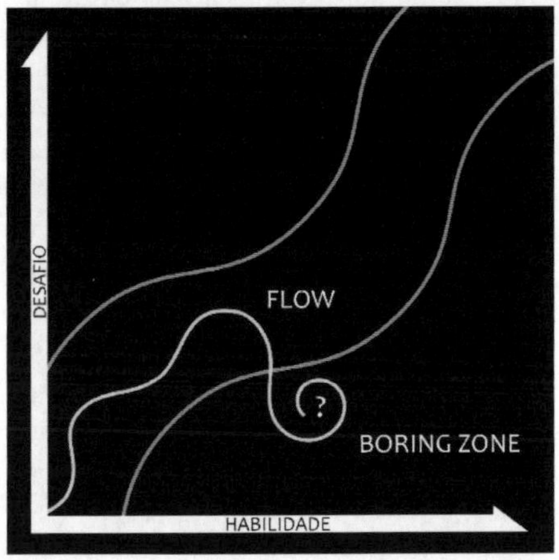

Figure 6. Excitement Becomes Frustration. Source: Flow. The Psychology of Optimal Experience, 1990

When the player gets lost and does not know what to do and it's about to give up, that the developers must think on the micro-flow, that is, factors that allow the player to go back to the flow.

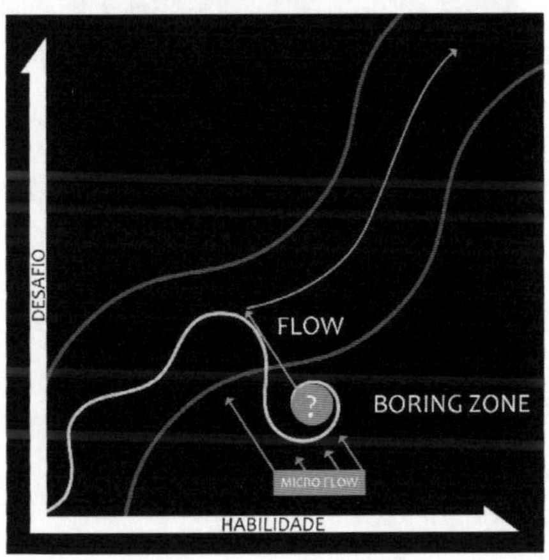

Figure 7. Micro-Flow Act. Source: Flow. The Psychology of Optimal Experience, 1990

For that we must think in some factors to develop the best ways to apply the Micro-Flow:

- What are the moments that might generate an abrupt redirection on the player's flow, such as for the anxiety zone as the boredom zone?

That because the use of micro-flow must be done with parsimony, so that the challenging feature of the game is still there.

- The bigger the time that the player can try this redirection without they in fact give up (after the player tries the micro-flow, the tendency is that they widen the bands that act as a boundary between the boredom and anxiety zone).
- How to fit the micro-flow in the narrative so that the player understands the context without the need of an explanation of that.

Let's imagine a classic situation in horror games- The player needs to find a key in the room they are at, in which the door closed itself, it has been a while and they cannot find where the key is hidden- The developers could think of something like- "If the plays cannot find the key in an determinate amount of time, the item starts to shine"- This thought, in fact, would corroborate for items 1 and 2 of the micro-flow considerations, but not for number 3, unless there was some justification for it to shine. In this way, a suggestion to solve this problem would be- "If the player cannot find the key in a determinate amount of time, the clock on the wall starts to make noise, like it possessed by an evil spirit, calling attention to the clock the player will see the key hidden there". Well, the game is horror and the suspense about the supernatural has already been made (or should have been) when the player sees that, they won't lose the subconscious immersion and starts to understand that they will never get stuck with not knowing what to do, generating a kind of **Barrier of Micro-Flow**, providing more empathy with the game.

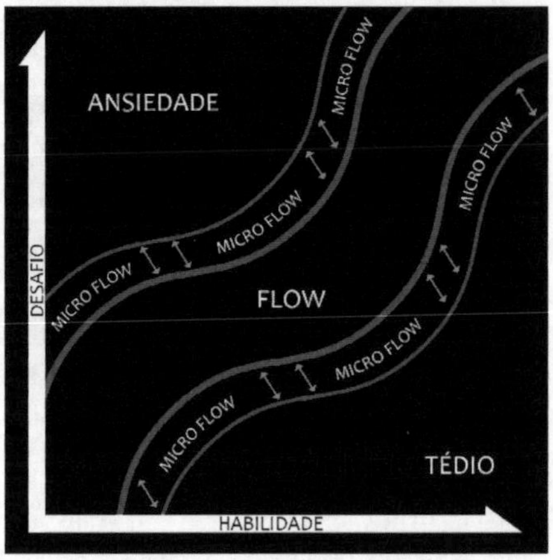

Figure 8. Barrier of Micro-Flow. Source: Flow. The Psychology of Optimal Experience, 1990

In this way, it can be understood that the micro-flow has as goal to be like a barrier, in order for the player to have more difficulty getting out of this psychological state that helps a game to succeed and win over many fans.

3. CONCLUSION

As we have seen, the micro-flow completes all understanding about game design decisions, became the last toll that provide in details an assistance to professionals in game design develop games that engagement target audience.

REFERENCES

Csíkszentmihályi, M. (1990). *Flow: The Psychology of Optimal Experience,* Harper and Row. NY

Ferrara, J. (2012). *Playful Design: Creating Game Experiences in Everyday Interfaces*, Louis Rosenfeld. Michigan.

Jenova, C. (2006). Implement Flow in Games – Dynamic Difficult Adjustment, San Francisco – GDC (Game Development Conference).

REFLECTION PAPERS

THE LUDIC SPECTACLE AND MEDIATIZED PARTICIPATION IN ESPORTS: POLAND AND HONG KONG

Mateusz Felczak
SWPS University of Social Sciences and Humanities, Chodakowska 19/31, 03-815 Warsaw, Poland

ABSTRACT

This study, conducted from February 2020 to February 2022, applies constructivist grounded theory approach to the data gathered during participant observation and ethnographical research connected with electronic sports in Poland and Hong Kong. The research involved looking at the data on selected Twitch channels as well as social media communication of leading eSports brands and incentives (including Talon Esports in Hong Kong and ESL Gaming in Poland). The overarching aim of the study was to compare the divergent dynamics of eSports cultures in various digital media ecosystems. Key contributions of this paper to eSports-oriented game studies involve the application of comparative approach and focus on the interconnectedness of fans' digital labor with the physical and digital spaces dedicated to electronic sports.

KEYWORDS

Electronic Sports, Poland, Hong Kong, Fan Culture, Identity, Grounded Theory, Streaming, Participation, Business

1. METHODS AND RATIONALE EMPLOYED IN THE STUDY

Electronic sports, or eSports, can be defined as "a form of sports where the primary aspects of the sport are facilitated by electronic systems; the input of players and teams as well as the output of the eSports system are mediated by human-computer interfaces" (Hamari & Sjöblom, 2017, 213).

The rationale behind the juxtaposition of the Repblic of Poland (later as Poland) and the Hong Kong Special Administrative Region of the People's Republic of China (later as Hong Kong) reads as follows: 1) similar chronology of the development in terms of eSports culture 2) the comparable video games market penetration and cultural impact of the eSports phenomenon 3) the same predominant live streaming platforms used in both regions for the live coverage of eSports events (especially Twitch).

The project implements grounded theory (Glaser & Strauss, 1967) as a methodological scaffolding. Grounded theory is considered one of the most thoroughly elaborated qualitative research methods and it allows to formulate and verify hypothesis on the basis of systematically gathered empirical data. It is flexible and sensitive to changes in the investigated phenomena, which makes it suitable for the analysis of the rapidly evolving eSports media landscape. As the grounded theory approach affords generating theory from data, the process involves the open coding phase (collecting the raw data and breaking it down into segments) and, subsequently, axial coding (to map different categories and the relations between them) and finally selective coding (Strauss & Corbin, 1998). The methods used in this paper rely on the constructivist approach to grounded theory (Charmaz, 2006; Mills, Bonner, & Francis, 2006), to take into account the personal involvement of the researcher and their idiosyncratic approach to the topic as a gamer and as an academic. In the field of game studies, grounded theory methods have already found some success in the analysis of online streaming media (Anderson, 2017).The three key subsections of this paper are a result of a preliminary coding phase and subsequent saturation of ideas and concepts.

This research considers two aspects of eSports: ludic spectacle and mediated participation. The first one involves an analysis of publicly available eSports events, such as tournaments and competitions of international rank. The goal of this part of the project is to describe, analyze and interpret the issues connected with ludic and social aspects of large eSports events, focusing especially on online/offline interplay, institutional factors, and identity issues pertaining fans and players alike. The mediated participation, that is the live-streamed broadcast via Twitch, YouTube gaming and other digital platforms. The examples of investigated largescale eSports events include Intel Extreme Masters in Poland and the largest Asian eSports Mong Kok hub, located in Hong Kong.

2. THE OFFLINE AND THE ONLINE EXPERIENCE

Due to the COVID-19 pandemic, the vast majority of scheduled live large-scale eSports events have either been postponed, moved online or forced to commence without the presence of the audience. An interesting example of this last instance concerned the 2020's IEM tournament in Katowice, in Poland, where organizers issued a last-minute statement denying anyone but the competing players and the necessary broadcasting crew members to enter the Spodek arena. Electronic Sports League (ESL) Vice President of Pro Gaming, Michał Blicharz, issued an emotional public statement addressed to the fans who bought tickets for the event and were expecting to personally attend the tournament. Broadcasting of the tournament without the audience revealed previously unexplored interconnections between the online and offline dimensions of the eSports spectacle. The special circumstances affected especially players' presentations and other elements of corporeal presence; the subsequent, pandemic editions of major eSports tournaments started experimenting with replacing players with their hologram avatars and moving the whole studio to the realms of a digital simulation, with mixed effects. The associated technical difficulties resulted in hosts and commentators and shoutcasters engaging in a more laid-back, humorous conversations, openly acknowledging their uncanny predicament.

Poland and Hong Kong curiously share quite similar, historical associations between the emerging eSports culture and a specific type of *internet cafés* – places where people can play video games, socialize and engage in activities which go beyond the eponymic usage of the Internet and coffee drinking. Such establishments are best known in their South Korean manifestation, the *PC bang*, but the Polish and Hong Kong iterations have much in common. As noted by Jun-Sok Huhh, "the pricing policy of PC bangs encouraged their visitors to play longer; the more you stayed on, the lower the hourly charge", which was the case in many Polish *internet cafés* [*kafejki internetowe*] (Huhh, 2008, 28). Significant cultural differences pertain food and drink policies. While Korean and Hong Kong establishments encouraged visitors to order and consume on site, Polish *cafés* were places almost exclusively devoted to one activity: gaming. According to Yaewon Jin and Veli-Matti Karhulahti, PC bangs have been a crucial factor in establishing a "ludic identity" of Korean gamers and are constantly evolving to provide a more diversified entertainment than just playing games with high levels of proficiency (Jin & Karhulahti, 2019).

The assessment of the CGA Esports Stadium in Mong Kok, in Hong Kong, a space designed to host professional eSports events and a multi-room *internet café*, offers an additional insight on the parallels and differences between eSports cultures in Poland and Hong Kong. Sporting a VR Zone as well as a Mobile Game Zone, CGA broadens the scope of eSports-related experiences including gaming activities rarely, if ever, seen during professional, sponsored events. Whereas Poland has its share in establishing and curating non-mainstream entries in the eSports media landscape (see next section), the Hong Kong example positions this region as being more focused on advancing digital technologies to draw in new eSports audiences, whereas in Poland the focus would be on re-invigorating the already existing gaming fandoms to adapt to the media strategies pushed by companies involved in the electronic sports business.

To sum up, the ludic element of eSports events has its roots in such informal gatherings of gaming enthusiasts. The enduring popularity of *BarCrafts*, that is events organized in bars and other drinking parlors to collectively watch *StarCraft* tournaments, has been witnessed throughout the heydays of this Activision Blizzard's title and is yet another example of this phenomenon.

3. INSTITUTIONAL FACTORS

Electronic sports in Poland and Hong Kong share a significant degree of interest from the officials. Jiang & Fung propose the term 'neo-techno-nationalism' to describe China's policy towards gaming companies (Jiang & Fung, 2019); the key element of this governmental strategy is to help popularize a certain, local product while leaving it susceptible to censorship and/or alteration of its content. In the context of eSports titles, such strategy may be difficult to execute, as developing or appropriating an electronic sport requires a significant degree of investment in terms of finances and intellectual property. China's recent regulations regarding the age of players and time spent on gaming impose an additional level of difficulty in creating a prospective environment for aspiring e-athletes. In the official, government-funded *Report on Promotion of E-sports Development in Hong Kong* it has been noted that

"a significant difference between e-sports and traditional sports is that in esports, the platform for the e-sports activity is proprietary. In e-sports, the company owning the intellectual property rights to the game can charge fees, or change the rule of the game anytime they like. E-sports operates with proprietary tools, and the Intellectual Property ("IP") owners have the right to alter the terms of play and impose royalty anytime they like."(CityU, 2020)

Understanding the importance of this remark is crucial to the future of eSports-related initiatives on any level. In Poland, with the gaming culture in its nascent years shaped by sharing the devices, PCs, and consoles among multiple players in social situations (Sitarski, Garda, Jajko, & Kirkpatrick, 2021), competitive titles employing the "hot seat" mode of play were preferred to the games (IPs) which required an impeccable Internet connection and were demanding in terms of required software and hardware. An example of the longevity of a title which in other regions is hardly recognized as an eSport-worthy game is *Heroes of Might and Magic III* (New World Computing 1999). This turn-based strategy game has a cult following in Poland and Eastern Europe, with the "world championship" level eSports tournament effectively being a rivalry between the top local players, despite the presence of competitors from other continents. The involvement of business partners of the event, Nvidia and Predator, suggests a level of professionalism extending beyond the fan-made one-off event; production values also embraced the visual conventions adopted from high-budget events hosted on Twitch (Perkowski, 2022). One of the findings of the study suggests that older games (IPs) are better suited to "organic", bottom-up nature of the eSports culture(s), with the caveat that they trade off the mass popularity for predictability and a relatively low entry point.

Among institutional, top-down factors influencing eSports future development are business-oriented conferences, featuring the latest trends and giving an insight into the industry's plans for the future. The most interesting – and telling – events that were part of the DELF2021 conference hosted in the Cyberport, in Hong Kong, were the Elderly Esports Experience Day and the Harry Potter: Magic Awakened tournament. These two events were accompanied by the FIFA tournament, a more traditional eSports game compared to the gaming iteration of the JK Rowling's franchise[1]. The increased interest in divergent age categories of gamers has two potential consequences. Firstly, it may be a sign of industry looking beyond the PC and major consoles as platforms for eSports titles, to pre-eminently counterbalance the market saturation. Secondly, it could be considered a step forward towards greater inclusivity, along other initiatives aiming at making electronic sports more appealing to the wider audience (Taylor, 2012) and contesting the culture of competing in video games as a never-ending festival of ruthless, cut-throat competition (Paul, 2018).

4. DISCOURSES OF IDENTITY AND COMPETITIVENESS

Identifying with a particular geographical region and being included as a part of sponsored team or organization are crucial, yet rarely explored factors in achieving success in eSports.

In the *StarCraft* section of the IEM Katowice 2022 tournament, players from Hong Kong (Gogojoey and Bistork) are attributed to the 'Taiwan' region, which defines against which players their achievements are being assessed. While eSports spectacles have previously been identified as vehicles for constructing the notion of national identity and pride (Szablewicz, 2015), relatively little attention has been devoted to the influence of the divergent gaming cultures in this area. Findings of this paper in that regard highlight the connection between the long-term, historical popularity of a particular genre and the opportunities of development for aspiring eSports players engaging with a particular title. For example, even though Polish *Counter-Strike* teams have not achieved any significant victories in the period of this study, this title still offers the most in terms of the number of teams recruiting new players, number of (local) tournaments and the sponsorship money. From 2006 to 2014 an all-Polish team assigned under a Russian organization Virtus.pro scored multiple World Cup

[1] https://delf.cyberport.hk/en/agenda

medals, and some of the team members have later become important eSports media personalities, effectively animating the scene after their retirement from in-game competitions on the highest level. This raises questions of the importance of national (self) attribution in electronic Sports, a potentially contentious and complicated issue which may impact the chances of players. The volatile rules of electronic sports are susceptible to impromptu, judicial interpretations, where ethical concerns may come into play (Chee & Karhulahti, 2020). In some eSports titles, there is an imbalance: players from one country are overrepresented and dominate over the more macro-defined 'region'. Historically, this was the case of players from South Korea, a homeland of competitive gaming, albeit recently this trend has shifted towards higher numbers of players from countries with a high-level infrastructure and gaming cultures that are susceptible to nurturing a competitive edge.

5. FURTHER DEVELOPMENT

The next steps in the study involve disentangling the differences between various types of the *internet cafés* and their connection with the eSports business. A time-sensitive mapping of the social media activities of the eSports business representatives is to be juxtaposed with the digital and non-digital activities of selected eSports fandoms.

REFERENCES

Anderson, S. L. (2017). Watching People Is Not a Game: Interactive Online Corporeality, Twitch.tv and Videogame Streams. *Game Studies*, *17*(1). Retrieved from http://gamestudies.org/1701/articles/anderson

Charmaz, K. (2006). *Constructing Grounded Theory: A Practical Guide Through Qualitative Analysis*. London: SAGE Publications.

Chee, F. M., & Karhulahti, V. M. (2020). The ethical and political contours of institutional promotion in esports: From precariat models to sustainable practices. *Human Technology*, *16*(2), 200–226. https://doi.org/10.17011/ht/urn.202008245642

CityU. (2020). *Report on Promotion of E-sports Development in Hong Kong*. Retrieved from https://www.ogcio.gov.hk/en/news/publications/doc/EN_e-sports_report.pdf

Glaser, B., & Strauss, A. (1967). *The Discovery of Grounded Theory. Strategies for Qualitative Research*. Chicago: Aldine.

Hamari, J., & Sjöblom, M. (2017). What is eSports and why do people watch it? *Internet Research*, *27*(2), 211–232.

Huhh, J. S. (2008). Culture and business of PC bangs in Korea. *Games and Culture*, *3*(1), 26–37. https://doi.org/10.1177/1555412007309525

Jiang, Q., & Fung, A. Y. H. (2019). Games With a Continuum: Globalization, Regionalization, and the Nation-State in the Development of China's Online Game Industry. *Games and Culture*, *14*(7–8), 801–824. https://doi.org/10.1177/1555412017737636

Jin, Y., & Karhulahti, V.-M. (2019). Evolution of PC Bangs: Traditions and Trends in South Korea. In *Proceedings of DiGRA 2019*. Retrieved from http://www.digra.org/wp-content/uploads/digital-library/DiGRA_2019_paper_78.pdf

Mills, J., Bonner, A., & Francis, K. (2006). The Development of Constructivist Grounded Theory. *International Journal of Qualitative Methods*, *5*(1), 25–35. https://doi.org/https://doi.org/10.1177/160940690600500103

Paul, C. A. (2018). *The Toxic Meritocracy of Video Games. Why Gaming Culture Is the Worst*. Minneapolis: University of Minnesota Press.

Perkowski, M. (2022, January). Za nami pierwsze w historii Mistrzostwa Świata w Heroes of Might and Magic III. *Esportnow.Pl*. Retrieved from https://esportnow.pl/esport/za-nami-pierwsze-w-historii-mistrzostwa-swiata-w-heroes-of-might-and-magic-iii/

Sitarski, P., Garda, M. B., Jajko, K., & Kirkpatrick, G. (2021). *New Media Behind the Iron Curtain: Cultural History of Video, Microcomputers and Satellite Television in Communist Poland*. Kraków: Jagiellonian University Press.

Strauss, A., & Corbin, J. (1998). *Basics of qualitative research: grounded theory procedures and techniques* (2nd ed.). London: SAGE Publications.

Szablewicz, M. (2015). A realm of mere representation? "live" E-sports spectacles and the crafting of China's digital gaming image. *Games and Culture*, *11*(3), 265–274. https://doi.org/10.1177/1555412015595298

Taylor, T. L. (2012). *Raising the Stakes. E-sports and the Professionalization of Computer Gaming*. Mass.: The MIT Press.

WE NEED TO FOCUS ON RULES

Luiz Cláudio Silveira Duarte and Adriano Furtado Holanda
Universidade Federal do Paraná, Brazil

ABSTRACT

We take a hard look at game rules and the moral significance of rules agency, going back to a landmark study by Jean Piaget.

We approach the relationship between game rules and players from an interdisciplinary perspective. Since our focus lies in games, we purposely refer to "rules" throughout, even when "norms" would be a more precise term. As for the different functions of game rules, we follow David Parlett's terminology (Parlett, 2005).

Our main interest is the ethical aspect of game rules themselves. However, our approach straddles the magic circle boundary, especially concerning rules agency, both before and during the game. We submit that rules agency, by itself, has ethical significance, which transcends the game.

This is not a proposal for any course of action; on the contrary, it is a quite theoretical reflection, intended as a contribution to the growing field of ethics in games, and a call -- a challenge, if you will -- for further reflections and discussions.

KEYWORDS

Game Studies, Game Ethics, Game Rules, Rules Agency

1. GAMES AND RULES

There are very few characteristics that can be said to be common to all games, as many philosophers have discovered to their chagrin. Ludwig Wittgenstein famously used games as the ur-example of fuzzy concepts (Wittgenstein, 1953/1986, secs. 66–71); and his contention still rings true, notwithstanding even kicks below the belt (Hurka, 1978/2005, p. 11).

Perhaps the one characteristic shared by all games is that they have rules. This, by itself, does not help to circumscribe and define games, as rules are intrinsic to several other fields of human interest. Indeed, rules helped Huizinga identify the play-element in other cultural activities: the magic circle itself is the locus in which the rules of the game not only exist but take precedence over the rules of the outside world (Huizinga, 1938/1980, p. 10).

Rules are an effective tool. The Latin word regula is the origin for both "rule" and "regular"; as a species, since time immemorial we have been creating rules for ourselves and looking for regularities in the world around us. *Homo sapiens* are also *Homo regulans*, those who create rules. Most human social activities are organized by rules and systems of rules (Burns et al., 2015).

In games, rules go beyond mere usefulness and become foundational elements. In a sense, a game *is* its rules (Schell, 2020, p. 189). Thus, it is worthwhile to examine rules a bit more closely, to better understand games. Fortunately, rules – or rather, norms – have already been the subject of choice for various thinkers, from fields such as Sociology, Law, or Ethics – and, naturally, Game Studies.

Johan Huizinga treated rules as fixed and absolute, and he supported this by quoting some words by Paul Valéry. Huizinga may have slightly misquoted Valéry; but the noted French poet was indeed castigating arbitrary and rigid rules which, in order to preserve the hallowed "classical art", worked to stifle creativity (Valéry, 2015, p. 35).

The operative characteristic, for Valéry, was arbitrary; but Huizinga did not mention it. It fell to another of the "Founding Fathers" of Game Studies, Roger Caillois, to identify arbitrariness as a characteristic of rules (Caillois, 1958/2001, p. 165). This should come as no surprise to game designers since much of their work is precisely to create and change rules. But "arbitrary" does not imply "haphazard"; indeed, the better the several rules in a game work together, the better the game – for its rules are now a system of rules, a normative system (Raz, 1975/2002, p. 113).

It would be tempting to think of the rules in a game as immutable, at least during actual play; both Huizinga and Caillois seem to think so, as do many others (Salen & Zimmerman, 2004, p. 122). But the world of games always manages to poke holes in certainties: in Peter Suber's *Nomic*, valid moves can not only change the rules but also create entirely new ones (Suber, 1990, appendix 3); and players in some "free-form" roleplaying games are quite at home with mutable rules.

Game rules may fulfill several functions (Parlett, 2005). The functions of rules in other normative systems may be different, but, in all cases, this has a direct impact on how rules are perceived, and on what expectations are created from them (Gibbs, 1965).

2. RULES AGENCY

All games control the agency of their players. But we must point out that there is players' agency over the rules themselves. In non-digital games, this agency includes learning, teaching, and enforcing the rules; but many digital games reduce the player's rules agency, often proudly presenting themselves as "intuitive".

However, there is one aspect of rules agency that may never be removed: the agency to decide to play, or not to play.

This agency has been considered a fundamental aspect of games. Both Huizing and Caillois saw games as voluntary activities (Huizinga, 1938/1980, p. 7; Caillois, 1958/2001, p. 6). There have been objections to this characterization – for instance, "if you are pressured by your friends into playing a game that you don't want to play, is it still a game?" (Salen & Zimmerman, 2004, p. 76). However, here we chose to deal only with games in which free will – the will to play – is a major component of players' agency.

The will to play is the same agency that Michel Foucault identified as the foundation of all power structures: "power is exercised only over free subjects, and only insofar as they are free" (Foucault, 1982/1983, p. 221). This is not a novel idea; it had already been wondered at by Étienne de la Boétie, in the XVIth century (De la Boétie, 1553/2002), and by David Hume, in the XVIIIth century (Hume, 1741/1994).

Any game can be understood as a power structure, in Foucault's sense (Sicart, 2009, Chapter 3), just as the modern state and several other cultural institutions. In his study, the French philosopher singled out two characteristics of the modern state: it is individualizing, and it is totalizing (Foucault, 1982/1983, p. 213). The two characteristics are shared by games.

In the modern state, totalization is exercised through "a very sophisticated structure, in which individuals can be integrated, under one condition: that this individuality would be shaped in a new form, and submitted to a set of very specific patterns" (Foucault, 1982/1983, p. 214). This description is perfectly adequate to games: it does not matter who the participants are outside of the game; inside the game, they are shaped in the new form of players, submitted to a set of very specific patterns, created by the game rules.

As for individualization: the foundational rules of a game create a dividing practice (Foucault, 1982/1983, p. 208), establishing some people as players – individuals –, and others as an undifferentiated mass of non-players. Generally, players have considerably more agency in the game than non-players. The players' agency is the exercise of power: certain actions by the players modify other actions and relations inside the game (Foucault, 1982/1983, p. 219) – effects which are determined by the operational rules of the game.

Both individualization and totalization are contingent on an act of free will. When someone decides to play a game, he is deciding to subject himself to the rules of that game – he is deciding to become a subject of that power structure, by this very act both becoming an individual in the game, and restricting his agency according to the rules of the game.

Furthermore, in the case of games, there is a very special aspect of this: the act of deciding to play creates the game. There is no game before it is created by some people agreeing to the proposal "let's play a game of…".

This holds true even when playing games with well-established rules – whether by their designers, their publishers, or their governing bodies. The rules agency of the now-players is the same, even if they decide to play by other than the "official" rules (house rules, variants, and so forth) – and also if they misremember a rule. Board game players like to joke that "there is no game police".

No rules exist by themselves; but more importantly, no rules can be self-implemented, or self-enforced. Law philosophers and practitioners often speak of "the will of the Law", or that "the Law enforces" something or other. But this is always a fig leaf under which we find voluntary acts by people in society (Hart, 1961/1994, p. 201).

The agency of subjection/creation of rules is the agency that no game can remove – both because it lies outside of the game, and because the existence of the game itself depends on it.

Players then, both create rules and subject themselves to the rules they created. What does that mean?

All rules are constraints. Even when a rule authorizes some action, it does so by constraining when and how that action may be performed. The foundational rules of a game create fundamental constraints: they define its limits, both in space and in time. The operational rules are constrained by the foundational rules and create further constraints of their own. This brings to mind Bernard Suits' formulation of games as "voluntary attempts to overcome unnecessary obstacles" (Suits, 1978/2005, p. 55). In other words, players voluntarily subject themselves to rules which constrain their agency.

The creation and subjection to rules is thus an act of self-restraint.

This is an act imbued with deep significance – the same significance which motivated Jean Piaget to use games as the starting point for his study on children's morality.

"All morality consists in a system of rules, and the essence of all morality is to be sought for in the respect which the individual acquires for these rules" (Piaget, 1932/1960, p. 1). Children are taught to respect the rules – and Piaget names this as a "supremely characteristic of human dignity" virtue (Piaget, 1932/1960, p. 2). More importantly, children are taught to create rules, enforce them – and change them.

The ability to change rules is not a trivial issue. When discussing her game *Train*, on the Holocaust, Brenda Romero asserted that "games are a good medium for approaching any subject, particularly difficult ones, because, by their very nature, they are abstract, invite interaction and allow us to confront and question things… particularly, rules that we may blindly follow" (Brophy-Warren, 2009).

Here we may look back on digital games and the purposeful reduction of rules agency. The fundamental rules agency – to play or not to play – may not be removed, but digital games often remove almost all other rules agency from their players. They do not create (or recreate) the rules, and they do not enforce the rules; occasionally, they can change some rules – by exploiting loopholes or even by design intent.

Perhaps Piaget would be appalled. Here are games that may be played with total disregard to rules because they are no longer relevant to the players. They cannot even disobey the rules; in such a game, the universe itself prevents any rule-breaking. They will not learn to create and to change rules. They will blindly follow whatever rules the universe enforces. In many digital games, there *is* a game police – an all-seeing, pervasive, uncompromising police.

In such games, players do not learn, or exercise, self-restraint – what Norbert Elias considered the foundation of civilization – the "constant restraint and foresight that they need for adult functions" (Elias, 1939/2000, p. 374).

3. FINAL THOUGHTS

Rule, after you have first learned to submit to rule.
– Solon of Athens

The ethical significance of rules is nothing new. Indeed, rules agency has already been used as a tool for investigating the ethical content of games, accepting that "games aren't an inert medium for conveying ideas but also a negotiated practice" (Koo & Seider, 2010).

However, previous investigations have mainly concerned themselves with the interaction between the meaningful content of games and their rules. Here, we submit that rules agency, by itself, has ethical significance, which transcends the game. Moreover, we assert that this subject deserves further attention and investigation.

We do not propose that all games are, or should be, moral teaching machines. Nonetheless, we contend that game designers ought to be aware of the ethical aspects of what they create – and they go well beyond content and gameplay.

REFERENCES

Brophy-Warren, J. (2009). The board game no one wants to play more than once. *The Wall Street Journal*. Retrieved from https://blogs.wsj.com/speakeasy/2009/06/24/can-you-make-a-board-game-about-the-holocaust-meet-train/

Burns, T. R. et al. (2015). The sociology of creativity, part I, Theory: The social mechanisms of innovation and creative developments in selectivity environments. *Human Systems Management*, *34*, 179–199. https://doi.org/10.3233/HSM-150839

Caillois, R. (2001). *Man, Play and Games*. (M. Barash, Trans.). Urbana: University of Illinois Press. (Original work published 1958)

de la Boétie, É. (2002). *The politics of obedience: The discourse of voluntary servitude*. (H. Kurz, Trans.). Montreal: Black Rose. (Original work published 1553).

Elias, N. (2000). *The civilizing process: Sociogenetic and psychogenetic investigations*. (E. Jephcott, Trans.). Malden: Blackwell. (Original work published 1939).

Foucault, M. (1983). The subject and power. In H. L. Dreyfus & P. Rabinow, *Michel Foucault: Beyond structuralism and hermeneutics* (2nd ed., pp. 208–226). The University of Chicago Press. (Original work published 1982).

Gibbs, J. P. (1965). Norms: The problem of definition and classification. *American Journal of Sociology*, *70*(5), 586–594.

Hart, H. L. A. (1994). *The concept of law* (2nd ed.). Oxford: Clarendon. (Original work published 1961).

Huizinga, J. (1980). *Homo ludens: A study of the play-element in culture*. London: Routledge. (Original work published 1938).

Hume, D. (1994). Of the first principles of government. In K. Haakonssen (Ed.), *David Hume: Political essays* (pp. 16–19). Cambridge (UK): Cambridge University Press. (Original work published 1741).

Hurka, T. (2005). Introduction. In B. Suits, *The grasshopper: Games, life and utopia* (pp. 7–20). Peterborough: Broadview. (Original work published 1978).

Koo, G., & Seider, S. (2010). Video games for prosocial learning. In K. Schrier & D. Gibson, *Ethics and game design: Teaching values through play* (pp. 16–34). Hershey: Information Science Reference.

Parlett, D. (2005). Rules OK. Retrieved March 14, 2022, from https://www.parlettgames.uk/gamester/rulesOK.html

Piaget, J. (1960). *The moral judgment of the child*. The Free Press. (Original work published 1932).

Raz, J. (2002). *Practical reason and norms*. Oxford: Oxford University Press. (Original work published 1975).

Salen, K., & Zimmerman, E. (2004). *Rules of play: Game design fundamentals*. Cambridge, MA: The MIT Press.

Schell, J. (2020). *The art of game design: A book of lenses* (3rd ed.). Boca Ratón: CRC Press.

Sicart, M. (2009). *The ethics of computer games*. Cambridge (MA): The MIT Press.

Suber, P. (1990). *The paradox of self-amendment: A study of law, logic, omnipotence, and change*. Bern: Peter Lang International Academic Publishers.

Suits, B. (2005). *The grasshopper: Games, life and utopia*. Peterborough: Broadview. (Original work published 1978).

Valéry, P. (2015). *Collected works of Paul Valéry, volume 11: occasions*. Princeton: Princeton University Press.

Wittgenstein, L. (1986). *Philosophical investigations*. (G. E. M. Anscombe, Trans.) (3rd ed.). Chichester: Blackwell. (Original work published 1953).

POSTERS

CO-EXPERIENCE AND DIGITAL INCENTIVES: UNDERSTANDING PURCHASE INTENTION IN THE P2E METAVERSE

Sujin Bae[1], Qiyuan Tang[2] and Ohbyung Kwon[3]
School of Management, Kyung Hee University, Kyung Hee Dae Ro 26, Dong Dae Mun Gu, Seoul 02447, Korea
[1]Research Professor
[2]Ph.D. Student
[3]Professor

ABSTRACT

The purpose of this study is to demonstrate the effects of co-experience and digital incentives, the main features of the Play to Earn (P2E)-type metaverse, on the successful operation of the metaverse. With consideration of the experience economy model, we propose a research model to elucidate participants' satisfaction, attitudes toward farming, and purchase intention for a P2E metaverse-type virtual farm. Analysis of data from questionnaires targeting real players confirmed the positive effects of co-experience and digital incentives on satisfaction and attitudes toward farming related to educational and entertainment experiences. We present theoretical and practical implications suggested by the results.

KEYWORDS

Virtual Farm, Avatar, Co-Experience, Experience Economy Theory, Satisfaction, Purchase Intention

1. INTRODUCTION

The use of virtual reality (VR) technology is increasing in various fields such as education (Hamilton et al., 2021), tourism (Tussyadiah et al., 2018), and exhibitions (Jin et al., 2021). Non-face-to-face situations such as those experienced frequently during the COVID-19 pandemic enable uninterrupted training by moving the real world to the virtual world (Albus et al., 2021). Virtual worlds are a type of metaverse created using VR technology that increase visitor satisfaction and allow users to experience things they might otherwise not be able to experience.

On a virtual farm, an avatar appears on behalf of the participant, providing enjoyment and learning-by-doing activities necessary to grow real crops, such as sowing, fertilizing, and watering (Karcher, 2018). Recently, the P2E (Play to Earn) farming experience has provided practical benefits to users, who can obtain real agricultural products depending on the outcome of their farming experience. A P2E-type virtual farm uses digital incentives and co-experience (Strokosch & Osborne, 2020) to increase user engagement and attitudinal change toward farming. However, no empirical studies have examined whether digital incentives and co-experience achieve the purposes of the developers of the P2E virtual farm.

The purpose of this study is to investigate the effects of digital incentives and co-experience on the satisfaction of users of virtual farms, their attitudes toward farming, and their purchase intention. In particular, this study examines whether the four types of experience identified in experience economy theory (Pine & Gilmore, 1999), education, entertainment, esthetic, and escape experience, play a mediating role between our two variables of interest, co-experience and digital incentives, and satisfaction with virtual farms and attitudes toward farming. This study has both academic and practical implications.

2. RESEARCH DESIGN

2.1 Virtual Farm as P2E Metaverse

P2E refers to a gaming or virtual experience in which experiencers can obtain economic benefits (Kaur & Gupta, 2021). P2E is different from the traditional P2W (Play to Win) gamification method (Stott & Neustaedter, 2013). In particular, as non-face-to-face culture is expanding due to the COVID-19 pandemic, the demand for farming experiences through VR is growing rapidly.

Virtual farms promote P2E-type services to increase the participation and satisfaction of experienced users. Typically, after a certain level of experience on a virtual farm has been obtained, real agricultural products are delivered to the home where the experiencer resides (e.g., 'Realfarm', as shown in Figure 1).

The most prominent features of P2E virtual farms are co-experience and digital incentives. Co-experience refers to "the user experience, which is created in social interaction" (Battarbee, 2003b, p. 1). Co-experience enriches learners' experience in an educational environment (Narayan, 2018) and enhances their enjoyment (Battarbee, 2003a). Digital incentives are actual benefits (free gift certificates, products, etc.) acquired as a result of efforts in digital settings such as VR or the metaverse. Digital incentives are known not only to satisfy people's economic needs, but also to contribute positively to changing attitudes and promote pro-social behavior (Perera, 2018).

https://game.naver.com/lounge/REAL_FARM/board/detail/444067 https://game.naver.com/lounge/REAL_FARM/board/detail/473280

Figure 1. P2E-based Virtual Farms

2.2 Research Method & Main Results

To examine whether co-experience and digital incentives provided by P2E virtual farms affect their success, we propose a research model for hypothesis testing, as shown in Figure 2. The targets of this study were real users of 'Realfarm', a representative virtual farm popular in South Korea. Participants in the survey had experience growing virtual crops in 'Realfarm' through their avatars. In January 2022, users responded directly during the event hosted by 'Realfarm'. In total, data from 309 respondents were obtained and analyzed.

To test the hypotheses of this study, we used PLS-SEM and smartPLS 2.0. The results confirmed the reliability and validity of the scale. After confirming the discriminant validity of the research model, we tested the hypotheses via bootstrapping, as shown in Figure 2.

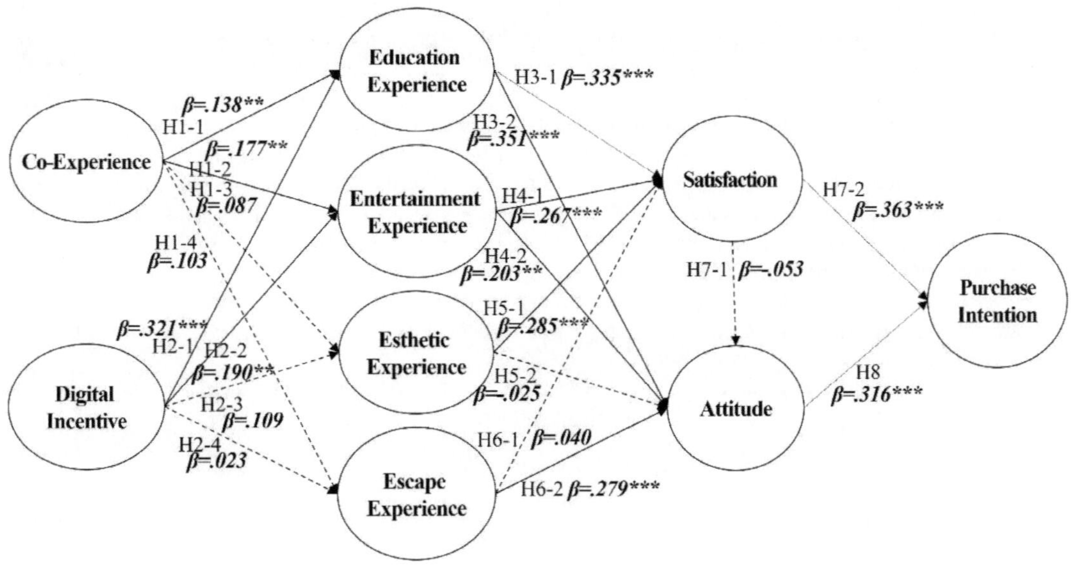

Figure 2. Research Model and the Results of PLS-SEM Bootstrapping

3. CONCLUSION

The results of this study demonstrated the positive effects of digital incentives and co-experience functions provided by the P2E virtual farm on both educational experience and entertainment experience; however, the hypotheses related to esthetic experience and escape experience were rejected. These results suggest that experience with online or offline friends in metaverse-type virtual farms brings more enjoyment and has better educational effects than experience alone. In addition, the fact that digital incentives, the core of P2E, contribute strongly to educational and entertainment experiences may indicate that the P2E experience is preferable to the traditional P2W experience. In this study, the experience economy model was useful to explain satisfaction and purchase intention related to P2E virtual farms. We will discuss the results in detail in the future based on the theory. Besides, we attempt to illustrate the meaning of this research through the additional analysis and suggest the academic and practical implications.

ACKNOWLEDGEMENT

This work was supported by the Ministry of Education of the Republic of Korea and the National Research Foundation of Korea (NRF-2020S1A3A2A02093277).

REFERENCES

Albus, P., Vogt, A., & Seufert, T. (2021). Signaling in virtual reality influences learning outcome and cognitive load. *Computers & Education*, 166, 104154.

Battarbee, K. (2003b). "Defining Co-Experience." In: Proceedings of the 2003 International Conference on Designing Pleasurable Products and Interfaces, Pittsburgh.

Battarbee, Katja. (2003a). "Co-experience: the social user experience." In CHI'03 extended abstracts on Human factors in computing systems, pp. 730-731. 2003.

Hamilton, D., McKechnie, J., Edgerton, E., & Wilson, C. (2021). Immersive virtual reality as a pedagogical tool in education: a systematic literature review of quantitative learning outcomes and experimental design. *Journal of Computers in Education*, 8(1), 1-32.

Jin, S., Fan, M., & Kadir, A. (2021). Immersive Spring Morning in the Han Palac e: Learning Traditional Chinese Art Via Virtual Reality and Multi-Touch Tabletop. *International Journal of Human–Computer Interaction*, 1-14.

Karcher, E. L., & Reid, P. (2018). The Use of Virtual Farm Tours in a Dairy Cattle Management Course. *NACTA Journal*, 62(4), 371-375.

Kaur, M., & Gupta, B. (2021). Metaverse Technology and the Current Market.

Narayan, B. (2018). Using a co-experience approach to improve international students' classroom experience: A practice report from within an Australian higher education setting. International Journal of Innovation, Creativity and Change.

Perera, S., Hardie, M., & Ratnasabapathy, S. (2021). Liquid Waste Management in the Construction Projects.

Pine, B. J., Pine, J., & Gilmore, J. H. (1999). *The experience economy: work is theatre & every business a st*age. Harvard Business Press, Massachusetts, USA.

Stott, A., & Neustaedter, C. (2013). Analysis of gamification in education. *Surrey, BC*, Canada, 8, 36.

Strokosch, K., & Osborne, S. P. (2020). Co-experience, co-production and co-governance: an ecosystem approach to the analysis of value creation. *Policy & Politics*, 48(3), 425-442.

Tussyadiah, I. P., Wang, D., Jung, T. H., & Tom Dieck, M. C. (2018). Virtual reality, presence, and attitude change: Empirical evidence from tourism. *Tourism Management*, 66, 140-154.

COMPARATIVE STUDY ON THE CHARACTERISTICS OF METAVERSE EXPERIENCE: AN EXPERIENCE ECONOMY MODEL PERSPECTIVE

Qiyuan Tang[1], Sujin Bae[2] and Ohbyung Kwon[3]
School of Management, Kyung Hee University, Kyung Hee Dae Ro 26, Dong Dae Mun Gu, Seoul 02447, Korea
[1]Ph.D. Student
[2]Research Professor
[3]Professor

ABSTRACT

The previous studies in areas of the experience economy investigate the relationship between 4 realms of experience and the consumers' attitudes or behaviors. However, with the development of Mixed reality and Metaverse, human-oriented experiences expanded from the physical world to the virtual world. Thus, there are critical changes in the ways people participate in the experience and the contents of the experience. In this study, we aim to explore whether there are any recent changes in the experience economy under the VR/AR context. We utilized the Term Frequency Inverse Document Frequency method (TF-IDF) to extract keywords from two datasets consisting of questionnaire items for related papers. The results show that the core contents of the 4 realms of experience have changed in the VR/AR context. This study provides inspiration for us to refine the classification of the experience economy and optimize the experience design.

KEYWORDS

Experience Economy Model, TF-IDF, Metaverse, Human Factor

1. INTRODUCTION

During the COVID-19 pandemic, people are relying on the internet more than ever before in their daily lives to socialize, study, and work (Deutrom et al., 2022). At the same time, with the mushrooming of technologies of virtual reality (VR), augmented reality (AR), and mixed reality (MR), Metaverse, as a virtual world that has attributes of seamlessness, scalability, sharedness, and persistence (Stucky et al., 2009), is noted by investors, scholars, and individuals as a new economic growth point (Verkerk, 2022) and a completely new way to achieve novel experiences (Trunfio et al., 2022). Specifically, the creators and operators of experience consist of not only independent individuals but also informally organized groups or commercially focused enterprises (Kiong, 2022). In addition, users in Metaverse with different regions, cultural backgrounds, and consumption levels (Mystakidis, 2022) make the demographic characteristics of consumers of experience no longer monolithic. Besides, Metaverse platforms provided with 3D content editors, such as the VOXEDIT of The Sandbox, the Create Section of the Decentraland, and the editing tools of the Cryptovoxels, facilitate users to create virtual scenes, virtual props, and digital arts (Kiong, 2022). The overall phenomenon shows that in terms of individuals, the contents of experience related to sensory and spiritual are richer. In terms of companies, experience preferences are more complex and less predictable. Therefore, this study aims to explore how the experience economy (Pine & Gilmore, 1999) is changing in VR/AR contexts will help the practice of the experience economy in the virtual world.

2. METHOD

In this study, we aim to explore the experience differences between two different experience contexts of virtual and physical. There are two datasets prepared for extracting the keywords and measuring the values for comparison. One dataset consists of the items of the questionnaire from 11 papers on the topics of "the VR/AR experience economy" published between 2015 and 2021, and the other dataset consists of the items of the questionnaire from 21 papers on the topics of "the non-VR/AR experience economy" published between 2007 and 2021. The measurement utilized in this paper is the Term Frequency Inverse Document Frequency method (TF-IDF), which is a statistical method used to measure the importance of a term in a document. The importance of a term has a positive relationship with the times that appeared in the document but has a negative relationship with the times that appeared in the corpus (Zhou, 2022). The process of extracting keywords includes dataset preprocessing, TF-IDF, ranking in descending order by TF-IDF value, and extracting the top 5 keywords for analysis. Among these, dataset preprocessing includes word segmentation, stopwords removal, stemming, and lemmatization. Results and analysis will be presented in the next section.

3. MAIN RESULTS

The overall results as shown in figure 1. Specifically, in terms of educational experience, there are five keywords that are common to both. However, we notice that the TF-IDF value of 'learn', 'new', and 'curios' in the VR/AR context is extremely higher. But the TF-IDF value of 'knowledg' is relatively higher in the non-VR/AR context. This probably implies that VR/AR could promote the learning effects and increase the intellectual curiosity of the individual, but the knowledge loading in the VR/AR environment is probably inadequate compared to the non-VR/AR context. With regards to entertainment experience, the TF-IDF value of 'amuse', 'captiv', and 'enjoy' is relatively higher in the non-VR/AR context. There are worth noting that 'avtiv' is unique to the non-VR/AR context. This probably suggests that individuals could freely and actively interact with surrounding or other people in a non-VR/AR context, but couldn't freely interact with their surroundings in a VR/AR context, which is probably limited by the operational or systems. 'entertain' is unique to the VR/AR context, this suggests that VR/AR context also has its own advantages that provide diverse and rich contents which could promote entertaining experiences. Concerning esthetic experience, the TF-IDF value of 'pleasant', 'harmoni', 'attent', and 'sens' is relatively higher in the non-VR/AR context. There are worth noting that 'attract' is unique to the non-VR/AR context, 'design' is unique to the VR/AR context. this probably implies that the esthetic experience in the VR/AR context could provide 'pleasant', but lack attractiveness, while in the non-VR/AR context, the esthetic experience is highly attractive but lacks 'design'. This probably suggests that the content in the VR/AR context is not so visually pleasing. Regarding escapism experience, the TF-IDF values of 'escap' hardly changed in both contexts, but one is highest in the non-VR/AR context, and the other only ranks third in the VR/AR context. The TF-IDF values of 'differ' change largely in both contexts, the highest in the VR/AR context and ranking third in the non-VR/AR context. besides, the keywords of the escapism experience in the non-VR/AR context also include 'routin' , 'daili', 'imagin'. While the keywords in the esthetic experience in VR/AR context include 'time', 'live', and 'place'. This suggests that the escapism experience in the non-VR/AR context largely helps individuals to escape from routine daily life. But the escapism experience in the VR/AR contexts largely provides a possibility that living in a different space-time. Escape is no longer important, what matters is different.

4. CONCLUSION

This study expects that the additional factors of experience confirmed as a result of the TF-IDF will be added to the existing experience economy and will be considered to apply to design or services. In terms of the research method, the results of TF-IDF centered on journals that dealt with experiential economy theory were presented. In the future, this study suggests examining whether it can be combined with the experiential economy theory by additionally examining theories related to human needs. It is expected that the results of this study will contribute to the development of social and human-centered technology and content development in an era where the metaverse coexists.

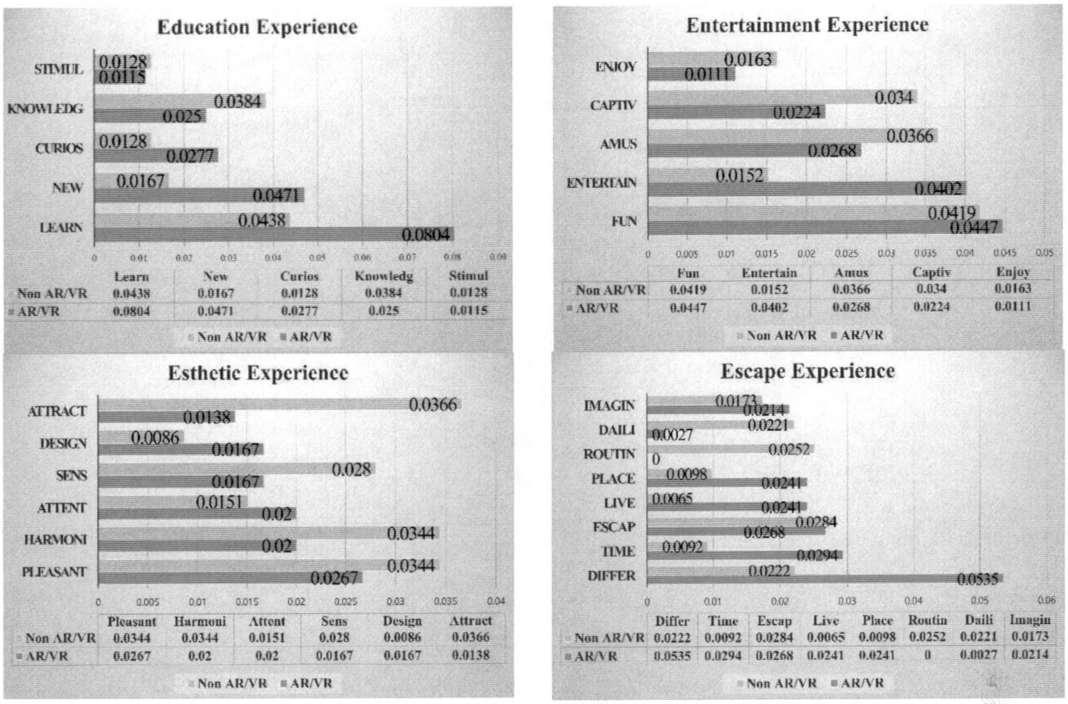

Figure 1. Keywords and the TF-IDF value of the experience economy in VR/AR context and in non-VR/AR context

ACKNOWLEDGEMENTS

This work was supported by the Ministry of Education of the Republic of Korea and the National Research Foundation of Korea (NRF-2020S1A5B8103855).

REFERENCES

Deutrom, J. et al, 2022. The Relationships between Gender, Life Satisfaction, Loneliness and Problematic Internet Use during COVID-19: Does the Lockdown Matter?. *International Journal of Environmental Research and Public Health,* Vol. 19, No. 3, pp. 1-14.

Kiong, L. V., 2022. *Metaverse Made Easy: A Beginner's Guide to the Metaverse: Everything you need to know about Metaverse, NFT and GameFi.* Independent pubulication.

Mystakidis, S., 2022. Metaverse. *Encyclopedia,* Vol. 2, No. 1, pp. 486-497.

Pine, B. J., Pine, J., & Gilmore, J. H., 1999. *The experience economy: work is theatre & every business a st*age. Harvard Business Press, Massachusetts, USA.

Stucky, S. U. et al, 2009. Virtual environments overview. *IBM ALMADEN RESEARCH CENTER SAN JOSE CA.*

Trunfio, M. et al, 2022. Innovating the cultural heritage museum service model through virtual reality and augmented reality: The effects on the overall visitor experience and satisfaction. *Journal of Heritage Tourism,* Vol. 17, No. 1, pp. 1-19.

Verkerk, V. A., 2022. Virtual Reality: A Simple Substitute or New Niche? *Information and Communication Technologies in Tourism 2022,* Vol., No. , pp. 28-40.

Zhou, H., 2022. Research of Text Classification Based on TF-IDF and CNN-LSTM. *In Journal of Physics: Conference Series*, Vol. 2171, No. 1, pp. 012021.

International Association for Development of the Information Society (IADIS)
Rua Sao Sebastiao Da Pedreira
No. 100, 30, 1050-209
Lisbon, Portugal

ISBN 978-1-7138-6090-7

CURRAN ASSOCIATES INC.
proceedings.com

3rd Jordan International Oil Shale Symposium and the 36th CSM Symposium 2016

Madaba, Jordan
21 - 22 November 2016

Ministry of Energy and Mineral Resources
The Hashemite Kingdom of Jordan